SLOW TRAVEL

South Devon & Dartmoor

Local, characterful guides to Britain's special places

Hilary Bradt & Janice Booth
Gill & Alistair Campbell

T0049665

EDITION 3
Bradt Guides Ltd, UK
The Globe Pequot Press Inc, USA

Third edition published March 2024
First published 2014
Bradt Guides Ltd
31a High Street, Chesham, Buckinghamshire, HP5 1BW, England
www.bradtguides.com
Print edition published in the USA by The Globe Pequot Press Inc, PO Box 480, Guilford,
Connecticut 06437-0480

Text copyright © 2024 Bradt Guides Ltd
Maps copyright © 2024 Bradt Guides Ltd; includes map data © OpenStreetMap contributors
Photographs copyright © 2024 Individual photographers (see below)
Project Manager: Samantha Fletcher
Cover research: Pepi Bluck, Perfect Picture

ISBN: 9781804691007

British Library Cataloguing in Publication Data
A catalogue record for this book is available from the British Library

Photographs © individual photographers and organisations credited beside images &
also from picture libraries credited as follows: Alamy.com (A); AWLimages.com (AWL);
Dreamstime.com (D); Shutterstock.com (S); Superstock.com (SS)
Front cover Bantham Bay, from Bigbury Bay (PAUL SHADDICK/A)
Back cover Kayaking on the River Erme (Chris Parker)
Title page Bowerman's Nose in Dartmoor National Park (Adam Burton/AWL)
Author photo Hilary Bradt (Lee Miller)

Maps David McCutcheon FBCart.S. FRGS.

Typeset by Ian Spick, Bradt Guides
Production managed by Zenith Media; printed in the UK
Digital conversion by www.dataworks.co.in

Paper used for this product comes from sustainably managed forests, recycled and
controlled sources.

AUTHORS

Hilary Bradt co-founded Bradt Guides in 1974, and now lives in semi-retirement in Seaton, East Devon. After 40 years of writing guidebooks to Africa and South America, she has embraced her chosen home to the extent of insisting that such a large, varied and beautiful county deserved three Slow guides, not just one. A keen walker, she has hiked many miles of the South West Coast Path

and inland footpaths, as well as enjoying Dartmoor on someone else's legs – on a horse. Most Saturdays see her taking part in one of Devon's parkruns (5k, but she's appropriately slow) and during the summer a swim in the sea, just a few minutes away, is always a pleasure. She is a productive member of the South West Sculptors' Association and lectures regularly on travel-related topics at libraries and literary festivals, both in Devon and further afield.

Janice Booth joined Hilary to research and write the first two editions of this book, combining her experiences and impressions so that the 'I' could be either author. Her interest in local folklore and history and her enjoyment of everything Devonian brought a special character to this series. Janice died in February 2023.

UPDATERS

Gill and Alistair Campbell have lived in the West Country for more than 19 years. During that time they have walked extensively in the area, often leading walks for local residents, tourists and foreign tour groups. They have hiked all the UK's national trails, including the South West Coast Path, as well as the Two Moors Way, the Macmillan

Way West and the Tarka Trail. They are both volunteer workers for the National Trust, where they restore ancient stone walls and help visitors

get the most out of their visits to the South West. They love to travel and have criss-crossed the world for most of their lives, both for work and for pleasure.

Alistair and Gill have written two walking guides, as well as being co-authors of the Bradt Slow Travel guide *North & Mid-Devon*.

CONTRIBUTORS

Alex Graeme runs Unique Devon Tours (⊘ uniquedevontours.co.uk), which offers tailor-made, small group guided tours of Devon. We have unashamedly used his knowledge and expertise for boxes (pages 16 and 334).

Joanna Griffin won Bradt's 'Perfect Day' competition for East Devon with her evocative description of wild swimming and was a finalist in Bradt's 2018 New Travel Writer of the Year award. She has researched wild swimming across the region; her suggestions can be found on pages 123, 215 and 292.

AUTHOR'S STORY

Hilary Bradt

I bought my little house in Devon in 2005, but it was a while before I could tear myself away from my roots in Buckinghamshire. Now I wonder why on earth it took me so long. It's always fascinating to look back at the process of getting to know a new place; I've done it often enough. It begins with your immediate neighbourhood, then gradually radiates out, like ripples, as locals tell you about, or show you, their favourite places. Devon has been different.

Because the predecessor of this book, *Slow Devon and Exmoor*, was researched within a year of moving here, the process has been more like one of those speeded up nature films where the greening of my

knowledge has quickly spread from one point to cover the whole landscape. It's a process that never ends, nor does the excitement at finding something new ever diminish. I remember the sheer elation when we discovered Kenn and walked on a spring day down its main street past the thatched cottages and library in a phone box, marvelling that no-one seemed to know about such an enchanting village. Conversely, our pleasure at experiencing the paddle steamer on the River Dart – a well-known tourist attraction – was just as fresh and untarnished by expectation. I feel so lucky to live here, and to have such a good reason to keep exploring.

ACKNOWLEDGEMENTS

People living in East Devon and Somerset can't pretend to know everything about another region of the West Country. But through friends, acquaintances and chance meetings at bus stops or shops, they can end a summer of research knowing a heck of a lot.

Author and ornithologist Tony Soper provided local information and the box on birdwatching (page 202) retained from previous editions. Likewise Philip Knowling gave prompt answers just when we needed them, and permission for some of his boxes on follies to be reused.

Hilary is particularly grateful to her old friends Bridget and Jerry Gurney, who provided exceptional accommodation and local knowledge in East Portlemouth, and her colleagues in the South West Sculptors' Association, who chipped in with warm recommendations for their home areas: Derek Cadle, Jenny Distin, Rose Ellis, Angela Holmes, Jean Lock, David Newman, Verity Newman, Luke Shepherd and Pippa Unwin, with an extra thank you to Pippa who introduced me to so much in the Aveton Gifford area, and Jenny and Jean, whose enthusiasm and way with words provided quotes from 'locals' around Galmpton and Kingsbridge. We would also like to thank Kez Paget at Powderham Castle and Suzy Bennett of Dartmoor Artisan Trail who both helped us with the update.

Finally we would like to thank Imogen Vignoles and the Mais Estate for kind permission to use extracts from *Glorious Devon* by S P B Mais.

FEEDBACK REQUEST

At Bradt Guides we're aware that guidebooks start to go out of date on the day they're published – and that you, our readers, are out there in the field doing research of your own. You'll find out before us when a fine new family-run hotel opens or a favourite restaurant changes hands and goes downhill. So why not tell us about your experiences? Contact us on ℰ 01753 893444 or ✉ info@bradtguides.com. We will forward emails to the author who may post updates on the Bradt website at ⬦ bradtguides.com/updates. Alternatively, you can add a review of the book to Amazon, or share your adventures with us on Facebook, Twitter or Instagram (@BradtGuides).

SUGGESTED PLACES TO BASE YOURSELF

These bases make ideal starting points for exploring localities the Slow way.

OKEHAMPTON page 260
Its dramatic 11th-century castle overlooks the Okement River. Nearby are unspoilt villages and the reopened Dartmoor Line.

CHAGFORD page 287
The perfect base for exploring northern Dartmoor, with its rich prehistory and scenic mix of wooded valleys and high moor.

TAVISTOCK page 326
This gracious town with its historic market is at one end of Drake's Trail for cyclists (Plymouth is the other end) and is the western gateway to Dartmoor.

WEMBURY page 204
Handy for Plymouth but very unspoilt, this is one of the best beaches in the region; it has excellent rock pools as well as sand, good coastal walks and surfing.

KINGSBRIDGE page 161
This very pleasant small town, only a short ferry trip from Salcombe, has a wide selection of inland footpaths and easy access to the coast path.

BIGBURY BAY page 178
The best combination of sandy beach, pretty villages and the coast path. You can surf at nearby Bantham, or take the 'sea tractor' to Burgh Island.

Cornwall

CHAPTER 7
page 251

CHAPTER 8
page 275

CHAPTER 5
page 189

CHAPTER 4
page 149

A3072
Okehampton
A30
A382
Chagford
Moretonhamps
A3079
A386
A30
Tavy
DARTMOOR
B3212
Widecomb
the-Moo
Tavistock
B3357
NATIONAL
Princetown
Tamar
PARK
Ashburto
Plym
Buckfastleig
A386
PLYMOUTH
A38
A379
Yealm
Erme
Avon
Wembury
Kingsbridge
A3
Bigbury
Bay
Salcombe

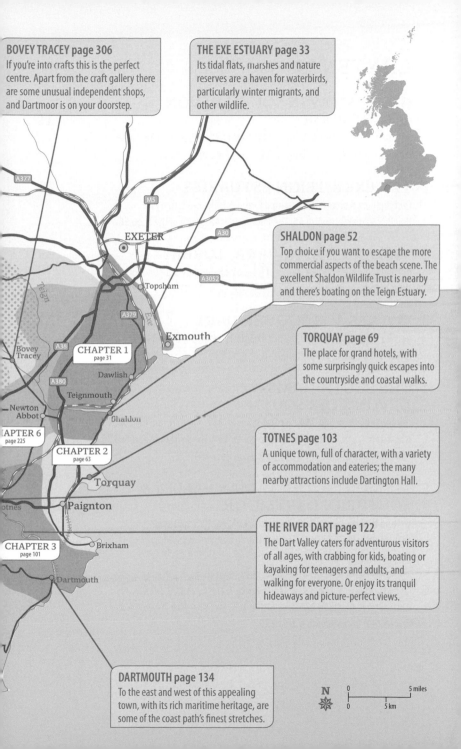

BOVEY TRACEY page 306
If you're into crafts this is the perfect centre. Apart from the craft gallery there are some unusual independent shops, and Dartmoor is on your doorstep.

THE EXE ESTUARY page 33
Its tidal flats, marshes and nature reserves are a haven for waterbirds, particularly winter migrants, and other wildlife.

SHALDON page 52
Top choice if you want to escape the more commercial aspects of the beach scene. The excellent Shaldon Wildlife Trust is nearby and there's boating on the Teign Estuary.

TORQUAY page 69
The place for grand hotels, with some surprisingly quick escapes into the countryside and coastal walks.

TOTNES page 103
A unique town, full of character, with a variety of accommodation and eateries; the many nearby attractions include Dartington Hall.

THE RIVER DART page 122
The Dart Valley caters for adventurous visitors of all ages, with crabbing for kids, boating or kayaking for teenagers and adults, and walking for everyone. Or enjoy its tranquil hideaways and picture-perfect views.

DARTMOUTH page 134
To the east and west of this appealing town, with its rich maritime heritage, are some of the coast path's finest stretches.

EXETER

Topsham

Exmouth

Bovey Tracey

Dawlish

Teignmouth

Newton Abbot

Shaldon

Torquay

Paignton

Brixham

Dartmouth

CHAPTER 1 page 31

CHAPTER 6 page 225

CHAPTER 2 page 63

CHAPTER 3 page 101

A377 M5 A30 A3052 A379 A38 A380

Teign Exe

N

0   5 miles
0   5 km

CONTENTS

GOING SLOW IN

SOUTH DEVON & DARTMOOR

[The holidaymaker] comes to Devon for what he cannot get anywhere else, clotted cream the colour of cowslips for breakfast, lunch, tea and dinner, scenery as rich as the cream, contact with a glorious past history and a very pleasant type of modern people. The way, and I think the only way, to see Devon, is to go slowly in and about her, to keep moving, but to keep moving at snail's pace.
S P B Mais, 1928

One thing that has been a constant pleasure when researching our three Slow guides to Devon is the way that early guidebook writers like S P B Mais anticipated our current appreciation of the Slow movement. Indeed, there's nothing new in Slow; it's a rediscovery of the perfect way to enjoy the most beautiful and intriguing parts of our country. It's about taking the time to visit a church, or watch the scenery unfold from a bus window, or observe a peacock butterfly fluttering from flower to flower, or sit gazing out to sea from the coast path, or plunge from the moor into one of those deep, wooded valleys we call combes. Indeed, that's where the county gets its name: *Dyfnaint* was the Celtic name for Devon, and means 'dark and deep valleys'.

A TASTE OF SOUTH DEVON & DARTMOOR

Cream teas and cider are the treats most associated with Devon, and indeed they're a big part of any holiday here. But foodwise there's so

◄ South Devon features mile upon mile of beautiful coastline for walking, such as around Gara Rock (page 170).

11

much more. With Devon's high rainfall (shh!) and rich and varied grazing, **meat** is of exceptional quality, and restaurants take pride in sourcing it from named local farms, so that what you're eating comes directly or indirectly from our fertile soil. **Seafood** also is superb, as you might expect in the only English county with two separate sea coasts. Restaurants often have their own suppliers, who rush the catch to them straight from their boat. If you're self-catering look in fishmongers for the 'catch of the day'.

Local dairies offer more calorific delights. The very best **clotted cream**, thick, velvety and yellow, comes from Devon and Cornwall, and its taste is quite unlike that of thinner creams. It can vary according to

THE SLOW MINDSET

Hilary Bradt, Founder, Bradt Guides

**We shall not cease from exploration
And the end of all our exploring
Will be to arrive where we started
And know the place for the first time.**
T S Eliot, 'Little Gidding', *Four Quartets*

This series evolved, slowly, from a Bradt editorial meeting when we started to explore ideas for guides to our favourite part of the world – Great Britain. We wanted to get away from the usual 'top sights' formula and encourage our authors to bring out the nuances and local differences that make up a sense of place – such things as food, building styles, nature, geology, or local people and what makes them tick. Our aim was to create a series that celebrates the present, focusing on sustainable tourism, rather than taking a nostalgic wallow in the past.

So without our realising it at the time, we had defined 'Slow Travel', or at least our concept of it. For the beauty of the Slow movement is that there is no fixed definition;

we adapt the philosophy to fit our individual needs and aspirations. Thus Carl Honoré, author of *In Praise of Slow*, writes: 'The Slow Movement is a cultural revolution against the notion that faster is always better. It's not about doing everything at a snail's pace, it's about seeking to do everything at the right speed. Savouring the hours and minutes rather than just counting them. Doing everything as well as possible, instead of as fast as possible. It's about quality over quantity in everything from work to food to parenting.' And travel.

So take time to explore. Don't rush it, get to know an area – and the people who live there – and you'll be as delighted as the authors by what you find.

the breed of cow and the preparation (milk is heated very slowly and then cooled, so that the cream rises to the top and can be skimmed off). A recent transatlantic visitor expected her 'Devon cream tea' to be a cup of tea with cream in it, so was surprised to receive freshly baked scones spread thickly with clotted cream and jam, accompanied by a generous pot of tea. In Devon, the jam usually goes on top of the cream, in Cornwall underneath. For those who like ice cream, local family-run Taw River Dairy (🇫) make both ice cream and sorbets, all the milk coming from their own herd of Jersey cows.

The **cheeses** range from hard and nutty to soft and squashy, and from raspingly strong to gently creamy; you'll find them on sale locally. They're enriched with all manner of herbs and flavours; different dairies have their own specialities, some dating back several centuries. For instance, Quicke's traditional mature cheddar comes from land near Exeter that has been farmed by the same family for over 450 years (⌂ quickes. co.uk); and Curworthy Farm near Okehampton (⌂ curworthycheese. co.uk) uses a 17th-century recipe. If you like some chutney with your cheese, look out for Hogsbottom (⌂ hogsbottom.co.uk), a small local company that produces excellent chutneys and jams.

Pasties are another temptation, and both their fillings (a mix of meat and vegetables) and their pastry vary according to the maker. You'll just have to sample a few to find your favourite! The aroma as they're taken from the baker's oven is hard to resist. In Devon, the crimp (closure) traditionally arches over the top; in Cornwall it's along the edge of the base.

CHEERS!

The mild climate and south-facing slopes are also conducive to wine-making, with **Sandridge Barton Vineyard**, home of Sharpham wines (page 126), leading the way with its wine tastings, vineyard tours and café. At **Old Walls Vineyard** (page 51) near Teignmouth you can 'rent' an area of vines and receive the fruits of its harvest once bottled.

South Devon also has some internationally famous **gin** distilleries: Salcombe Gin (page 168) has won many awards, as has Plymouth Gin (page 193), made traditionally by one man in one Victorian copper still, and Thunderflower Gin (⌂ thunderflowergin.com) is a true craft gin that is worth seeking out. Devon's first single malt **whisky** distillery

can be found in Bovey Tracey (page 306). Several breweries around the county, small and larger, have their own ranges of ales: you'll find them in shops and pubs, together with plentiful local advice as to which you should try.

Cider

Two types of cider are brewed in the UK – in eastern counties, Kent and East Anglia, and in the west in Devon and Somerset. We in the West Country have a valid claim that ours is the best. True cider apples are only grown here, and most cider producers use varieties that date back hundreds of years, with evocative names such as Fair Maids of Devon, Pig's Snout, Tail Sweet, Devon Crimson and Slack-Ma-Girdle. The distinctive cloudy cider, which is unfiltered and unpasteurised, is produced in Devon, as is the famous high-alcohol scrumpy.

Cider enthusiasts can fuel their interest through the website *∂* real-cider.co.uk. A few of the region's cider producers are below.

Gray's Devon Cider Tedburn St Mary *∂* 01647 61236 *∂* graysdevoncider.co.uk. Some 21 acres of orchards with 50 varieties of apple are tended by the Gray family to make their cider; the family has been doing it since 1640. Cider can be ordered online, or visit the farm and they will help you blend a bespoke cider to suite your own taste (booking essential). They wassail their trees every January (page 16) and a film of their wassail can be found at *∂* heres-to-thee.org.uk.
Heron Valley Drinks Loddiswell *∂* heronvalley.co.uk. One of the largest of the region's producers, with their own mobile bar, they make a variety of juices and cider vinegar, as well as a range of ciders either bottled or bagged.
Hunts Cider page 89
Luscombe Organic Drinks Buckfastleigh *∂* luscombe.co.uk. Well known for their range of organic fruit juices and soft drinks, Luscombe also make a medium-dry cider.
Ron Barter Dunsford *∂* 01647 252783 *✉* lowleyfarm@aol.com. Here is something completely different. Ron is part of the Dartmoor Artisan Trail (page 284), producing cider using one of the UK's oldest working cider presses in a barn that dates back to Saxon times,

◄ **1** Rolling fields and pastures are a reminder of Devon's strong cattle farming tradition. **2** Enjoy fresh seafood all along the coast, for example at one of Rockfish's restaurants (page 97). **3** You won't struggle to find cream teas on the menu! **4** Quicke's cheddar comes from land farmed by the same family for centuries (page 13). **5** Locals gather to help with the apple harvest at South Zeal (page 256).

WASSAILING

Alex Graeme

Imagine leaving your house after dark and walking by night along lanes and across fields, with the distant beat of drums drifting through the still air. Then from down in the valley ahead you start to hear other sounds – stringed instruments, laughter, bellows of excitement, and the clacking of wood hitting wood. 'Old apple tree, old apple tree, we wassail thee…' reaches your ears, and there's no doubt as to where you're heading. It's the ancient pagan festival of wassailing, and it doesn't get much more atmospheric than in the depths of Devon.

The tradition began a very long time ago, somewhere in the Dark Ages. A wassail is a ceremony where offerings are made to the apple trees, in the hope their next harvest will be large enough to make plenty of cider. Wassails traditionally take place in January, on the old 12th night (either the 5th or 16th of the month), although nowadays different wassails are held on different nights around Devon.

To appeal to the spirits of the apple trees and deter evil spirits, singing, dancing, chanting and toasts are the order of the night – I've experienced Mummers' plays, shotguns being fired, and sometimes the trees being doused in cider. Thankfully I haven't as yet observed any sacrifices,

full of antique cider-making tools and equipment. Tours can be arranged, including cider tasting; booking essential.

Sampford Courtenay Cider ⬦ devoncider.com. Make a good variety of ciders, which can be bought online, and you'll find them in many farm shops in the area.

Orchard Drinks and **Yarde Cider** ⬦ orcharddrinks.co.uk. Two family businesses that came together in 2023 to produce award-winning organic craft cider, mead, nettle vodka and a range of sparkling country wines and natural fruit juices. They also hold a wassail (see above) in January.

GETTING THERE & AROUND

It goes without saying that Slow Travel favours public transport above the car, and in Devon this isn't just because it's better for the environment. Although Devon actually has more miles of road than the whole of Belgium, many of these are car-unfriendly single-track lanes with high banks and hedges where you rely on intuition rather than eyesight to deal with oncoming cars. S P B Mais recognised the problem for drivers: 'If you keep to the road you will not see Devon at all, only a succession of whitewashed thatched cottages red with fuchsia clustered round a tall although I suspect they may have taken place once upon a time. Anything to protect the apple harvest!

Wassails are held throughout Devon, although they are fairly scarce these days. My favourite is at the village of Lustleigh, where the old orchard and the Cleave Restaurant and Bar are the focal points for this great tradition. Here the Beltane Border Morris Dancers defy many of the traditional stereotypes, with their blackened faces, fast and hard dancing, and seemingly vicious swinging of their wooden sticks! There is something quite primeval about the whole experience; as the spectators wander together into the orchards to address the trees, a collective warmth spreads among the crowd, and the wassail songs and blessings begin. By this stage the sticks have become flaming torches, and the flickering light catches eyes that are both wary and cheerful: slightly unnerved by the strangeness, but joyous at attending such a timeless ritual.

Do try to experience at least one wassail. It's so special, and the memory will stay with you for a very long time. Drinking the cider that the very same trees you are blessing helped create the year before is part of the cycle of life. Each year we take our children, and often their friends, and it really is one of the highlights of our winter.

grey granite church tower at three- or five-mile intervals as you bore your way through green tunnel after green tunnel.'

It is entirely possible to enjoy a holiday in Devon without a car. Transport to the area is good, and there are usually local buses to get you to the places of interest. Each chapter has specific information on public transport. A useful organisation for **planning journeys by bus and/or train** is Traveline (☏ 0871 200 2233 ♂ traveline.info). If you are stuck at a bus stop with no bus and only an unsmart mobile phone, you can phone the number (which is also shown on most bus stops) for help and advice. Another excellent **website** for all forms of travel – bus, train, cycle, walking – is ♂ traveldevon.info. Its interactive bus map is particularly useful.

Local buses are a boon for bus-pass holders, but even for paying passengers there are often special deals such as the DevonDay bus ticket, which gives unlimited bus travel throughout Devon. Praiseworthy community-run buses such as Tavistock Country Buses (page 281) are an extra bonus. Devon County Council publishes a series of regional bus timetables as well as a bus map of the county. We list relevant ones in each chapter and they can be picked up in most tourist information centres (TICs) and some shops or newsagents.

SINGLE-TRACK ROADS

You can get to all sizeable towns in South Devon on good main roads, but if you visit more remote areas you may well have to drive on single-track roads with passing places. They're perfectly manageable if you remember three things.

- As you drive past passing places, make a mental note of where they are, so that you know how far you've got to go if you need to reverse.
- When you're reversing, rather than pulling sideways into the passing place as you reach it, you may find it easier to continue reversing straight back on the crown of the road until you've passed it and then drive forward into it. Visibility is often better.
- Whether you're reversing or driving forward, and whichever side the passing place is on, keep to the left so that the oncoming driver passes on your right. And remember to use your indicators.

CYCLING & WALKING

These are now combined in each chapter under the heading *Self-powered travel*.

This part of Devon has a good range of dedicated **cycle paths** as well as the 99-mile Coast-to-Coast (National Cycle Network or NCN Route 27) from Ilfracombe to Plymouth. A Croydecycle map (see opposite) covers the whole route. Other NCN routes that pass through this region include the NCN 28 running 78 miles from Okehampton to Plymouth and the NCN 2 which crosses South Devon from Exeter to Plymouth, the whole route running 378 miles from Dover in Kent to St Austell in Cornwall (⊘ sustrans.org.uk). See also ⊘ traveldevon.info.

Among the most popular **cycle trails** are Drake's Trail, the Dart Valley Cycle Way, the Granite Way, the Stover Trail and the Dartmoor Way. These, and others, are listed in the relevant chapters.

For **walkers**, there's the **South West Coast Path** (⊘ southwestcoastpath. org.uk) from Starcross to Plymouth, a distance of almost exactly 100 miles. Some of the best walks in all of Devon are here, with the most rewarding short stretches described in each relevant chapter. Those tackling the whole trail, or planning to walk for several days, would do well to use the services of a luggage transfer company so they can walk unencumbered. **Luggage Transfers** (⊘ luggagetransfers.co.uk) will also arrange walker-friendly accommodation for you. Likewise,

Dartmoor is the starting/finishing point for the **Two Moors Way** (⊘ twomoorsway.org), a stiff but hugely rewarding challenge linking Dartmoor and Exmoor, which can now be extended to Wembury to make a coast-to-coast trail.

If you fancy the idea of letting someone else do all the planning, organisation and luggage transfer, the tour operator **On Foot Holidays** (⊘ onfootholidays.co.uk), which specialises in self-guided walking holidays in Europe, has an appealing six-day inn-to-inn walk, *A tale of two rivers*, taking you from Dunsford on the River Teign to Dartmouth. The longest days are about 12 miles but these can usually be shortened.

Walking (& cycling) guides & maps

There are plenty of **guidebooks** for walkers. Some are listed in the relevant chapters; Pathfinder's *South Devon and Dartmoor* by Sue Viccars is particularly useful, covering as it does the same area as this book. The best guide to the South West Coast Path is Trailblazer's *Dorset and South Devon Coast Path*, by Henry Stedman and Joel Newton, which has detailed maps and suggestions for accommodation.

The 1:25,000 Ordnance Survey Explorer **maps** covering Dartmoor and South Devon are huge, double-sided affairs, prefixed OL (the scale means they are great for detail but very unwieldy – we dubbed them 'the table cloth'). Much more useful are the series produced by Mike Harrison under his Croydecycle imprint (⊘ croydecycle.co.uk) at a scale of 1:12,500 (about five inches to a mile). Personal (Mike Harrison walks or cycles every road and path), idiosyncratic (plenty of observations to help the walker, such as the condition of the footpath or little nuggets of history) and small-pocket-sized, these cover all of the coastal areas in this book and some popular inland places such as Totnes and Kingsbridge. In 2023 Mike added six Dartmoor maps to his list, which is excellent news. These are Lustleigh, Haytor, Holne, Bellever, Chagford and Fingle. The relevant maps are listed in each chapter and are widely available from TICs and gift shops. Mike is also the brains behind the excellent *South Devon* map at 1:100,000 which, despite its relatively small scale, is my map of choice for finding my way around the region. It almost exactly corresponds with the area covered in this book and manages to pack in more detail, including town plans, than any other map.

SOME FAVOURITE VISITS

EXCEPTIONAL CHURCHES

S P B Mais wrote: 'We are now beginning to discover in a quickly changing England that almost our only link with the past lies in our churches…[They] bring back memories of our ancient stock. I make no more apology for turning aside into every church than I do for exploring every stream and river.'

We have turned aside into many churches and described them with enthusiasm for the same reason that so moved Mr Mais. From their monuments and tombstones to the present day's flower rota and village-life kneelers, they represent an unbroken link with the past. Churches are also repositories for important art (just how important is illustrated by the theft in 2013 of Torbryan's treasures; page 233). Devon's intricately carved wooden screens with their panels of painted saints are exceptional; there are more complete ones here than in any other county, so we can be forgiven for describing them with such affection. Likewise, carved bench ends and stained-glass windows, which show us the mindset of a medieval craftsman whose life was dominated by the twin fears of God and the law, as well as his deep understanding of the rural life he was familiar with. And when asked to portray an animal he had never seen, he did his best.

Some of our favourites are Combeinteignhead (page 56) and Haccombe (page 58), Bere Ferrers (page 212), Doddiscombsleigh (page 227) and Higher Ashton (page 228), as well as the unique Victorian St Raphael's Chapel in Dartmoor (page 321).

BEACHES

When I say I live in Devon, the response is often 'Oh lovely! We used to go there every year for our holidays', and indeed Devon's beaches rival any in England. Many beaches have the Blue Flag award for highest water quality, good facilities and safety and environmental

---

1 A Dartmouth Steam Railway train travels past Goodrington Sands (page 88).
2 Pygmy goat kids at Totnes Rare Breeds Farm (page 110). **3** There are plenty of spots to go crabbing, including in Kingsbridge (page 161). **4** Painter Amy Jobes takes part in Devon Open Studios (page 24). **5** One of Devon's beautiful gardens in the National Garden Scheme (page 24). ▶

THE BELL RINGERS OF DEVON

If you're a 'church crawler' like us, you start to notice unusual features. I was struck, for instance, by the floor-level bell ropes in some churches, including Lustleigh, and wondered if they were a rarity. Usually, I thought, the bell ringers climb up to the tower. The opportunity to learn more about this and bell ringing in general came when I met David Trist in the pub at Lustleigh. 'There are a lot of ground floor rings in Devon,' he said. 'This arose because the fashion in Devon was for relatively short, solid towers as opposed to Somerset which liked tall towers. The Devon fashion may well have sprung from the local building materials, in this case granite, being both difficult to work and very heavy.' I joked that I knew everything about bell ringing because of a storyline in *The Archers*. 'You're thinking of method ringing,' said David. 'That's not what we do. In Devon we do call-change ringing.'

'What's the difference?'

'Call-changes are a repeated pattern of ringing which then introduces a slight change. Method ringing does not repeat its patterns and is constantly changing its sound on every stroke of the bell. Our tradition of call-changes is probably what all churches used to ring.' David went on to explain that the tradition was passed down through families and communities, but because ringing the old bells was hard work, it used to be the 'working' community that did it. Old rules that survive on tower boards state that it was an offence to swear, curse, fight and draw knives or pistols in church. This says a lot about the bell-ringing community. The gentry and clergy decided to take up bell ringing in order to introduce a more sophisticated style, better suited to people with an education. This was a blatant attempt to exclude the rougher element.

Devon was barely affected by the changes of population brought about by the agricultural and industrial revolutions in other counties, so a strong tradition of ringing continued to be handed down through families – something that continues to this day with the Trouts, Sharlands, Pascoes and Adams dynasties. 'As a result,' said David, 'we maintained our tradition, which is now recognised throughout the country as being uniquely skilful.'

management. Blackpool Sands (page 142), Dawlish Warren (page 45), Paignton's Broadsands (page 88) and Preston Sands (page 88), Torquay's Meadfoot (page 77) and Oddicombe (page 68), Teignmouth's Town Beach (page 51) and Brixham's Breakwater Beach (page 95) have all been awarded a Blue Flag. Unlike sandy North Devon, many in the south are shingle or a mixture of shingle and sand, but any slight disadvantage is offset by their setting, tucked into coves and framed by greenery. Some (such as Wembury, page 204) have rock pools to explore; others (for example Anstey's

Cove, page 71) have exceptionally beautiful pebbles. We describe South Devon's best Slow beaches in the relevant chapters, but to get an overview the excellent website ⊘ devonbeachguide.co.uk locates and describes every beach in the county, illustrating them with photos.

ANIMALS & WILDLIFE

Some visitors are bored by birds but adore zoos, while others abhor zoos but would happily spend all day in a hide. We love both, so have catered for both types of enthusiast.

Exceptional spots for **birdwatching** include the Exe Estuary (page 33), Dawlish Warren (page 45), Berry Head (page 97), Slapton Ley (page 152), Charleton Marsh (page 162) and the Tamar Estuary (page 202).

Birdwatchers and other wildlife enthusiasts should check out the **Devon Wildlife Trust** (⊘ devonwildlifetrust.org), an active, 50-year-old charity with wildlife reserves and other conservation projects throughout Devon. The **RSPB** (⊘ rspb.org.uk) also manages several reserves here and organises birdwatching events.

Foremost among the area's **zoos**, **aquariums** and **farm attractions** are: Shaldon Wildlife Trust (page 53), Paignton Zoo (page 87), Totnes Rare Breeds Farm (page 110), the National Marine Aquarium in Plymouth (page 194), Dartmoor Zoo (page 221), Buckfastleigh's Otters and Butterflies (page 245) and Pennywell Farm (page 248).

GOOD TIDINGS

Devon's beautiful stretches of coastline are particularly tempting for visitors fascinated by cliffs, beaches and the seashore. However, lifeboats all too often have to rescue people trapped by the incoming tide. These call-outs can be dangerous and costly, and are avoidable by checking the **tide tables** (available in local shops and TICs) before any seashore wander.

Non-seawise visitors don't always realise how much the extent and times of tidal ebb and flow vary with the moon's phases. The fact that you could walk past those rocks yesterday at midday and return safely doesn't mean you can do the same tomorrow: the tide may not ebb so far, or may rise higher, and you'll be trapped. (If this happens, don't try wading; there can be dangerously deep pools close to rocks.) These differences vary from place to place and from day to day, throughout the year, so – better safe than sorry!

DOG-FRIENDLY DEVON

South Devon is a great place to come with your dog, with endless opportunities for walks along the coast or through unspoilt countryside. The book *Dog Walks: South Devon and Dartmoor* by Deb Bridges describes 20 good walks, many with dog-friendly pubs en route.

There are, of course, places that do restrict dog access, so it is advisable to check before you head out. The best website for information on whether a beach allows dogs is the Devon Beach Guide (⊘ devonbeachguide.co.uk), which covers every South Devon beach.

Visit Devon has a section on their website that is devoted to dog-friendly activities, attractions and places to stay, from lovely old hotels to award-winning campsites (⊘ visitdevon.co.uk/explore/dog-friendly).

NATIONAL GARDEN SCHEME (NGS) & OPEN STUDIOS

The NGS (⊘ ngs.org.uk) started in 1927: householders across England and Wales open their gardens to the public on various dates each year to raise money for nursing charities. This offers visitors the perfect way to get under the skin of Devon and to understand Devonians or – if you are visiting from overseas – the English. We consider ourselves the most passionate gardeners in the world and Devon, with its rich soil and mild climate, makes enthusiasts out of even reluctant horticulturists. There are now more than 3,700 participants with homes of every size, from manor houses to semi-detached cottages. And it's not just their gardens you'll enjoy. Almost every householder taking part in the scheme adds to the money raised by providing coffee and tea with a wonderful array of home-baked cakes. There are gardens opening at different times throughout the year, from January to December, although more, of course, in spring and summer. Some open only for one weekend so you need to plan ahead. The NGS annual publication, *The Garden Visitor's Handbook* (known as 'the yellow book'), gives a complete countrywide list and can be bought via the NGS website, but there are separate county lists too. The Devon one can usually be picked up free at tourist offices and other local outlets.

Devon Open Studios (⊘ devonopenstudios.co.uk) is a fortnight-long event that takes place annually in September. This is an initiative of the Devon Artist Network (⊘ devonartistnetwork.co.uk), a non-profit organisation set up in 2004 to promote the visual arts and create opportunities for local artists and craftspeople; more than 300

BOOKS & MEDIA

participating studios around the county are listed on its website. The range of these is vast and the opportunity to purchase truly original art direct from the artist in the setting where it was created is one not to be missed. Look out for their yellow arrows that show you the way.

BOOKS & MEDIA

NEWSPAPERS & LOCAL RADIO
The *Western Morning News* (⊘ westernmorning.news) has been published six days a week since 1860 and is an excellent paper for Devon-based visitors, with lots of information and reports on local events, as well as politically unbiased international news. Taking the longer view is the monthly magazine *Devon Life* (⊘ devonlife.co.uk), with in-depth articles on a range of town and country issues.

Radio Devon (◧), broadcast since 1983 from the BBC studios in Plymouth, is one of the most listened-to of the BBC's local radio stations. Tune in to hear traffic news as well as local-interest stories and interviews. *Devon Live* (⊘ devonlive.com) is a useful online source for local news, sport and entertainment ideas from community correspondents and columnists around the county.

BOOKS
The books below have been particularly useful for our research – and the list is church-oriented because Devon's little village churches are such an integral part of its history. A good website for finding out-of-print editions is ⊘ abebooks.co.uk.

In print
Devon W G Hoskins (Collins, 1954); frequent reprints by Phillimore & Co. Hoskins is the authority on Devon and his gazetteer is comprehensive.
The Devon Cook Book Kate Reeves-Brown (Meze Publishing, 2017). A celebration of Devon's food; good recipes.
Devon's Fifty Best Churches Todd Gray (The Mint Press, 2011). Some fine photos of the churches and their carvings, accompanied by location maps and informative text.
England's Thousand Best Churches Simon Jenkins (Penguin, 1999). The essential companion for any churchophile; 33 of Jenkins's choices are in Devon.
The Pilgrim's Guide to Devon's Churches (Cloister Books, 2008). A practical and sturdy little handbook, systematically listing and describing all of Devon's Anglican churches.

FAIRS & FESTIVALS

These are very much a part of Devon life, some of them deeply traditional and others with a modern touch. You'll come across far more than we've listed here, particularly during the summer months.

April
Blackawton Festival of Wormcharming
nr Totnes ⊘ wormcharming.co.uk
Toby's Garden Festival
Powderham (page 43)

May
Brixham Pirate Festival (page 92)
Dart Music Festival Dartmouth
⊘ dartmusicfestival.co.uk

June
Bovey Tracey Craft Festival
⊘ craftsatboveytracey.co.uk
Teignmouth Folk Festival (page 50)
Shaldon International Music
Festival ⊘ shaldonfestival.co.uk

July
Ashburton Medieval Ale-
Tasting & Bread Weighing
⊘ discoverashburton.info (page 238)
Galmpton Gooseberry Pie Fair (page 90)

Kingsbridge Fair Week
⊘ kingsbridgefairweek.co.uk
Salcombe Town Regatta
⊘ salcombeinformation.co.uk

August
Dartmoor Folk Festival (page 256)
Dawlish Carnival
⊘ dawlishcelebratescarnival.co.uk
Plymouth International Firework
Championship ⊘ britishfireworks.co.uk
Shaldon Regatta (page 52)
Shaldon Water Carnival
⊘ shaldonwatercarnival.co.uk

September
Ashburton Food Festival (page 237)
Marldon Apple Pie Fair (page 79)
Widecombe Fair (page 314)

October
Dartmouth Food Festival (page 141)
Powderham Food Festival (page 43)

The South Devon Coast Charles G Harper (Chapman & Hall, 1907); reprint Hardpress Publishing, 2013. A lengthy and often entertaining look at Devon a hundred years ago.
Wild Guide to the South West Daniel Start, Tania Pascoe and Jo Keeling (Wild Things Publishing, 2013). Over 500 wild places across the South West – from caves to castles and campsites.
Wild Swimming Walks: Dartmoor & South Devon Sophie Pierce and Matt Newbury (Wild Things Publishing, 2016). Practical guide of walks, wild-swimming spots and good pubs along the way.

Out of print

A Cloud of Witnesses (2011 & 2013) and *Showing the Path to Heaven* (2014) Diane Wilks (Azure Publications). Descriptions of medieval panel paintings of saints in Devon churches.

Crossing's Guide to Dartmoor William Crossing (1909). Second-hand copies of the 1990 paperback edition (Peninsula Press) are widely available. Practical, authoritative and informative, with a good index.

Devon: A Shell Guide Ann Jellicoe and Roger Mayne (Faber & Faber, 1975). The erudite research and literary style that you would expect in a Shell Guide.

Early Tours in Devon and Cornwall R Pearse Chope ed. (James G Commin, 1918); reprint by David & Charles, 1967. Fascinating reports from early travellers in Devon, including John Leland (travelling 1534–43), Celia Fiennes (1695), Daniel Defoe (1724) and Robert Southey (1802).

Glorious Devon S P B Mais (Great Western Railway Company, 1932). In his very readable style, Mais brings the scenery and people affectionately and enjoyably to life.

The King's England: Devon Arthur Mee (Hodder & Stoughton, 1928 and later). Arranged alphabetically as a gazetteer, Mee's descriptions include some unusual details and a sprinkling of old tales and legends.

Some Old Devon Churches John Stabb (Simpkin, Marshall, Hamilton, Kent & Co, three volumes, 1908–16). Careful descriptions of many of Devon's finest churches, with grainy old black-and-white photos.

HOW TO USE THIS BOOK

If you look at a map of Devon, you'll see that you can extract an Africa-shaped chunk from the Exe Estuary and the A30 and A386 roads that run around the northern perimeter of Dartmoor to Plymouth. This is what we have (mostly) done in *South Devon and Dartmoor*, though some villages north and west of the main road have been described – because they deserve to be. Chapter divisions are relatively arbitrary; the largest (penultimate) chapter covers Dartmoor National Park and some villages beyond its perimeter. We have put the villages and attractions around the western and eastern sections of the national park – some still technically inside the park but with a different character – in separate chapters. Divisions in the south of the county are dictated by water, either the sea or rivers.

MAPS

Each chapter begins with a map with **numbered stopping points** that correspond to numbered headings in the text, and the relevant regional maps – large-scale maps for cyclists and walkers – are listed under the *Self-powered travel* headings.

FOOD, DRINK & ACCOMMODATION

We've listed some of our, and local people's, favourite pubs, cafés, restaurants and farm shops – anywhere supplying particularly good or unusual food or drink or because they're in a convenient location. Just be aware that such places close or change ownership frequently so check before setting out for that special meal.

The last chapter of this book lists a few recommended places to stay – or camp – out of the many hundreds in South Devon & Dartmoor. The hotels and B&Bs featured in this section are indicated by ♠ under the heading for the town or village in which they are located. Self-catering is indicated by ⌂, campsites by ⛺ and glamping by ⛺. For full descriptions of these listings visit ⌀ bradtguides.com/southdevonsleeps.

OPENING TIMES

Where they are useful, we have given the opening times of pubs, restaurants, tourist offices and attractions. They're correct at the time of writing but some may well change during the life of this book, so if they're important for your planning, do double-check before visiting. The same applies to the times of public transport.

ℹ FURTHER INFORMATION ON SOUTH DEVON & DARTMOOR

Visit Dartmoor ⌀ visitdartmoor.co.uk

Visit Devon ⌀ visitdevon.co.uk. Provides detailed information for visitors, with regional sites focusing on the most popular areas.

The English Riviera ⌀ englishriviera.co.uk

Visit Exeter ⌀ visitexeter.com

Visit Plymouth ⌀ visitplymouth.co.uk

Visit South Devon ⌀ visitsouthdevon.co.uk

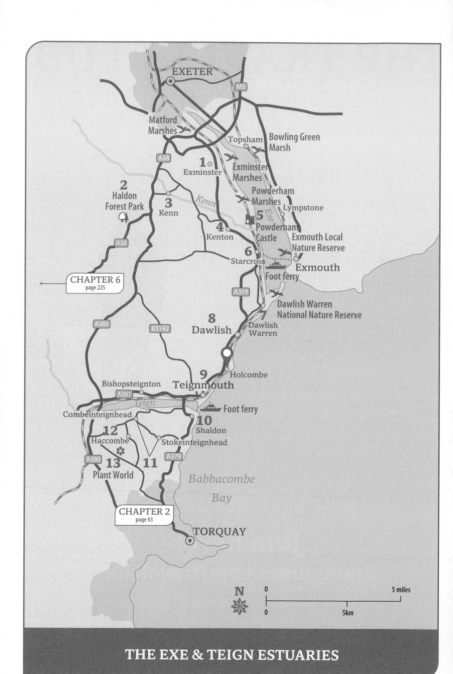

THE EXE & TEIGN ESTUARIES

1

THE EXE & TEIGN ESTUARIES

This area may not often hit the touristic headlines but it has some of South Devon's loveliest views and best birdwatching. Flatter than much of the county, it is friendly to walkers and cyclists, and its lack of main roads and large 'attractions' makes it well and truly Slow. Into a smallish space it packs rivers, thatched cottages, small ancient churches, beaches, cliffs and coastal views; while local museums and heritage centres offer glimpses of a fascinating rural past. The Exe and Teign estuaries host an exceptional variety of birdlife, and the rail journey southward from Exeter includes one of Britain's most scenic stretches.

 WET-WEATHER ACTIVITIES

Exeter Cathedral & **Royal Albert Memorial Museum** (page 33)
Avocet Line (page 35)
Powderham Castle (page 40)
Dawlish Museum (page 48)
Teign Heritage Centre & **art galleries** (page 50)

GETTING THERE & AROUND

The obvious gateway town is Exeter, with its airport, M5 motorway and rail links to London, Bristol and the north, but if you're travelling northward from Cornwall the area is equally accessible from Plymouth. Coming by **car** the area lies between the fast A380 and the slower A379, so everywhere mentioned here is easily accessible – and with not too many single-track roads, unless you take cross-country short cuts. Views while driving are pleasant but without the drama of Dartmoor.

Slow **trains** from Exeter St Davids stop at Starcross, Dawlish Warren, Dawlish, Teignmouth and Newton Abbot (expresses go direct to Newton Abbot) and offer wonderful estuary views. Leaving from

Exeter, sit on the left-hand side. **Buses** B from Exeter High Street and 2 from Exeter Bus Station between them serve all of the above, as well as Exminster and Kenton (for Powderham Castle); the number 22 runs between Dawlish Warren and Paignton daily via Shaldon. On Wednesday and Friday the 886 links Shaldon and Newton Abbot twice daily each way via Stokeinteignhead and Combeinteignhead, while the 366 runs once each way Monday–Saturday between Exeter and Kenn. Exeter is also the eastern terminus of the **Dartmoor Explorer** ($\mathcal{O}$ firstbus.co.uk/adventures-bus), which runs twice a day in each direction across the moor to Tavistock, stopping at all the towns and villages in between. The Devon bus timetable that you need is *Teignbridge*; timetables and routes are available from $\mathcal{O}$ traveldevon. info, as is information about rail travel and cycling. **Small foot ferries** will carry you and your cycle across the Exe (between Exmouth and Starcross, page 36) and the Teign (between Teignmouth and Shaldon, page 50).

SELF-POWERED TRAVEL

The award-winning **Exe Estuary Trail**, a part of National Cycle Network (NCN) route 2, is the cherry on this chapter's cake, offering some fabulous views and birdwatching across the water. The 16-mile cycleway/walkway, much of it off-road, follows the edge of the estuary from Exmouth on the east bank round to Dawlish Warren on the west bank, past nature reserves and waterside towns. For an excellent downloadable map and details, see $\mathcal{O}$ exe-estuary.org. The **South West Coast Path** and the Starcross/Exeter stretch of the Exe Valley Way also pass through this chapter's area, which is covered by OS Explorer map 110 and OS Landranger 192.

ESSENTIAL EXETER

Tourist information: The Custom Hse (46 The Quay, EX2 4AN $\odot$ Apr–Oct daily, Nov–Mar Thu–Sat) has tourist information that focuses on the quay & the estuary. There are also events & temporary exhibitions here, all free

Strictly speaking this guide starts just south of Exeter, but we're including the city briefly in case you pass through. For fuller coverage see our companion guide to this one, *Slow Travel East Devon & the Jurassic Coast*.

The two must secs are the cathedral (about five minutes' walk from the central railway station) and the Royal Albert Memorial Museum (only about two minutes). From St David's Rail Station they're a stiffish walk uphill (20–25 minutes) but there are buses from the station to the city centre. From the central bus station both are about ten minutes' walk, and on the way you can visit the tourist information centre.

The **Royal Albert Memorial Museum** (Queen St ✆ 01392 265858 ⊘ rammuseum.org.uk ☉ Tue–Sun; free entry) is an imposing Gothic building, completed in 1868 and extensively redeveloped in 2010–11. In 2012 it was named the UK's Museum of the Year by Art Fund, the national fundraising charity for art, and described as 'quite simply a magical place'. It claims to be 'home to a million thoughts', and indeed its million-odd exhibits do cover a massive range. As you might imagine, it's strong on the history of Devon and Exeter, from the prehistoric to the present, but also includes international cultures (with some rare West African art), ceramics, natural history (various birds, bugs, mammals and seashells), the 18th- and 19th-century global explorers and many other changing exhibits. Wonderful for a browse – but allow plenty of time.

The great crouching bulk of **St Peter's Cathedral** (✆ 01392 285983 ⊘ exeter-cathedral.org.uk), with its massive carved frontage, was started by the Normans in 1114 and remodelled in decorated Gothic style in 1270–1369. It's hunkered solidly on Cathedral Green, the weight of centuries pressing it into Exeter's earth; yet when you step inside your eye swings instantly up to the space and grace of its amazing roof: the longest unbroken stretch of Gothic vaulting in the world. When you've recovered from the impact of the building's size and splendour, you can focus on small, intimate details: animals on the choir stalls, sweet-faced angels playing musical instruments, sad swans with entwined necks, intricate roof bosses and the centuries-old hole in the door of the north tower to allow access for the cathedral cat.

You may want simply to gaze and absorb the atmosphere, but, if you'd like to learn more, the cathedral shop has guidebooks. The entrance fee helps to maintain this treasure-house of Exeter's history.

THE EXE ESTUARY

This broad stretch of water tethering Exeter to the sea is a haven of birdlife, with nature reserves, easy trails for cyclists and walkers, and

exceptional views. The eastern side is outside the range of this book, but we're including some practicalities about it to help you with overall planning. Buses and trains serve towns along both banks. Seasonal foot ferries criss-cross between Exeter, Exmouth, Topsham, Starcross and Old Topsham Lock (page 36). Different operators offer different concessions, so ask when you're booking.

From Exeter, two train journeys either side of the Exe Estuary are far more scenic than the same routes done by road. Both have sections running very close to the water. On the eastern bank, the short stretch to Exmouth is known as the **Avocet Line** ($\hat{\mathcal{O}}$ avocetline.org.uk) – and with good reason. In winter, thousands of waders and waterbirds come to the estuary, and the train windows offer a tremendous view. During the 30-minute journey you're likely to spot a variety of species – including avocets if you're very lucky – and even the occasional peregrine as it seeks out its prey. Numbers dwindle in summer, but the view is wonderful anyway. The little two-coach train takes up to two cycles if there's room but can be jam-packed with Exeter commuters at peak times, so travel off-peak if possible. From the Paignton/Plymouth train on the western side, you'll see the wetlands taking over from Exeter's urban compactness, Lympstone nestling between its red cliffs, colourful yachts scattered against the distant backdrop of Exmouth, Dawlish Warren's ancient sand dunes and the estuary gradually widening into the open sea of the English Channel. Starcross and Dawlish stations are so close

"In winter, thousands of waders and waterbirds come to the estuary, and the train windows offer a tremendous view."

to the water that at high tide it laps just below the platforms. After Teignmouth (pronounced Tin-mth) the train turns away from the sea to travel along the northern bank of the River Teign (pronounced Teen) to Newton Abbot, with peaceful views across to the southern bank.

Running from Exeter's historic quayside to Turf Lock (by the Turf Inn) is the four-mile **Exeter Ship Canal**, opened in 1566 on behalf of Exeter traders to improve access for shipping, which had been blocked by weirs. It was the first canal to be built in Britain since Roman times. The

◀ EXETER: **1** The River Exe flows through the city centre. **2** The amazing Gothic roof of St Peter's Cathedral. **3** Hop on a boat to explore the waterways around the city. **4** The Royal Albert Memorial Museum is excellent for rainy days.

big trading vessels have long since departed and now it's a peaceful spot for walkers, cyclists and boaters; the Exe Estuary Trail follows its bank, and bikes, canoes or kayaks can be hired on the quayside (see below).

⚓ FERRIES & BOAT TRIPS

Exeter Cruises ☏ 07984 368442 ⌖ exetercruises.com ⊙ Jul–Aug daily, Apr–Jun & Sep weekends only. Scenic 30-minute round-trip on the canal from Exeter Quay to Double Locks Inn. Also private hire.

Exmouth–Starcross Ferry ☏ 07934 461672 ⨍ ⊙ Mid-May–late Oct hourly daily, timetable on Facebook; carries cycles (including tandems).

Stuart Line ☏ 01395 222144 ⌖ stuartlinecruises.co.uk ⊙ year-round. Birdwatching & other cruises, including wildlife on the Exe Estuary, a coastal trip from Exmouth to Torquay & Brixham, & guided winter bird cruises that benefit the Devon Wildlife Trust (page 23).

Topsham Ferry ☏ 07801 203338 ⊙ Apr–Sep Wed–Sun, winter just weekends & bank holidays, plus Tue in school holidays. Times depend on tide; for details check Exeter Port Authority Facebook or phone. Runs from Ferry Road in Topsham to Topsham Lock on the Exeter Canal/Exe Valley Way (for Exminster Marshes).

Topsham to Turf Ferry (*Sea Dream II*) ☏ 07778 370582 ⌖ topshamturfferry.com ⊙ late May–mid-Sep daily, Easter & Apr weekends only, times on website. From Topsham at Trout's Boatyard to Turf Locks for the Turf Inn; takes cycles. Also private birdwatching & river cruises.

🚲 CYCLE & CANOE HIRE

Route 2 Bikes Topsham Quay ☏ 01392 879160 ⌖ route2bikes.co.uk ⊙ closed Sun. Cycle hire including electric bikes & a tandem.

Saddles & Paddles Exeter Quay ☏ 01392 424241 ⌖ sadpad.com ⊙ daily (check for off-season changes). Canoe, paddleboard & kayak hire (for Exeter Canal) plus bike hire, sales & repairs.

1 EXMINSTER

The avian attractions here are the RSPB's Exminster Marshes Nature Reserve (on the Estuary Trail) and Powderham Marshes. You can also walk or cycle to the Turf (page 38), one of the few pubs in the country that can't be reached by car, which has been providing refreshment to lock keepers and passing vessels since 1827.

Powderham Marshes are accessed (courtesy of Palmers brewery) via a track from the car park of the convenient Swan's Nest Inn just south of Exminster; the left turn from the A379 to the Swan's Nest is clearly signposted, at a roundabout. The one-mile trail leads through arable fields managed for farmland birds, including the rare cirl bunting. Brent geese gather there, and finches, including goldfinches and linnets, flock to feed in the stubble in winter. The observation platform at the end of the trail gives views across the estuary; bring binoculars.

Exminster Marshes are on the cycle trail; by car continue along the Swan's Nest turning until the narrow road crosses the railway, then almost immediately there's a sharp turn right to the free RSPB car park. It's at the start of a 2½-mile circular trail that takes you through fields alongside the railway – occasional trains whoosh by unnervingly – to the Turf pub on the edge of the Exeter Ship Canal. After pausing here for a drink and to admire the estuary view, follow the cycle trail northward for a peaceful, train-free return alongside the canal, the silence broken

BIRD RESERVES AROUND THE EXE ESTUARY

Walking or cycling round the estuary will take you past some of the best mudflats and wetland habitats in Devon. In spring you can see lapwings and redshanks and – if you're seriously dedicated – listen for the rare Cetti's warbler; but autumn is the most rewarding time, when thousands of waterbirds, including dark-bellied brent geese, fly from the freezing Arctic to overwinter there. As winter approaches other wildfowl crowd into the estuary to feed – look out for huge flocks of widgeon and graceful pintail ducks, as well as black-tailed godwits and shoveler ducks.

The ace in the pack, however, is the avocet and you have a good chance of seeing some in the winter (in spring they go to East Anglia and the Netherlands to breed), especially on the special birdwatching cruises run by the RSPB and the Stuart Line from Topsham, Exmouth or Starcross (see opposite).

The RSPB (⌀ rspb.org.uk) has four reserves along the estuary. On the eastern side is **Bowling Green Marsh**, in the pocket of wetlands south of Topsham between the River Clyst and the Exe; in summer, Topsham Ferry connects it to **Exminster Marshes** and **Powderham Marshes** on the western side. The smaller **Matford Marshes** is close to the A379 in the surprisingly green outskirts of Exeter, on the edge of the floodplain. Near Exmouth is the extensive and accessible **Exmouth Local Nature Reserve**, one of Devon's largest, with its constantly changing tidal mudflats and sands; and on the western side the **Dawlish Warren National Nature Reserve** (page 46) is centred on a 1½-mile sand-spit at the estuary's mouth. The Exe Estuary Management Partnership (⌀ 01392 382236 ⌀ exe-estuary.org) produces a series of leaflets, *Exe Wildlife*, *Exe Explorer*, *Exe Heritage* and *Exe Activities*, available online and from tourist information centres. These are excellent, providing maps and useful details of walks, birds and ferries.

only by fish sploshing to the surface, coots scuttling through the reeds and an occasional bird-call. Watch out for kingfishers and, in spring and early summer, hairy dragonflies (*Brachytron pratense*). An observation platform part-way along gives you a view inland; binoculars are helpful here, to identify birds in the fields and ponds, possibly lapwings, kestrels, buzzards, herons, egrets, brent geese, finches and more. After almost a mile, at a small private car park on your left (visitors' parking is allowed, in the marked bays), you can either turn left and return up the lane that led past the RSPB car park or else continue a little further to the Topsham Ferry.

"The silence is broken only by fish sploshing to the surface and coots scuttling through the reeds."

Next to the Swan's Nest, on the site of the old Exminster railway station, is **Toby's Reclamation Yard** (✐ 01392 833499 ☕ tobysreclamation. com), a cornucopia of a place with rooms full of interior and exterior furniture, statuary, building materials, antiques, doors, fireplaces, objets d'art… Happy browsing!

⊪ FOOD & DRINK

The Turf Exeter Canal, Exminster ✐ 01392 833128 ☕ turfpub.net ☉ roughly Apr–late Nov. The sign on its wall says The Turf Hotel, but this popular pub, on the edge of the estuary & looking straight across the water to Exmouth, is known locally as the Turf or the Turf Inn. It's a rambling old place, with thick walls & a feel of the sea about it, accessible to visitors only by kayak, boat or ferry (page 36) or by foot and/or cycle – from the RSPB car park or private car park mentioned above, or along the footpath from Powderham Church (about 25 minutes). Despite its isolation, the Turf bustles in summer & at weekends. Camping, B&B & a yurt are also available.

2 HALDON FOREST PARK

Kennford EX6 7XR ☕ forestryengland.uk/haldon-forest-park

This is a well-managed 3,500-acre woodland with clearly marked and graded trails for walkers, runners, cyclists and horseriders. Open every day except Christmas Day, entrance is free with paid car parking.

Youngsters can follow the 1½-mile Superworm activities trail and discover lots of interesting facts about tiny creatures. An extensive orienteering trail is more of a challenge for all the family. For an adrenalin rush, Go Ape has zip wires and high-level walkways through the treetops; it looked scary even from the ground. Perhaps renting a Segway to ride around the forest is more in keeping with Slow travel; they also rent out bikes and trampers.

The Ridgeway Café serves a wide range of snacks, cakes and drinks and has indoor and outdoor seating. There are also many lovely peaceful spots for a picnic.

3 KENN

Tucked away in a green landscape only five miles from Exeter, and perhaps a mile from the busy A38, Kenn presents itself as the perfect Devon village. Well, almost perfect; there's no village shop, but the library, housed in the old phone box, makes up for this. Villagers are invited to borrow a book, read it and return it, and to add more.

A little brook runs past thatched cottages ending with The Ley Arms, also thatched. Opposite the pub a mature chestnut tree, speckled with red 'candles' or dropping conkers, depending on the time of year, shares a grassy circle with a white wooden signpost. Up on a hill, and framed by trees, is the tall tower of the red sandstone church. An illustrated board by the graveyard points out the flora and fauna found there, and its ancient yew tree is splendid: huge and cathedral-like with its pillars of surviving trunk around a hollow centre.

The church smells right – and that's important – with the indescribable scent of old oak, flowers and mildew that defines our country churches. Part of the font comes from Oberammergau, there's a fine barrel roof with painted bosses, some hand-hewn dark-oak benches and pew shelves, and a finely carved alabaster pulpit with a portrait of St Andrew and his distinctive cross. But the glory of this church is the wooden screen. Lavishly carved with entwining foliage, the niches contain some of the best-preserved painted saints in the county. There's St Sebastian, so cluttered

"The church smells right, with the indescribable scent of old oak, flowers and mildew that defines our country churches."

with arrows that it's hard to make out his body; St Apollonia, patron saint of dentists and toothache (page 230); and the four evangelists, who are so holy even the animals at their feet have halos, including a very cute lion. Most unusual is St Mary of Egypt, one of only two depictions in the country (the other is in Norfolk). Mary had a colourful life in the fleshpots of Alexandria, but repented her sins and wandered off into the desert with only three loaves of bread to sustain her and her long hair to keep her warm.

If you visit the church expressly to look at the painted niches, a torch is useful to pick out the details.

4 KENTON

The car park in the centre of this pleasant but not especially picturesque village is handily near the 14th-century church of All Saints, described by John Leland (c1540) as 'a right goodly church': an impressive listed building of red sandstone whose 120ft tower is the second tallest in Devon. (St Nectan's in Hartland, North Devon, beats it by 8ft.) Don't be put off by the modern entrance; the interior includes a fine rood screen (mentioned in Simon Jenkins's *England's Thousand Best Churches*), some attractive carving and an unusual wooden 15th-century pulpit that in 1882 was rescued from a cupboard, in pieces, by the ubiquitous Sabine Baring-Gould (page 266) and reassembled. From the outside this church is strikingly similar to St Andrew's in Kenn, only a few miles' drive away.

5 POWDERHAM CASTLE

Kenton EX6 8JQ ✆ 01626 890243 ⌂ powderham.co.uk ◷ castle & grounds Apr–Oct 11.00–16.30 Sun–Fri plus occasional Sat; 50% discount on admission for National Trust & English Heritage members

Entered from the A379 in Kenton, Powderham Castle, dating back to 1391, has been the home of the Earl and Countess of Devon for over 600 years. The present Earl (the 19th, and the 28th generation of Courtenays to live in the castle) inherited the title when his father died in 2015. The castle was besieged during the Wars of the Roses and badly damaged by parliamentary forces in the Civil War, and, as all good castles should, has its share of ghost stories, notably of a 'grey lady' on the landing and shutters which were mysteriously screwed back into place after being opened to provide blackout during World War II.

Like so many stately homes, it now earns its keep by opening to the public for part of the year, but remains very much a family home,

---

1 The nature reserves around the Exe Estuary include Matford Marshes. **2** Powderham Castle has been home to the Earl and Countess of Devon for over 600 years. **3** In Starcross you can find an old pumping station from Isambard Kingdom Brunel's atmospheric railway. **4** Wintry walking in Haldon Forest. ▶

with the earl's two young children sometimes mingling with visitors. Guided tours of the interior (its beautifully proportioned rooms from a variety of architectural periods include some opulent furnishings and fine 18th-century Rococo-style plasterwork) are held throughout the day and prove very popular in summer; one of the enthusiastic guides told me that he barely has time to draw breath. No wonder, when they tell so many anecdotes! The kitchen, as old as the house itself, has been restored, with lots of gleaming copper utensils, to reflect its condition in Victorian times. In 2017 the medieval solar (the old family room, focus of home life through many generations) was also restored.

Among the ancient oak, chestnut, lime and cedar trees that surround Powderham, an unexpected find is a Wollemi pine, planted by the earl's father; this prehistoric tree became world-famous following its rediscovery in Australia in 1994. The well-kept grounds offer peaceful strolls, beautiful views and various family-friendly attractions (pets' corner, birds of prey, nature trails), while on some days (check the website for the current programme) a tractor-trailer carries groups on 'safari' to the surrounding deer park with its 600-odd fallow deer and other wildlife. When I was last there a medievally clad storyteller had a string of children trailing, pied-piper-like, behind him. The licensed (dog-friendly) **Courtyard Café** offers snacks, light lunches and diet-busting cream teas; or visitors can use the picnic tables set up in the grounds. Also in the courtyard, the **gift shop** has imaginative souvenirs and crafts, and leads to the **Courtenay Gallery,** with ancient treasures from the castle's archives and an interactive digital display exploring 1,000 years of history, as well as a copy of the Courtenay family Bible which, published in 1626, is one of the earliest editions of the King James Version.

"The well-kept grounds offer peaceful strolls, beautiful views and various family-friendly attractions."

The peaceful and appealing little **chapel** was originally built around 1450 as a 'grange' or accommodation for visitors to the medieval castle. Its 16th-century carved pew ends come from St Andrew's Church in South Huish near Kingsbridge, which is now a ruin looked after by (this sounds so sad) the Friends of Friendless Churches. In 1866, when parts of it were already 500 years old, the parishioners of St Andrew's decided that the repairs it needed were far beyond their means (a window had just been blown in by a storm during Divine Service) and it was abandoned. However, some of its 'organs' were transplanted to give new life elsewhere: the 14th-century font went to a new church being built in Galmpton (page 90), near South Huish, and the pew ends were given to the 11th Earl of Devon, who converted the Powderham grange into the present chapel in 1874. Outside the chapel is a large mulberry tree with a notice warning visitors that the fallen fruit underfoot can be messy – and also saying 'help yourself', which I did and they were delicious. Manna from Heaven?

Various events throughout the year (fairs, festivals, music…) include, in April, the popular **Toby's Garden Festival** (⊘ tobygardenfest.co.uk), run by Devon-born gardener, TV presenter and author Toby Buckland; and in October the **Powderham Food Festival** (⊘ powderhamfoodfestival. com) with a mass of local contributors. The castle can be busy in summer, so for Slow visitors off-season visits are recommended.

At the top of the castle grounds next to Kenton's main street is a small group of shops, open year-round. The huge **General Trading Company**, run by Bovey Tracey's House of Marbles (page 307), stocks old-fashioned toys and games (including, of course, numerous and multi-coloured marbles), wonderfully soft alpaca knitwear and other stylish clothing, books, jewellery, toiletries, furnishings, bags and souvenirs. The **Orangery Restaurant** (⊘ 01626 891639, also run by House of Marbles) covers the range, from breakfasts through lunches to cream teas, and is popular locally. When I called in for coffee, the venison sausages and homemade fishcakes looked (and smelt) tempting. **Urban and Rural Plants** (⊘ 01626 891133) is a well-stocked garden centre, with plants helpfully classified according to their favoured conditions (wet, dry, sunny, etc). Finally, **Powderham Farm Shop** (⊘ 01626 891883) has a great range of locally produced goodies – cheeses, preserves, pâtés, wine, baking, meat, and organic fruit and vegetables – and treats from further afield too, depending on season and availability. It also has a small café.

6 STARCROSS

Starcross is an unassuming little place, clinging so closely to the edge of the estuary that from the platform of the railway station, at high tide, you can look straight down into the water. Its value for visitors is the Exmouth–Starcross Ferry (page 36) which docks just a stone's throw

THE ATMOSPHERIC RAILWAY IN DEVON

The possibility of using air pressure to provide propulsion for a vehicle or train came to life early in the 19th century, although Thomas Newcomen (page 138) had pointed the way with his atmospheric pumping engine 100 years earlier. In 1812 George Medhurst of London proposed somehow blowing passenger carriages through a tunnel but unsurprisingly the idea didn't catch on. In 1838 gas engineer Samuel Clegg and marine engineers Jacob and Joseph Samuda jointly took out a patent for a new improvement in valves and at this point atmospheric propulsion with pumping engines became feasible. They set up a working model in Southwark in 1839 and ran a half-mile demonstration track at Wormwood Scrubs from 1840 to 1843. Things were moving fast, with many top-level railway technicians expressing both interest and criticism; the first atmospheric railway opened in Ireland in 1844, followed by one on the outskirts of Paris. Another was started in 1846 on five miles of the London and Croydon Railway, but it encountered too many problems and in 1847 was scrapped.

Among experts keeping a close eye on progress was Isambard Kingdom Brunel, who had been appointed engineer to the South Devon Railway in 1844; he recommended using the system on a much longer stretch, from Exeter to Torre and Totnes. The trains literally ran on air, with a combination of partial vacuum and atmospheric pressure; they were practically silent, and with no nuisance caused by steam or smuts. At stations along the route, including Exeter, Turf, Starcross and Dawlish, pumping houses were built and steam-driven pumping engines were installed in them. The first train ran in September 1847, between Exeter and Teignmouth.

There were always difficulties. Among others, the pumping engines used far more coal than expected, communication between pumping houses was poor, and the leather flap valves sealing the traction pipes deteriorated from use and the salty atmosphere. Treated with oil to prevent this, they then attracted hungry rats and mice, which got sucked into the tube and thus jammed the piston – at which point third-class passengers might have to dismount and push the train to the next station. At the system's peak, nine trains a day ran between Exeter and Teignmouth at up to 70mph; but the cost and the many operational problems proved insurmountable. The last train ran in September 1848, gradually the machinery was removed, and the pumping houses were closed and dismantled. The one at Starcross is the only one that has survived in situ, although its machinery was stripped out long since.

from the station; walk down the platform and along a pier and you're there. Combining this with the good bus and rail services (page 31), plus cycling and/or walking, offers you a variety of circular trips around the two shores of the estuary.

The reddish building with a tower was the old pumping station of Isambard Kingdom Brunel's atmospheric railway (see opposite). The chimney was once much taller, but was damaged in a storm in the 1890s. The Atmospheric Railway Inn has – appropriately – some related memorabilia around the walls: old photos, newspaper cuttings, lamps, models and so forth.

¶¶ FOOD & DRINK

The **Atmospheric Railway Inn** (✆ 01626 906290 ⬛) is on the main street near the railway station & ferry. Interesting menu featuring local beef & fish; even the gin & rum are made locally.

Teigh Bean Starcross car park ⬿ teighbean.co.uk. Independent take-away coffee & home-made cakes. Handy for both the station & the ferry.

The Anchor Inn ✆ 01626 890203 ⬿ anchorinncockwood.com. This deservedly popular 17th-century inn, a mile or so south of Starcross, on the edge of Cockwood's tiny harbour, specialises in seafood – in fact I counted 14 mussel dishes on its menu!

DAWLISH WARREN & DAWLISH

Here the estuary opens out into the English Channel. Bustlingly busy in the summer, with some very un-Slow 'amusement' areas and tourist paraphernalia, these two small resorts, just a couple of miles apart, retain a flavour of old-time seaside, with long, windswept beaches, ice creams, beach huts and promenades. They're far more peaceful out of season. Below the tideline (gritty sand at Dawlish, finer at Dawlish Warren) *"You can beach-comb for shells, sea-smoothed glass and other salty treasures."* you can beach-comb for shells, bleached driftwood, cuttlefish 'bone', sea-smoothed glass and other salty treasures, and swimming is safe. The flat walk between them along the sea wall and cliff path is a constant pleasure – beware of waves in stormy weather – and you can do part of it on the beach at low tide. The waterside rail journey from Exeter is the most memorably scenic in this book, and at its most dramatic during winter storms when trains can get thoroughly soaked. As you approach Dawlish, you can see the repairs to the sea wall made after storm damage in February 2014 left the rails dangling precariously above the waves. Buses 2 and 2B run from Exeter to Dawlish and buses 22 and 222 run from Dawlish Warren through Dawlish and on to Teignmouth.

7 DAWLISH WARREN

🏠 **Brunel Holiday Park** (page 336)

Tourist information: 🖉 dawlishwarren.info

Apart from its Blue Flag beach, the attraction of Dawlish Warren is its 500-acre **National Nature Reserve** (🖉 dawlishwarren.info, follow links), an area of grassland, sand dunes and mudflats centred on a 1½-mile sand-spit/beach stretching across the mouth of the Exe Estuary. It's a wild, peaceful and windswept place where (out of season) you can wander without spotting another soul. Parking is outside, near the entrance.

The long, sandy, dune-edged shoreline is superb and an internationally important area for wildlife: the main roosting site for the huge numbers of wading birds and wildfowl (dunlin, grey plover, bar-tailed godwit, oystercatcher, brent geese, widgeon and teal, among others) that spend the autumn and winter on the estuary. Other habitats include salt marsh, freshwater ponds, wet meadows and woodland.

The reserve is also designated a Special Area of Conservation (SAC) for its dune grassland, humid dune slacks and the tiny, rare 'petalwort' that grows there. In spring the ancient dunes blossom with wildflowers, including the spectacular blue sea holly and the yellow evening primrose with its large crinkled petals. With luck and sharp eyes you might also spot the little lilac-coloured sand crocus (*Romulea columnae*), whose only other known location on the British mainland is at Polruan in Cornwall. A small visitor centre (🖉 01626 863980) with information and displays is open most weekends from October to March, and most days (irregularly) from April to September. Rangers run guided walks from there. About a mile beyond the visitor centre is a bird hide, excellent for watching the waders and wildfowl in winter. Viewing is best two hours either side of medium-high tides. Dogs must be kept on a lead and are not allowed in some areas.

To get to the reserve from the centre of Dawlish Warren, go through the little railway tunnel by the station, turn left past the amusement area with its arcades and razzmatazz, and continue through the car park to the gate at the far end.

---

1 Dawlish has a long, sandy beach between sandstone cliffs. **2** The town is lit up by its annual carnival in August. **3** There are plenty of activities for children at Dawlish Museum. **4** A sanderling at Dawlish Warren's nature reserve. **5** All aboard the Teignmouth–Shaldon foot ferry. ▶

Beyond the amusement area are some useful shops and the only toilets on the reserve. Warren Trading Co sells some good outdoor and indoor clothing and there is a restaurant and some seasonal food and drink outlets. For rail buffs there's some unusual self-catering accommodation at the Brunel Holiday Park (page 336) – in old railway carriages, facing seaward across the line where the atmospheric railway once ran.

8 DAWLISH

🏠 **Lammas Park House** (page 336)

> Half village, half town, it is – pleasant but smallish,
> And known, where it happens to be known, as Dawlish;
> A place I'd suggest
> As one of the best
> For a man breaking down who needs absolute rest,
> Especially, too, if he's weak in the chest.
> R H D Barham, 1867

I wish I could, as local residents seem to, come to terms with the garish amusement complex dominating the main square, because without it Dawlish could be a pretty town. A brook flanked by gardens, Dawlish Water, runs through the centre, there are some pleasingly twisty streets and attractive buildings, the beach is long and mostly sandy between red sandstone cliffs and there's a friendly feeling of bustle. Oddities are appealing: Dawlish Community Transport runs a little red minibus called Rosie, black swans and various other exotic waterbirds display themselves on Dawlish Water, and the busy railway station café, improbably named Geronimo's Diner, is decorated with Wild West artefacts.

In the early 20th century, Dawlish became famous for the popular perfume Devon Violets, and hundreds of varieties of violet were raised in market gardens – you may still spot them growing wild in the area. Jane Austen holidayed here in 1802 and complained about the 'particularly pitiful and wretched library'. Today she could enjoy **Dawlish Museum** (✆ 01626 888557 🌐 devonmuseums.net 🕐 run by volunteers, variable opening hours), with its three floors of wonderfully miscellaneous memorabilia linked to Dawlish and Devon: anything from a penny-farthing bicycle to bagpipes, 19th-century bridalwear and an ancient mousetrap. The late Queen's 90th birthday is featured, as is the great storm of 2014 which demolished the local rail line, and there are plenty of activities for children.

South of the main beach (which you enter via a tunnel under the railway) is the smaller Coryton Cove, sheltered and pleasant for swimming. In the days of segregated bathing this was the gentlemen's beach; the ladies had their bathing pavilion towards the other end. At holiday time the beaches and indeed the whole town can become uncomfortably busy.

⫴ FOOD & DRINK

Daisy's Tea Room 25 The Strand ✆ 07793 209045 ⬛. A friendly, traditional place with cream teas, wonderful homemade cakes, salads, snacks & light meals.

Gay's Creamery & Pie Shop 20 Brunswick Pl ✆ 01626 863341 ⬛. Pies, pasties, top-class ice creams, homemade cakes, cream teas, salads & hot snacks. Take-away service but there are benches & tables nearby where you can sit & watch the black swans. Also a good range of local preserves, confectionery, cider & souvenirs.

Salty Dog Kiosk Smugglers Ln, Holcombe ⬧ saltydogkiosks.business.site ⬛ ◷ Feb–Oct 09.30–16.00 Wed–Mon. Excellent coffee & snacks by the sea. The owner posts daily updates every morning on Facebook for weather conditions, tides & whether the seawall footpath is walkable.

The Smugglers Inn 27 Teignmouth Rd (1.2 miles from Dawlish on A379) ✆ 01626 862301 ⬧ thesmugglersinn.net. A spacious restaurant & bar with an outside terrace & panoramic coastal views. Daily carvery with meat from an award-winning local butcher.

Sticky Rice Lawn Hill ✆ 01626 437343 ⬧ thestickyrice.co.uk. Delicious Thai food to eat in or take away; we can recommend the pad med ma muong & the beef massaman curry.

THE TEIGN VALLEY

For there's Bishop's teign
And King's teign
And Coomb at the clear Teign head –
Where close by the stream
You may have your cream
All spread upon barley bread...
John Keats, 1818

9 TEIGNMOUTH

🏠 **Yannon Towers** (page 336)

Teignmouth was granted its market charter in 1253 and in the early 14th century was Devon's second-largest port, smaller only than Dartmouth. It has known smuggling and shipwrecks, and in 1690 was left in ruins by a French raid, recalled on a panel at the corner of French Street:

> **On the 26th day of this instant July 1690 by foure of the clocke in the morning your poor petitioners were invaded by the French to the number of 1,000 or thereabouts, who in the space of three hours tyme, burnt down to the ground the dwelling houses of 240 persons of our parish.**

The arrival of Brunel's railway in 1846 brought a huge increase in tourism, and Teignmouth today is a well-laid-out and organised seaside resort with a range of attractions: Victorian pier (now given over to 'amusements'), gardens, clean sandy beach, heated lido and the excellent **Teign Heritage Centre** (✆ 01626 777041 ◈ teignheritage.org. uk ⊙ Tue–Sat), opened in an eye-catching modern building in 2011. Its extensive displays run from prehistory to the present, and include an Edwardian bathing machine, relics from a 16th-century shipwreck, old pier slot machines and other local memorabilia. History walks are organised from here and it's a good source of local information. On the northern edge of town, accessed from the promenade just past the lido, **Eastcliff Park** offers some pleasant clifftop strolls, beautiful sea views, carefully tended lawns, a walled garden dating back to around 1825, and a subtropical valley garden, the Dell, created some 100 years ago.

For me, Teignmouth doesn't have the endearing quirkinesses of some smaller resorts, but its classic Georgian crescents are attractive and visitors return year after year. The back streets are fun, with twisting little alleys and some original small shops. The area around Northumberland Place, where Keats is said to have lived in 1818, is becoming known as an **arts quarter**, with various galleries, of which **TAAG** (Teignmouth Arts Action Group ✆ 01626 779251 ◈ teignmoutharts.org) at No 4/5 is particularly worth visiting, with a constantly changing programme of exhibitions. At No 43 is the independent, family-run **Quayside Bookshop** (✆ 01626 775436), with new, secondhand and rare books. It's particularly strong on transport.

Teignmouth holds an **International Folk Festival** (◈ teignmouthfolk. co.uk) in June and its regatta in July/August. Walks are varied and plentiful, whether along the coast or up into the countryside; and the 18-mile Templer Way to Haytor on Dartmoor starts here.

The **Teignmouth–Shaldon foot ferry** (✆ 07896 711822 ◈ teignmouthshaldonferry.co.uk ⊙ times vary seasonally) has been running in various forms since at least the 13th century and is said to be Britain's oldest such service. It carries cycles and dogs, starts from

Back Beach near the lifeboat station and runs year-round except over Christmas. Also based on Back Beach, **Riviera Cruises** (*🖉* 07921 761224 ☉ seasonal) take passengers on bay cruises, River Teign cruises and mackerel fishing trips. Their boat *The Restless* was the Teignmouth auxiliary lifeboat for many years. At the other end of Back Beach, behind New Quay Inn, is **Devon Sea Safari** (*🖉* 07931 291191 *𝓭* devonseasafari. com) offering one- to two-hour coastal tours in their Humber RIB boat; it is a great way to see marine wildlife including dolphins, porpoise and seals.

An alternative to the ferry is to **walk to Shaldon** across the A379 bridge; when the first – a wooden one – was built in 1827 it had 34 arches and was said to be the longest in the country. A span at the Teignmouth end could be raised to let tall vessels pass through. The centre collapsed in 1838, having been eaten by ship-worm, and again in 1893. The bridge was completely rebuilt in 1927–31, using steel for the piers and main girders and concrete for most of the deck, and allowing for subsequent repairs that's the one you see today. It occasionally whistles when winds catch it from a certain direction.

A couple of miles from Teignmouth, tucked away among fields, is the little ruined 13th-century **chapel of St Mary**, protected by a rusty iron railing with a sign saying Lidwell Chapel. I'm reminded of Tennyson's 'a chapel near the field, a broken chancel with a broken cross' from *Morte d'Arthur*, but this old story is far grizzlier: of a medieval monk living there who murdered visiting travellers and threw their bodies down a well. R H D Barham, son of the author of the *Ingoldsby Legends*, wrote a light-hearted poem about it (*The Monk of Haldon*) in 1867, by which time it was already the stuff of legend, so who knows what's true. To reach it, drive out of Teignmouth up the B3192 and, just after the golf course (on your left), a steepish footpath on the right leads down to it. The ground can be very muddy. It's marked on OS Explorer map 110, near Lidwell Farm (♥ SX924762). There's not much to see – only the west wall is still standing and the rest has crumbled – but it's a pretty and peaceful place and a listed monument. Beyond is private land, so you need to return the same way.

Just outside Bishopsteignton on Old Walls Hill is **Old Walls Vineyard** (*🖉* 01626 770877 *𝓭* oldwallsvineyard.co.uk). It's surprisingly historic: the Romans are thought to have planted vines on the same south-facing slopes and made wine there 2,000 years ago, and the name refers to the nearby remnants of old walls, which are all that's left of the 13th-century bishop's palace (*Bishop's-teign-ton*, you see?). Full-day vineyard tours run throughout the year (booking essential) and show the whole winemaking process from vines to wine and include lunch and a tasting of Old Wall's still wines. A small shop sells their wine and a good range of local food and drink. Also available is 'Rent a Vine', an innovative idea where you can 'rent' specific vines and, after the harvest, receive the wine they produced. There is a bistro on site (☉ Wed–Sun) as well as a few holiday lodges set in the vineyard.

¶ FOOD & DRINK

Elizabethan Inn Fore St, Luton TQ13 0BL ✆ 01626 775425 ⌂ elizabethaninn.co.uk. About three miles northwest of Bishopsteignton in the little village of Luton, this historic inn offers traditional food with an extra touch of class.

Crabshack 3 Queen St (near Back Beach) ✆ 01626 879202 ⌂ crabshackonthebeach.co.uk. Very strong on seafood, locally & sustainably caught, from luxury to relatively inexpensive. Pleasant & efficient staff. It's a light & bright place but not large, & it gets busy, so booking is advised at popular times. There's also a self-catering apartment above the restaurant.

The Owl & the Pussycat 3 Teign St ✆ 01626 775321 ⌂ theowlandpussycat.co.uk ☉ 18.00–21.00 Fri–Sat. This restaurant has been notable for elegant but informal dining for more than 13 years. You are guaranteed amazing food, all beautifully presented. The short menu features locally caught seafood and beef steaks from South Devon farms. The pan-fried scallops starter is reason enough to dine here. Good value. Booking recommended.

10 SHALDON

🏠 **The Ness** (page 336)

Tourist information: Ness Drive (in the car park) ✆ 01626 873723 ☉ May–Sep 10.30–16.30; the very helpful staff are volunteers so times may vary. A useful website is ⌂ shaldon-devon.co.uk.

This appealing village has a superb location, perched between the Teign Estuary and the sea, and a surprising number of **events** for such a small place: a small international classical music festival in June (⌂ shaldonfestival.co.uk), a water carnival (⌂ shaldonwatercarnival.co.uk) and popular nine-day 200-year-old regatta (⌂ shaldonregatta.com) in August, various watersports on the Teign Estuary and other local activities to suit the season. On summer Wednesdays a Craft Fair is held, with craftspeople in medieval costume.

At **Ness Cove** there is a pleasant beach of sand plus shingle (covered at high tide) which you approach through a tunnel – lots of fun for children – often called the **Smugglers' Tunnel**, though it seems a little too well built for that. The beach also has rock pools.

Towering over the shore is a red headland, **Ness Point**, and tucked neatly on it is a delightful little zoo, the **Shaldon Wildlife Trust** (✆ 01626 872234 ⌂ shaldonwildlifetrust.org.uk), which specialises in small animals such as marmosets, margays and tamarins from South America, meerkats from Africa and lemurs from Madagascar. There is also a small collection of reptiles and invertebrates, and a tropical house with poison dart frogs and tiny geckos. Perhaps their most unusual animal is a binturong, also known as a bear-cat, from south Asia and about six feet long. The spacious enclosures are cleverly designed to maximise space, and the animals are well cared for.

The **Homeyards Botanical Gardens** (⌂ shaldonbotanicalgardens. org), a stiff-ish climb up from the waterfront, were created by the energetic Maria Laetitia Kempe Homeyard with the money made from the invention by her husband, William Newcombe Homeyard, of Liqufruta, a garlic-based cough remedy that was revered as a cure-all in the early part of the 20th century. Entry to Homeyards is free, and it is maintained by a dedicated team of volunteers. The gardens are natural rather than manicured and pleasant for strolling, with some unusual shrubs and trees and an Italianate garden. They also offer terrific views over the Teign Estuary. There's a substantial 'summer house' designed to look like a castle, where Mrs Homeyard used to entertain guests to tea and which is now used for community events. It is not to be confused with the limestone grotto where the local witch Old Mother Gum is said to come at dusk for a furtive cuppa. The restored gardener's hut is now a roost for swallows and lesser horseshoe bats. Volunteers have been working hard to improve and develop the gardens, and arrange various activities.

"This appealing village has a superb location, perched between the estuary and the sea, and a surprising number of events."

If you take the road to the west along the estuary, about half a mile from Shaldon village centre you'll come to a tiny **church** – **St Nicholas** – dozing at the end of an alley with its back to the Teign. The writer W H Hoskins dismisses it as containing 'nothing of note', although the font is thought to be Saxon. We visited in early evening, well after closing time, but two parishioners were busy hoovering. And Hoskins was right, there's nothing of much note inside the church, but one of the ladies couldn't wait to show us a special gravestone outside: to William Newcombe Homeyard. When he died in 1927 his widow Maria Laetitia wanted the brand name of his great achievement to be put on his gravestone, but it was vetoed by the vicar as inappropriate advertising. She then asked if she could put a Latin inscription instead and that was approved. So forget the Saxon font and seek out the three-tier commemorative cross with Gothic letters proudly spelling out ATURFUQIL on the top stone, in the 'unfading' memory of its creator. No, it's not Latin, just Liqufruta spelt backwards!

Bus-assisted walk: Holcombe to Ness Cove

✻ OS Explorer map 110; start: the Ness car park, TA14 0HP ♀ SX93807188; just over three miles; mostly level, with one short steep-ish climb to the bus stop at the start.

After the bus ride, the walk follows perhaps the easiest 1½ miles of the whole 630-mile South West Coast Path, but that makes it no less rewarding. Then a short trip on the Teignmouth–Shaldon ferry and a final smugglers' surprise.

Friendly volunteers run a tourist information cabin in the Ness car park. There is also the excellent ODE café, which serves organic meals, snacks and good coffee (see opposite).

Walk up the track behind the café, which leads you to the main Torquay Road. Down to the right and across the road is the bus stop for the number 22 which runs hourly, at about ten minutes past the hour. It is a 20-minute ride north to Holcombe.

In Holcombe, take **Smugglers' Lane** – it is the first turning on the right as the bus enters the village. The lane runs steeply down to the sea and, at the bottom, you'll find the **Salty Dog Kiosks** coffee shop (◆ ☺ closed Tue). It is worth looking on their Facebook page before you set out, as every morning, the owner posts the weather and tide conditions. In very stormy weather or when there is an extreme tide, the wall may be overtopped by waves, making it unsafe for walkers.

After refreshments at the Salty Dog, it is a level stroll all the way to Teignmouth along the sea wall. The walk is strangely isolated with just the English Channel on one side and the red sandstone cliffs on the other… and the odd passing train. While this can be a wild walk if the tide is in and the waves are high, on a calm day, with the tide out, you can choose to walk most of the way on the sandy beach.

FOOD & DRINK

Café ODE In the Ness car park near the TIC, Ness Drive ⌀ 01626 873427 ⌀ odetruefood. com ⊙ Wed–Sun. A thoroughly organic place (their motto is 'Good food that doesn't cost the Earth' & even the cutlery is compostable), & the manager told us: 'If we're sent vegetables that weren't grown locally we just send them back.' A good range of hot & cold meals & snacks with indoor & outdoor seating. The **ODE Restaurant** at 21 Fore Street (⌀ 01626 873977 ⊙ 19.00–21.00 Fri–Sat) offers very fine dining with extensive tasting menus.

The Ferry Boat Inn The Strand ⌀ 01626 872340 ⌀ theferryboatinn.co.uk. Run by a local couple Matt & Michelle, close to the ferry & with a beautiful view over the estuary. A real local's local with a reasonably priced menu & good selection of beer & wine. Live music some evenings & a terrace overlooking the estuary.

As you arrive in Teignmouth a second excellent coffee shack, the **Teign Bean**, is the first place to greet you. In fact, the town has no shortage of places for food and drink. The sea wall slowly becomes more of a promenade and passes the **pier**. The prom is a popular location for pop up events – Punch and Judy and a circus-themed band when we last walked along. After passing around the car park at the Point, you reach the **Teignmouth–Shaldon ferry** (page 50). In a couple of minutes it brings you on to the beach in **Shaldon**, once a tiny fishing and boatbuilding community   which may explain why there are so many public houses. Turn left on to Marine Drive to follow the shore. As the houses peter out you pass Sea Sentry, once part of the naval defences and now a tiny self-catering retreat for two.

Soon Marine Drive curves right and uphill to pass **the Ness hotel**; the Ness is also the name of the headland behind it. Lady Elizabeth Clifford bought the Ness headland and much of Shaldon after the death of her husband Thomas, 1st Baron Clifford of Chudleigh, in 1673. The hotel was built around 1810 as a summer home for many generations of the Clifford family. You may feel the need to stop for a drink on its terrace, just to enjoy those unsurpassed views of the Teign Estuary. But the final wonder of this walk is still ahead of you.

Rumour has it that the family subsequently enlarged their considerable fortune through smuggling and, to facilitate this, in the 1860s the 8th Lord Clifford had a **tunnel** built through the cliffs to reach Ness Cove. The tunnel is now open to the public, just a little way up the road beyond the hotel and past the car park on your right.

We did not meet any smugglers, but descending the tunnel's steps to the red sand beach below is definitely a bizarre and unmissable end to this lovely walk. Today, the beach is more popular with picnickers than pirates.

Strand Café The Strand (near the ferry) ℘ 01626 872624 ⌀ thestrandcafebistro.co.uk. Breakfasts, popular brunches (including homemade pancakes with various toppings), cream teas & good baking. Nice terrace overlooking the harbour.

SOUTH OF THE TEIGN

This smallish strip of countryside manages to contain three exceptional little churches and extremely pretty traditional villages. The lanes between them may be twisty but they're well worth the effort.

11 STOKEINTEIGNHEAD & COMBEINTEIGNHEAD

⚐ **Rocombe Valley Retreat** (page 336)

The alternative spellings, Stoke-in-Teignhead and Combe-in-Teignhead, give a clue to the pronunciation of these two attractive villages. The 'in-teign-head' part is said to come from 'in ten hide', *hide* being an Anglo-Saxon measurement of area. Deep in the countryside yet a stone's throw from Teignmouth and Newton Abbot, they have good pubs, thatched cottages, and interesting churches. Arch Brook, which runs into **Stokeinteignhead**, gives the village some extra charm, which it has in bucketfuls anyway. There's a particularly attractive row of white houses lined up along the combe, and St Andrew's Church has allegedly the oldest screen in the country. Certainly it seems to be a simpler design than usually seen, and there's a brass dated 1375 which makes it the oldest in Devon. On the other side of the main street a community shop, rescued by the villagers from closure, has a good supply of home baking, local vegetables and other necessities.

Combeinteignhead also has an absolute treasure in its 13th-century church of All Saints, which you'd never guess when approaching its shocking pink door and seeing the even more inappropriate pink wall-tiles inside, which make it look like a municipal swimming pool. It's only when you get to the north transept (to the left of the altar) that you see the carved bench ends, just a few of them, hiding their light under a bushel of hymnbooks and other paraphernalia. The wooden pews in the rest of the church are plain and relatively modern, but these date from Elizabethan times and are fascinating in their subjects

1 Ness Point towers dramatically over the shore. **2** Combeinteignhead's church of All Saints is a 13th-century treasure. **3** Vines on the hillside at Old Walls Vineyard. ▶

as well as the bold carving and beautiful dark oak. There are saints galore, including St Catherine with a big crown and her wheel, a very serious St Peter with exuberant flowing locks and a giant key, St George in full armour spearing a tiny, dog-like dragon, and one of those really obscure saints that turn up in Devon churches from time to time: St Genesius, dressed in a fool's costume of cap and bells. Two strange men, side-by-side, seem at first glance to be dressed in densely pleated costumes, but it's much more likely to be fur (the lion's mane is done the same way). Each is holding a club, or escutcheon, and has a mop of unruly hair. These are probably 'wild men' or wodwo (woodwose), which appear quite frequently in old church carvings, perhaps representing untamed nature. There is a recognisable lion, but what are we to make of the 'poppy-head' carving (upright on the top of the pew rather than in a panel),

"The horseshoes on the door are said to be relics of an ancient wager as to who could ride furthest out into the sea."

which looks like a lion until you notice its long back legs and huge feet clutching a branch? Could it be a baboon? An animal the carver had never seen but had described to him? It has the deep shine of old wood that has been caressed by many hands. There is also an utterly indefinable animal, or possibly it's a fox, carrying off a goose flung over its shoulder – an image that is quite often seen in churches. They make it well worth braving the pink.

Near the church are traditional almshouses built of red sandstone, given to the village by William Bouchier, Earl of Bath, in 1620; also Fowlers Cottage and The Old Bakery, recalling former trades, and the 17th-century cottage that is home to the Wild Goose Inn (page 60).

12 HACCOMBE

This is a very worthwhile diversion but only on a Wednesday in April to September, when the little, peach-coloured **church of St Blaise** is generally open from 14.00 to 16.00, or for a 09.00 service on Sunday mornings. It's awkward to find; set your satnav to postcode TQ12 4SJ rather than to Haccombe. Since medieval times the church has been associated with the adjacent manor, originally lived in by the Haccombe family and later by the Carews. The present Georgian building (now converted to flats) replaced the original mansion at the end of the 18th century.

The horseshoes on the church door – only one and a half of them now, although there used to be four – are said to be relics of an ancient wager made between a George Carew, Earl of Totnes, and Sir Arthur Champernowne of Dartington, as to who could ride furthest out into the sea at Torbay. Carew won the gruelling challenge and, on returning to Haccombe, removed his horse's shoes and nailed them to the door, declaring that the brave beast should work no more but live out its days in pasture. So the story goes. Or possibly they were fixed to the door to deter witches, as happened in other churches? Believe what you will!

The church's tiny interior is a treasure-trove of memorials and other ecclesiastical goodies. To put you in the right frame of mind, there's a 'wool-comb' with fearsome nails; St Blaise was martyred by being flayed with a carding comb used to process wool, and then beheaded. Despite this, as a physician he managed to dislodge a fishbone from a child's throat, so is now patron saint of the wool trade and of throat ailments. He is also the patron saint of Dubrovnik, where a reliquary supposedly contains some of the saint's body parts – and a fish bone.

The biggest memorial is for Sir Hugh Courtney, who died in 1425, and his wife Philippa; the miniature alabaster memorial nearby is possibly of their son, Edward, who died while a student at Oxford. His feet rest on an appealing dog but sadly his hands are missing. The size suggests that this was a 'heart burial' and that the rest of the body was interred elsewhere. Sir Stephen de Haccombe, the knight who built the church in gratitude for his safe return from the Crusades in 1233, is also there along with his wife Margaret. A rather cute lion cushions his crossed feet. Beneath the carpet by the altar is a fine set of Carew brasses. There's some good medieval stained glass; the east window is 17th-century Flemish. Note, too, the lovely uneven medieval floor tiles.

Unusually, rather than a vicar the church has an archpriest, who reports to the Archbishop of Canterbury rather than a bishop and is entitled to wear a fur stole. This dates from the founding of a college of six chantry priests, with an archpriest at their head, in 1335. At the time of writing, the role of archpriest is vacant after the retirement of Revd Church, St Blaise's first female archpriest. Former incumbents included the renowned botanical artist, the Reverend W Keble Martin, appointed to the church when it was little more than an ivy-covered ruin, with only visiting birds to listen to his services. One such was a wren that nested in the pulpit. No-one would dream of removing it! Keble found Haccombe slow after the busy industrial parish he'd just left, and apparently upset his parishioners by visiting all of them twice in one week. His great work, *Concise British Flora in Colour*, published in 1965 when he was 88, was in fact anything but concise, containing 1,400 meticulous watercolours.

St Blaise's processional cross contains wood from the ancient flagship *Mary Rose*. After she was raised in 1982, two small pieces of her timber were given to the church in memory of her final captain, Sir George Carew, who drowned when she sank in 1545.

13 PLANT WORLD

St Marychurch Rd, TQ12 4SE ♂ 01803 872939 ♂ plant-world-gardens.co.uk ⊙ Apr–Sep

In the 1980s Ray and Linda Brown sold their nursery in the Scottish Highlands and moved in their Cortina estate to Devon, towing a horsebox full of their plants behind them. Initially they grew strawberries and fuchsia to bring in an income, then in 1986 laid out the garden, the first in the country to be arranged as a world map. Now they have a nursery with a great selection of unusual plants for gardening enthusiasts, and a four-acre garden carved out of a steep hillside showcasing a cottage garden and the flora of four continents in Gardens of the World. Apart from on-site sales, their catalogue contains a wide selection and attracts orders from across the globe. Well laid out and clearly labelled, the gardens are worth the small charge to visit. There's also a café.

Plant World is signposted at the Penn Inn junction on the A380 from Newton Abbot to Torquay, and good directions are on the website.

🍴 FOOD & DRINK

Church House Inn Stokeinteignhead TQ12 4QA ♂ 01626 872475 ♂ thechurchhouseinn. pub. In the spacious dining room of this 13th-century inn, you'll find a strong emphasis on locally sourced food: fish from Torbay, meat products from Shaldon. Good menu, loads of atmosphere.

Plant World (see above). The café serves light lunches & homemade cakes, with beautiful views over the Teign Estuary.

Wild Goose Inn Combeinteignhead TQ12 4RA ♂ 01626 872241 ♂ wildgoosedevon.com ⊙ noon–15.00 & 17.30–22.00 Wed–Sat, noon–16.00 & 19.00–22.00 Sun. A welcoming, family-run pub next to All Saints' Church, with an innovative British menu. Run as a pub since 1840, its current name refers to the geese of a 1960s landlord which tended to chase the customers.

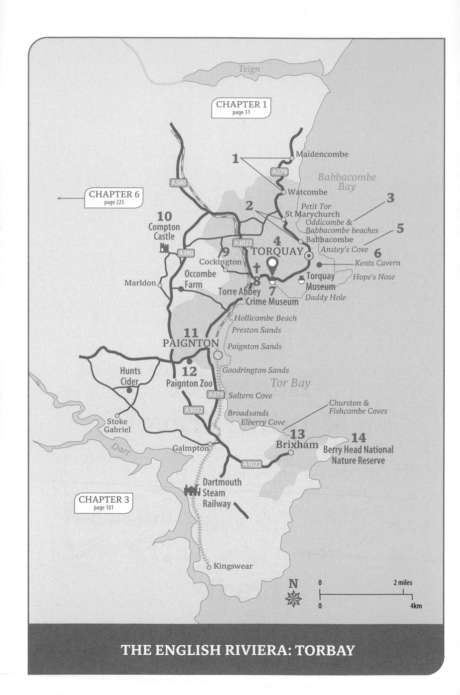

THE ENGLISH RIVIERA: TORBAY

2

THE ENGLISH RIVIERA: TORBAY

The wide, curved deep-water harbour of Tor Bay has played a regular part in history, as well as attracting more recent visitors to its mild climate and sandy beaches. W G Maton, writing in 1794, reported: 'The bay appears to be about twelve miles in compass [four miles as the gull flies], and is reckoned one of the finest.' The Napoleonic Wars (1803–1815) elevated the area still further, partly because the Channel Fleet was anchored in Tor Bay for a while, with Napoleon aboard en route to exile on St Helena, and partly because the war in Europe prevented the nobility from doing the Grand Tour abroad so some used the Devon coast as a substitute. Indeed, Napoleon may have inadvertently promoted the area as a holiday destination. On seeing the bay for the first time he is said to have exclaimed: '*Enfin, voilà un beau pays!*' ('Finally, this is a beautiful country!'). Suddenly, **Torquay** was fashionable and, once the Great and the Good started coming here, they never really stopped.

The bay area with its linked towns is officially known as Torbay, but the marketing people prefer 'The English Riviera'. Torquay has one downside – traffic jams – and Slow visitors may find **Paignton** hard to love, but if you know where to go and what to see there are all sorts of pleasures to be found: excellent art exhibitions, the spookily fascinating **Kents Cavern** (Torbay is a UNESCO Geopark – the term given to areas of exceptional geological interest), and surprisingly rural lanes folded into the hills behind the town. Tucked behind craggy **Berry Head** and **Hope's Nose** are quiet beaches and small, pebble-and-sand coves, with more secluded beaches further north towards Teignmouth.

 ## WET-WEATHER ACTIVITIES

Poppins Painting Studio (page 66)
Bygones (page 66)
Kents Cavern (page 73)

Torquay Museum (page 73)
Crime Museum (page 75)
Torre Abbey (page 76)
Paignton Zoo (page 87)
Compton Castle (page 80)
Brixham Fish Market Tour (page 92)
The *Golden Hind* (page 95)
Brixham Heritage Museum (page 95)

GETTING THERE & AROUND

The South Devon Highway (A380) has shortened the **driving** time from Exeter to a handy 40 minutes. Once in Torquay you would do well to leave your car in a long-term car park and use public transport to avoid the traffic jams.

The **bus** service into the town and along the coast is excellent, particularly the Hop 12, which runs between Newton Abbot and Brixham every 10–20 minutes until late at night. Paignton and Torquay are also accessible by **rail** via a branch line from Newton Abbot. Coming from the River Dart, there's the wonderfully picturesque **steam train** which runs between Kingswear and Paignton, a perfect route for window gazing and a stunning introduction to the beauty of Torbay when approached from the south. A 'Round Robin' ticket enables you to include a cruise on the River Dart to Totnes and return to Paignton by double-decker bus.

Ferries run frequently between Torquay and Brixham, and a day cruise runs from Torquay or Brixham to Dartmouth (⊘ westernladyferry.com).

SELF-POWERED TRAVEL

In Torbay itself a **bicycle** is an efficient means of transport rather than a source of enjoyment; it's ideal for covering the long stretch of waterfront between Torquay and Paignton, and gives you quick access to Cockington or Marldon. Electric bikes can be rented from E-ridez (137 St Marychurch Rd, TQ1 3HW ✆ 01803 302337 ⊘ eridez.co.uk).

For such a populated area there is a good selection of **long-distance walking trails**. Wending its way round the area for 35 miles, the **John Musgrave Heritage Trail** starts at Maidencombe, north of Torquay, heads inland following paths and lanes to Cockington, then continues through Totnes to Brixham. The most rewarding section of the **South West Coast Path** is round Berry Head to Kingswear and the stretch north of Torquay.

NORTH OF TORQUAY

Heading north from Torquay (or south from Teignmouth) you'll find a lovely stretch of coast path, giving sudden views of this deeply indented coastline and access to the region's hidden beaches, and quite near Torquay are quieter alternatives to the wide Torbay stretch of sand. For organised enjoyment the satellite towns of St Marychurch and Babbacombe have plenty to see and do.

1 MAIDENCOMBE & WATCOMBE

⋔ Orestone Manor (page 337)

Best known for its beach, **Maidencombe** feels a world away from the hustle of Torquay. Its oldest building, the Court House, dates from the 14th century and the primrose-yellow pub, the Thatched Tavern, is picture-postcard pretty. It has links with literary history as well: Rudyard Kipling lived here for a couple of years at Rock House, a spacious mansion with superb views. So why no longer than two years? Because he and his wife were afflicted with 'a gathering blackness of mind and sorrow of the heart' whenever they entered the house. 'It was the Feng-shui – the Spirit of the house itself – that darkened the sunshine and fell upon us every time we entered, checking the very words on our lips.' You can see his point, actually. The house has a grey, glowering exterior, in contrast with the welcoming **Orestone Manor** hotel next door.

The beach is perhaps the most appealing in the whole region – at least for lovers of Slow. The sand is the colour of a roan pony, mixed with a sprinkling of shingle, with large sedimentary rocks below the red sandstone cliffs and a good supply of tide pools. And Café Rio (⌀ caferio-maidencombe.co.uk) is a great find. As well as an interesting selection of snacks and light meals, they rent out kayaks and stand-up paddleboards.

Watcombe Beach, a mile further south, is even prettier. If coming by car be warned that it is a very steep walk down from the (free) car park, but it's a lovely, more or less level walk from Maidencombe along the South West Coast Path. The steps to the beach were washed away and access was closed for some time, a fate that has befallen other beaches on this coast. In 2023 work started on the restoration of the access path. These two beaches are perfect for lingering on during school holidays when the other Torbay beaches get crowded.

2 ST MARYCHURCH & BABBACOMBE

🏠 **Albaston Boutique B&B** (page 337)

St Marychurch is notable for its pedestrianised centre, giving visitors the chance to browse at leisure in the small, independent shops. On Fore Street there's a bookshop, Fables (✆ 01803 323923 ⊘ 15.00–18.00 Tue, Thu & Sat), a paint-your-own-pottery place, Poppins, and, for a touch of luxury, Lloyd and James (⬦ lloydandjameschocolate.co.uk), purveyors of fine chocolates. Almost hidden among the shop fronts is **Bygones** (see below), a chance to slip back into the past. In St Marychurch, despite its name, is **Babbacombe Model Village** (⬦ model-village.co.uk), while the Tessier Gardens off Manor Road are a peaceful haven full of flowers and closed to children and dogs. When I was there, each bench was occupied by a person quietly sitting listening to the birdsong. Balm for the soul.

East of St Marychurch, towards Torquay, is **Babbacombe**, where the **church of All Saints** gets a mention in Simon Jenkins's *England's Thousand Best Churches* for its Victorian aplomb. It is flamboyantly in keeping with the English Riviera surroundings. Jenkins points out that the church interior is built of 'no fewer than 50 varieties of Devon marble, in addition to marbles from Belgium and Sicily'.

Bygones

Fore St, St Marychurch TQ1 4PR ✆ 01803 326108 ⬦ bygones.co.uk

The modest frontage of this delightful exhibition is easy to overlook as you walk down Fore Street, but it's well worth a visit, especially on a wet day. The cliché 'transported back to the past' is hard to avoid as you stroll down a Victorian street with Queen Vic herself glaring unamusedly down at you. Even those of us who grew up in the 1950s will recognise the authenticity of the sweet shop with its tempting

---

1 The pretty village of Maidencombe has a picture-postcard pub, the appropriately named Thatched Tavern. **2** Tessier Gardens in St Marychurch are a peaceful haven. **3** A Victorian Street in the fascinating Bygones exhibition. **4** Striking red cliffs overlook Babbacombe Beach. ▶

goodies in large glass jars (and we have our own dollop of nostalgia in the Fabulous Fifties exhibition). There's a cobbler and a tobacco shop with a range of cigarettes and pipes (remember them?), an ironmonger and an apothecary, among other businesses. Each shop is stuffed with authentic items bringing memories to anyone over 60 and curiosity for the youngsters. Upstairs the displays are themed: a nursery, bathroom, parlour and kitchen; and a dentist showing sadistic delight in extracting a rotten tooth. Doors lead to a reconstruction of a WWI trench, and an almost whole locomotive snugly contained in the railway room. Bygones was created in 1987, and a recording by the founder is played in the background to put everything into context.

3 ODDICOMBE & BABBACOMBE BEACHES

⌂ The Cary Arms & Spa (page 337)

Charles Harper in 1907 found the walk down to the beach too challenging for comfort: 'There are winding walks down to Babbacombe, but for all their circumbendibility they are so steep that by far the easiest way to descend would be to get down on to your hinder parts and slide…the walking down jolts the internal machinery most confoundedly.'

Now, fortunately for those worried about their internal machinery, there is a funicular railway, the **Babbacombe Cliff Railway** (Babbacombe Downs Rd *☎* 01803 328750 *⌂* babbacombecliffrailway.co.uk *☉* Feb–Dec 09.00–16.45 daily; adult/child £3.50/£2.50, cards only) to transport visitors up and down the steep cliff.

It opened in 1926 and has been running ever since, only stopping during World War II and occasionally for refurbishment; it is now owned by a community interest company. The name is misleading since it actually deposits you on Oddicombe Beach. Compared with its quieter neighbour, **Oddicombe Beach** is a 'happening' beach, with the Three Degrees West café and bistro (*⌂* oddicombebeach.co.uk *☉* high season daily, off season Wed–Sun), watersports and occasional live music festivals. Ideal for families, there's enough red sand for sandcastles and good swimming off the pebble-and-sand shore. Winding, jungly paths take the energetic up to the road or to Babbacombe Beach. The shorter, surfaced walkway to this more upmarket beach hugs the cliff, with access to slipways and

"Ideal for families, there's enough red sand for sandcastles and good swimming off the pebble-and-shore."

rocks for adrenalin-fuelled jumps into the sea. The Cary Arms (✆ 01803 327110 ⬠ caryarms.co.uk) has been there for several hundred years and is now a boutique hotel with an excellent restaurant.

From Babbacombe Beach you can walk 'over the downs' to Anstey's Cove (page 71), a beautiful leafy stroll of about two miles.

¶¶ FOOD & DRINK

Angels Tea Room Babbacombe Downs Rd, TQ1 3LP ✆ 01803 324477 ⬠ angelsatbabbacombe.co.uk. A very popular (so often crowded) traditional tea room with some of the best coastal views in the southwest. The jam & scones are excellent, & there is a good selection of teas.

Hanbury's Fish Restaurant 24 Princes St, TQ1 3LW ✆ 01803 329928 ⬠ hanburys.net. Highly rated for fish & chips & their own beer & lager; take-away only.

Labrow's Bistro Bay 131 Reddenhill Rd, TQ1 3NT ✆ 01803 311911 ⬠ labrowsbistrobar. co.uk; ◷ year-round 09.00–15.00 Tue–Sat & summer Fri–Sat evenings. During the day this is a wonderfully welcoming café that attracts locals for all-day breakfasts & good coffee. On Friday & Saturday nights, Neil & Wayne offer a wide range of home-cooked tapas & cocktails. Their food & service are exceptional; we can recommend the Madeira chicken & the tempura prawns.

4 TORQUAY & AROUND

🏠 **The Haytor Hotel** (page 338), **Heathcliff House** (page 337) & **The 25 Boutique B&B** (page 338)

Tourist information: 5 Vaughan Parade, Torquay ✆ 01803 211211 ⬠ englishriviera.co.uk ◷ 10.00–17.00 Mon–Sat, 10.00–14.00 Sun

Visitors have been holidaying in Torquay for hundreds of years. Dr W G Maton wrote happily in 1794: 'Torquay far exceeded our expectation in every respect. Instead of the poor, uncomfortable village that we had imagined, how great was our surprise at seeing a pretty range of neat, new buildings, fitted up for summer visitors, who may certainly here enjoy convenient bathing, retirement, and a most romantic situation.' A visitor burbled to Bishop Phillpotts that Torquay was like Switzerland, to which he replied: 'Yes, only there you have mountains and no sea, and here we have sea and no mountains.' There are, however, hills which give the upper town its attractive, layered look, and some splendid mansions overlooking the bay. The seafront and marina are attractive – you can walk right around the latter by crossing the shiny steel lift bridge – and there is a sandy beach – at least until the high tide chases the sunbathers on to the esplanade.

Just along from the marina is the **English Riviera Wheel** (☉ Easter–Sep) which takes you over 150ft up above the famous **Pavilion Gardens**. The view across the town, the harbour and marina and out to sea is truly breathtaking.

Perhaps the gloss came off with the arrival of the trams, as predicted by Charles Harper in 1905: 'Presently there will be electric tramways at Torquay! Conceive it, all ye who know the town. Could there be anything more suicidal than to introduce such hustling methods into Lotus-land?' The hustling methods of the modern motor car have anyway done for Lotus-land, but stick with it because there are plenty of escapes.

An interesting way to explore the waterfront is to pick up the Agatha Christie Mile leaflet (page 132) and seek out 14 locations associated with her extraordinary life in Torquay. Take the advice of S P B Mais, writing in the 1920s: 'At the back of the inner harbour is the shopping centre. There will be time for this on a wet day. The wise tourist will cling to the coast to explore the outer edges before venturing inland.' I agree: for me the most attractive and interesting area of Torquay is the knob that includes Hope's Nose.

BEACHES

There are beaches galore in this region, but it is the secluded coves that are the most rewarding for those looking for beauty as well as swimming. They can be divided into the mostly sandy stretches at the southern, Brixham, end of the bay, and the pebble-and-sand coves north of Hope's Nose.

In the south, apart from the large and popular sandy beaches at Paignton and Goodrington, the most accessible smallish one is Broadsands, with reddish sand and rewarding rock pools at the southern end at low tide. But it's the little coves, sheltered by red cliffs, that can only be reached on foot which most appeal to me. Accessible from the South West Coast Path as you head south from Teignmouth, there's Maidencombe and Watcombe, then the popular Oddicombe and Babbacombe beaches.

Beyond Paignton, heading towards Brixham, is Elberry Cove (about 15 minutes' walk), a quiet pebble beach, and then Churston Cove, a delightfully secluded sand-and-shingle beach tucked into the wooded hillside. Fishcombe Cove is tiny, equally scenic and secluded, only 15 minutes from Brixham, with the added advantage of a café in summer (page 91).

MONTY PYTHON, FAWLTY TOWERS & TORBAY

In 1969 the BBC launched a comedy show that many claim changed comedy and television forever. Over the next five years, 45 episodes of *Monty Python's Flying Circus* were broadcast and many of the seaside sketches were filmed in Torbay.

While filming, the Python team stayed in the Gleneagles Hotel, run by retired naval officer Donald Sinclair and his wife, Beatrice. Donald was quite eccentric, berating the team for their incorrect use of cutlery and throwing one of the team's ticking suitcases over a wall, assuming that it contained a bomb rather than an alarm clock.

Most of the team swiftly moved out but John Cleese stayed on at the hotel with his wife and co-writer, Connie Booth.

They had decided to write a new comedy, *Fawlty Towers*.

Only 12 episodes were written about Basil and Sybil Fawlty's hotel in Torquay but *Fawlty Towers* is remembered as one of the greatest British comedy sitcoms ever. Sadly, Donald Sinclair died in 1981 and the Gleneagles Hotel was demolished in 2007 to be replaced by a rather bland block of apartments. They bear the name Sachs Lodge, named after the late actor Andrew Sachs, who played Manuel, the Spanish waiter, in the series. In 2017 a Blue Plaque was placed on the building to record its link with comedy history. If you wish to take a look, Sachs Lodge is on Asheldon Road, TQ1 2ER, just a five-minute walk from Kents Cavern.

5 ANSTEY'S COVE

This tiny bay is an unexpected delight so close to Torquay. A steep path runs down from the car park to a broad concrete esplanade with its modest but very good café and a few tables overlooking the pebble-and-rock 'beach' which pretty much disappears at high tide. The pebbles here are the most beautiful in South Devon and the joy of this peaceful place is poking around to find the most perfect one. They are as colourful as marbles, red and white mixed with greens. In summer there are sun-loungers for hire and also sit-on-top sea kayaks and stand-up paddleboards in the peak holiday months. People come

"The pebbles here are the most beautiful in South Devon and the joy of this peaceful place is poking around to find the most perfect one."

here to sit dreamily looking out to sea and at the view of high red-and-green cliffs with the dramatic spike of Long Quarry Point at its northern end. This is manmade, the result of quarrying in Victorian times for the high-quality limestone, similar to marble, which was used to build some of Torquay's finest houses.

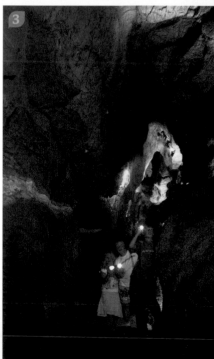

6 KENTS CAVERN

91 Ilsham Rd, TQ1 2JF ✆ 01803 215136 ⏣ kents-cavern.co.uk

I've had quite a few depressingly commercial and dumbed-down cave experiences and feared that Kents Cavern would be all entertainment and no education. Well, I was wrong. It's wonderful! We were lucky to be on the last tour of the day, with only one enthusiastic family, so our excellent guide was able to match his commentary to our interests. He told us that they can have as many as 30 people, which would not only make it hard to hear the explanations but also diminish the genuine feeling of awe at being in a place inhabited by our human ancestors and animals for around 350,000 years, and where modern man, *Homo sapiens*, sheltered some 30,000 years ago. The prize find at the cavern was a fragment of *Homo sapiens* jawbone, dated to almost 40,000 years ago, making it the oldest fossil of modern man found in Britain. We learned about William Pengelly, an amateur cave scientist, and his work excavating and identifying the bones found here. There's a model of the great man, frock coat and all, which highlights the difficulty of maintaining Victorian decorum in these conditions. Among the animal remains found in the cave were the teeth of woolly mammoth and scimitar-toothed cat, as well as a large number of hyena bones. Recent evidence suggests that the humans using the cave may have been cannibals: marks from flints used to butcher animals were found on human bones.

The stalactites and stalagmites make Kents Cavern visually superior to the caves at Buckfastleigh (page 242) and knowing that it took them 60,000 years to get that way adds to one's appreciation. There was once an almost complete pillar of stalagmite and stalactite. Now it's just a stub next to its taller companion. The stalactite and stalagmite had nearly met, and only needed another three or four centuries to bridge the gap, when a visitor fell against them and broke them off.

TORQUAY MUSEUM

529 Babbacombe Rd, TQ1 1HG ✆ 01803 293975 ⏣ torquaymuseum.org ⏲ 10.00–16.00 Tue–Thu & Sat

There's a miscellany of permanent and temporary exhibits here, including a reconstructed Devon farmhouse, some artefacts excavated

◄ 1 Torquay's attractive marina and English Riviera Wheel. 2 Go hunting for pebbles at beautiful Anstey's Cove. 3 Join a long history of explorers as you look around Kents Cavern.

THE EXPLORERS OF KENTS CAVERN

Humans have been living in Kents Cavern, on and off, for nearly 40,000 years, and tourists have been visiting the caves since at least 1571. We know that because William Petre carved his name and the date into the soft limestone walls, and other visitors followed suit in 1615 and 1688.

By the time Dr W G Maton paid a visit in 1794 there was a guardian to prevent such abuses. Maton describes 'Kent's Hole' as 'the greatest curiosity in this part of the country'. He was guided by two women with candles and tinderboxes. 'The lights, when viewed at a distance, gleaming through the gloomy vaults, and reflected by the pendant crystals, had a most singular effect. We began to imagine ourselves in the abode of some magician, or (as our companions were two ancient females, and not the most comely of their years) in the clutches of some mischievous old witches…'

Although William Pengelly is the name associated with scientific excavation of the caves, he wasn't the first. In 1824 a Mr Northmoore broke through the lime deposits on the floor to the clay below and recognised the bones of extinct animals. The following year the chaplain of Tor Abbey, the Reverend J MacEnery, started three years of excavation and discovered 'the finest fossil teeth I had ever seen!' He also collected many bones and some flint implements. Both these men paved the way for William Pengelly's scientific exploration of Kents Cavern between 1865 and 1880, and his conclusion that 'man was, in Devonshire, the contemporary of the mammoth and other extinct cave-mammals; and that, therefore, his advent was at a much earlier period than has commonly been supposed'. After Pengelly had enlarged the caves and sparked worldwide interest, more people wanted to make a visit. Charles Harper took a look in 1905 or thereabouts. 'A limestone bluff, shaggy with bushes, trees and ivy, rises abruptly to the right of the road, and in the side of it is a locked wooden door, upon which you bang and kick for the guide, who is guide, proprietor, and explorer in one. When he is not guiding, he is engaged in digging…'

from Kents Cavern and unusual fossils, and an Agatha Christie gallery which includes many items from TV adaptations of her books. In fact it's a great little museum, and repays the time spent reading the information boards and getting to grips with Torbay's prehistoric world. Here are remains of woolly rhino and mammoth, an explanation of the Ice Age and descriptions and fossils of the wolves and cave lions that inhabited South Devon. An Explorers' Gallery shows eminent Victorian explorers including Colonel Fawcett, and mineral lovers will learn a lot about Devon marble, quarried at Petit Tor, which was valued nationwide for its variety of colours.

The number 22 bus stops outside the museum, but there are usually parking spaces at the roadside.

7 CRIME MUSEUM

23 Victoria Parade, TQ1 2BD ✐ the-real-crime-museum.business.site

This little museum is owned by George Bamby, which probably means nothing to most people but, in his 40s, George discovered that he was the son of Charles Bronson, said to have been the most violent prisoner ever held in a British prison.

The museum is hidden in an alley and housed in a set of underground bunkers last used in World War II. The collection does have a full history of Charles Bronson – including his award-winning artworks – but other exhibits focus on the Great Train Robbery (with postcards home from Ronnie Briggs, safe in Brazil), a recreated cell from HMP Dorchester and artefacts from drugs smugglers, serial killers and gangsters.

The museum gives an insider's view of the criminal underworld. Don't forget to bring your reading glasses.

¶¶ FOOD & DRINK

As you would expect in the English Riviera, there are plenty of excellent places to eat in and around Torquay. This is just a selection of local favourites to suit all palates and budgets.

Blue Walnut Café Walnut Rd, TQ2 6HS ✐ 01803 392522 ✐ bluewalnuttorquay.co.uk. What makes this place special is that it is an arts café, with live music & performance poetry, & is also home to an original 25-seat nickelodeon, making it one of the smallest functioning cinemas in the world. There are occasional Friday-night film viewings. They also host regular art shows.

The Elephant 3–4 Beacon Terrace, Harbourside, TQ1 2BH ✐ 01803 200044 ✐ elephantrestaurant.co.uk. This Michelin-starred restaurant is probably the best in Torquay, with 'gracious dining' in an informal atmosphere. Chef Simon Hulstone loves ingredients grown & reared on the restaurant's dedicated farm. Dishes are scrumptious & prices high.

Le Bistrot Pierre Abbey Crescent, Torbay Rd, TQ2 5HB ✐ 01803 221213 ✐ bistrotpierre.co.uk. Normally we'd avoid chains, but this French restaurant with views across the bay is excellent. The fixed-price lunches are great value, & with seating for nearly 200 people, you'll always find a table even on the busiest days.

Number 7 7 Beacon Terrace, TQ1 2BH ✐ 01803 295055 ✐ no7-fish.com. An unpretentious seafood restaurant overlooking the harbour. Daily specials.

A walk from Torquay to Anstey's Cove via Daddy Hole & Hope's Nose

✺ OS Explorer map 110; start: The Strand, Torquay TQ1 2AA ♀ SX918634, or Anstey's Cove car park, TQ1 2QP ♀ SX934645; four miles; moderate, with a few steep climbs.

A quick escape from Torquay is provided by taking the footpath to Daddy Plain and on to Hope's Nose, the rocky headland that forms the northern limit of Tor Bay.

The walk starts from **The Strand** in Torquay but if you need to park then it is best to do so at the end of the walk in the Anstey's Cove car park and then catch the number 22 bus to the start.

Walk around the marina, keeping it on your right, and then fork left up **Beacon Hill**. Soon fork right, passing the front of the **Imperial Hotel** (which featured in at least three of Agatha Christie's murders). You'll see the path ahead, waymarked with the acorn of the **South West Coast Path**, and it's a most agreeable walk, with good sea views including 'London Bridge', an eroded rock arch, benches to rest on, plenty of wildflowers, and peeps into the gardens of the millionaires' homes that overlook the sea.

Above the curiously named **Daddy Hole** (Daddy was a colloquial name for Devil or Demon who was allegedly responsible for the landslip that created the hole) is Daddy Plain, an expanse of flat grass, popular with families and their dogs, backed by a row of picturesque houses.

The Orange Tree Restaurant 14–16 Park Hill Rd, TQ1 2AL ✆ 01803 213936
⌂ orangetreerestaurant.com. With prices on the high side this is not a place to rush; true Slow Food of the highest quality, & the wine list is very well chosen.

WEST OF TORQUAY

8 TORRE ABBEY

The King's Drive, TQ2 5JE ✆ 01803 293593 ⌂ torre-abbey.org.uk ⌚ 10.00–17.00 Tue–Sun

A great deal of thought, time and effort have gone into the restoration of Torre Abbey, with admirable success. The abbey was founded in 1196 and at the time of the Dissolution of the Monasteries was the wealthiest Premonstratensian house in England. Some of the ancient monastic buildings remain, including an early 14th-century gatehouse and a tithe barn, now known as the Spanish Barn because it rather improbably played a part in the Spanish Armada. In 1588 Sir Francis

From Daddy Hole the path descends to join Meadfoot Sea Road; look for the café on your right at the start of the beach, before climbing through a little wood on to Ilsham Marine Drive. This is a proper walk, with ups and downs, and gorgeous sea views.

After a while the path turns right through Thatcher's Pines to round **Thatcher's Point**, with Thatcher's Rock off shore. The two islands to the left are Lead Stone – also called, rather unimaginatively, Flat Rock – and Ore Stone.

When the path rejoins the road look for the path to the right, opposite Thatcher's Avenue – we're sensing a theme here – which takes you to the tip of **the Nose** where you have a fine view across to the other horn of the bay, **Berry Head**. On the rocky shore below there are fossils, but it's strictly forbidden to damage or remove any; this is a Site of Special Scientific Interest, managed by Torbay Coast and Countryside Trust.

Returning to the road, cross on to the signed path above it to continue along the coast. Eventually the path drops and crosses the road on to Bishop's Path, which leads through the woods of **Black Head** and then to the **Anstey's Cove** car park. There is a path to your right that leads down to the cove (page 71).

To return to Torquay follow the road right under two little bridges to reach Babbacombe Road; the bus stop for the 22 is just on your right.

Drake, on board the *Revenge*, captured the 1,000-tonne Spanish man-of-war *Nuestra Señora del Rosario*. An oil painting of the Spanish captain surrendering to Drake is in Buckland Abbey (page 216). The crippled *Rosario* was towed into Torbay, where almost 400 of her crew were held prisoner in the tithe barn while she was repaired enough to be used as a floating prison. These prisoners are said to have included a young woman who had disguised herself as a sailor so that she could go to sea with her beloved husband. During their two weeks of imprisonment in the barn she caught a chill and died; it's claimed that her ghost is sometimes seen and heard there, lamenting her fate.

After the dissolution, the abbey passed through many hands before being bought by Sir George Cary in 1653. It remained in the hands of this Catholic family until 1930 when it was bought by Torquay Corporation to be used as a museum and art gallery.

Most of Torre Abbey is now a museum, housing a very good collection of art, including ceramics. There is something here to appeal to everyone, well displayed and free from crowds. Treasures include William Blake's engravings for the *Illustrations to the Book of Job*, and paintings by William Holman Hunt and Edward Burne-Jones. Other rooms are preserved as they were when it was the Carys' private residence, with some of their loaned furniture. You can also see the secret chapel, used regularly through the times when Catholicism was banned.

Take time, too, to visit the peaceful and immaculately kept gardens and their palm and cactus houses. The 'Potent Plants Garden' is inspired by poisons used in the plots of Agatha Christie's books; several plants are rich in cyanide, castor oil plants produce deadly ricin and there are even opium poppies. Having a snack in the café is, we're sure, quite safe.

9 COCKINGTON

Initially we were a bit suspicious of Cockington. With all the spontaneously charming villages in Devon this seemed to be more or less manufactured for tourists. However, we were wrong. Yes, Cockington is chocolate-box pretty, yes, it's packed with coach parties and tourists, but Cockington Court is also full of interest and to be able to escape Torquay within minutes and walk through spacious parkland beside a brook is not to be sneered at.

Although you can drive here there are much better alternatives: the Cockington Tripper bus (number 62) runs five to seven times a day from Torquay Strand (Harbourside). It's also a very enjoyable 20-minute walk up Cockington Lane, opposite Livermead Beach; the lane crosses the railway line and Old Mill Road, then you'll see the Watermeadow Walk on the right, running parallel to the lane almost all the way to the village less than a mile away.

In 1935, Torquay Corporation bought Cockington and the town has owned it ever since, preserving the traditional thatched cottages and forge as in a time warp. Even the Drum Inn, designed by Sir Edwin Lutyens in 1934, is perfectly in keeping. The historic house and church are on the edge of the village, in a peaceful area of the old deer park. A long stretch of lawn in front of the house is shaded by trees and village cricket matches are still played there. But the main interest here is **Cockington Court** (⊘ cockingtoncourt.org) and its church. This elegant mansion was once owned by the Cary family, but is now a centre for crafts, and very good ones too. In the old stable yard there are many workshops including glass-blowing. They were giving a demonstration while I was there, turning out impressively good stuff in front of the clicking cameras. Beyond the workshops is a delightful walled rose garden, an ideal place to relax. Before heading across to the church, take a right turn up to the modern studios where skilled crafts are still practised; we found some seriously fine jewellery, handmade chocolates and even an upholsterer.

In the main house there is a small Kitchen Gallery, full of giant metal insect sculptures on our last visit, and the Seven Dials café – some of their food is grown in the garden. Every summer there is a sculpture trail around the grounds.

When you've finished with the crafts and the gardens, there's the church to visit. The ornate and unusual pulpit is said to include decorated timbers taken from the Spanish flagship *Nuestra Señora del Rosario*, which was captured by Sir Francis Drake during the Armada (page 200). It consists of various pieces of screenwork, some from the 15th century, others possibly from the early 16th, and the bookrest from still later. Parts may be from the front of a rood gallery. The whole effect is colourful and a little bizarre. There seem to be cherubs with wings sprouting from the sides of their heads, bringing the disconcerting mental image of heads flapping around the Devon countryside. It is said that the originals may have been portraits of captains or clergymen with huge ears to show that they 'heard all', but were converted to something more appropriate for their new home. Maybe.

MARLDON

⚑ **Brownscombe** (page 338)

Marldon merits a mention because of the welcome speed with which you can lose yourself in the little lanes leading to it, and also for Occombe Farm and for Compton Castle, a splendid fortified manor house. The village celebrates an **Apple Pie Fair** each July (🛈).

Occombe Farm

TQ3 1RN ✆ 01803 696250 ⌖ occombe.co.uk

This is a working, organic farm which is open to the public. It is a wonderfully relaxed place where you can wander around admiring the vegetables and animals, including goats, chickens, ducks and some cheerful pigs, or take the 1.2-mile nature trail and see what wildlife you can spot. There are plenty of informative signs about food production and no human hassle – you are free to do your own thing. The farm runs an impressive shop with a huge deli, a bakery, a dairy, a butchers, a greengrocers and more. Some of the profits go to the Torbay Coast and Countryside Trust which protects Torbay's wild places, including Berry Head. The café has indoor seating and an outdoor terrace; it is particularly popular for its substantial cooked breakfasts.

10 COMPTON CASTLE

TQ3 1TA ✆ 01803 661906 ⊙ Apr–Oct 10.30–16.30 Tue–Thu; National Trust
🏠 **Long Barrow** (page 338)

This medieval fortress is sometimes cited as the finest building of its kind in Devon. It certainly makes a dramatic impression when you round a corner and suddenly see it, its huge castellated walls towering above you in an appropriately threatening way. The house belonged to the Gilbert family from the 1300s to 1800, and again in 1930 when the run-down estate was purchased by a descendant of the original Gilberts and painstakingly restored before being handed over to the National Trust. The estate has strong connections with America: in 1583 Sir Humphrey Gilbert proclaimed Newfoundland a colony in the name of Queen Elizabeth and in the same decade his half-brother, Sir Walter Raleigh, started planning the Roanoke Colony in North Carolina. The family has named their eldest son Walter Raleigh ever since.

"Wherever you go, there are squirrels: carved in wood, as stuffed animals in odd corners, and on the coat of arms."

There is plenty of interest in the house and garden. Visitors are given an informative guide to take them through the attractive walled Rose Garden and the ornamental Knot Garden as well as the orchard.

Only a few rooms in the house are open to the public, but wherever you're allowed to go, there are squirrels: carved in wood, as stuffed animals lurking in odd corners, and on the Gilbert coat of arms. The reason? Sir Humphrey's ship when he sailed to Newfoundland

---

1 The beautifully restored Torre Abbey was founded in 1196. **2** Traditional thatched cottages have been preserved in Cockington. **3** Medieval Compton Castle has a pretty walled rose garden. ▶

MIRAPHOTO/S

PAULA FRENCH/S

PATRICIA HOFMEESTER/D

was called *The Squirrel*. The family motto is *Semper ciurus*, 'always provident', a squirrely characteristic. One item that particularly caught my eye was a magnificent silver centrepiece depicting General Gilbert taking the surrender of the Sikhs in the Anglo-Sikh War of 1848–49. It shows some turbaned and bearded mounted Sikhs throwing down their weapons in front of the rather bored-looking general. It was presented to Sir Walter Gilbert, an officer in the British East India Company, by the officers who served under him in the war; it must have cost them a pretty penny.

Don't miss the kitchen, standing separate from the house because of the fire risk, with its enormous range, vast cooking pots and high barrel ceiling to help disperse any smoke that escaped the chimney.

Children are well catered for, with Tudor games such as croquet and quoits, and costumes to try on. During the school holidays you are likely to be greeted by ladies in Tudor costume giving a gratifyingly deep curtsy.

PAIGNTON TO BRIXHAM

11 PAIGNTON

🏠 **Redcliffe Hotel** (see opposite and page 337)

Once upon a time Paignton was a small fishing village surrounded by huge apple orchards. It was the centre of Devon's cider industry, and the harbour, built in 1837 to enable the export of cider all over the country and beyond, kick-started the town's development; the arrival of the railway in 1859 completed the job. I learned about the cider industry from Roger Hunt (page 89); his family has been making cider for eight generations, so he should know.

"The steam railway is a dollop of nostalgia, with some of the best scenery in Torbay passing slowly before your eyes."

For the casual visitor Paignton is a long stretch of sand hemmed in by the traffic-clogged main road and holiday complexes. Even its pier, erected in 1879, now glitters with slot machines and 'amusements'. However, to look no further than the seafront does Paignton a disservice. Like Torquay, it has its quiet attractions tucked away inland where the old town still has some good shops, Victorian houses, a thriving theatre and a historic cinema currently being lovingly brought

REDCLIFFE HOTEL

Philip Knowling

On the seafront where Paignton ends and Preston begins, the Redcliffe Hotel was built as a private residence in 1856 by Colonel Robert Smith. He had found success in India, and to mark the fact he built in the Indian style – or a fantasy version of it, known as Hindoo. It's a great grey confection of Eastern arches, exotic turrets, pointed windows and Arabesque crenellations. The Hindoo style stems from the Mughals of central Asia, descendants of Genghis Khan, who founded a golden age of science, arts and architecture; one of their greatest achievements was the Taj Mahal. Mughal architecture uses columns and courtyards, marbles and mosaics, arches, domes and turrets. To the Western eye it is romantic, evocative and elegant but in Torquay Smith's creation must have shocked and bemused the locals. When Smith started work on his grand design in the 1850s Paignton was a small fishing village. He took an early 19th-century coastal defence tower set on an outcrop of red sandstone among the dunes and marshes and turned it into a sumptuous new home, Redcliffe Towers, with 23 bedrooms and five acres of gardens.

After Smith died aged 86 in 1873, the property changed hands; it was owned for a time by Paris Singer, whose father built nearby Oldway Mansion, and it took in troops during the Second Boer War. Smith lived an exotic life and left us an exotic legacy. A Torquay amusement arcade is perhaps the only other local example of the Hindoo style. Its proximity is surely no coincidence.

back to its former glory, and the extraordinary Oldway Mansion (page 84).

For family outings **Paignton Zoo** is one of the country's finest, and the **steam railway** to Dartmouth (page 135) is a dollop of nostalgia and a chance to watch some of the best scenery in Torbay passing slowly before your eyes.

A symbol of ancient Paignton survives in the Bishop's Tower, a fragment of the palace of the bishops of Exeter, 'Lords of the Manor of Peintona' (1050–1549). The last to live here was Myles Coverdale, who was made a bishop in 1551. Coverdale's name lives on as the first translator of the Bible into English, a predecessor to the King James version. There is no evidence to support the local belief that he worked on the translation while living in the palace, but the Bishop's Tower was formerly known as the Coverdale Tower. In 1549, during the Prayer Book Rebellion in Devon and Cornwall (page 264), Coverdale played a prominent part in attempts at pacification.

The **church of St John** finds itself in *England's Thousand Best Churches* on the strength of the Kirkham Chantry Screen, though Simon Jenkins also commends the 'jolly use of red piers and white plaster. The effect is appropriately seaside.' Jenkins describes the Kirkham screen as one of the most remarkable monuments to survive in any church in England, but I must admit that I was underwhelmed by this austere church and the jumble of decapitated stone apostles, angels and other holy folk which comprise the screen. Cromwell's men laid about them with their hammers with disastrous effect. Indeed, hammers weren't their only weapons: three Cromwellian cannonballs are on display. Created in the late 15th century as a screen for the tombs of the Kirkham family, the carvings deserve a close examination; some are intact and the detail is extraordinary. The Norman font here is the oldest in Devon, and there is an exceptionally horrible 15th-century stone depiction of a cadaver of an Irish bishop, a memento mori, carved in unsparing detail.

"The old Paignton picture house is steeped in history and was a favourite with Agatha Christie."

One of Paignton's most important historic buildings is the old **Picture House**. Back in 1915 this was described as 'the coolest house in Paignton' due to having air conditioning. One of the earliest cinemas in the country, it closed its doors in 1999 but is now set again to become the coolest house in Paignton, but in the modern sense. The Paignton Picture House Trust (⊘ paigntonpicturehouse.org) is bringing the building back to its former glory of red plush chairs and intricate stained glass. The place is steeped in history and was a favourite with Agatha Christie. The plan is to use it for a wide range of entertainments while remaining faithful to its original purpose.

Oldway Mansion

This once-splendid building was the creation of sewing machine magnate Isaac Merrit Singer and remodelled on the Palace of Versailles by his architect son, Paris. In 1909 he invited his American lover, the dancer Isadora Duncan, to Oldway, making much of its splendour. She went expecting, she said, 'a glorious time'. It didn't happen. She wrote to a friend: 'I had not reckoned on the rain. In an English summer it rains all day long. The English people do not seem to mind at all. They rise and have an early breakfast of eggs and bacon and ham and kidneys and porridge. Then they don mackintoshes and go forth into the humid country until lunch, when they eat many courses, ending with Devonshire cream.'

Meanwhile Paris had suffered a stroke; under the care of a doctor and nurses, he spent most of his time in his room on an invalid's diet of rice, pasta and water. Isadora was banished to the opposite end of the building for fear of 'disturbing' him. Isolated from her lover, she practised her dancing and entertained herself as best she could, soon ending up in the arms of the conductor and composer André Caplet. Shortly afterwards she returned to France, with very few happy memories of Paignton.

THE PUDDEN' EATERS OF PAIGNTON

When King John granted the town's charter in the early 13th century, Paignton's residents offered a giant suet pudding in part payment – and thus became nicknamed 'pudden' eaters' by other folk in the area. For a while a pudding was made annually, but eventually only every 50 years or so. It was boiled in a cloth, with a recipe of flour, suet, raisins and eggs.

One made in 1819 for the annual show took 64 hours to boil and was paraded around the town on a wagon drawn by eight oxen. The largest – weighing 1½ tonnes – was the centrepiece of a great feast to celebrate the coming of the railway to Paignton, in August 1859. It was shaped like a giant pyramid, 13ft 6in at the base and 5ft around the apex. An uninvited crowd of almost 18,000 people turned up and fights broke out as they surged forward, many of them fuelled by the two wagon-loads of cider that the 'feast' also included. The police tried valiantly to protect the pudding but were outnumbered: soon only the crumbs remained. Post-office workers reported that a number of squashy, greasy little parcels were dispatched the following day.

Smaller commemorative puddings are still occasionally made. One in 1968 marked the original granting of the town's charter, with almost 1,550 portions sold for charity in small souvenir dishes; another, in 2006, celebrated the 200th anniversary of Isambard Kingdom Brunel's birth. For the Paignton regatta in August 2009, a solid, suety, seven-tiered pyramid weighing 154lb was chuffed into the town by the Paignton and Dartmouth Steam Railway, then paraded in a 1947 Bedford lorry as the town crier called on the inhabitants to come and eat.

Finally, in August 2014, some 900 years after its creation, came arguably the pudding's finest hour. Sue Perkins explored its origins (and an 11-tier replica was baked) for no less a television programme than *The Great British Bake-Off*. Fame had come at last for this chunky lump of calories, whose recipe probably pre-dated the Magna Carta!

The house, described in the Shell Guide as 'a rollicking extravaganza in hundreds of thousands of tonnes of pale pink stone' was used as council offices and a wedding venue until 2013. The mansion then lay neglected until 2019 when the council teamed up with the Oldway Mansion Trust and the Friends of Oldway to restore it to its former glory.

Progress on the house is likely to take years but restoration of the 23 acres of gardens is well underway. A team of dedicated volunteer gardeners (oldwaygardens.co.uk) has transformed them and they are now an oasis of quiet formal beauty, with the magnificent house providing a backdrop. There is a small café run by the Friends of Oldway (closed Thu & Sun) serving good coffee and locally made cakes.

12 Paignton Zoo

Totnes Rd, TQ4 7EU 01803 697500 paigntonzoo.org.uk

This distinguished zoo, which celebrated its centenary in 2023, is one of England's best. It is a constant pleasure; however often you visit it, there is always something new to see, and a feeling of space and greenery. It was the country's first combined botanical and zoological garden, not always an easy relationship: 'I hate animals,' the former curator of plants once said cheerfully, 'they eat all my plants.' This hasn't changed. We were told there is constant dynamic between gardeners, animal keepers and the public. The former are enraged when the free-range peafowl eat the seedlings (although when we were there they spent their time displaying sexily to visitors), animals need the privacy that large trees and high vegetation give them, and the public want as clear a view as possible. And, for their own safety, to be kept away from the 'dangerous animals'.

Paignton Zoo has solid conservation credentials, helping projects in Nigeria, Zimbabwe, Tanzania, Indonesia and the UK. It has some impressive African primates, including Hamadryas baboons and lowland gorillas. 'They're all males,' I was told. 'Because gorillas live in complex social groups, these chaps need to learn how to be gorillas here, before going to other zoos where they can breed. They arrive as youngsters and develop with just what a growing male gorilla needs – tough love.'

◀ **1** The beautiful formal gardens at Oldway Mansion. **2** Hollicombe Beach is enclosed by red cliffs. **3** The Manor Inn in Galmpton is the hub of the village – and hosts its annual Gooseberry Pie Fair. **4** The Hindoo-style Redcliffe Hotel.

The zoo is home to some of the rarest species including black rhinos, Sumatran tigers and Bornean orangutans – all critically endangered.

Our favourite place was the Reptile House. Not only was it lovely and cosy on a chilly spring day and reminiscent of the Eden Project with its rainforest flitting with free-range tropical birds, but it houses some of my favourite animals, such as poison dart frogs and the leaf-tailed gecko from Madagascar. The Crocodile Swamp is also as attractive to humans on a cold day as it is to warmth-loving crocs.

The zoo is part of the Wild Planet Trust, a conservation charity with a wide range of projects in the area including conserving the seagrass meadows in Torbay.

PAIGNTON'S BEACHES

All the beaches between Paignton and Brixham are shingle and red sand, disliked by some visitors since it can stain your clothes. Perhaps for this reason **Preston Sands** and **Paignton Sands**, which together make up the long stretch of beach next to the B3201, are never crowded. They offer all the requirements for a family outing: car parking close by, toilets, fast food and amusements. **Hollicombe Beach** to their north ticks most of the boxes for a Slow beach, being a small cove enclosed by red cliffs, and you have to walk here through Hollicombe Park or at low tide from Preston Sands. And it's open in winter to dogs.

To the south **Goodrington Sands**, between the promontories of Roundham Head and Three Beaches Headland, is a long sandy beach with cafés and beach huts to rent. Behind the beach are a water park, for those who seek the thrills of flume rides, and Youngs Park, with a traditional boating lake.

"For lovers of undeveloped beaches, it starts to get exciting, with the coves that give Three Beaches its name."

Then, for lovers of undeveloped beaches, it starts to get exciting, with the coves that give Three Beaches its name. First, and really the only accessible one, is **Saltern Cove**, a designated SSSI (Site of Special Scientific Interest) within the Geopark. It's a nature reserve that extends underwater to a depth of 411 yards. The cove can only be reached from the South West Coast Path, down steep steps. Come at low tide when there are rock pools and a larger area of sand.

Continuing south you'll come to **Broadsands,** with its line of multicoloured beach huts. Unlike the busier beaches to the north, there is no main road nearby (but parking is conveniently close) so it's relatively peaceful, though the narrow strip of sand above a seaweedy expanse of pebble-mix belies its name. It has two cafés, toilets and so on, safe swimming for children since it shelves very gradually, and lots of rock pools for them to explore. Little **Elberry Cove** is further from the car park, so even quieter. And that's it until the approach to Brixham.

HUNTS CIDER

You can tour the orchards and cider-making operation near Stoke Gabriel (TQ9 6PU ☏ 01803 782422 ⊘ huntscider.co.uk) with prior booking, usually at 14.00 on Wednesdays. The farm also has a campsite, Broadleigh Farm Park.

Devon is known for its cider so, en route to visit a friend in Aish, on the road to Stoke Gabriel, it was easy for me to give in to temptation and follow a sign to Grove Orchard and its cider sales. I was greeted by Richard and Annette Hunt who told me that the Hunts had been making cider for eight generations and that he himself had been involved in the business for 40 years. Clearly I wasn't just going to buy a bottle and leave; as I was shown round the state-of-the-art cider barn, I learned a lot about cider. The Hunts have been farmers and part of Paignton's cider industry since 1805 when the family was based at Crabbs Park, Paignton, although they were making cider in a small way from 1771. Orchards were bought and sold, but the family remained in South Devon, and finally they moved to their present place with 400 acres, 16 of those given over to apple orchards, on the fringes of the Paignton district. Only traditional Devon varieties of apples are used, with evocative names such as Paignton Marigold, young trees flourishing beside the mature ones planted by Richard's great-grandfather.

Up to 80 tonnes of apples are harvested or bought in (but only from Devon) each year to make the six varieties of cider, from a lowish-alcohol one, Clinker (3.8%), for people like me who want a lunchtime tipple without falling asleep, to the more traditional 6% ones like Wobbler (medium-sweet) and Thrasher (dry, 6.2%). The latter, along with Andsome Bay (4.8%), won Gold in the 2017 Taste of the West Awards. A pink one caught my eye – this is a brightly coloured raspberry cider. Bull Walloper is a rather alarming 7.2% alcohol.

A tour of the orchards and cider-making building shows what a high-tech business this is these days. The old wooden presses straining the juice through straw are now in museums; it's all computerised now, although the basic technique is the same: pick, wash, press, store, remove sediment, ferment, pasteurise, bottle.

Richard and Annette are particularly pleased with the pouches with a tap at the bottom, allowing you to drink small quantities without the cider losing its freshness, since air is never introduced.

🍴 FOOD & DRINK

The Old Manor 10 Old Torquay Rd, Paignton TQ3 2QZ ℘ 01803 551157 ⬛. It comes as something of a surprise to find a Grade II-listed pub in Paignton, but the 17th-century thatched inn has been pleasing visitors for many years. The food is classic pub food, nothing fancy but well cooked, & there's a beer garden for the summer & log fires in winter. Live music most Fridays.

GALMPTON

Jenny Distin, a resident, says: 'I chose to move to Galmpton because I worked out it has the finest public transport service of any place in Devon not on a bus or train timetable!' The reason is that the station and the bus stops are all called Churston not Galmpton. Even the locals can't work out where Churston ends and Galmpton starts; in my mind the two communities divide roughly into Golfers and Gardeners.

The highlight of the village year is **Gooseberry Pie Fair** (⬛; usually the first Sunday in July) when a specially baked giant gooseberry pie arrives by steam train with a military escort from Dartmouth Royal Naval College. It is paraded through the village followed by pre-school children dressed as gooseberries, blessed by the vicar, then cut by a naval officer with a ceremonial sword before being dished out with clotted cream to the villagers and visitors – who are then entertained with various village fête events. It's been going on since 1873 and is hosted by the **Manor Inn** (⬧ manorinngalmpton.co.uk), which is the hub of the village.

The Hop 12 bus between Brixham and Newton Abbot runs via Galmpton every ten minutes or so until late at night.

ON FOOT OR BUS FROM PAIGNTON TO BRIXHAM

If you have time, an alternative to driving into Brixham is to park at Broadsands car park, and either walk up to the bus stop or follow the coast path for a bit over two miles to Brixham. To go by bus, take the coast path north from the far end of the beach and under the viaduct to Broadsands Park Road. Follow this uphill to Dartmouth Road and you'll see the bus stop on the left.

Walkers will follow the coast path through woodland to **Elberry Cove**. This is a popular beach for waterskiing and powerboats so can be noisy. Now comes about a mile of attractive woodland, with steep ups and downs as well as level stretches, until you come to one of the nicest beaches (or rather two beaches) of southern Torbay. **Churston Cove** and **Fishcombe Cove** are curves of shingle separated by a headland and enclosed by steep cliffs. Swimmers will need beach shoes to protect their feet, although there's access to deep water from rocks and steps. Being only accessible on foot down a very steep path makes them particularly appealing to Slow enthusiasts. Fishcombe has a café and toilets, and dogs are allowed.

Directly above Fishcombe Cove is the **Brixham Battery Heritage Centre** (brixhambattery.net 14.00–16.00 Sun, Wed & Fri). Renovated in 2016 and run by an enthusiastic and dedicated band of volunteers, this is for WWII enthusiasts. The museum houses displays of uniforms, weapons, posters and other items such as the Mickey Mouse gas mask that I remember from my childhood, and a lady's gas mask handbag. Visitors are allowed to handle the weapons and are invited to share their memories and interests. As well as the museum, there's the Battery Observation Post and the main gun emplacement.

The path continues to Brixham, skirting the yacht harbour and passing fish merchants David Walker and Son (see below) to emerge at The Quay.

13 BRIXHAM

 Faithful (page 338)
Tourist information: Ula, The Quay, TQ5 8AW (unmanned)

Brixham pushes out towards Berry Head, the southern prong of Tor Bay, and the start of one of the South West Coast Path's most spectacular sections: to Kingswear. In the mid 1500s John Leland described it as 'a praty Towne of Fischar Men, caullid Brixham'. It's still pretty – at least its setting is – and it still has a flourishing fishing trade.

On my last visit I met two Scottish visitors who used to know Brixham a decade or so ago. The elderly man shook his head: 'So much has changed.' Indeed, so visitors need to be prepared for the extensive building and renovation required to bring Brixham up to the standard that the fishing industry requires and visitors to the English Riviera expect. A state-of-the-art **fish market** keeps the catch fresh, and **David Walker and Son** (01803 882097 davidwalkerandson.com 09.00–15.00 Mon–Fri, 08.00–13.00 Sat), who justifiably claim to 'offer the finest fresh fish in the world', provide a range of take-home fish to satisfy your inner Rick Stein. There are also amusement arcades, fish-and-chip shops galore, and all the offerings that help separate visitors from their money.

If you are in Brixham at the beginning of May, you will have the chance to join in the annual **Pirate Festival** (∂ brixhampiratesfestival. com). The whole town goes pirate-crazy and most people dress up for the occasion. There is street theatre, shanty singing and lots of live music.

There is also a quiet, reflective side to Brixham. Walk down the south side of the harbour and you will find a row of benches from where you can watch the harbour activities and observe the busy little turnstones competing with the gulls for scraps. Further along the walkway are lobster traps stacked neatly against the wall and other paraphernalia associated with the fishing trade. Here trawlers set out to catch the fish that end up in so many of the country's best restaurants. Indeed, Brixham has the highest-value catch in the country. If you want to see the real Brixham, unchanged for hundreds of years, you need to be an early riser. The fish auction begins at 06.00 with around 40 different kinds of fish on offer. The **Fish Market Tour** currently takes place every Wednesday in July and August, and less frequently in September and October. Its

"For the annual Pirate Festival, the whole town goes pirate-crazy and most people dress up for the occasion."

price includes a fish breakfast at Rockfish (page 97) and the tour must be booked in advance (∂ therockfish.co.uk/products/fish-market-tour).

Among Brixham's visitor attractions are a replica of Sir Francis Drake's *Golden Hind* (page 95) and a statue of William of Orange, who landed here in 1688 and changed the course of history (see opposite). A plaque on the harbour wall reproduces a wonderfully grovelling message from the humble folk of Brixham to Prince William Henry, Duke of Clarence and recently appointed Lord High Admiral, on the occasion of his visit in 1828. They obviously had high hopes that his new position would benefit Brixham and felt that they'd better get in quick with their praise: 'We felicitate ourselves on having this opportunity of expressing our Respect and Attachment', with a gift of an 800-year-old oak chest containing – gasp – part of the stone on which King William III placed his foot on his arrival at Brixham 140 years earlier. The prince was ecstatic, commending 'this Beautiful and Magnificent bay' and promising to preserve the stone as a 'precious Relick', a reminder of the 'benefit conferred on this TRULY HAPPY ISLAND' by the arrival of his ancestor from the Netherlands.

All summer there is a local art and craft market on the quayside (☉ 10.00–16.00 Wed–Sat), and set back from the tourist-busy Quay are quieter streets with uncrowded shops and restaurants. Hidden along King Street is the surprisingly shaped blue building known as the **Coffin House**. It gets its name from its shape: that of a coffin standing on its end. The story goes that a young lady of the town had set her fancy on a young man who in no way met with her father's approval; in fact, he had told the suitor that he'd sooner see him in his coffin than married to his daughter. So the young man bought the 'coffin house' and showed it to his sweetheart's father – who apparently relented in the face of such ingenuity and gave his blessing to their marriage. A little plaque gives its former name and date (1736), but the building is now occupied by

WILLIAM OF ORANGE

In 1688 England was in a bit of a mess, with Protestants hating Catholics and Catholics fearing Protestants, and the Protestant monarchy established by Henry VIII looking decidedly shaky. After the Civil War and Republican rule by Oliver Cromwell, Charles II restored the monarchy and the Stuarts, but had too many Catholic sympathies to ensure stability; religious tolerance was not popular in 1660. It didn't help matters that Charles signed a secret treaty with Louis XIV of France, a Catholic monarch who was starting to throw his weight around, on the promise that he would convert to Catholicism – which he did on his deathbed. To strengthen his Protestant credentials he arranged for his niece Mary to marry William of Orange (William III of the Netherlands), grandson of Charles I. Childless (at least by his wife), Charles was succeeded by his brother, the Catholic James II, which threw everyone into a tizzy of paranoia. An openly Catholic monarch would not do. So most of the country welcomed the arrival of William and his invading army. He had a legitimate claim to the throne and impeccable Protestant credentials (he had chased Louis XIV out of Holland). His wife Mary was herself a Protestant and the daughter of King James, who was persuaded to give up the throne. When he changed his mind a few years later he was soundly defeated, with his Catholic followers, in Ireland at the Battle of the Boyne. The Orange Order has been stirring up trouble there ever since. James fled to France while William and Mary ruled together, with reduced powers through parliament's new Bill of Rights. The constitutional change that their rule brought about is known in history as The Glorious Revolution.

the Destiny Mystical Shop, which seems to have escaped from Totnes, offering tarot reading, crystals, faeries, angels and a yoga and juice bar.

Tucked away in the old police station on New Road is the **Brixham Heritage Museum** (✆ 01803 856267 � brixhammuseum.uk ⊙ Tue–Sat), which houses an eclectic mixture of items mostly illustrating the town's maritime and railway history. There's also a Victorian parlour and nursery, and archaeological exhibits.

Next door is Brixham's splendid and independent **theatre** (� brixhamtheatre.co.uk). Run entirely by volunteers, the 250-seat theatre is part of the Victorian Town Hall. It stages everything from films and live music to touring theatrical groups throughout the year.

One of the pleasures of Brixham is the variety of transport options. It's much nicer to visit without a car, and there are frequent bus services to and from Paignton and Kingswear, allowing you to combine a visit here with the steam train from Kingswear. Ferries also run from Brixham to Paignton and Torquay. If you do drive into town, I'd recommend parking at the Oxen Cove car park to the north, or the Breakwater car park to the east, both with access to the coast path leading into Brixham past the yacht harbour. It's a lovely approach to the town.

Between the Breakwater and Berry Head is the **Shoalstone Seawater Pool** (Berry Head Road ⌀ shoalstonepool.com ⊙ May–Nov; £2.50 donation), a 173ft salt water swimming pool. It has been used almost continuously for bathing since Victorian times. In the 1920s and 1930s, the start of the season was marked by a local woman, Minnie Bowman, jumping off the diving board wrapped in the union flag. Today a charity runs the pool and there is a lifeguard present during the day from May to September. There are showers and changing rooms for bathers and deckchairs and sun loungers to hire for those who just want to watch. In the season there is a fish restaurant, Shoals (⌀ shoalsbrixham.co.uk), above the pool, run by a local fishing family.

THE *GOLDEN HIND*
✆ 01803 856223 ⌀ goldenhind.co.uk

Prominent in the harbour is this replica of Sir Francis Drake's original ship in which he circumnavigated the globe, a feat that brought him

---

◀ BRIXHAM: **1** & **2** The town's busy harbour, which includes a replica of Sir Francis Drake's *Golden Hind*. **3** Get up early to catch the fish auction. **4** Nearby Berry Head is a peaceful oasis.

lasting fame. The fact that his mission was to rob ships carrying treasure (in other words, he was a pirate) is rather glossed over, with the excuse that half of his booty was given to Queen Elizabeth, enabling her to pay off the national debt and earning him his knighthood as well as enough wealth to buy 40 properties including Buckland Abbey (page 216). His crew – the ones that survived the voyage – were well rewarded too. The value of the treasure that was off-loaded in the West Country in 1580 was a mind-boggling £478 million in today's money, and comprised not only Spanish silver and gold, but 3 tonnes of cloves from the Spice Islands (Indonesia). Originally he had taken on board 6 tonnes but was forced to jettison half this cargo when the *Golden Hind* was caught on a reef. Geographical exploration was never the purpose of the voyage, but when Drake failed to find the Northwest Passage in Alaska he had no choice but to sail west across the Pacific to avoid the Spanish lying in wait for him in South America.

"The treasure comprised not only Spanish silver and gold, but 3 tonnes of cloves from the Spice Islands."

Barely 100ft long, the ship is packed with interest, particularly for children who can collect stamps to show what they've seen and be awarded a poster giving them honorary pirate status. And they can walk the plank, although sadly for desperate grandparents, it is only a safe simulation.

Adults will marvel at the cramped space that could house 70 men, ten of them officers. Only Drake had a cabin; the rest bedded down wherever they could. Among the well-labelled displays are weaponry, entertainments (the ship carried a band for part of the voyage), cooking facilities, and little nuggets of information such as why birds were kept captive: if the ship was lost they were released and would instinctively fly to the nearest land; the ship would then follow in the same direction. It's a rewarding visit and worth the admission price.

¶¶ FOOD & DRINK

Beamers Seafood Restaurant 19 The Quay, TQ5 8AW ✆ 01803 854777 ⊙ beamersrestaurant.co.uk ⊙ closed Tue. In an enticing location overlooking the harbour & above the Ula gift shop & tourist information centre, this has an extensive seafood menu, as well as steaks with a choice of homemade sauces.

The Curious Kitchen 14–16 Middle St, TQ5 8ER ✆ 01803 854816 ⊙ thecuriouskitchen. co.uk. In a quiet street away from the tourist bustle of the quay, this is a lovely restaurant of scrubbed wooden tables serving 'real food', with a good choice of vegetarian dishes, home-made brioche, doughnuts & excellent coffee. The portions are huge, but they do kids' portions (half size, half price) which are still enough for smaller appetites.

Rockfish Restaurant & Takeaway New Fish Quay, TQ5 8AW ✆ 01803 850872 ⏶ therockfish.co.uk. Their slogan is 'Tomorrow's fish is still in the sea', a claim that won't be challenged, not in Brixham. With the best location in town & the best range of seafood, this is the place for a special treat. They also serve their own craft beers & cider. Rockfish also have an equally excellent restaurant on the quayside in Torquay. If you are self-catering & fancy a night in, Rockfish also offer next-day delivery of fresh fish to your door; order on their website.

14 BERRY HEAD NATIONAL NATURE RESERVE

Gillard Rd, TQ5 9AP ✆ 01803 882619 ⏶ countryside-trust.org.uk/explore/berry-head ⏱ year-round, although the visitor centre closes during quiet times

This is a blissful oasis where nature and history are the focus, not commerce. The story of Berry Head begins 400 million years ago, when the tropical reef around this chunk of land started its slow progress from seashells to Devonian limestone. Heaved up by geological forces and further sculpted by ice and storms through millions of years, its exposed position left it free from human settlement until man had developed the means to blast his enemies with cannon fire. It is the two fortresses from the time of the Napoleonic Wars that the visitor sees first, with picture-book crenellations and cannons peeping through the gaps. More blasting, this time for the quarrying of valuable limestone, left caves beneath the cliffs.

The combination of the work of man and nature has made this a perfect environment for birds and rare limestone-loving plants and their accompanying wildlife. Twenty-eight species of butterfly have been recorded here, but it is the bird population that is the main draw, with around 200 species seen. A huge colony of guillemots nest on the cliffs; visitors can follow their everyday lives on the CCTV cameras at the visitor centre,

"The combined work of man and nature has made this a perfect environment for birds and rare limestone-loving plants."

or from the bird hide, which has posters to help with identification and recent sightings. In the small auditorium in the visitor centre an excellent slideshow describes the geological and human history of the site as well as the wildlife.

A path runs from the fort to the lighthouse at the end of Berry Head where you can admire the 360-degree view. The caves below are also an important roost for greater horseshoe bats (page 246). Finally, the licensed **Guardhouse Café** is something special, a favourite with locals as well as visitors: 'You can watch all this wildlife sitting at a picnic table (or inside if it's windy) eating a delicious breakfast, coffee, lunch or tea,' says a friend who lives nearby. 'Everything is freshly made, imaginative and served with a smile, and it is dog-friendly in a popular walking area. They also do quirky one-off events like a 05.00 breakfast to watch the sunrise at the summer solstice.'

There's no public transport here but it's a very rewarding walk from Brixham along the South West Coast Path, which takes you through woods and out to the cliffs with a gorgeous view of the bay before you arrive at the fort. There is a closer (paying) car park, however.

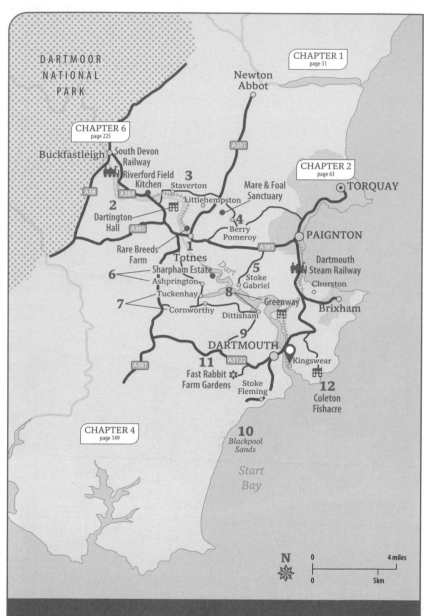

DARTMOOR NATIONAL PARK

Newton Abbot

CHAPTER 1
page 31

CHAPTER 6
page 225

Buckfastleigh

South Devon Railway

Riverford Field Kitchen

3 Staverton

Littlehempston

Mare & Foal Sanctuary

CHAPTER 2
page 63

TORQUAY

2 Dartington Hall

4 Berry Pomeroy

1 Totnes

PAIGNTON

Dartmouth Steam Railway

6 Sharpham Estate

Ashprington

5 Stoke Gabriel

Churston

7 Tuckenhay

Cornworthy

8

Dittisham

Greenway

Brixham

9

DARTMOUTH

11 Fast Rabbit Farm Gardens

Stoke Fleming

Kingswear

12 Coleton Fishacre

CHAPTER 4
page 149

10 Blackpool Sands

Start Bay

N

0   4 miles

0   5km

TOTNES & THE RIVER DART

3
TOTNES &
THE RIVER DART

The **Dart** is one of the loveliest rivers in England and, like Devon's three other great rivers, the Exe, the Plym and the Taw, has played an important part in shaping the county's history. It rises in Dartmoor and meanders down to Dartmouth for 42 miles, with the lower 11 miles tidal. **Totnes**, at the upper navigable end, has been a prosperous town since at least the 10th century, and continues the trend thanks to the energy and creativity of its inhabitants. Of all the larger towns in Devon, this is perhaps the most rewarding to visit, so provides a perfect starting or finishing point for a walk or cruise down/up the Dart. Although Totnes is as far inland as you can go by passenger boat, the Dart is still a significant presence north of the town, and **Dartington Hall**, with its focus on sustainability and the arts, perfectly complements the spirit of Totnes. The **South Devon Railway** follows the river upstream as far as Buckfastleigh.

As the river snakes its way south, it passes small villages or grand houses that flourished as a result of their location and then subsided into tranquillity when water transport ceased to be viable. Now they are an ideal base for exploring this exceptionally scenic part of Devon, and for refreshment while walking the **Dart Valley Trail**. At the river mouth is **Dartmouth**, and its twin town **Kingswear**, which have been enchanting travellers for centuries, and to the east and west stretches the **South West Coast Path**.

 ## WET-WEATHER ACTIVITIES

Totnes museums (page 105)
China Blue Totnes (page 105)
Dartington's The Barn cinema (page 113) & **Cider Press Centre** (page 114)
South Devon Railway (page 240)
Dartmouth Steam Railway (page 123)

GETTING THERE & AROUND

Of all the regions in this book, this is the one where you really can leave your **car** behind and enjoy the variety of public transport on offer. For those with strong legs there are footpaths galore and one of the best short(ish) walking and cycling trails in the county.

Totnes is served by frequent **buses** from all parts of the county and is on the mainline **railway** from Exeter to Plymouth. The region is blessed with two **steam train** lines: the South Devon Railway between Totnes and Buckfastleigh, with a stop at Staverton, and the Dartmouth Steam Railway between Kingswear and Paignton. (The original trains on this line lost money so regularly that it was closed in 1958 even before Dr Beeching axed his way through all the little unprofitable railways of Britain. It was reopened as a preserved steam line by Beeching himself in 1960.)

By far the most enjoyable way of getting between Dartmouth and Totnes is the **river ferry** (page 138) and there are other vessels and **river boats** calling at villages along the Dart.

In short, bring your car if you must, but you may regret it. Many of the lanes are single-track.

SELF-POWERED TRAVEL

Totnes is full of enthusiastic cyclists, and using the **bicycle** as a means of transport is accepted practice. For recreational cycling, the **Dart Valley Cycleway**, part of the NCN 2 Coast-to-Coast route, provides outstanding river views along largely traffic-free paths. The Totnes–Dartington stretch is 3½ miles in total, going to Dartington and on to Hood Barton in the direction of Staverton and Buckfastleigh. The three-mile ride from Totnes to Ashprington is largely traffic-free, but quite hilly. Much of it runs along the old Sharpham carriage drive and crosses the estate (page 127) on the way to Ashprington.

There's a wonderful variety of **walks** here, mostly with views of water: either river or sea. **The Dart Valley Trail** is described opposite, and there are various **South West Coast Path** options. You can also walk the **John Musgrave Heritage Trail** from Totnes to Torbay. The **Franklin Totnes**

THE DART VALLEY TRAIL

This walkers' trail links Dartmouth to Totnes, and Greenway to Kingswear. In total it's 17 miles, but is linked to buses, ferries and the steam train so is easy to do in sections. With some planning, you can take in all that is typical of the area: river views (of course), small villages with impossibly narrow streets (you'll be glad you're on foot) and ancient oak woods. The main options are: walk beside the lower Dart from Dartmouth to Dittisham and across the river to Greenway, then back to Kingswear (nine miles); ferry from Dartmouth to Dittisham and walk back on either side of the river (about five miles); or walk from Totnes to Dittisham, taking in the villages of Ashprington, Cornworthy and Tuckenhay, and take the ferry back (about nine miles).

Trail is a seven-mile circuit of Totnes, taking in most of the places of interest in the area as well as the lovely riverside path.

A look at the OS Explorer map OL20 will inspire other ideas, although by far the best maps for walkers are the Croydecycle ones (page 19) at a scale of 1:12,500 (five inches to a mile). For this area: Totnes includes Berry Pomeroy and Ashprington, and there are two versions of the Dartmouth map. Each has Dartmouth and Kingswear on one side, including the confusing streets of Dartmouth itself; *Dartmouth & Slapton* covers the region south, and *Dartmouth, Dittisham & Coast to Brixham* is for the north. *Dittisham & Cornworthy* continues up the river as far as Totnes, including the cycle route. As in all these maps, not only is every geographical detail covered but there are helpful notes such as 'stone base' or 'grazed fields'.

The **South Devon Area of Outstanding Natural Beauty** (southdevonaonb.org.uk) has details of many local walks, which can be downloaded.

There are plenty of opportunities for **canoeists and kayakers** on the River Dart (page 124), with the option of renting or bringing your own canoe/kayak.

1 TOTNES

Ashley's Shack, between Totnes & Dartmouth (page 338)
Kilbury Manor, between Buckfastleigh & Totnes (page 338)
Tourist information: Market Sq, Totnes ✆ 01803 269190 ⊘ visittotnes.co.uk ⊙ Apr–Oct 10.00–15.00 Mon–Fri

A few years ago a hand-painted addition to the town sign summed up the image of Totnes perfectly: 'Totnes, twinned with Narnia'. But Totnes is no fairytale. Its success in creating a genuine alternative to 'clone towns' is built on the knowledge that the world's supply of oil is dwindling, and that a different, less consumerist lifestyle is not only inevitable but enjoyable. Transition Town Totnes, or TTT, is the result, outlined in *The Transition Handbook* by Rob Hopkins.

Totnes is blessed with a perfect position. Its location at the navigable limit of the River Dart ensured its place in early history, with Brutus of Troy (page 111) allegedly making a rather giant leap for Britain here. The town minted its own coins in the 10th century and had its own currency, the Totnes Pound, from 2007 to 2019. It grew rich on the cloth trade and in Tudor times was second only to Exeter in the wealth of its citizens.

"There are said to be more listed buildings per head of population in Totnes than in any other town in England."

Daniel Defoe described it as having 'more gentlemen in it than tradesmen of note' and an 18th-century visitor wrote approvingly that Totnes 'abounds in good shops'. There are said to be more listed buildings per head of population here than in any other town in England. This has helped ensure that it still has plenty of good shops, since large chains look for large premises. Among the more unusual shops (both at the upper end of the High Street) are the **Devon Harp Centre** (⊘ devonharpcentre.co.uk) and the **Zero Waste Shop** (⊘ thezerowasteshop.co.uk), which aims to cut waste by eliminating unnecessary packaging. The shop is owned and run by former footballer Richard Eckersley and sells only vegan and organic produce. Bring your own container, or buy a reusable one in the shop, and serve yourself from a huge range of products. You decide how much you want, rather than the producer deciding for you, and you can even grind your own peanut or almond butter. It's a great idea and very Totnes.

Apart from shopping – and eating in the many cafés and restaurants – there is plenty to engage visitors. The circular, crenellated **Norman castle** (Castle St ⊙ Easter–Oct 10.00–17.00 daily & Nov–Easter weekends only; English Heritage) sits, like a child's drawing, on a hill and the 15th-century red sandstone **church of St Mary** competes for attention. The rood screen here was carved from Beer stone, rather than the more usual wood, at the command of the town corporation, who wanted it to rival Exeter Cathedral. The **Guildhall**, behind the church, started life as the refectory of the Benedictine priory, but was rebuilt during the height of the town's wealth in the mid 16th century for the Guild of Merchants. It has been the home of the town council ever since and is open to visitors in the summer (☉ Apr–Oct 11.00–15.00 Mon– Fri) – you can get married there too.

About halfway down the High Street on the left-hand side a flattish, rough stone is set into the pavement; this is the so-called 'Brutus Stone' (page 111). Legend apart, another possibility is that it was the *bruiter's* stone (to *bruit* meaning to report or proclaim, often by rumour) where news was announced by the town crier or equivalent.

At the north end of town, across the Town Bridge in Bridgetown, is the **Steamer Quay** (TQ6 9PS) from where you can catch the river ferry to Dartmouth (page 138). It's a lovely walk of about a mile on a leafy footpath alongside the river from the mainline train station (TQ9 5JR). Close to the station is **China Blue** (✆ 01803 860908 ⊘ china-blue. co.uk). Here you can paint your own pottery, browse a huge selection of ceramics in the shop, or enjoy a good meal in the café. It's a great place.

MUSEUMS, MARKETS & SPECIAL EVENTS
Museums
Totnes has four unusual and excellent museums, so there's plenty to keep you interested on a wet day. Starting at the top, opposite Market Square, is the **Fashion and Textiles Museum** (43 High St ✆ 01803 862857). It houses the Devonshire Collection of Period Costume and is extraordinarily complete, with clothing ranging from 1650 to the present day. On the first floor is a temporary exhibition which changes each year. At the time of writing, the museum was closed for refurbishment, but planning to re-open soon. Check their website for opening hours.

The **Timehouse** (69 Fore St, just below the Eastgate Arch ✆ 01803 862109 ⊘ the-timehouse.business.site ☉ Apr–Sep 11.00–16.00 Thu– Sat) is unique and gloriously Slow. It really does need time, ideally over an hour, to appreciate the 'individually themed installations designed to stimulate all the senses and film presentation areas to stimulate the mind'. You enter, appropriately enough, through a shop called Narnia Totnes, but the museum is more Tardis than Narnia, being a complete immersion in 20th-century England, with a few sorties abroad. The colonisation of Australia is put under the lens with a disturbing

1

2

3

4

5

slideshow showing the fate of Indigenous Australians from Cook's arrival to the present day (in a room called Cloud 9). Each room is full of the items typical of an era or subject, arranged seemingly haphazardly but with great artistry. Films include life as a child during World War II, a look at environmental disasters, and a mini Odeon cinema. There's a Beatles room and a Moroccan bazaar where you can drink mint tea. The museum is the result of the enthusiasm and dedication of artist Julie Lafferty, who put her life savings into the project. It's a great achievement.

"Each room is full of the items typical of an era or subject, arranged seemingly haphazardly but with great artistry."

One of the Tudor houses on Fore Street contains the **Totnes Museum** and the **Elizabethan House** (70 Fore St ✆ 01803 863821 ⌨ totnesmuseum.org ☉ Mar–Sep 10.30–16.00 Mon–Fri), whose 13 little rooms overflow with an eclectic mix of furniture, local history and childhood. Charles Babbage, credited with the invention of the first computer (page 107), has his own room here.

The **Totnes Image Bank** (Town Mill, Coronation Rd, next to Morrisons supermarket car park ⌨ totnesimagebank.info ☉ 10.00–16.00 Tue & Fri) is housed in the restored old water mill. An exhibition of panels shows the history of Totnes from Saxon times to the present day, and upstairs in a separate gallery are displays of some of the 45,000 or so photos documenting the more recent history of the town, which have been collected, scanned and catalogued by their team of volunteers. Computers are provided for research and photographic prints are for sale.

Markets

The excellent **weekly market** is held on Fridays and Saturdays in Market Square, spilling over into Civic Square. The large range of stalls include bric-a-brac, two bakers and a butcher, fruit and vegetables, plants, seashells and fishing reels, everything to make your own willow baskets, oriental rugs and kilims, and new and secondhand clothing.

◀ TOTNES: **1** The circular Norman castle overlooks the town. **2** The unique Timehouse museum is just below Eastgate Arch. **3** Totnes holds an excellent weekly market. **4** The Sea Change Festival celebrates music, art and conversation. **5** Merlin, a rare East Siberian eagle owl, at the Rare Breeds Farm.

CHARLES BABBAGE, INVENTOR EXTRAORDINAIRE

Charles Babbage hated music, and was tormented by the barrel organs, buskers, fiddlers and other rough-cast musicians who enlivened London's 19th-century streets. He bombarded *The Times* with angry letters and engineered a parliamentary bill to curb the noise. The objects of his fury retaliated by playing for hours outside his house; in his obituary in 1871 *The Times* commented that he had 'reached an age, [in] spite of organ-grinding persecutors, little short of 80 years'.

Street musicians apart, his interests were wide-ranging. Statistics fascinated him. His writings covered such subjects as how to lay the guns of a battery without exposing men to enemy fire, the causes of breaking plate-glass windows, and the boracic acid works of Tuscany. For all that, he is best known for the difference engine he invented in the 1820s: a massive calculating machine, designed to produce accurate results for logarithmic and other mathematical tables. For lack of funds it was never built in his lifetime, but a version built in 1991 from his plans by London's Science Museum (where half of his brain is also preserved – the other half is in the Hunterian Museum at London's Royal College of Surgeons) worked as he had forecast. In the 1830s he followed it with his analytical engine, based on a punched-card system and the precursor of today's computers.

Jonas Fishmonger's van (🖉 jonasfishmongers.co.uk) is there selling fish fresh from Brixham, and there's a reasonable choice of hot food and a fresh coffee stand.

In the same location on the third Sunday of the month you'll find the amazing **Totnes Good Food Market** with over 60 stalls. There is local produce of every kind – cheese, meat, wine, cider, bread and on and on – plus a good range of hot-food-to-go stalls where the cuisines span the globe.

In the summer Totnes holds an **Elizabethan Market** every Tuesday morning, when the stallholders dress up in Tudor costumes. It's organised by the Totnes Elizabethan Society, which runs a series of special events. The tourist office has leaflets, or ✉ elizabethansociety@outlook.com if this is your special interest.

Special events

The **Totnes and District Show**, on the last Sunday in July, is one of the biggest one-day agricultural shows in the county, dating back 100 years and highlighting the region's farming roots. Unique to the town

Born in 1791, Charles was from an old Totnes family, and Totnes claims him as one of its 'sons'. The Elizabethan House (page 107) has a room devoted to him.

Apart from his 'engines', his many inventions included a prototype submarine, an occulting light, a system for deciphering codes, and more prosaically the cow catcher on the front of American trains. In 1831 he founded the British Association for the Advancement of Science and was also instrumental in founding the Royal Astronomical Society and the London Statistical Society.

In 1833 he met Ada Byron (Lord Byron's daughter, sometimes described as the first computer programmer), later to become Countess of Lovelace; she was fascinated by his 'engines' and contributed to his work on them – but died in 1852. In 1864, the ageing and increasingly grumpy Charles wrote his obsessive *Observations of Street Nuisances*, recording 165 of them in less than three months, but achieved little else before his death. However, his name lives on in several university buildings and the Babbage crater on the moon, and there's a commemorative blue plaque on the wall of his former home in the London Borough of Southwark. Since he loved trains, he might be happy that in the 1990s British Rail named a locomotive after him; also perhaps that his lunar crater is well out of reach of noisy street musicians...

is the **Orange Race** on the third Tuesday in August, when locals pursue the fruit down the hill, the speed (and danger) of the pursuit dictated by the age of the contestants; there are races for all age groups, from just four to over 60. If you want to see the true definition of breakneck speed, watch the adult men's group. Apparently Sir Francis Drake started the ball rolling, so to speak, when he knocked over a delivery boy's basket, sending dozens of oranges tumbling; the local children were quick to race after the exotic fruit. The **Sea Change Festival** (⊘ seachangepresents.co.uk) of 'music, culture and high times' takes place usually in May. Contact the Totnes information centre (page 103) for more information.

⁋ FOOD & DRINK

Some of the most famous food places in the area are **Ben's Farm Shops** (⊘ bensfarmshop.co.uk). They were formerly under the umbrella of Riverford, but changed their name in 2017 since not all products are strictly organic (remember *The Archers*? They had the same problem). But the produce is still locally grown, fresh, varied and irresistible.

Their Totnes shop (38 High St ⊖ closed Sun) sells produce and take-away light lunches including soup, pasties and cakes. As you would expect in such a buzzy town, there are plenty of good places to eat.

The Curator 2A The Plains, TQ9 5DR ✐ 01803 865570 ⚐ thecurator.co.uk ⊖ daily. This Italian restaurant is winning plaudits for its morning coffee & the quality of the meals. A small menu but cooked to perfection. They also have a pop-up coffee shop at 51 High Street, inside Butterwalk (⊖ closed Sun).

Pie Street 26 High St ✐ 01803 868674 ⚐ piestreet.co.uk. A perennial favourite for its excellent pies (of course!), chips & other substantial meals; there is a café, a restaurant & a bar. You can also buy pies to take away or bake at home.

Rumour Kitchen & Bar 30 High St ✐ 01803 864682 ⚐ rumourtotnes.com ⊖ closed Sun. For many years this has been the place to go for a treat: all scrubbed wooden tables & cheery diners. The menu is varied & imaginative, with steak & pizza a speciality.

Seeds 2 40 High St, just below Market Sq ✐ 01803 865101 ⚐ seeds2totnes.co.uk ⊖ closed Sun. Advertising themselves as 'healthy fast food', this is just what this vegetarian/ vegan restaurant does. A choice of tasty self-service dishes ensures that there's no waiting for your order to be taken. Very good value: you can eat well for under £11.

Totnes Brewing Company 59a High St 🗗 ⊖ 17.00–midnight Mon–Wed, noon– midnight Thu–Sun. A local micro-brewery with lovely premises which suggests, 'You bring the food, we'll bring the drinks'.

THE TOTNES LITTLEHEMPSTON STEAM RAILWAY STATION & RARE BREEDS FARM

The charmingly nostalgic station and this appealing little animal centre (✐ 01803 840387 ⚐ totnesrarebreeds.co.uk ⊖ Easter–Nov) are opposite each other across the railway tracks. With its limited space the centre doesn't try to do too much; it just does it small-scale and very well. Along with the garden café there are domestic animals such as angora goats which look like gone-wrong sheep with floppy ears and stuck-on horns, plump pygmy goats, Welsh mountain sheep and Berkshire pigs. Some very tame rabbits and remarkably relaxed guinea pigs await a cuddle from children and, at Easter, orphan lambs arrive for them to bottle feed.

It is birds, however, that make this place special. Not only the rare breeds of chicken such as the Light Sussex hens, which are as snazzy as a Japanese painting, and Silkies with feathery feet and topknots, but a unique collection of nine species of owl. Most were hatched from eggs

BRUTUS OF TROY & TOTNES: A NEW TAKE ON AN ANCIENT TALE

As one version of the legend goes, the grandson of Aeneas (hero of Troy and of Virgil's *Aeneid*) struck up an illicit affair with the niece of a princess. The local soothsayer foretold that any child born to them would cause the death of both its parents and would then wander through many lands before gaining great honour. The mother did indeed die in childbirth, and the boy, Brutus, later killed his father with an accidental arrow while out hunting, having rather improbably mistaken him for a stag.

Consequently Brutus was exiled to Greece, whence, as an adult, he set sail with a group of other Trojans to seek new lands. After two days and one night they came to an island where they found a shrine to the goddess Diana, at which they offered libations and prayed for guidance. That night, the goddess appeared to Brutus in a dream. She told him of an empty island far away beyond the sunset, once peopled by giants, where he and his group could settle. He would breed a race of kings there, whose power would spread around the earth. Onward the group sailed, westward and then north, passing strange and savage shores.

After many months they came to a coastline of ragged grey cliffs, rising from sandy bays. It was the coast of Cornwall, in the land then known as Albion. Easing their ships carefully up a sheltered river, they reached a bay overlooked by a wooded hill. Brutus set off instantly to survey the area, which is now Totnes. A boulder – the Brutus Stone – on which he stepped as he sprang ashore can be seen to this day, in Fore Street. Satisfied, he called his people to inhabit their new home.

Later Brutus set out to seek a site for the capital of his domain. Finally selecting the Thames, he built on its banks the rough wooden settlement that became today's London. It's said he was buried there when he died, 23 years after reaching Devon, in around 1100bc, no doubt with due ceremony and pomp. His three sons divided Britain between them, creating their own kingdoms of England, Scotland and Wales. And thus – as happens in all good legends – the early prophecies were fulfilled.

Main source: Geoffrey of Monmouth's *The History of the Kings of Britain (Historia Regum Britanniae)*, c1136

so have only known captivity, including Lady Jane, the magnificent great grey owl who arrived in 2012. The rarest in the collection is Merlin, the East Siberian eagle owl. There are only 12 of this species in the UK, all his relatives. You get the chance to gently stroke the feathers of the owls and feel their density (one reason they can fly so silently), and learn their stories and some surprising facts from their handler. I learned, for instance, that the body weight of the biggest owl, Lady Jane, is half that of the smaller European eagle owl; she's all feathers.

Many of the enclosures can be entered; the owners feel that it is so important for children from cities to get the chance to meet animals they may never have seen before.

Jacquie Tolley and her husband bought two acres of jungly land in 1999 and then set up the farm, which opened to the public four years later. In 2015 they handed the farm on to Sam Adams, who had been their farm manager. New owners Julie and Simon Forster and their son James took over in 2023 and have great plans for the farm, including the introduction of some new rare breeds, as well as more animals to the petting farm for everyone to enjoy.

There is no car park at this steam railway station; the mainline station is your best option or, if full, there's parking at the Pavilion (follow signs from the A385 roundabout at the northern end of town), though it's quite a long walk along the pleasant footpath to the steam train station and Rare Breeds Farm. If you are taking the steam train – and it's a lovely journey – it's better to start from Buckfastleigh (page 240), where parking is free.

DARTINGTON & AROUND

🏠 **Cott Inn** (page 338) & **Dartington Hall** (page 338)
🛖 **Dartington Hall** (page 339)

Although the road signs ask you to drive slowly through this unremarkable village, you would be hard put to remember it the next day. But Dartington is Dartington Hall and what a special place that is!

2 DARTINGTON HALL

TQ9 6EL 🖉 01803 847000 🖔 dartington.org

Dartington Hall has been a significant part of this corner of Devon for at least a thousand years. The FitzMartin family owned it in the 12th century and probably built the church, now ruined apart from the tower. By the mid 14th century it had reverted to the Crown and Richard II granted it to his half-brother John Holland, who built the first great country house here.

In 1559 a prominent Devon family, the Champernownes, bought the estate. By the beginning of the 20th century, however, their family fortunes, and the buildings, were in ruins. Leonard and Dorothy Elmhirst saw Dartington's potential and bought it in 1925. He the son of a Yorkshire clergyman and she an American heiress, they shared a vision of rural regeneration through the arts. Leonard had done missionary work in India and studied agriculture in order to improve farming methods there. Returning to India later he became secretary to Rabindranath Tagore, the Nobel-Prize-winning writer and social reformer, an appointment that sowed the seed for establishing Dartington Hall as a place of 'experiment and new creation' and restoring it to its former glory. He and his wife (who shared his enthusiasm for radical causes) aimed to bring 'economic and social vitality back into the countryside' as well as creating

"Their interest in the arts made their house a magnet for artists and musicians from around the world."

one of the finest gardens in Devon. They also founded the progressive Dartington Hall School (now closed) and their interest in the arts made their house a magnet for artists and musicians from around the world.

The Dartington Hall Trust (⌀ dartington.org) continues the work done by the Elmhirsts, supporting various projects and the Schumacher school, under the umbrella of sustainability and social justice.

One of Dartington's many success stories is **Landworks** (⌀ landworks. org.uk), a prisoner resettlement scheme that gives prisoners and ex-prisoners the opportunity to learn about working the land, or working with the produce of the land (including woodworking). One statistic says it all: nationwide, 46% of prisoners reoffend within one year of release; the comparable reoffending rate for Landworks trainees is 4%.

Dartington is also a centre for **agroforestry**, where Martin Crawford runs the Agroforestry Research Trust to tap into the edible or medicinal products of trees and plants and how best to manage them.

Dartington always has plenty going on – a sculpture exhibition, informal talks and lectures, book sales and sustainably sourced food, as well as concerts, films and theatre. There is also a continuous programme of craft and skills courses that runs throughout the year; courses last from half a day to six months – there are even some that are online.

Even when there are no events, Dartington is a wonderfully gentle, peaceful place to visit, just to stroll around the grounds, to take a look at the Great Hall and to eat at one of the restaurants (page 115). Perhaps also watch a film at their independent cinema, **The Barn**.

The Grade II-listed **gardens**, behind the Great Hall, are open year-round dawn to dusk; they are partnered with the Royal Horticultural

Society whose members get free entry. The gardens' most notable features are the enormous trees, which have had hundreds of uninterrupted years to grow to maturity, and the lawn terraces which lead to the sunken garden. Sculptures are dotted here and there, including a Henry Moore. Just north of the Hall is their walled **Deer Park**, first established in the 1500s and enclosed with a wall in 1738. There are a couple of short trails in the park – pick up a map in the Welcome Centre. A one-mile trail leads to a medieval observation platform, which offers a great view of the fallow deer. The longer trail, two miles, continues to pass alongside the River Dart – keep your eyes open for kingfishers and dragonflies. Both trails are tramper- and wheelchair-friendly.

For longer visits, Dartington Hall has 50 comfortable rooms (page 338), and all profits from the accommodation go to the trust to help their work; Hall residents get free admission to the gardens and discounts on everything else. The Elmhirsts would be happy to see how their inspiration has lasted.

The Cider Press Centre (TQ9 6EL) is the commercial wing of Dartington, but all profits go to furthering the trust's aims, and the spirit is very much Dartington, with an emphasis on local art, craft and organic produce. Notable among them is The Food Shop, which sells a huge range of local, mostly organic produce. Not cheap, but that's not the point. There's also a very popular café and restaurant, Bayards Kitchen, which has indoor and outdoor seating. An inter-connected run of stores – we weren't sure where one ended and the next began – offers a wide range of high-quality kitchenware, home furnishings, glass, pottery and jewellery. There is also a small art studio and gallery run by Pam Neaves, focusing on local artists. Devon Distillery offers hands-on gin- and rum-making classes on site in an old American school bus. You get to take your unique bottle of gin or rum home with you.

"The longer trail continues to pass alongside the River Dart – keep your eyes open for kingfishers and dragonflies."

Dartington Hall and The Cider Press Centre are easily reached on foot via a leafy riverside walk from Totnes or Staverton, from where you can catch a South Devon Railway steam or diesel train to Buckfastleigh or Totnes. The Croydecycle *Totnes* map shows numerous walking possibilities. Bus 165 runs roughly every two hours from Totnes to Dartington Hall.

¶¶ FOOD & DRINK

Almond Thief Bakery Cedar Units, Shinners Bridge, Dartington TQ9 6JY ✆ 01803 411290
⊘ thealmondthief.com. This deserves the cliché of 'best-kept secret'. You're not going to find
this terrific bakery by accident. In the corner of an industrial estate, marked by a few shabby
outside tables crammed with people tucking into breakfast, brunch or lunch, or chatting
over 'the best coffee in South Devon', the Almond Thief sells sourdough bread, pastries &
the fullest of full English breakfasts as well as lunch. Take the road towards Plymouth at
the Dartington roundabout; Cedar Units is on the left, just beyond the Cider Press Centre &
Texaco garage.

Cott Inn Cott Ln, Dartington TQ9 6HE ✆ 01803 863777 ⊘ cottinn.co.uk. One of the oldest
(1320) & most beautiful thatched inns in the county – perhaps the country – & the place
to go for a special treat. They are famous for their meals, with a varied menu & beautifully
presented dishes emphasising local produce. They also have rooms (page 338).

The Green Table Dartington 🛱. Located near the car parks at the heart of Dartington Hall,
with indoor & outdoor seating, this restaurant offers an interesting selection of breakfast
& lunch dishes, always including vegan, vegetarian & gluten-free options. There's a choice
of soups, a frittata & a selection of salads. A children's menu is offered at half price for
a half-portion.

New Lion Brewery Shinners Bridge, Dartington TQ9 6JD ✆ 01803 226277
⊘ newlionbrewery.co.uk ⊙ daily, times vary. A community-owned & community-run
brewery that is co-located with…

Pizzalogica ✆ 07726 320177 ⊘ pizzalogica.uk ⊙ from 17.00. An independent, family-
run pizza restaurant. The brewery & restaurant combo took over the ground floor of a disused
community building & the result is great pizza, great beer & lots of fun. There is often live
music. You can eat & drink inside, outside or take away.

White Hart Bar & Restaurant Dartington ✆ 01803 847116 🛱. Located
adjacent to Dartington's Great Hall, this friendly pub serves classy food, beautifully
presented, at reasonable prices. Tables inside, on the terrace & often in the Great Hall;
booking recommended.

LITTLEHEMPSTON

⚐ Hemsford Yurt Camp (page 339)

Across the river from Dartington Hall and tucked into rural surroundings
only a five-minute drive from the bustle of Totnes, Littlehempston is no
run-of-the-mill village. First, one of its pubs, the **Tally Ho** (TQ9 6LY
✆ 01803 862316 ⊘ tallyhoinn.co.uk ⊙ Tue–Sun plus bank holidays),
is South Devon's first community-owned pub, rescued by the villagers
from conversion to a private home and opened in April 2014. The

Grade II-listed building is thought to date from the 17th century or earlier, and to have been built originally as a church house. By 1841 it was already an inn.

Funds for its purchase were raised largely by the sale of shares, with shareholders also cooking, pulling pints, scrubbing floors and tending gardens. In 2018, Kelly and Mike Joiner became the tenant landlords with their son Isaac and in 2019 it was CAMRA's South Devon Rural Pub of the Year, followed by South Devon Pub of the Year in 2022. Littlehempston's other pub, the **Pig and Whistle** (✆ 01803 863733 ⌂ thepigandwhistleinn.co.uk), is also highly praised for its food, local beers and the wide selection of wines and spirits.

Next door to the Tally Ho, an innovation in the 15th-century **St John the Baptist Church** could well be copied by any ancient churches seeking to maintain their historic charm while meeting their communities' practical and social needs. Enter the church and all seems traditional: a fine screen, a well-preserved wagon roof, a seven-sided Norman font, stone effigies dozing on the windowsills and carved Victorian pews. It's the pews that hold the secret: they've been mounted on castors, so that they can be pushed aside or repositioned for local concerts, social events and suchlike without permanently damaging the church's appearance and atmosphere.

The Mare & Foal Sanctuary
TQ9 6LW ✆ 01822 854477 ⌂ mareandfoal.org

Between Littlehempston and Berry Pomeroy (see opposite) is Coombe Park, the centre for this busy charity which rescues, retrains and rehomes horses and ponies. A visit here on one of their open days is bliss for horsey types. There are behind-the-scenes guided tours of the yard and you can meet the horses waiting for adoption. Refreshments are available and there is a gift shop.

3 STAVERTON
⌂ **The Sea Trout Inn** (page 338)

The village has a good pub but its main attractions are the railway station and the ancient packhorse bridge nearby. The bridge, built in the early 15th century, is considered the best medieval bridge in the county and is unusual in that cars are allowed to cross it – provided they are no wider than 6ft 6in. Two metal posts, decorated by scrapes of multicoloured car paint, act as a gauge. Staverton means 'the village by the stony ford', which suggests that the village existed before the bridge.

The **South Devon Railway** between Buckfastleigh and Totnes stops at this delightfully vintage station. It is how people like to remember the 1950s, although I doubt the busy station in those days had so many flowers. It is cared for by volunteers from the Staverton Preservation Group, and there is also a wagon repair workshop here to keep the rolling stock on the rails.

Trains run frequently enough for you to alight here and take the riverside footpath to the Sea Trout (nearly a mile away), or cross the river to take a longer but lovely walk along the Dart to Dartington Hall and thence to Totnes (the Croydecycle map, *Totnes*, gives you plenty of options). Alternatively, if you are having a day out with the children, there's a lovely safe swimming pool in the river (page 123).

¶¶ FOOD & DRINK

Ben's Farm Shop TQ9 6AF ✆ 01803 762851 ⟨⟩ bensfarmshop.co.uk. Just off the A384 & formerly Riverford Farm Shop, you'll find seasonal & mostly organic fruit & vegetables, plants & a large variety & choice of groceries. There's a very good deli, bakery, butchers, a café with outdoor seating, & a picnic area.

Riverford Field Kitchen Wash Barn, TQ11 0JU ✆ 01803 227391 ⟨⟩ fieldkitchen.riverford. co.uk ⟨⟩ brunch Sat, lunch Wed–Sun, supper Wed–Sat. Emphatically more than just a restaurant, this is part of the pioneering organic farm that first introduced the concept of veg boxes, where seasonal vegetables are delivered to local homes as well as hotels & restaurants. Lunch or dinner consists of dishes just continually appearing for you to share. Diners sit together at large tables so a desire to be convivial should accompany a good appetite (you help yourself from the communal dishes). Dining here is a unique experience & gastronomically very rewarding. Advance booking is mandatory & there is only one sitting.

The Sea Trout Inn Staverton TQ9 6PA ✆ 01803 895395 ⟨⟩ seatroutinn.co.uk. A friendly 15th-century pub and restaurant; look out for daily specials on the blackboard. You have the choice of eating in the smart restaurant or in the more relaxed & dog-friendly Stag Bar. The menu has a selection of traditional dishes, making use of fresh local ingredients. The inn also has good en-suite accommodation (page 338).

4 BERRY POMEROY

The tiny village – just a few cottages, a school and a church – lies only a mile from Totnes, with the castle a further mile away, so although there is free parking at the castle it's rewarding to walk there, using part of the area's long-distance footpath, the **John Musgrave Heritage Trail**. The ancient path through woodland leading to the castle along Gatcombe Brook is particularly lovely (shown on the Croydecycle *Totnes* map). It is a three-mile walk to the castle from Totnes and a further 1½ miles on to Berry Pomeroy, from where you can return to Totnes by the bus number 149 (three times a day on weekdays). If you drive you will pass close to the Mare and Foal Sanctuary (page 116), well worth a visit for horse lovers.

Berry Pomeroy has been in the possession of only two families since the Norman Conquest, the Pomeroys and Seymours, who came over with William the Conqueror. Ralf or Ralph Pomeroy was given the baronial estate by William I, and his family owned it until 1548 when his fortunes collapsed and he was forced to sell it to Edward Seymour, Duke of Somerset.

The Pomeroys built a defensive castle in the late 15th century, ideally situated in a deer park so hunting could be enjoyed as well as a lifestyle appropriate to their station. The Seymours considered themselves even more elevated, not without reason, since the Duke of Somerset was the brother of Jane Seymour, the third wife of Henry VIII, and the only one of six wives to bear him a son, the future Edward VI, who ascended the throne

"Berry Pomeroy has been in the possession of only two families since the Norman Conquest, the Pomeroys and Seymours."

when he was only nine. The duke, his uncle, was appointed protector until the boy reached maturity but Edward died at the age of 15, so being king in all but name, the duke was a man of immense power and wealth. However, his rise in fortune was followed by an abrupt fall: he was overthrown as protector by political enemies in 1549 and beheaded two years later.

His son, also Edward, made Berry Pomeroy his home and set about building the finest mansion in Devon within the walls of the original castle. The work was continued by a son and grandson, so four generations of Edward Seymours have left their mark on the village, its church and its castle.

---

1 The romantic ruins of Berry Pomeroy Castle. **2** Dartington Hall's Grade II-listed gardens include terraced lawns. **3** Staverton's 15th-century bridge is considered the best medieval bridge in the county. **4** Enjoy a scenic journey on South Devon Railway's steam train. ▶

DARTINGTON HALL

GRAHAM WOOD

MICHAEL LOVEROCK

Royalists like the Seymours had a difficult time in the Civil War but their fortunes were restored, along with the monarchy, and the 6th duke welcomed William, Prince of Orange, to Berry Castle after he had landed at Brixham in 1688.

The church, **St Mary's**, stands on its own, overlooking a glorious view. The first thing you notice is the vaulted porch, with some interesting faces carved on the bosses. Inside, the exposed brickwork is unusual, and the finely carved gilded screen stretching the full width of the nave catches the eye. The saints painted on the panels have been defaced, presumably at the time of the Reformation, leaving their eloquent hands to do the talking.

There's a memorial stone to the Reverend John Prince, author of *The Worthies of Devon* (see opposite), but the glory of the church is its Seymour Chapel with the memorial to Lord Edward Seymour, son of the protector, and his son (another Edward) with his wife Elizabeth Champernowne, who was not known for her chastity. John Prince referred to her disapprovingly as 'a frolic lady'. All are lying on their sides, propped on an elbow. Elizabeth looks particularly uncomfortable, but is sustained by a prayer book clutched in her hand. She has two of her 11 children with her: a baby in a cradle at her head and at her feet a little girl, described in the information sheet as 'an imbecile child', sitting in a chair. Lined up below are the kneeling figures of the nine surviving children.

Berry Pomeroy Castle

TQ9 6LJ ✐ 01803 866618 ☉ Apr–Nov & winter weekends 10.00–17.00; English Heritage

This romantic ruin had earlier writers in rhapsodies. At the end of the 18th century, W G Maton wrote, 'the principal remains of the building... are so finely overhung with the branches of trees and shrubs that grow close to the walls, so beautifully mantled with ivy, and so richly encrusted with moss, that they constitute the most picturesque objects that can be imagined.' S P B Mais, in the mid 1920s, refers to the 'exquisite' ruin with ivy covering every inch of the walls, confirmed by an accompanying photo, and W G Hoskins (1954) describes it as 'one of the most romantically beautiful ruins in Devon, almost buried in deep woods on the edge of a cliff'. It is still romantically beautiful and still almost buried in deep woods, but the ivy has now been removed and quite a bit of clearance must have been done by English Heritage to bring the castle to its present rather austere state. It's worth taking the time to explore properly, with the audio guide, to give your imagination full rein and visualise the castle in its heyday, when a succession of Sir Edward Seymours were striving to make it the grandest mansion in Devon before running out of money, or enthusiasm, and abandoning it to the elements and nesting swallows. Berry Pomeroy is also famed as being one of the most haunted castles in Britain, and almost yearly there are reports of someone seeing a ghost here, usually the White Lady. For some first-hand accounts check out ⊘ ghost-story.co.uk. The **café** at the castle serves very good snacks.

By the entrance to the car park and the footpath leading to Gatcombe Brook is a pollarded beech tree, its roots reaching down to the eroded path below. This is what used to be the **Wishing Tree**.

WORTHY OF BEING A WORTHY OF DEVON

John Prince was vicar of Berry Pomeroy from 1681 to 1723, during which time he researched the history of Devon's noble families. His book *The Worthies of Devon* was published in 1701 and makes delightful reading – for the language as much as the content. Here are some extracts from his description of the life of the third Sir Edward Seymour:

The occasion of his being born there [in the Vicarage]...was that Berry Castle...was then a rebuilding: and his Lady-Mother, not likeing the Musick of Axes and Hammers (this Gentlemans great delight afterward) chose to lay down, this her burthen in that lowly place.

He had no sooner passed the care and inspection of the Noursery, but that he was put abroad to School (it enervates youth to keep it too long at home under the fondling of a Mother)...[At Sherborne] he met with a severe Master, tho a good Teacher: the Memory of whom, would often disturb his sleep long after he was a Man.

...it pleased almighty God, in just Punishment of a Nation whose sins had made it ripe for Vengeance, to let loose upon it, a most dreadfull Civil War. A War founded upon the glorious pretences of Liberty, Property, and Religion...And when matters brake out into open violence between the King and Parliament, this Gentlemans native Principles of Loyalty soon instructed him which side to take.

[Sir Edward, then a colonel, was taken prisoner at Modbury before making his escape] by fileing Off the Bars of the Window, and leaping down, upon the back of the Centinel that stood under; who being astonished by so unexpected a rancounter, the Colonel wrested his Musket out of his hand, and gave him such a sound Rebuke as hindered him, for the present, from following after him, or making any Discovery of him.

I first visited the castle with a friend who, in the late 1960s, used to take her children there to make a special wish. 'We had to walk backwards – very tricky with three little children in wellies. They kept falling over. One year we made a special journey [from Guildford] because all three were about to take exams.' There is now no sign indicating the magical powers of this sadly diminished beech, but I found this description in a 1963 Devon guide: 'According to local tradition, to walk backwards round this tree three times will bring the fulfilment of any desire…[but] as the earth has fallen away from the far side, the slope is now too steep to admit of perambulation round the tree – either backwards or forwards.' You can still do a half-perambulation and make a half-wish.

THE MIDDLE & LOWER RIVER DART

The claim that the Dart is the loveliest river in England is not misplaced. Ancient oak forests line the banks (the name Dart is derived from the Old English for 'oak', which is probably why there are two Dart rivers in Devon; the other one joins the Exe at Bickleigh), drooping their gnarled trunks towards the water. Where the trees end the hills begin, chequerboard fields of red earth and green pasture rising steeply up to the horizon. Sometimes the river widens so it feels more like a lake, and at other times it's so narrow you could throw a stone to the other side. Small villages of whitewashed cottages hide along the arms of creeks, and splendid mansions are just visible through the trees. Clusters of sailing boats lie moored at Dittisham and Stoke Gabriel, and a variety of passenger-carrying vessels use the river as a highway.

Perhaps the perfect way to get to know the river is to walk from Totnes to Dartmouth on a lovely nine-mile section of the Dart Valley Trail. You can take the river ferry for the journey back.

ON (& IN) THE RIVER DART
FOR TRANSPORT OR PLEASURE

The line between a pleasure cruise and transport is blurred on this river. Price is the main difference. The most elegant and expensive way of travelling between Dartmouth and Totnes is by the **paddle steamer** *Kingswear Castle* (✆ 01803 555872 ⊘ kingswearcastle.org; page 126), but you'll find an assortment of cheaper boats. The

Dartmouth Steam Railway and River Boat Company (✆ 01803 555872 ⏀ dartmouthrailriver.co.uk) are the leaders, with a good commentary and the option of including the steam train to Paignton and bus back to Totnes. Whichever boat you catch, the hour-long trip most delightfully combines getting from Dartmouth to Totnes, or vice versa, with an overview of the sights along the river. You'll see a reasonable amount of birdlife, including cormorants and herons, and if there's a commentary, you'll hear about the wildlife and history of the houses and villages en route. All River Dart boats can only operate within a few hours of high tide, so timetables vary.

For shorter journeys the good-value **Greenway Ferry** (✆ 01803 882811 ⏀ greenwayferry.co.uk) runs between Dartmouth and Dittisham (page 131).

If you're a keen **swimmer**, you can sign up to the Outdoor Swimming Society's **Dart 10k** (⏀ outdoorswimmingsociety.com) in September, from Totnes to Dittisham. This is probably the oldest 10k open-water swim in Britain and attracts over 1,000 swimmers every year. They welcome swimmers of all abilities and stress that it is 'a journey, not a race'.

WILD SWIMMING IN THE RIVER DART

Joanna Griffin

The River Dart is one of Devon's most popular rivers for swimming. Its clear waters, stained the colour of dark red amber by the peaty soil, rush down from the high moor, cascading over large, smooth stones and widening towards Totnes where the river becomes tidal. A popular stretch on Dartmoor itself is around Newbridge. From here, the beautiful **Sharrah Pools** are a 40-minute walk upstream through the National Trust's Holne Woods. Closer to Newbridge itself, the river is shallow and turbulent, thrust into small waterfalls as it courses over large boulders, but there are still some lovely deep, calm parts to be found on the left bank, perfect for a swim between the banks of birch and ancient oaks.

Once the Dart has left Dartmoor, there are numerous swimming spots en route to Totnes. A favourite along this stretch is **Still Pool**, a wide, calm and reasonably deep section outside the village of Staverton (page 116), just below the weir. Parking is in the old station car park and it is a lovely 10–15-minute riverside walk through the woods to the pool, where there is access from the riverbank or a small beach. This can be a popular spot in the warm weather and you might find you're not alone in the water, but it is pretty and easily accessible.

Paddling or sailing the Dart

What better way of getting to know this wonderfully unspoilt river than on a hired kayak or dinghy? There is a good choice of companies offering everything from sit-on-top kayaks to stand-up paddleboarding, and from sailing dinghies to cabin cruisers. Operators offering kayaks and canoes are based in the small villages on the upper river, where there is a selection of pubs to visit (always an important consideration!) as well as the best scenery and quietest water. Six hours is generally considered a full day's hire.

⚓ BOAT HIRE

Canoe Adventures ✆ 07706 343744 ⎙ canoeadventures.co.uk. Guided tours exploring the Dart aboard a fleet of six canoes, each taking six to eight adults plus up to four children. Based at Tuckenhay & Stoke Gabriel.

Dartmouth Boat Hire Centre ✆ 07545 518546 ⎙ dartmouth-boat-hire.co.uk. Boat hire for all levels of experience, from motor launches to cabin cruisers suitable for two to eight people.

Dittisham Boats ✆ 07711 177124 ⎙ dittishamboats.co.uk. Motorboats, sailing boats, kayaks & stand-up paddleboards from Dittisham.

Totnes Kayaks ✆ 07799 403788 ⎙ totneskayaks.co.uk. The kayak specialists, with sit-on-top kayaks, paddleboards & open canoes. Hire one of these for an hour or the day. Guided trips are also available. Operate from Stoke Gabriel.

RIVERSIDE VILLAGES

Although all these villages are accessible by road, approaching them from the river or on foot gives a unique perspective of their evolution before the age of the motor car.

5 STOKE GABRIEL

⌂ **Sandridge Boathouse** (page 338)

A village of confusingly winding lanes funnels traffic down to the riverside car park, where the salmon fishermen used to mend their nets and where boat-hire people now ply their trade. The Rivershack (⎙ therivershackdevon.co.uk), right on the quay, serves good local food and there is excellent crabbing for children from the dam at low tide.

THE RIVER DART: **1** & **2** Rent a boat or try a paddleboard to enjoy the river fully.
3 The *Kingswear Castle* paddle steamer travels between Totnes and Dartmouth. ▶

KINGSWEAR CASTLE

THE SLOW WAY TO SEE THE RIVER DART & AREA

Take a tip from us. Leave your car in Totnes or Torbay and spend a heavenly day enjoying some of Devon's best scenery rather than trying to find that elusive Dartmouth car park. The Round Robin ticket gives you the river, rail and bus journey between Totnes, Dartmouth and Paignton in one day. Contact the Dartmouth Steam Railway and River Boat Company (✆ 01803 555872 🖥 dartmouthrailriver.co.uk).

In 2013 paddle steamer *Kingswear Castle* (🖥 kingswearcastle.org) was welcomed back to her original home, having spent time in the Isle of Wight and the Medway. Built in 1924, she spent the first decade or so of her

life carrying up to 500 passengers between Dartmouth and Totnes, before the more efficient propeller boats took over. She has been repaired, restored and refurbished many times, having more than £500,000 spent on her in 2022. The *Kingswear Castle* is now the last remaining coal-fired paddle steamer in operation in the UK. All polished brass and wood, with sleekly pumping pistons keeping the wheels turning ('Nigel's down there shovelling coal,' said the commentator), this is the best-looking boat on the river. Even the loo is gorgeous: almost a throne (raised on a platform, at any rate) with the white ceramic bowl and cistern decorated with blue flowers.

The village itself is contained in one steep, narrow street with the post office and general store. Indeed, this is the only shop, although there's a craft gallery and two pubs, the **Castle Inn**, a crenellated Victorian folly, and Church House Inn.

The church is large and, for Devon, relatively uninteresting apart from the striking wooden pulpit which is partly painted in green and gilt, and the rood screen with its intricately carved leaf design. The glory of the church is the **yew tree** that stands – or rather sprawls – in the graveyard. It is reckoned to be between 800 and 1,300 years old and is feeling its age. It stands hunched and droopy, with every limb supported on a pillar or draped across a tombstone.

"The yew tree that stands – or rather sprawls – in the graveyard, is reckoned to be between 800 and 1,300 years old."

Just a mile southeast of the village, **Sandridge Barton Estate** (✆ 01803 732203 🖥 sandridgebarton.com ☉ Mar–Oct 10.00–17.00, Nov–Dec 10.00–16.00) produces top-quality wine and their own cheeses. They offer a variety of tours as well as having a restaurant and a shop selling their produce. Tours, optionally with a guide, range from a wine and cheese tasting to a 'Vine to Wine' tour (☉ May–Sep 15.00) which takes you behind the scenes to learn all

We took the hour-long river cruise, which starts by doing a circle round the river mouth. Our guide pointed out the sights, including the two castles from where the great chain was stretched across the river in the 15th century to thwart invaders. Then up the river for a look at Greenway and Dittisham before heading back to Dartmouth. Although Danny the dolphin hasn't been seen for a while, we did watch an indolent Atlantic grey seal.

The steam train complements the river trip perfectly. The brass is polished to mirror-shininess, and the trains wear their names with pride. Ours was *Hercules*. Most trains go via Greenway, over the Brunel Viaduct, giving you a chance to visit Agatha Christie's former home (page 133). If you want to see the river views sit on the left, but for a real *wow!* experience find a seat on the right where you steam and toot past Longwood, with its sessile oaks, and on to Churston. It is shortly after this station that the train rounds a corner and, suddenly, there is Torbay. On the sunny October day that we did the trip, the sea was a Mediterranean blue and Broadsands Beach, contained within a semicircle of red cliffs, looked irresistible. Then on to Paignton and the option of taking double-decker bus number 100 back to Totnes.

there is to know about how they make their wines. You'll get to taste four wines on the way plus a couple of cheeses from Sharpham Dairy, which is just upriver. There are also three self-catering cottages on the estate.

The village is not on the Dart Valley Trail so driving is the easiest way of getting here. It's served by bus number 125 from Paignton. Get off at 'Four Cross Lanes' if you are going to Sandridge Barton.

6 ASHPRINGTON & THE SHARPHAM ESTATE

The picturesque village of **Ashprington** sits at the top of a hill, the tall, slender tower of its church dominating the scene and its pub, The Durant Arms, a welcome sight for those who've walked or cycled the three miles from Totnes.

The church of St David was thoroughly done over in the 19th century, but still retains some interesting features. Even before entering the graveyard I was struck by the lychgate, which has a resting slab for the coffin – often considered to be a medieval feature, although this one dates from the 19th century. The tower, too, is unusual. Probably dating from the 13th century, it is constructed in four sections, each slightly smaller than the last, giving it a tapering appearance, and there's an external staircase to the belfry. On entering, the first thing you notice is the wooden pulpit. This is by the noted Devon woodcarver Herbert Read (or his son, also called Herbert), and is intricately carved with all manner of flora and fauna: vines, birds and even a snail, as well as the Virgin Mary and other biblical Marys (it was given in memory of Mary Cottam Carwithen of Ashprington House).

The monuments are particularly eye-catching. Three generations of Bastards are commemorated without shame: it was the surname of the family that inherited Sharpham Estate in the 19th century, following the death of Captain Philemon Pownoll, whose monument is in the church (see below).

CAPTAIN PHILEMON POWNOLL

Philemon Pownoll (or Pownall, or Pownell) was born in 1734 in Plymouth, the son of a master shipwright, so he naturally went to sea to seek his fortune. At the age of only 28 Philemon struck gold – literally. War between Britain and Spain broke out in January 1762 and His Majesty's sloop *Favourite*, to which he had recently been promoted captain, was one of several warships despatched to guard Cape St Vincent. On 15 May, *Favourite* and the frigate *Active* spotted the Spanish man-of-war *Hermione* returning home to Cádiz from Lima; she responded aggressively to their challenge so they let loose their guns and took her. It then emerged that *Hermione* was no simple warship: she also carried bags of dollars, gold coins, ingots of gold, silver and tin – and, more prosaically, a large stock of cocoa.

The prize money from this capture was massive: in total over £500,000, of which Pownoll's share was £64,872. Even the ordinary seamen from the two ships received around £480 each, a sum they would have taken over 30 years to earn. More than 20 wagons were needed to carry all the booty to London.

Pownoll and his fellow captain from the *Active*, Herbert Sawyer, had earlier been courting the two daughters of a merchant from Exeter, who had refused their suits because of their inadequate financial status. Now the men rapidly married their sweethearts and even settled an annuity on the merchant.

Pownoll spent his money lavishly. He had his portrait painted by Sir Joshua Reynolds and started building his manor at Sharpham. The house was laid out in the Adam style with gardens designed by a follower of Capability Brown. The estate has a river frontage of nearly three miles. It was his daughter Jane who married the unfortunately named Edmund Bastard. They had no sons, so the Bastard line ended there.

Pownoll remained in the navy and in 1780 was killed by cannon fire while engaging a French privateer. Admiral John Jervis wrote in tribute that he was 'the best officer, & most excellent kind-hearted man in the Profession'.

Sharpham House, Captain Pownoll's former estate, enfolded in a loop of the river, was purchased in 1961 by Maurice and Ruth Ash. She was the daughter of Dartington Hall founders the Elmhirsts, so it is no surprise that development of the estate took a spiritual and sustainable path, with quality food production just part of their work. It is now owned by the **Sharpham Trust**, which runs three- to ten-night **retreats** at the Barn, Coach House, in the woodland and in the main house (🖱 sharphamtrust.org). Many retreats are themed – mindfulness, walking, gardening, Buddhist or silent – there could not be a better place to experience the inner stillness that the Slow concept is all about. The trust also runs a variety of outdoor events including nature events on the estate; booking is essential.

The views over the Dart from the long, steep lane down from Ashprington are such that drivers will need real concentration to stay on the road. Both the Dart Valley Trail and NCN 2 pass the entrance to Sharpham Estate before reaching Ashprington.

FOOD & DRINK

The Durant Arms Ashprington TQ9 7UP ☎ 01803 732240 🖱 durantarms.co.uk. Hearty pub fare in a typical village inn; walker-, dog- & cyclist-friendly, with a log fire in the winter, & three en-suite guest rooms.

Emma's Stoke Gabriel TQ9 6RU ☎ 01803 782697 f ⏲ lunch Sat–Sun & dinner Wed, Fri, Sat. This small family-run restaurant in the middle of the village has gained a five-star reputation for superb cooking & great service. It's 'bring-your-own-booze' but the pub is across the road if you forget to bring wine.

7 TUCKENHAY & CORNWORTHY

Tuckenhay Mill (page 338) & **Duck Cottage** (page 338)

The tiny, elongated village of **Tuckenhay**, squeezed between the River Wash, Bow Creek and a steep hillside, makes an agreeable and peaceful base for exploring the middle section of the river. It's hard to believe that until 1970 this was an important industrial centre, with the paper mill providing local employment, and ships plying the river to transport its high-quality paper throughout the realm. It was used, among other things, to make banknotes. During wartime, when the raw materials were hard to get, local people were asked to save their rags and printed paper for the factory. They had to divide them into three bags: wool, cotton and paper – an early version of today's coloured

bins. The mill and its outbuildings have been converted into luxury self-catering accommodation.

An enjoyable circular walk from Tuckenhay takes you along Bow Creek, past benches for the weary and picnic places for the hungry. You return via **Cornworthy**, which has a pub and the ruined Augustinian priory of St Mary, reportedly founded for seven religious women. It was a victim of the Dissolution of the Monasteries and abandoned in 1539. Nothing much remains except the gatehouse with its rather splendid arch, large enough to allow the passage of horse-drawn carriages, framing Cornworthy in the valley below. Nearby is a humbler doorway for pedestrians. The Croydecycle *Dittisham & Cornworthy* map shows this walk.

¶¶ FOOD & DRINK

Maltster's Arms Tuckenhay TQ9 7EH ☎ 01803 732350 ⌂ the-maltsters.co.uk. *The* riverside pub & deservedly popular. The food is excellent & the setting sublime. If possible arrive by river, rather than tackling the nerve-rackingly narrow lanes by car. Booking advisable.
Waterman's Arms Bow Bridge (between Ashprington & Tuckenhay), TQ9 7EG ☎ 01803 732214 ⌂ thewatermansarms.net. A 17th-century hotel & restaurant with tranquil outdoor seating next to the Harbourne River. The food is standard pub grub but you come here for the location. Also B&B.

8 DITTISHAM & GREENWAY

The river is at its narrowest between these two places, a delightful village and Agatha Christie's holiday home, with a motorboat acting as a ferry from one to the other. There's no particular schedule, you just ring a large bell when you're ready to cross and by and by the boatman will appear (⌂ greenwayferry.co.uk).

Dittisham
⚑ **Dittisham Hideaway** (page 339)
Pronounced locally as 'Ditsum', this sailing centre is reminiscent of Cornwall, with a hillside of tightly packed, steeply stacked white cottages with slate roofs. If you arrive here by car, avoid heading straight

◀ **1** Stoke Gabriel sits right on the River Dart. **2** Agatha Christie bought the Georgian house Greenway in 1938. **3** Cornworthy's church tower peeks out from the valley. **4** The Sharpham Estate holds wonderfully Slow retreats.

down to the quay – there's no parking and your car may end up in the pub or the river. Look for the car park in the upper town (the Ham) which overlooks the river. This is just below the church, which is worth a look for its colourful and unusual pulpit carved of stone rather than wood. It dates from the 15th century and is intricately carved, gilded and painted, entwined with fruit and foliage, with some very gloomy saints or apostles in the niches. From the car park you can walk through the park and then along the shore (at low tide) to the quay.

Sightseeing as such may be limited but there is plenty to enjoy. Dittisham is said to be the best place on the Dart for crabbing (off the pontoon) or just pottering. Most visitors seem to spend their time sprawled happily with a pint of beer in their hand in front of the **Ferry Boat Inn** (𝄞 01803 722368 🖉 fbidittisham.co.uk), known by locals as the FBI. It is a wonderfully traditional pub which invites lingering. As does the excellent **Anchorstone Café** (𝄞 01803 722365 🖉 anchorstonecafe.co.uk), more of a licensed restaurant than a

AGATHA CHRISTIE

Dame Agatha Christie – born Agatha Miller in Barton Road, Torquay, in September 1890 – is the best-selling novelist of all time. Sales of her work top 2 billion, in more than 60 languages, surpassed only by Shakespeare, the Bible and the Koran. Her play *The Mousetrap*, which opened in London in 1952, has by now become the longest-running theatre play in history.

The play came about because the BBC asked Queen Mary how they might best celebrate her 80th birthday on radio. She requested something by Agatha Christie – who obligingly wrote a short sketch, *Three Blind Mice*, broadcast in 1947, which she then adapted for the stage as *The Mousetrap*.

On Christmas Eve in 1914, as World War I was breaking, Agatha Miller married Captain Archibald Christie of the Royal Flying Corps; they honeymooned in Torquay's Grand Hotel. During the war Torquay Town Hall served as a hospital and she worked there, picking up useful details about poisons and meeting Belgian refugees, the blueprints for Hercule Poirot. The Christie Gallery in Torquay Museum (page 73) and the Agatha Christie Mile commemorate her connections there. The marriage was not happy, and in December 1926 Britain's newspapers were buzzing with the news that she had 'disappeared'; amid murmurs of foul play a massive search was mounted, with rewards offered for information leading to her return. Eleven days later she was spotted: it turned out she had travelled by train to Yorkshire and checked in to a hotel in Harrogate, using the surname (Neele) of her husband's current mistress. She traditional café, serving delicious food on a terrace overlooking the river.

North of the village is the blunt peninsula, Gurrow Point, which you can walk right round (with some difficulty) at low tide.

Greenway
Galmpton TQ5 0ES ✆ 01803 842382 ⊙ Mar–Oct 10.30–17.00; National Trust

The Georgian house was built in the late 18th century, but its predecessor, Greenway Court, was the home of Sir Humphrey Gilbert, half-brother to Sir Walter Raleigh and owner of Compton Castle (page 80). The young Walter spent holidays there as a boy, and as an adult allegedly sat by the river smoking his silver pipe with the first tobacco seen in England. Understandably, this act was misinterpreted by a servant who, seeing his master apparently on fire, threw a jug of ale (or maybe water) over him.

Agatha Christie bought the house in 1938 for £6,000. She took a break from writing while on holiday here, but the sloping grounds, with

claimed amnesia, but more probably had been reacting to her husband's affair. They divorced two years later.

In 1930 Christie married archaeologist Max Mallowan, and *Murder on the Orient Express* was inspired by one of her rail trips with him to his excavations in the Middle East. Asked what marriage to an archaeologist was like, she is said to have replied: 'Wonderful – the older you get, the more interested he is in you.' In 1938 they bought the Greenway estate on the River Dart (see above).

Burgh Island Hotel in Bigbury Bay (page 179) is the setting for her best-selling novel (and the world's best-selling mystery) *And Then There Were None*, written in 1939. The 'writer's hut', reputedly built for her there in the 1930s, was rebuilt in 2007; now called 'The Beach House', it's one of the hotel's

luxury bedrooms. Kents Cavern in Torquay appears as Hempsley Cavern in her novel *The Man in a Brown Suit*: her father helped to finance excavations there and was an enthusiastic volunteer on the dig.

Christie died in 1976, but constantly gains more fans through the many new adaptations of her work, while the annual International Agatha Christie Festival (⊘ iacf-uk.org) in Torquay attracts ever-larger audiences.

Poet and novelist Sophie Hannah has been chosen by the Christie estate to continue her legacy by writing new stories featuring Hercule Poirot: five have been published over the last ten years and are already pleasing her fans, and more are promised. Like *The Mousetrap*, the 'Queen of Crime' is still a very long way indeed from reaching her final curtain.

glimpses of the river through the trees, provided settings for some of her murder mysteries. If you are an Agatha Christie fan you'll love your visit to the house, marvelling that you are looking at the actual Steinway piano she played, and appreciating the papier-mâché tables that she collected. In fact the place is stuffed with Agatha Christie memorabilia, not all of which were here originally. You can listen to an interesting recording of a radio interview with Dame Agatha where she describes the process of writing her books. If your interest is more towards archaeology than murder mysteries, you'll enjoy the collections from Christie's second husband, Sir Max Mallowan, who organised digs in Iraq and other Middle Eastern sites. My lasting impression was of coupledom. The Mallowans clearly loved doing things together and Agatha was an enthusiastic helpmate on Max's archaeological trips. And it would be hard not to be happy in such a setting. The garden is lovely, well worth a visit for its peacefulness and some unusual plants.

"It would be hard not to be happy in such a setting. The garden is lovely, well worth a visit for its peacefulness."

Plonked in the river opposite Greenway's boathouse is the Anchor Stone, which doubled as the site of a ducking stool for disobedient wives.

Visitors are encouraged to come to Greenway a green way if possible: on foot, bike, bus, steam train or boat. Car parking has to be booked in advance and is strictly limited. This is no great hardship when a large part of the house's attraction is its position overlooking the river and gorgeous surrounding scenery. The five-mile walk here from Kingswear is particularly rewarding, passing as it does through the oaks of Longwood. Alternatively you can take the steam train (it doesn't always stop at Greenway but you can walk from Churston, about two miles), take the Greenway Ferry (⊘ greenwayferry.co.uk) from Dartmouth, or park in Dittisham and cross the river. In fact, you're spoilt for choice.

DARTMOUTH & AROUND

It is rare for a town to combine a rich and interesting history with present-day beauty. Usually the accidents of geography that gave it strategic importance a few hundred years ago also caused its later industrialisation. Dartmouth and Kingswear (page 143), placed either side of the steeply banked estuary, have escaped this fate, probably because the planned-for railway never happened. The writer W G Maton, although sometimes given to hyperbole, describes his arrival in the late 1700s in words that could still be used today:

> We were in some measure prepared for the enchanting scene which our passage across the Dart opened to us…On our left appeared the castle, which stands at the mouth of the river, surrounded by a rich mass of oak, and the steeple of an adjoining church just peeps above the branches. Opposite to us was the town, situated on the declivity of a craggy hill, and extending, embosomed in trees, almost a mile along the water's edge…The rocks on either side are composed of a glossy purple slate, and their summits fringed with a number of ornamental plants and shrubs. Enraptured with so lovely a scene, we arrived insensibly at the quay of Dartmouth.

A couple of centuries later, S P B Mais, arriving at night, wrote: 'As you step on to the cobbled quay and dimly glimpse the medieval, richly carved, gabled houses bending courteously to greet you, you feel that you have been transported not merely to another land but to another century.'

Kingswear is equally attractive in a smaller way, and the walk from here to **Coleton Fishacre (page 145)**, or to Brixham if you can manage the 11 miles, is one of the best on Devon's South West Coast Path.

9 DARTMOUTH

🏠 **Anzac Street Bistro** (page 338) & **Dart Marina** (page 338)
Tourist information: The Engine House, Mayors Av ✆ 01803 834224 ⚘ visitdartmouth. uk. Very helpful, with a good selection of leaflets & printed matter for sale.

Present-day visitors should endeavour to arrive, as Maton and Mais did, by water, or via the coast path or steam train towards Kingswear, for the enchanting view across the Dart. Arrival by car, in the summer, may only result in frustration and the inevitable backtracking to the park-and-ride car park, which may be the only place you can leave your car for longer than four hours. If you do drive into the centre of town, ignore your satnav or you could find yourself wedged in one of those impossibly steep, narrow and oh-so-picturesque approach lanes. Off-season parking is easier: free along the riverfront and there's a short-stay car park near the little inner harbour. One time you definitely don't want to drive into Dartmouth is during the annual August **Regatta**.

Seen across the river the view is much as Maton describes it, with the castle at the furthest point of the cliff, and white houses set into the hillside among dark trees contrasting with the terraces of multicoloured homes arranged along the waterfront. On a sunny day it is one of the loveliest sights in Devon. And on a wet day you can happily fill a couple of hours under cover.

At the time of the Domesday Book (1086) the River Dart was under the control of the Lord of Totnes, Dartmouth coming into its own only with the arrival of decked sailing ships. The Second and Third Crusades sailed from here in 1147 and 1190, and, for the 300 years that Bordeaux was under English rule, trade was brisk between the two countries, with wine the main import, and wool, carried down the river from Totnes, the export. John Hawley (page 139) built up his business through this two-way trade. Royal favour was guaranteed to this maritime town when privateers could fight the king's battles for him and enrich both themselves and their monarch. Richard II, a weak, effete king if we are to believe Shakespeare, seems to have been particularly grateful for the services of Hawley and his followers in protecting the shores from French invasion. In the 15th century the town was kept safe from invaders by a chain that was raised across the harbour mouth during the night, from Gommerock, south of Kingswear, where the hole can still be seen, to Dartmouth Castle, where remnants of the hoist still exist.

"In the 15th century the town was kept safe from invaders by a chain that was raised across the harbour mouth."

After England lost Bordeaux in 1453, Dartmouth's prosperity declined, but the great explorers of the Elizabethan era revived it and from 1580 it profited from the cod fishery in Newfoundland. The Civil War took its toll and the town sank into relative obscurity until the building of the Royal Naval College in 1899–1905. Its strategic importance during World War II ensured that it was extensively bombed; the town sent 485 ships to Normandy for D-Day. The planned railway never reached Dartmouth so industrialisation also passed it by. We can be thankful for that.

Much of the Dartmouth you see today is on reclaimed land. Even before John Hawley's time the industrious inhabitants were harnessing

DARTMOUTH: **1** The castle sits grandly at the entrance to the estuary. **2** Explore the town's picturesque pedestrianised streets lined with colourful houses. **3** One of the impressive brasses at St Saviour's Church. ▶

REBECCA WRIGHT/A

the tides to provide power to their mill. Sea water ran into an inlet known as the Mill Pool through an artificially narrow entrance. Then at high tide a sluice gate was dropped, diverting the receding water to turn the mill wheel. The former Mill Pool now provides the only flat land in town.

Dartmouth was the birthplace of **Thomas Newcomen** (1663–1727), whose atmospheric engine was one of the forerunners of the Industrial Revolution. It was used to remove water from flooded mines, which hitherto had been hauled out by teams of horses. Take a look at the reconstructed engine by the tourist office. And if you really want to understand how it worked, look at the neat animation on ⊘ animatedengines.com.

Car ferries connect Dartmouth and Kingswear. You can take the Lower Ferry, on the B3205, or the Higher Ferry, less than a mile upriver on the A379. Both ferries carry cycles and foot passengers as well as cars. River cruises around the harbour or to Totnes, Dittisham or the castle are booked at one of the several kiosks along the quay.

Exploring the town

Most people arrive en masse on the quay, disgorged either from a river ferry or a bus, so the riverfront (North Embankment) is always crowded. The wise visitor heads uphill to the pedestrianised streets to look at some of the specialist **shops** and have a snack in the market, before going to the museum and the church to be immersed in Dartmouth's rich history.

In Foss Street you'll find the Canvas Factory (⊘ canvas-factory. co.uk) with a great range of old-fashioned holdalls, and you can smell Roly's Fudge Pantry from a block away; you might as well give way to temptation. Next door is the Dartmouth Bookseller, a good independent bookshop, and further along is Simon Drew's gallery (⊘ simondrew. co.uk), full of his distinctive, quirky political caricatures and cards.

Opposite the Visitor Centre is the **Dartmouth Museum** (𝄢 01803 832923 ⊘ dartmouthmuseum.org ⊙ 11.00–15.00 daily) housed in the timber-framed Butterwalk, dating from 1635. Dartmouth lost some of its finest medieval buildings in a road-widening scheme in the 1800s, but this house is still there, bending courteously towards visitors, and rich with enigmatic carvings. The museum is well worth a visit. Staffed, as are many Devon museums, by volunteers, it contains a variety of exhibits. Model ships illustrate the maritime history of Dartmouth from the wine trade to Drake's *Golden Hind* and the *Mayflower*, which put in for repairs here before taking the Pilgrim Fathers to America. Look out for the amazing man-of-war carved from bone by Frenchmen incarcerated in Dartmoor Prison during the Napoleonic Wars. There is also an extensive collection of ships in bottles, and some hands-on exhibits for younger visitors, including those in the reconstructed studio of naturalist William Cumming Henley.

JOHN HAWLEY, A 'SCHIPMAN OF DERTEMOUTHE'

John Hawley was one of those hugely successful entrepreneurs who shaped the history of England and ensured that their name lived on in brass. Born around 1340 into a prosperous Dartmouth family, Hawley built up his ship-owning business until he had about 30 vessels. This asset came to the attention of Edward III, who was involved in the interminable wars with France which later became known as the Hundred Years' War.

Hawley was granted a privateer's licence by the king in 1379. This meant that he could attack enemy ships, which might just happen to be carrying valuable cargo, and share the proceeds with the king. The arrangement worked well on both sides, and Hawley clearly gained the respect of his fellow citizens, since he was elected mayor of Dartmouth a total of 14 times, and also served twice as the town's MP.

Of course sometimes the line between 'enemy' and 'valuable' became a bit blurred and, as the description of Hawley in St Saviour's notes, 'There seems little doubt that he was also a pirate'.

Hawley is believed to be the inspiration for Chaucer's 'schipman of Dertemouthe', a somewhat shady character. He will have met Chaucer when the latter was customs officer for Edward III. Any illegal business of Hawley's was far outweighed by the benefits he brought to Dartmouth, however, during his tenures as mayor. He successfully kept the strategic port safe from enemy attack by building fortresses on each side of the mouth of the Dart and stretching a huge chain across the harbour to repel enemy ships.

The story goes that after a particularly successful sortie into French waters, from which he returned laden with booty, he declined to accept any personal reward, asking that the king's generosity be visited on his native town instead. Hence Dartmouth has a particularly charming coat of arms: Edward III, flanked by two lions, all perched precariously on a very small boat.

Hawley died in 1408, in his late 60s. His elaborate memorial brass in St Saviour's is not excessive given his larger-than-life contribution to the town's prosperity and status. And anyway, he built the chancel.

If you do no other sightseeing in Dartmouth, go to **St Saviour's Church** and look at the door inside the south entrance. It's thought to have been made in 1372 but the vigour and artistry of the ironwork would be amazing even for 1972. Two slinky lions leap through leafy branches, claws out, eyes bulging, mouths snarling. Equally impressive and dramatic are the huge brasses near the altar, sometimes hidden under the carpet but often on display. A print taken from a brass rubbing is on the west wall, so you can examine them as a whole. They commemorate John Hawley and his two wives. He is in full armour, with his feet on a feisty lion, chastely holding the hand of one wife (he outlived them both). Often church brasses and memorials are of people whose deeds have been forgotten, but not so John Hawley. Privateer, pirate, MP and 14 times mayor of Dartmouth, he shaped the history of the town (page 139) and paid for 'his' end of the church.

"Thought to have been made in 1372, the artistry of the door's ironwork would be amazing even for 1972."

Other notable features are the splendid screen, with its fan vaulting, painted in muted gold and charcoal grey, and the early 16th-century painted carved stone pulpit, similar to the one in Dittisham, covered with bold clumps of foliage. The figures of saints were hacked off during the Reformation, to be replaced by secular emblems of the Kingdom: England, Scotland, Ireland and Wales.

On the southern outskirts of town, beyond a cobbled quay with benches for gazing at the view or just hanging out, is **Bayard's Cove**, a ruined fortress built to protect the town from pirates and other enemy ships, which has proved too sturdy to demolish to make way for development. **Dartmouth Castle** (☉ Apr–Oct 10.00–17.00 daily, Nov–Mar 10.00–16.00 Sat–Sun) is a further mile away. Now owned by English Heritage, it was built in 1488 on the site of one of John Hawley's fortifications to guard the narrow opening to the estuary. The church of St Petroc is incorporated within the castle grounds. The Castle Ferry from the centre of town provides an alternative to walking.

A town landmark if approaching from the river or Kingswear is the imposing **Britannia Royal Naval College** (✆ 01803 677565 ⌂ britanniaassociation.org.uk), set high on the hillside. Completed in 1905, this is now the only naval college in the country, training naval cadets from all over the world. Visitors can pre-book a walking tour (☉ Feb–Nov 10.00 Mon & Wed) taking just over two hours. In 1939 the

13-year-old Princess Elizabeth was shown round the college by one of the cadets, Prince Philip. So who knows who you will meet?

¶¶ FOOD & DRINK

Alf Resco's Lower St, in the southern part of town ✆ 07775 911369 ⌂ cafealfresco.co.uk. Famous for its breakfasts & brunches. Very popular so can get busy in the holiday season.

Anzac Street Bistro Anzac St, off Victoria Rd ✆ 01803 835515 ⌂ anzacbistro.co.uk. The menu is small, with around five main dishes & a couple of specials, some with a Polish twist; all are hearty & unusual including vegan & imaginative vegetarian options. Booking essential. They also have three rooms (page 338).

Cherub Inn 13 Higher St ✆ 01803 832571 ⌂ the-cherub.co.uk. The oldest building in Dartmouth, dating from 1380, all black timbers, old oak beams & hanging baskets, & just oozing history (it was once a merchant's house). The food is good, with daily specials & proper English desserts such as bread & butter pudding.

Dartmouth Food Festival ⌂ dartmouthfoodfestival.com ☉ Oct. Celebrates the best of the southwest with tastings, workshops, seminars & over 120 exhibitors. No entry charge.

Dartmouth Ice Cream Company The Good Intent, 30 Lower St ✆ 01803 832157 ⌂ dartmouthicecream.com. Scrumptious ice creams & sorbets made on the premises. Also fudge & clotted cream. It has a good online shop too – clotted cream or a complete Devon hamper delivered to your door.

Devonishly Good ✆ 01803 411216 ⌂ dartmouthfinefoods.co.uk. Fresh or frozen Devon meals delivered to your self-catering accommodation with full instructions: from picnics to banquets, Dartmouth crab & pollock to vegetarian Wellington & mushroom ragu.

Rockfish 8 South Embankment ✆ 01803 832800 ⌂ therockfish.co.uk. One of six Rockfish restaurants in Devon, its motto is 'Tomorrow's fish is in the sea'. Serves a great range of fish dishes but its fish & chips are famous. There's a separate take-away outlet.

Seahorse Restaurant 5 South Embankment ✆ 01803 835147 ⌂ seahorserestaurant. co.uk ☉ noon–16.00 Tue–Thu, noon–20.00 Fri–Sat. Founded by Mitch Tonks, the Seahorse is famous for its terrific seafood in classy surroundings. Lunches are great value. Come here for that special treat, & book ahead.

The Singing Kettle 6 Smith St ✆ 07519 004635. Seriously good cream teas, & lunches too, in a traditional Dartmouth building.

SOUTH OF DARTMOUTH

The South West Coast Path lures you away from the town to the castle, and then along the cliffs to a pretty little shingle beach, **Compass Cove**, where you can swim. Continue round the cliffs or take the short cut via Little Dartmouth, until you pass the delightfully named cluster of rocks, the Dancing Beggars. **Stoke Fleming** is the next village. It has an interesting church whose tall tower used to be an aid to guide ships into Dartmouth harbour, and which has one of the oldest brasses in Devon, dated 1361. The great-grandfather of Dartmouth's Thomas Newcomen was rector here in the 17th century. Beyond the village is the surprisingly named beach of Blackpool Sands, scene of John Hawley's last battle.

The walk here from Dartmouth is about six miles – but only three by road. Bus number 93 runs hourly back to Dartmouth.

10 Blackpool Sands

TQ6 0RG ✏ 01803 771800 ⚲ blackpoolsands.co.uk

Blackpool Sands is a deservedly popular privately owned beach. Like Slapton, the 'sands' are actually fine shingle so no good for sandcastles, but there is a sandpit for children with the real stuff. The bay is exceptionally beautiful, framed in a semicircle of woods, cliffs and green pasture. There is a small café with an area under cover, an outdoor terrace and a take-away hatch so you can eat your picnic on the beach. Toilets, showers, shop, watersports, lifeguards… This is firmly geared towards upmarket holidaymakers, and does it very well. No dogs are allowed in the holiday season.

Above the beach, on the opposite side of the main road, is a subtropical **garden** (○ Apr–Sep 10.00–16.00 daily) of the type that grows so well on Devon's south-sloping shores. Sir Geoffrey Newman, owner of Blackpool Sands, understands the allure of a secret garden: you enter through a green door, overhung with fuchsia. Trees and plants from the southern hemisphere thrive in this sheltered place, as does native vegetation. Informative labels tell you what you're looking at, and if you are looking for some peace after the bustle of Dartmouth and the beach, you'll find it here on the gentle, shaded walkways. A ticket should be purchased from the car-park attendant.

Blackpool Sands is easily accessible by the hourly number 93 bus from Dartmouth. The bus stop is on the hill on the approach to the Sands; easy to miss.

11 Fast Rabbit Farm Gardens

TQ6 0NB ✏ 07813 504490 ⚲ fastrabbitfarm.co.uk ○ 11.00–17.00 daily

I know I'm not the first to assume from the name that this was some sort of attraction for children. When I located the owner, Alan Mort, hoeing a terraced flower bed in the evening sun, he told me a coach had once drawn up in the car park and a heavily accented voice had asked 'Excuse me, can I see the fast rabbits?' In fact the name derives from the need to teach an ageing collie that 'Look, there's a hare!' was as exciting as the familiar 'Rabbit!' 'When told it was a "fast rabbit" both the puzzlement and the collie vanished.' You are welcome to bring your dog into the gardens but it must be kept on a lead.

The farm's 43 acres are as good as it gets for lovers of beautiful views, flowers and walking (you can easily cover a mile here without noticing), and parts are also accessible for those with more limited mobility. Every month has something special: daffodils, bluebells, primroses, camellias and rhododendrons. The grounds are laid out with broad paths running through meadows and woodland, and alongside streams, lakes and ponds. There's also a more formal Mediterranean garden. Among regular events are wildlife walks (check the website) but the gardens no longer host 'clothing optional' days for an Adam and Eve experience. I've lost count of the number of times a place has described itself as 'Devon's best-kept secret' but Fast Rabbit Farm really does qualify. It took me five years to find it.

"The farm's as good as it gets for lovers of beautiful views, flowers and walking. Every month has something special."

Locals come here for the huge range of plants for sale, with several large polytunnels to browse through; free entry.

KINGSWEAR & THE COAST TOWARDS BRIXHAM
🏰 **Kingswear Castle** (page 338)

Kingswear, directly across the water from Dartmouth, is little more than the ferry terminal, a steam train station, a pub, a village shop, and a car park (at the Kingswear Marina, up the steep hill towards Paignton). Like Dartmouth, it has multicoloured terraced houses backed by green cliffs up which the road towards Brixham climbs in a series of hairpin bends. It is also the starting point for a particularly worthwhile, though strenuous, stretch of the coast path. When I did it in April the cliffs were splashed with purple and yellow from violets, primroses and gorse, and newborn lambs were gambolling in the fields. But any time of year it would be lovely if you're fortunate with the weather. It's 11 miles to Brixham, with opportunities to stop off for refreshment, and the 18 bus

runs hourly to return you to the start. Alternatively, you could consider taking a taxi (Devon Taxis ℰ 01803 833778) from Kingswear to Coleton Fishacre, enjoying the house, garden and tea, and then walking back to Kingswear. It's less than four miles and you'll be bowled over by the view of Dartmouth as it gradually appears through the trees, particularly if the sun is shining on those multicoloured houses.

12 COLETON FISHACRE

Brownstone Rd, TQ6 0EQ ℰ 01803 842382 ⊙ mid-Feb–Oct 10.30–17.00 daily, Nov–mid-Feb weekends only; National Trust

The National Trust acquired this house and garden in 1982, initially to link the unconnected sections of the South West Coast Path, which now runs through the lower garden. It was built in the 1920s as a holiday home for Sir Rupert D'Oyly Carte, the son of Richard D'Oyly Carte who struck up such a lucrative friendship with the lyricist W S Gilbert and the composer Arthur Sullivan. The contrasting personalities of the barrister Gilbert and the young composer meant that if the partnership were to survive, they needed a manager of great diplomacy. Richard D'Oyly Carte was that man, encouraging them to follow their one-act operetta *Trial by Jury* with others that combined witty words, outrageous plots and catchy tunes, and founding the D'Oyly Carte Opera Company in 1878. Richard moved from one successful enterprise to another, building the Savoy Theatre (specifically for the eagerly awaited Gilbert and Sullivan productions) and the Savoy Hotel.

Richard D'Oyly Carte died in 1901 a very wealthy man, and that inheritance allowed his son Rupert, who took over the business, to continue to make money – and to build Coleton Fishacre. His architect Oswald Milne, formerly assistant to Sir Edwin Lutyens, was influenced by the Arts and Crafts movement which, at the turn of the century, highlighted the skill of individual craftsmen as an antidote to mass production.

You need to be something of a connoisseur to fully appreciate the inside of the house. Only the built-in features are original; Bridget D'Oyly

◀ **1** The sweeping bay of Blackpool Sands is framed by woods and has a café under the trees. **2** The gardens of Coleton Fishacre feature steep descents down a series of terraces. **3** Fast Rabbit Farm offers 43 acres of beautiful views. **4** There's some beautiful walking along the South West Coast Path around Dartmouth and Kingswear.

Carte, who inherited the house from her father and sold it in 1949, left very little furniture. It's worth taking time to read about the fixtures that remain from the original house – like the Art Deco Lalique uplighters in the dining room, the tide indicator in the hall, and the splendid Hoffman painting of Coleton with an accompanying wind dial in the library. The polished limestone fire surround in the sitting room is also fascinating: the stone comes from Derbyshire and is impregnated with fossils. I was also intrigued by the 1930s map of the Great Western Railway network in the butler's pantry: it would be the job of a gentleman's gentleman to look up the guests' trains.

The **garden** of Coleton Fishacre is absolutely gorgeous. It slopes steeply down in a series of terraces to Pudcombe Cove, where the D'Oyly Cartes had their private bathing pool and jetty. Stone was quarried from the grounds to use in the building of the house, allowing for the dramatic use of level areas and steep descents. Lady Dorothy, Rupert's wife, was a keen gardener and plant enthusiast, and the grounds are an appealing mixture of native, untended vegetation and exotics such as tree ferns and Persian ironwood. A stream runs down to the sea, providing a natural water feature. A local artist and frequent visitor says: 'I can't be the only person who wants to roll the whole garden up like a magic carpet and take it home!'

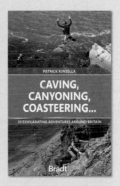

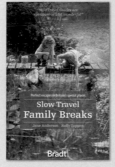

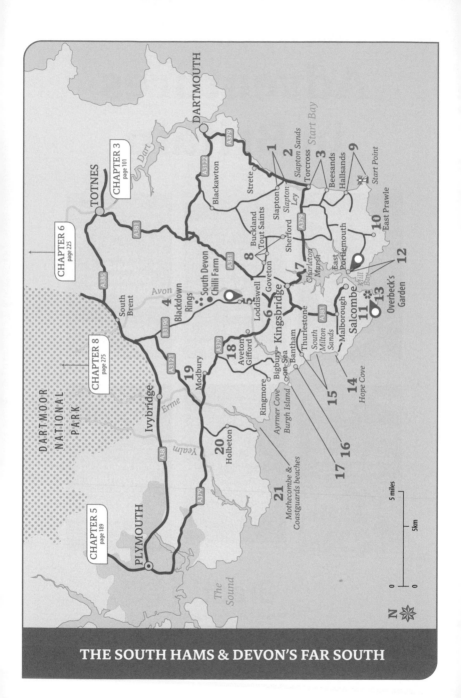

THE SOUTH HAMS & DEVON'S FAR SOUTH

4
THE SOUTH HAMS & DEVON'S FAR SOUTH

The extreme south of Devon has its roots planted firmly in the sea; the coast and all it can offer is the magnet for visitors here, with **Salcombe** its epicentre. From here you can hire a boat and putter around the estuary, select some of the most scenic stretches of the South West Coast Path, or spend the day on one of the sandy beaches. This is an enduring favourite family destination.

Coming from Dartmouth in the east, the first place of special interest is **Slapton**, with its long beach that stood in for Normandy in practices for the D-Day landings (page 156). But hereafter visitors gravitate south, below the A379. Here, in the South Hams, Devon points two knuckles towards Brittany, bifurcated by the estuary up which a weekly steamer used to carry merchandise to and from Kingsbridge. The name **South Hams** probably derived from the Saxon *hamm*, which meant peninsula but also a homestead or village. Some take it literally, and there are plenty of piggy references in the coastal landscape here: Pig's Nose, Ham Stone, Gammon Head.

Among a clutch of likeable and highly photogenic villages on the southwest coast are **Thurlestone** and the enchantingly named **Inner** and **Outer Hope**. Cross the River Avon, with its trick pronunciation (page 175), to reach **Bigbury-on-Sea** and walk or take the sea tractor at high tide to **Burgh Island**.

The sea isn't the only attraction in the region, however. If you're heading south from Dartmoor and the A38, you'll pass through **Loddiswell**, little known but with plenty to see and do.

 ## WET-WEATHER ACTIVITIES

The South Devon Chilli Farm Loddiswell (page 159)
Cookworthy Museum Kingsbridge (page 161)
Maritime Museum Salcombe (page 168)

GETTING THERE & AROUND

There is really only one main road in the region: the A379 from Dartmouth to Kingsbridge and on to Plymouth, connecting with the A381 to Malborough and Salcombe. The narrow lanes that link the villages south of this line evolved through foot and hoof traffic and are not designed to transport holidaymakers. If you are visiting the area in July and August you would do well to leave your **car** at home, or at least drive as little as possible. You can access the area by public transport by taking the **train** to Totnes or Plymouth and then the hourly **bus** 164 from Totnes to Kingsbridge, the 'capital' of the region, or the hourly number 3 from Plymouth to Kingsbridge. From Kingsbridge the 164 continues to Salcombe. The most satisfying mechanised way of arriving in Salcombe is by **ferry** from Kingsbridge. Normally the *Lady Mary* runs several times a day from April to October, dependent on the tides (✆ 07967 57527 ♢ kingsbridgesalcombeferry.com).

Once you get into the South Hams, however, you'll find that buses rarely venture south of the A379. When they do, they are utterly delightful, and can be used for bus-assisted walks as well as just the pleasure of riding in them. A few favourite walks are described in this chapter but you can easily devise your own. The bus timetable for the area is *South Hams*, or use the excellent interactive map on ♢ traveldevon.info.

SELF-POWERED TRAVEL

A maze of small lanes meander up and down the relentlessly hilly, switchback South Hams, and the gradients can make it tough and slow-going for **cycling**. Route 28 of the **National Cycle Network** (NCN) runs from Yealmpton to Totnes, taking in the most scenic places; from Totnes you can continue on the NCN 2 to Plymouth. You can take your bicycle on the passenger ferry between East Portlemouth and Salcombe (on the NCN 28), giving you a chance to explore the East Portlemouth prong, and a bicycle is also ideal for touring the other southern lumps and bumps, which are isolated between river estuaries connected only by bicycle-carrying passenger ferries.

Most **walkers** will head for the **South West Coast Path** and this southern stretch is certainly one of the very finest, being far from a main road yet with enough accessible refreshments to keep body and soul together, and enough beaches, some sandy, to encourage you to carry your swimsuit. The coast path west of Salcombe between Thurlestone and Hope Cove is broad and pushchair-friendly, while sections further east by Soar Mill Cove, Bolt Head and around Prawle Point have significant ups and downs. Fewer walkers do the more isolated rugged stretch of the coast path west from Thurlestone, partly because of the lack of public transport. There are no buses until you reach Newton Ferrers, a tough 13 miles or so away with a tricky river crossing. This is the additional challenge on this part of the path: working out the timing so that you cross the rivers when the ferries are running (if they're running) or, in the case of the Erme, at low tide when you can usually wade across. Carry a tide table.

In contrast to the coast, there are some beautiful riverside walks through woodland along the Avon, particularly recommended in the springtime.

Walking maps, guides, information & websites

The two-sided OS Explorer map OL20, scale 1:25,000, covers all this region. However, by far the best maps for walkers and cyclists are the Croydecycle maps (⊘ croydecycle.co.uk) produced by Mike Harrison at a scale of 1:12,500 (five inches to a mile). They cover most of the South Hams and are widely available in shops and TICs. Not only is every geographical detail marked in, but so are helpful footpath notes for walkers, such as 'can be muddy' or 'grassy and rutted'. For those walking the coast path, by far the best guide is *Dorset and South Devon Coast Path* (Trailblazer), which describes and maps the trail in great detail, as well as listing places to eat and stay. Also useful is *Shortish Walks: the South Devon Coast* (Bossiney Books). The excellent website for South Devon's Area of Outstanding National Beauty, ⊘ southdevonaonb.org. uk, also describes good walks, with clear directions, advice on access and maps, as well as having information on ferries, buses, taxis, parking and tide times.

BEACHES

Devon's south coast is ringed with beaches, varying from powdery yellow to coarse grey sand and shingle. Some are accessible only to walkers but others are family beaches with car parking and facilities. With the South West Coast Path linking all of these, and a (mostly) fairly decent bus service, you can spend a day walking the cliffs and pausing for a dip at a variety of beaches and coves. Heaven!

THE SLAPTON AREA

The first view of Start Bay is of a spectacular stretch of coarse sand/ fine shingle on one side of a scrub-bordered road and a lagoon on the other, both places of current and historical interest. **Slapton Ley** is one of Devon's most prized nature reserves, and **Slapton Sands** played a pivotal role in World War II (page 156).

John Leland, travelling in the mid 16th century, described Slapton as having 'a very large Poole 2 Miles in length. Ther is but a Barre of Sand betwixt the Se and this Poole; the fresch Water drenith into the Se thorough the Sandy Bank, but the Waite of the Fresch Water and Rage of the Se brekith sumtime this Sandy Bank.' And so it is today. The A379 runs along a narrow spit of land between the 'large Poole' and the sea, and is breached from time to time despite modern engineering providing an outlet for the lake water. In 2001 a severe storm destroyed the road and isolated the village of Torcross and its neighbours for four months. Another severe storm badly damaged the road in 2018 and Natural England, which shares responsibility for the area with local councils, says that next time may be the last; it's just too expensive to repair.

1 SLAPTON LEY & SLAPTON

A hundred years or so ago the **Ley** was of commercial and sporting interest, providing reeds for thatching, and waterfowl and fish for shooting and angling. When it looked as though it was going the way of so much of Devon's coastal landscape, with holiday development taking precedence over scenery and wildlife, it was bought by the conservationist Herbert Whitley, founder of Paignton Zoo, as a wildlife sanctuary.

"Slapton Ley is one of Devon's most prized nature reserves, and Slapton Sands played a pivotal role in World War II."

The Ley, the largest freshwater lake in Devon, is now leased to the Field Studies Council (FSC) by the Whitley Trust.

The nature reserve is well known among birdwatchers for its rare species. The checklist produced by the FSC, and available from TICs,

1 & **2** Browse for beach pebbles at Slapton Sands or visit the Sherman tank memorial to the US troops killed in 1943's Exercise Tiger. **3** Spot birds such as Cetti's warblers at Slapton Ley. **4** Torcross sits on the narrow spit that separates Slapton Ley from the sea. ▶

lists 107 species. There are two bird hides looking out over the reed beds, with information on the species most commonly seen as well as a checklist of recent sightings. For those who like to spot their wildlife while on the move, a trail runs through the reserve, sometimes along boardwalks, with a choice of exit points so you can decide on your preferred length. The maximum, if you want to include Slapton on the route, is about three miles.

Starting at the car park at Slapton Bridge, the path runs round the northern shore of the lake, then gives you a choice of two short routes to Slapton or a longer one via Deer Bridge. Watch out for the intricately carved handrail on the wooden viewing platform during the early part of the walk. The FSC runs a variety of guided walks, courses and events (slnnr.org.uk).

"There are two bird hides looking out over the reed beds, with information on the species most commonly seen."

You will enjoy **Slapton** itself far more if you walk into it, rather than try to drive; the narrow road forms a fearsome bottleneck in the summer. It's an attractive village and both its pubs offer a warm welcome. The Chantry Tower dates back to the religious foundation set up in 1372 by Sir Guy de Brian who bore the standard of Edward III at the siege of Calais. The foundation was dissolved in the Reformation, and the stone of the associated chapel was used to build the house, also known as The Chantry, in whose garden the tower stands. You can't visit the tower, but can see it from outside the Tower Inn. It is home to a noisy congregation of jackdaws and herring gulls.

At Stokeley Barton, a few miles away, is the excellent **Stokeley Farmshop** (TQ7 2SE 01548 581605 stokeleyfarmshop.co.uk), which has a restaurant, deli and butchery as well as lots of fruit and veg and, in season, PYO strawberries. They also brew their own beer and hire out electric bicycles.

FOOD & DRINK

The Kings Arms Strete 01803 770027 kingsarmsatstrete.co.uk. This community pub is owned by the village & serves local beers & ciders & homemade food. There is a nice garden too & lovely views.

The Queens Arms Slapton 01548 580800 queensarmsslapton.co.uk. Good, honest pub food including fish & chips & homemade steak & mushroom pie. It has an intimate walled garden, plus the ultimate prize in Slapton: a car park.

Start Bay Inn Torcross ℰ 01548 580553 ⊘ startbayinn.co.uk. A 14th-century beachside tavern serving outstanding fish & chips. Very busy in the summer.

Torcross Boathouse Torcross ℰ 01548 580747 ⊘ torcrossboathouse.com ⊙ Apr–Sep. Family-friendly, in nautical surroundings. A local resident told me: 'Forget fine dining – my favourite dinner in Devon is nipping to Torcross Boathouse on a summer's evening, getting take-away fish & chips or the yummiest beanburger I have ever tasted, & sitting on the beach watching the boats sail past & the sun set.'

Tower Inn Slapton ℰ 01548 580216 ⊘ thetowerinn.com. Has a garden overlooked by the Chantry Tower & a rooftop view of Slapton. The 14th-century flower-bedecked building has low-beamed rooms & flagstones, & gourmet food. Parking is awkward.

2 SLAPTON SANDS

The 'sands' are not that inviting, being fine shingle so not the sort of stuff you can build sandcastles from. Swimming is 'bloody cold' according to a resident, because the shore shelves steeply so you are quickly out of your depth and the sun has little effect (however, these two aspects make swimming here particularly attractive to keen 'wild swimmers'). For families it's perfect browsing territory for beach pebbles, with plenty of flat stones for skimming. The northern part of the Sands is popular with naturists.

"For families it's perfect browsing territory for beach pebbles, with plenty of flat stones for skimming."

Near the middle car park is a monument presented to the people of South Hams by the US army as a thank you to the 3,000 villagers who vacated their homes to allow for the military exercises that led up to D-Day (page 156). The Sherman tank at the Torcross end is a memorial to the American troops killed during Exercise Tiger. Through the enthusiasm and financing of a local hotelier, Ken Small, it was retrieved from the sea in 1984.

3 FROM TORCROSS TO BEESANDS VIA THE CLIFF PATH

⌂ **The Cricket Inn** (page 339)

This short but varied and scenic walk takes you over the cliffs, with good views of Start Point lighthouse, through some woods, and on to the long shingle beach at Beesands. The beach is beloved of mackerel fishers, families seeking seclusion, and also foodies, for the wonderful fresh fish at the unassuming **Britannia @ The Beach** café.

EXERCISE TIGER

In November 1943 the inhabitants of nine villages in the Torcross area were ordered to leave their homes for an indeterminate period. Slapton Sands was similar to a beach in Normandy, codenamed Utah Beach, which would be used for the D-Day landings, and the American troops needed to practise. The locals, however, were told only that the area was needed for 'military purposes'. Just imagine what was being asked of these 3,000 villagers: Torcross, Slapton, Stokenham, Chillington, Frogmore, Sherford, Blackawton, East Allington and Strete were farming communities: their winter and spring crops had been planted, winter fodder was stored in the barns, and their ration of coal in the shed. They had to decide what to do with their cattle or sheep, and how to move heavy farm machinery. Then there were the churches to worry about. The little village church has always been at the heart of the rural English community, and in those days most villagers would have been churchgoers. Church valuables, including the carved wooden screens, were dismantled and removed to a place of safety, those that couldn't be removed were sandbagged, and in each church was pinned the following notice:

To our Allies of the USA. This church has stood here for several hundred years. Around it has grown a community, which has lived in these houses and tilled these fields ever since there was a church. This church, this churchyard in which their loved ones lie at rest, these homes, these fields are as dear to those who have left them as are the homes and graves and fields which you, our Allies, have left behind you. They hope to return one day, as you hope to return to yours, to find them waiting to welcome them home. They entrust them to your care meanwhile and pray that God's blessing may rest upon us all.

Charles, Bishop of Exeter

Charles Harper, writing at the beginning of the 20th century, described the villagers keeping chickens in upturned decaying boats. 'They are the most trustful cocks and hens in the world, and follow the fishermen into the inn and cottages like dogs.' He goes on to describe the Newfoundland dogs of Beesands, and neighbouring Hall Sands, which were trained to swim out through the surf to meet the incoming fishing boats. The dogs would grab the end of the rope and bring it to the beach so the boats could be hauled on shore.

Cyclists and drivers can reach **Beesands** (TQ7 2EN) via a network of narrow lanes; it has a large car park.

Various exercises were held from March to April, all involving heavy bombardment of the beach area. To replicate the Normandy landings as closely as possible, live ammunition was used. Exercise Tiger took place between 26 and 29 April 1944, as a full rehearsal for Operation Overlord planned for June. The first exercise went without a hitch, but during a routine patrol of the English Channel German E-boats discovered the vessels preparing for the second assault and fired on two ships with torpedoes, setting fire to one with the loss of at least 749 lives. The radio message that could have summoned help in time to save some of them was delayed because a typing error gave the wrong frequency. Accounts suggest that around a thousand Americans were killed during the months of exercises, some through 'friendly fire'.

Everyone involved in Exercise Tiger was sworn to secrecy; Operation Overlord was imminent and proved to be the beginning of the end of the war. The villagers started to trickle back to their damaged and rat-infested homes a few months later. Some never returned.

An annual memorial service is held at the Sherman tank in April to commemorate those who lost their lives in Exercise Tiger.

FURTHER READING

The American Forces at Salcombe and Slapton during World War Two Muriel March (Orchard Publications)

Exercise Tiger: the D-Day Practice Landings. Tragedies Uncovered Richard T Bass (Tommies Guides)

The Forgotten Dead Ken Small (Bloomsbury)

The Invasion before Normandy: Secret Battle of Slapton Sands Edwin P Hoyt (Scarborough House)

The Land Changed its Face: the Evacuation of the South Hams 1943–44 Grace Bradbeer (Harbour Books)

¶ FOOD & DRINK

Beesands has an excellent pub, The **Cricket Inn** (✆ 01548 580215 ⌂ thecricketinn.com), with exceptionally good food. It is amazing that the Cricket Inn is still here: it has survived numerous storms, a Second World War bomb and a mudslide that went right through the building. It is, however, the **Britannia** (✆ 01548 581168 ⌂ britanniaatthebeach.co.uk), now rebranded as Britannia @ The Beach, that has fish enthusiasts jostling for a table. It was previously known as 'The Shack', and still is by locals, but it has evolved over the years to become a smart wooden beach restaurant. With the same team in place, the food – a freshly caught selection of seafood dishes – should be as good as ever, but serving more customers. Reservations are recommended.

APPROACHING THE SOUTH HAMS FROM DARTMOOR

Heading south from South Brent (page 223) along the B3196, you'll pass several rewarding places to stop before reaching your probable destination of Kingsbridge or Salcombe. The area around **Loddiswell** is worth exploring and makes a good base away from the summer crowds at the beach resorts.

4 BLACKDOWN RINGS

This Iron Age hillfort is worth a visit for the views, the bluebells in the spring and the interest of a well-preserved prehistoric site which dates from around 400BC. In addition to the fort there are the remains of a more recent medieval castle, built in the motte and bailey style. There is no record of who built it or why. Good explanation boards are dotted around the place, with illustrations of how it probably looked over a millennium ago.

A walk up the River Avon

✳ OS Explorer map OL20 or, better, the Croydecycle *Kingsbridge & Loddiswell*; start: Avon Mill car park, TQ7 4DD ♥ SX727482 (if Avon Mill is closed park in Loddiswell and start the walk by taking the lane past the church to turn right at step **5**); three miles; easy

The upper reaches of the river that meets the sea at Bigbury, pronounce it Avon or Aune, are enchanting, running through woodland pungent with wild garlic in the spring, when I had the thrill of seeing a stoat cross my path. The Avon Valley woods which incorporate Woodleigh Wood are managed by the Woodland Trust; it has provided boardwalks over excessively muddy stretches (nevertheless, boots are recommended after rain) and steps up steep sections. There's a variety of circular walks including a circuit through the very pretty Watkins Wood, named after the founder of the Woodland Trust, and returning through Woodleigh with its interesting church. The one described here is just a taster.

1 From **Avon Mill**, cross the river via the stone bridge and take the footpath to the left to reach the road. Keep left, under the railway bridge, to the old station.

2 Just beyond Station House is a footpath to the left. Then it's just a question of following one of the paths – there's a high one and a low one – to **Silveridge Bridge** in about a mile.

The access lane to Blackdown Rings is easily missed. It's signposted on the left, shortly after California Cross if heading south. The large car park tells you you've arrived.

THE SOUTH DEVON CHILLI FARM

Wigford Cross, Loddiswell TQ7 4DX ☎ 01548 550782 ⚲ sdcf.co.uk ⊙ Apr–Sep 10.00–16.00 daily, Oct–Mar 10.00–15.00 Tue–Sat

From the small beginnings of a few rented acres in 2003, this unique farm now has around 200 varieties of chilli on a ten-acre site, producing around ten tonnes of chillies in large polytunnels. Visitors are welcome to visit the show tunnel during the summer months, see the different varieties and learn how the sauces and chocolates are made. In the farm shop you can buy a huge range of chilli products, including chilli chocolate made on the premises, which is addictive after the initial shock – cautious buyers can taste a free sample first. Seeds, seedlings and plants are available by mail order as well as on the premises (seeds all year, plants Apr–Sep). The plants are labelled in detail: where they come from,

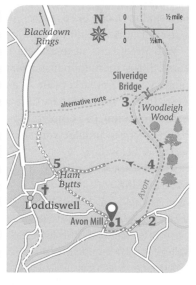

3 Cross the bridge (note the fine stone and brickwork) and take the left-hand footpath initially through a meadow and then beside the river. The path is up and down, but there are steps so it's not difficult, though you may have to duck under fallen tree trunks from time to time.

4 After less than a mile the path veers away from the river and crosses meadows dotted with old oak trees, then over a stream via a plank bridge and along its left-hand side. When you reach the access road to **Reads Farm** it's an uphill slog to **Ham Butts**.

5 Turn left down a green lane to Station Road and steep downhill back to Avon Mill and a deserved lunch or cream tea.

what they look like when mature and – most important – the degree of hotness. The very hottest is Carolina Reaper at around 2 million Scoville heat units, but there are plenty of milder ones too. Guided tours of the farm run in the summer – call the farm to check when.

The café serves a good range of food, for all tastes, with indoor and outdoor seating. There are activities and a play area for children (including a chilli-themed play tractor).

The best months to visit are July to October, when the chillies are ripening and at their most colourful.

5 LODDISWELL & AREA

🏠 **The Signal Box** Loddiswell (page 339)

Loddiswell is a surprisingly large village given the narrow lanes that serve it. It has a post office and general store, a pub and a large church that benefited from the medieval wealth of white gold: wool. In the 19th century copper was mined locally, but it was the arrival of the railway in 1893 that put the place on the map. Loddiswell was a stop on the branch line between South Brent and the port in Kingsbridge. Known as the Primrose Line because of the profusion of flowers along its embankment, it was beautiful but not profitable so inevitably closed in the Beeching cuts of 1963. Parts of the old station have been restored and the signal box converted to self-catering accommodation.

Well Street runs steep and narrow down to **Avon Mill** (⌀ avonmill. com). This is more than just a garden centre. Within the extensive plant nursery is an upmarket café, a gallery, a craft barn and a boutique. It hosts theatre from time to time and craft courses, and provides B&B accommodation (a complete apartment) for two people. This is the perfect place to indulge yourself before or after doing the Avon Valley walk (see below).

⑪ FOOD & DRINK

Avon Mill Café TQ7 4DD ⌀ 01548 550338 ⌀ avonmill.com. The menu varies during the day from breakfast through brunch to lunch & even a selection of cakes & scones for afternoon tea. Courtyard with outdoor seating, or glassed-in tables.

Valley View Café Rake Farm, TQ7 4DA ⌀ 01548 559126 ⌀ aunevalleymeat.co.uk. Part of the butchery & farm shop run by Aune Valley Meat. Terrific breakfasts & snack lunches overlooking the Aune (Avon) Valley.

DEVON'S FAR SOUTH

With the towns of **Kingsbridge** and **Salcombe** dominating, this most southerly part of Devon is the honeypot of the South Hams. It has all the attractions that holidaymakers need: sandy beaches, boats, fishing, walking, and the mildest climate in Devon. There is also the small little-known pocket of South Hams, north of Kingsbridge, where the villages of **Goveton**, with its thatched cottages, **Buckland Tout Saints** and, to the east, **Sherford** lie tucked into folds of the hills.

6 KINGSBRIDGE

🏠 **Bowcombe Boathouse** (page 339)

Tourist information: The Quay ✆ 01548 853195 ⌂ hellokingsbridge.co.uk. Exceptionally helpful centre where the staff offer lots of local advice. Good website too.

These days the only shipping that calls here is the *Lady Mary*, which plies the estuary between Kingsbridge and Salcombe, but in the early 20th century a 'market packet' steamer ran between Kingsbridge and Plymouth, calling at Salcombe on the way. Limestone was brought by ship from Plymouth, and its by-product, quicklime, was produced in the limekilns that are still to be found between Kingsbridge and the sea.

Kingsbridge is at the top of a narrow tidal creek and it is pleasant to walk along the edge of the water, with plenty of benches for watching the boats sail by. The town retains a lot of charm, its steep Fore Street the very antithesis of Clone Town Britain, with varied and interesting shops. There's also a museum, a cinema and regular happenings throughout the year. The **Cookworthy Museum** (⌂ kingsbridgemuseum.org.uk) is a restored 17th-century grammar school, still in use in the early 1900s, which gives insights into what life was like in Kingsbridge and area over the centuries. It's named after William Cookworthy, who discovered china clay in Cornwall and went on to develop porcelain manufacturing in England.

"It is pleasant to walk along the edge of the water, with plenty of benches for watching the boats sail by."

An artist friend who lives in Kingsbridge extols the town's virtues. 'For me the absolute focus has always been **Harbour House** (⌂ harbourhouse. org.uk), a wonderful centre set up as a charitable trust for the benefit of the town. It is an important centre of the arts, with a fantastic exhibition area. There's an art studio at the top of the building which is used by anyone who wants to paint, draw or experiment in any media. It has rooms where any group can hold meetings, practise yoga, sing songs, exercise the mind or the body, write poetry, or solve crossword puzzles. And it has a lovely garden and a vegetarian café. There's even a Friday morning drop-in art group with a model for life drawing.'

Five minutes' drive northwest of Kingsbridge, near the village of Churchstow, you can rent your choice of electric bicycles from e-Xplore Devon (TQ7 3QH ℰ 01548 859745 ⊘ e-xploredevon.co.uk) for half-a-day, a full week or longer. E-Xplore is on the NCN 28 so you have the choice of heading south to the coast at Salcombe or north to the Avon Valley and on to Dartmoor.

Kingsbridge and Salcombe are linked by the enjoyable *Lady Mary* ferry, which takes 35 minutes.

¶¶ FOOD & DRINK

A **farmers' market** is held on The Quay on the first and third Saturday of the month.

Crabshell Inn Embankment Rd, Kingsbridge ℰ 01548 852345 ⊘ thecrabshellinn.com ⊙ daily for lunch & dinner. A lovely place with very good, mostly crab-based, food, a short kids' menu & an interesting selection of pizzas. Or you can order from the Zest Deli menu which has a Moroccan slant. Great views overlooking the creek (they have mooring as well as parking).
Harbour House Café Harbour House, Promenade ℰ 01548 855666 ⊘ harbourhouse.org. uk ⊙ 10.00–16.00 Mon–Sat. A tasty range of vegetarian & vegan lunches & snacks in this centre of creativity.
The Old Bakery Promenade ℰ 01548 855777 ⊘ theoldbakeryrestaurant.co.uk ⊙ 18.00– late Tue–Sat. Great large tapas & sharing dishes with a Mediterranean & Persian twist. Vegan & gluten-free options. Booking recommended.

7 CHARLETON MARSH

🏠 **Maberly House** (page 339)

A couple of miles southeast of Kingsbridge is the village of **West Charleton** from where narrow Marsh Lane leads south down to a birdwatcher's

---

1 A lighthouse tops the dramatic peninsula of Start Point. **2** The Iron Age hillfort of Blackdown Rings. **3** Go for a stroll along Kingsbridge harbour. **4** Loddiswell's impressive church. ▶

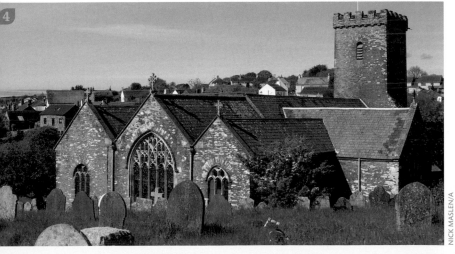

delight: a hide looking out over reed beds and the Kingsbridge Estuary. There is limited parking at the bottom of Marsh Lane if you only want to go to the hide about half a mile's walk away, but there are a couple of options for making this a very enjoyable longer walk.

The route to the hide is across private land where the farmer works with conservationists to preserve wildlife. Dung beetles are encouraged to flourish and these, in turn, provide food for greater horseshoe bats. You'll spot birds as you walk towards the estuary: mallards, shelduck and maybe a heron or two. The Chris Rogers Memorial Hide is round to the right (no dogs allowed); access can be tricky when it has been very wet, so wear good boots. It is both comfortable (cushions!) and full of information, with a logbook describing recent sightings. Cirl buntings are quite often seen here, as well as reed buntings, and sedge and reed warblers.

To make a longer walk, and spot more wildlife, cross the stile at the end of the field to the edge of the estuary. It's usually possible to walk around Wareham Point (avoid high tide) to pick up the footpath that runs to **East Charleton** or Frogmore (the Croydecycle map *Kingsbridge & Loddiswell* shows this clearly). From East Charleton there's a choice of steep lanes and tracks giving wonderful views over the estuary to bring you back to West Charleton, or you can continue to **Frogmore** with its pub, the Globe Inn, and catch the hourly bus (number 93) back to your car. The circular walk is about six miles.

"There's a choice of steep lanes and tracks giving wonderful views over the estuary to bring you back to West Charleton."

8 BUCKLAND TOUT SAINTS, GOVETON & SHERFORD

The linguistically odd name of **Buckland Tout Saints** apparently comes from the Toutsaint family, who owned the land in 1238. It seems that it had nothing to do with saints but rather with health: as in the French *sain* meaning healthy, so something like 'all-healthy'. **St Peter's Church**, its chunky little silhouette on a hilltop easily visible as you approach from Kingsbridge or Goveton, was rebuilt on its present site in 1778 to serve the family and staff of Buckland Manor House and surrounding villages. Although it has no single feature of particular historic interest, this is a much-loved and tranquil little church. A fine tapestry kneeler in front of the altar portrays the life of the parish, and there is a wildflower area in the churchyard.

The 17th-century **Buckland Manor** was substantially remodelled in the late 19th century and is now the luxury Buckland Tout Saints Hotel.

The village of **Goveton** is worth seeking out for its exceptionally pretty thatched cottages. **Sherford** caught my eye with its brown sign advertising a 14th-century church. It's a lovely place and the church of St Martin is indeed interesting. A worm-eaten door lets you into a light interior where the restored screen, financed by a lottery grant, is the main focal point. Painted in the 16th century, in the Flemish Renaissance style, the saints now glow in their original colours.

"Painted in the 16th century, in the Flemish Renaissance style, the saints now glow in their original colours."

Don't confuse this lovely village with the new town, Sherford, which is being built on the eastern outskirts of Plymouth.

9 THE EXTREME SOUTH: HALLSANDS TO START POINT

For cliff-path walkers, the first place for a rest stop along the stretch after Beesands is **Hallsands**, which is also accessible by road. Charles Harper describes the village which, when he visited (probably 1905), was beginning the process of falling into the sea. Half of the only inn had already gone 'while the landlady was making tea' and it was only a matter of time before the rest of the village met the same fate. This entirely preventable disaster was caused by the commercial dredging of shingle for the construction industry (Plymouth breakwater), with the result that the beach was about 12ft lower by the time they stopped in 1902. Without their natural defences, the cottages were exposed to every storm and, on 26 January 1917, during a particularly ferocious storm, they had almost all gone; the destruction was completed two days later during the spring tide. Only one cottage remained inhabitable. *The Kingsbridge Gazette* headline stated: 'The beach went to Devonport and the cottages went to the sea.' Amazingly, there were no casualties, but perhaps less surprisingly there has never been any compensation despite the villagers' efforts. In 2017, to mark the centenary of the disaster, a plaque was erected near the coast path. A look-out platform over the former village provides detailed information on this sad history.

Continuing along the coast path you'll reach **Start Point** (TQ7 2ET ♀ SX820375), about four miles from Torcross. The name comes from the Saxon *steort*, which means tail, as for example in redstart. It's a dramatic, rocky little peninsula topped by a lighthouse, which sometimes offers tours (✆ 01803 771802). There is no public transport in this area, so walkers either continue to Salcombe Harbour or take the easy option: leave their car at Start Point's car park and make a circular walk to the point and back.

10 EAST PRAWLE

This is the southernmost village in Devon, far from anywhere and approached by miles of narrow lanes, through rather desolate scenery (though cyclists will find it mercifully flat). Prawle Point is a significant corner on the coast where there is a daily watch on shipping and a good visitors' centre. The village is perched some 370ft above sea level, and six paths radiate like spokes to different parts of the coast offering a great selection of short or long circular walks. Within a short range you can explore soaring cliffs, ragged rocky headlands, secluded coves and picture-perfect small sandy beaches, conveniently facing south. From Prawle Point car park try Gammon Head with adjacent Maceley Cove (low tide best) or walk further to other beaches.

"You can explore soaring cliffs, ragged rocky headlands, secluded coves and picture-perfect small sandy beaches."

East Prawle village also offers useful facilities: the quirky **Pig's Nose** pub, an excellent shop/café, parking, toilets and basic camping. There is the charm of old buildings and a slow-changing history with a real sense of community. However, before making the pilgrimage be warned that the magnificent views are only achieved by walking. It's rarely level and of course the rain often lashes in from the ocean. Authentic Devon, in other words.

Walkers and cyclists will continue to **East Portlemouth** (page 170) and thence by ferry to Salcombe. Drivers will take the road to Kingsbridge.

¶¶ FOOD & DRINK

The Pig's Nose East Prawle TQ7 2BY ✆ 01548 511209 ⊘ pigsnoseinn.co.uk. An idiosyncratic place as popular with locals as visitors. Every corner is crammed with stuff – on the windowsill by my table was Barbie riding a stuffed pheasant. Walkers & cyclists can have a shower here, there are 'books to go', & board games if you're stuck in a rainstorm & looking for entertainment. Plus it's decidedly dog-friendly; there were seven there when I visited. The pub is famous throughout the region for its live music.

MALBOROUGH

This must be one of the most frequently misspelled village names in Devon. It's an attractive village with a good number of thatched cottages and at least two pubs. The large church, with its spire, dominates the view from miles around and makes a handy landmark for walkers. I found it too austere for my taste, but there are some nice touches inside such as the floor-stone in memory of William Clark, with a misspelling and some letters seemingly inserted as an afterthought.

Malborough's post office sells OS maps and a leaflet, *Footpaths in Malborough Parish*, which details all the car parks in the area as well as a selection of footpaths connecting to the most glorious section of the South West Coast Path between Bolt Head and Bolt Tail. Thus drivers can avoid the hassle of parking in Salcombe.

11 SALCOMBE

🏠 **Victoria Inn** (page 339)

Tourist information: Market St, TQ8 8DE 🖉 01548 843927 🖑 salcombeinformation.co.uk. Very helpful, with a good selection of books, maps & free brochures. They also publish a map of a self-guided walk around town.

Salcombe is boats. The town has always looked seawards, building its prosperity from fishing and maritime trade and, in recent times, from hobby sailors. Most people who come here regularly love messing about in boats, and just about everyone will take an estuary cruise or at least one of the ferries, to either Kingsbridge, East Portlemouth or South Sands. Do-it-yourself sailors can hire a sailing boat, a self-drive motorboat, or a kayak. As befits this book, there is a speed limit in the estuary, so forget about hiring a speedboat. And it's actually not a *real* estuary since there's no river; it's a flooded valley, or 'ria', hence the name, which derives from Salt Valley.

"Most people who come here regularly love messing about in boats, and just about everyone will take an estuary cruise."

Estuary cruises are good for wildlife spotting. With a knowledgeable guide you will see ducks and waders, and also learn what lies under

SALCOMBE GIN

⊘ salcombegin.com

If you thought that gin had something vaguely to do with juniper berries but mostly to do with tonic, think again. Two chaps in Salcombe have come up with a recipe for gin which is wowing connoisseurs around the world. Angus and Howard describe Salcombe Gin as 'the perfect balance of aromas and flavours between the heady, earthy and resinous pine notes of the finest Macedonian juniper…combined with the warming spiced citrus notes from English coriander seeds grown by one of our suppliers and fresh citrus peels, peeled by us immediately prior to distillation.' Goodness. This is clearly no ordinary gin, and its quality has been internationally recognised with a clutch of major awards. First came Gold at the World Drinks Award in 2016, where it won World's Best Gin in two Design sub-categories. Then, at the San Francisco World Spirit Competition in 2017 and 2020 they were awarded a Double Gold. Not bad for a company that only began trading in 2016.

You can taste and of course buy the gin in the Gin Bar at The Boathouse on Island Street or, for that special treat, you can sign up for a day at Gin School to produce your own bottle of gin.

the water – huge fan mussels, for instance, and even sea horses. Their relatives, pipe fish, are sometimes found in rock pools, along with cushion stars, brittle stars and anemones.

The town itself is a maze of little streets, alleys and independent shops, and has a two-room **Maritime Museum** (free admission *⊘* salcombemuseum.org.uk ⊙ Apr–Oct) with a display of shipwrecks around the Salcombe coast and paintings of the old sailing ships built in the 19th century in Kingsbridge and Salcombe. The Salcombe Fruiters were schooners, designed for speed, which carried citrus fruit from the Azores and Mediterranean for the markets in London. Later, larger, safer vessels carried pineapples from the Bahamas and other foods from further afield. There is also a **Lifeboat Museum** (⊙ Mar–Dec) on Union Street with intricate scale models. Distinctive Salcombe yawls were built here up until 2017 when the last boat builder, Mike Atfield, retired,

1 Plenty of boats fill the estuary around Salcombe, East Portlemouth and Mill Bay.
2 Salcombe's Maritime Museum explores this important side of its history. **3** East Prawle offers secluded coves and beautiful beaches. **4** The subtropical gardens at Overbeck's, complete with palm trees. ▶

having completed more than 30 yawls during his 55-year career. An easy walk south from Salcombe takes you to **North Sands**, a pleasant beach with its Winking Prawn restaurant (page 174), and beyond it is **South Sands** and Bo's Café, best reached from Salcombe by the half-hourly ferry (⊘ southsandsferry.co.uk ☉ Mar–Nov).

North of the town is **Snapes Point**, a National Trust-owned peninsula which juts into Salcombe Harbour. A footpath runs round the peninsula with lovely views at every step. The full circuit from the car park is about two miles.

Salcombe's popularity and narrow streets make driving here something of a nightmare. Use Park and Ride at Batson Cross off the A381.

⚓ BOAT HIRE

Salcombe Dinghy Sailing ✆ 07809 556457 ⊘ salcombedinghysailing.co.uk. Sailing courses & tuition.

Sea Kayaks Salcombe South Sands ✆ 01548 843451 ⊘ seakayaksalcombe.co.uk. Kayak & paddleboard rentals. Own safety boat for added security.

Singing Paddles Kingsbridge & Salcombe ✆ 07754 426633 ⊘ singingpaddles.co.uk. Guided canoe tours.

Whitestrand Boat Hire 1 Strand Court, Salcombe ✆ 01548 843818 ⊘ whitestrandboathire.co.uk ☉ Apr–Oct. A variety of power boats, paddleboards & electric bikes for hire; also estuary cruises & fishing trips.

12 EAST PORTLEMOUTH & MILL BAY

⌂ **Gara Rock** East Portlemouth (page 339)

A passenger ferry (✆ 01548 842061) plies the estuary between Salcombe and **East Portlemouth**, where there are some particularly inviting sandy coves. Most of the sand is covered at high tide so a tide table is handy if you want to spend time here with the family building sandcastles. An easy and scenic walk of five miles or so can be done by following the coast path from the ferry to Gara Rock, where the Gara Rock restaurant provides the ultimate in indulgence and views (page 174).

You can return via the less scenic 'high path'. We did this walk on Boxing Day, revelling in the lack of crowds and clear views.

A variation, possible only at low spring tides in the early afternoon, is to walk from the ferry along the foreshore all the way to a sand bar called **Hipples** at the harbour's entrance. It is only exposed for a couple of hours. If the tide is not quite low enough there is access from the cliff path.

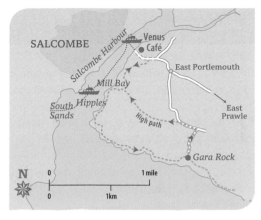

On the way you will cross **Mill Bay**, where the Americans were based during World War II, bringing a sparkle to the eyes of local girls. During the preparations for D-Day, in 1944, the estuary was full of American ships, with landing craft concealed under the trees along the shores of the estuary. Over in Salcombe, Normandy Way and the Normandy Pontoon are named to commemorate their embarkation.

Back at the ferry, a cannonball was discovered in the foundations of a wall. It is now proudly on display in the Village Hall.

Next to the ferry landing stage is the **Venus Café**, a great place to take on some energy-boosting calories before climbing the 138 steps to East Portlemouth village. As you go through the five-barred gate at the top of the path, look to your left and enjoy one of the most spectacular views the region has to offer. The estuary lies below you, right up to Kingsbridge. On a clear day the southern fringe of Dartmoor can be seen. Pass the

"As you go through the gate, look to your left and enjoy one of the most spectacular views the region has to offer."

cottages on your right and, at the top of the hill, you will find the 12th-century **church of St Winwaloe** (St Guénolé), whose followers came over from the Abbey at Landévennec in Brittany. He is also patron saint of at least six churches in Cornwall. The medieval screen, with its panels of saints and fine carving, was restored in the 1930s.

FOOD & DRINK

Dick & Wills Fore St ☎ 01548 843408 🖰 dickandwills.co.uk 🕒 closed Sun. A favourite with discriminating locals, this waterside brasserie serves very good food, with seating inside or in a glassed-in outdoor area (great for views).

A walk from Overbeck's

✵ OS Explorer map OL20, or Croydecycle Hope; start: National Trust Overbeck's car park, TQ7 3DR ♥ SX727374, or National Trust East Soar car park, TQ7 3DS ♥ SX712375 and start at step 8; around five miles; a few ups and downs but not unduly strenuous

This walk takes you along some of the most dramatic coastal scenery in South Devon, much owned by the National Trust. There are great views along the coast and the Salcombe estuary, and plenty of flora, birds and butterflies. Along the route, you'll pass two war relics, one a tower from the 18th century and the other a bunker from the Cold War. Make sure you have time to visit Overbeck's Garden (page 174).

1 Walk down the road from **Overbeck's** car park to the junction with the coast path.

2 Here turn right on to the track, signed to Bolt Head, although the path first loops around **Sharp Tor**. Looking back before Sharp Tor, there is a lovely view down the **Salcombe–Kingsbridge estuary** and, if it is low tide, you may see the sand bars at the entrance to the estuary that have snagged many unwary ships. You may also see gannets here, diving for fish in the estuary mouth.

3 The coast path continues around the small bay to climb Bolt Head, passing through a gate at the top. Suddenly the view west comes into sight with the impressive 400ft cliffs above **Off Cove**. The path stays high, passing through a second and then a third gate.

These cliff heaths are alive with wildlife. It is an untouched environment and attracts many insects; keep an eye out for silver-studded blue butterflies in July and August. Insects attract birds so, as well as the fulmers and gulls overhead, you may see smaller heathland birds including the rare cirl bunting.

4 At the third gate, fork right, leaving the coast path to follow the wall slightly away from the coast. The path soon passes the restored farmstead of **Middle Soar**, but keep ahead; you are heading for a path by the prominent stone tower.

5 Turn right through the small gate – there is a yellow waymark arrow. This lonely **tower** was built in 1794 as a watchtower and signalling station, ready to warn of revolutionary French ships approaching. Signals were shown on a 50ft-high flagpole with cross spars, rather like a sailing ship's mast. Flags and black balls were raised and lowered on these spars to convey coded information to ships and neighbouring stations; there were once 25 stations along this coast, but this is one of the few that have survived.

Follow the field boundary along the edge of three fields and then through a gate.

6 The path then bears right and downhill towards **Lower Soar**, which can be seen ahead. The next gate takes you into a hedged lane, which brings you to the hamlet of Lower Soar and the large thatched Olde Cottage. Here turn right and, at the next junction, fork right to stay on the lane. It soon leads to Higher Soar, another little cluster of houses.

7 Turn right again to reach East Soar car park, the alternative start point for this walk.

The airfield to your left is all that remains of **RAF Hope Cove**, a World War II airfield for fighter aircraft and, from 1941, a secret radar station. The airfield closed in 1947 but in 1959, during the Cold War, one of the UK's 17 nuclear bunkers was built here. It, too, was closed in 1992 and the airfield and bunker are now privately owned.

8 Turn left, signed to Overbeck's.

9 When the track turns sharp right, keep ahead, still signed to Overbeck. As the path starts to descend, there are some great views left to the estuary once more. A final gate and sign bring you into a track that takes you downhill to pass Overbeck's house and gardens and soon reaches the car park once more.

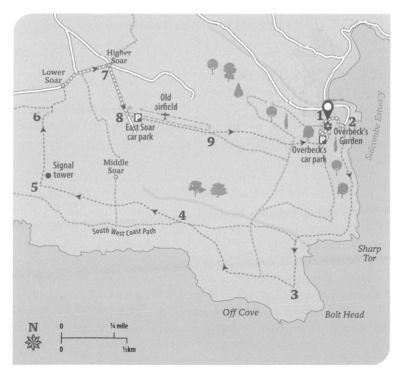

Gara Rock East Portlemouth ✆ 01548 845945 ⬦ gararock.com. Wonderful food & the best clifftop view in the South Hams! Walk here for the full impact, but you can also drive. Dogs & children welcome. Also has rooms (page 339).

Millbrook Inn South Pool TQ7 2RW ✆ 01548 531581 ⬦ millbrookinnsouthpool.co.uk ☉ closed Mon–Tue. Under new ownership (2021) but reportedly as good as ever. Accessible at high tide by boat, otherwise by car down narrow lanes.

Sailor V Ice Cream Parlour & Café Fore St ✆ 01548 843555 ⬦ cafesailorv.co.uk. Next to the ferry to East Portlemouth, with a range of sweet & savoury goodies – a real treat for all ages.

Victoria Inn Fore St, Salcombe ✆ 01548 842604 ⬦ victoriainnsalcombe.co.uk. A picturesque, central & very popular inn where you can bring your dog into the bar area. It's an exceptionally cosy place, with a log fire burning on cool days, & several small rooms for dining. Their multi-award-winning meals are traditional pub fare with interesting additions like the seafood sharer, Malaysian laksa & vegan battered banana blossom & chips. Also has rooms (page 339).

The Winking Prawn North Sands TQ8 8LD ✆ 01548 842326 ⬦ winkingprawn.co.uk. This beachside café at the cove just south of Salcombe is a relaxed place – a welcome pitstop for coast path walkers.

13 OVERBECK'S GARDEN

Sharpitor, TW8 8LW ✆ 01548 842893 ☉ Apr–Oct; National Trust

Otto Overbeck (1860–1937) was an eccentric chemist of Dutch ancestry, and an early advocate of electrotherapy, including 'the rejuvenator', which he claimed would keep you young by passing an electrical current through your body!

The subtropical Arts and Crafts gardens were created by Edric Hopkins, who had the house built. The next owners, the Verekers, extended the garden and, when Otto Overbeck bought the house in 1928, he continued to add rare and tender plants. The result of this work over the last 100 years is an exceptional and extensive garden that is now Grade II-listed. The garden drops down the hillside in a series of terraces, each with its own character and plants, and with views over the Salcombe Estuary. There are fuchsias, banana palms, myrtles, daturas, agaves, agapanthus, cannas and kniphofia – and lots of labels and descriptions. In the banana garden is a 'silent space' where you can sit and listen to the sounds of nature around you. No dogs.

The easiest means of getting here without a car is by the ferry to South Sands, but be warned that it's a steep climb up to the garden.

THE SOUTHERN BEACHES

South Devon is rightly famous for its beaches, and there is something for everyone here, from family-friendly stretches of sand with parking nearby and amenities, to more isolated coves that can only be reached on foot. From Hope Cove to Bantham, on the River Avon (Aune), they stretch in a tempting line, linked by the coast path. And that's the thing – to reach them by car is often a tortuous business, with lots of reversing up single-track lanes. Let the number 162 bus take the strain and spend the day the slow, relaxing way, swimming and walking. The bus runs in a loop from Loddiswell to Inner and Outer Hope three times a day, on weekdays only.

These beaches are famous for watersports: the best surfing is at Bantham, with South Milton known for wind-surfing – and its outstanding beach café (page 177).

14 HOPE COVE

Sandwiched between Inner Hope and Outer Hope is one of the most popular beaches in South Devon. The view from the hill where the bus deposits you in Inner Hope, and where there's a small car park, will make your spirits soar. There are thatched cottages hugging the curve in the road, and a steep hill down to the shore. Ahead is a forested cliff where the trees have been forced into retreat by the wind, creating a natural amphitheatre, around which the South West Coast Path sets walkers on their way to Salcombe. Those who have arrived on foot from Salcombe will find welcome refreshments at the Sun Bay Hotel.

"The beach is particularly attractive, with boats drawn up on to the sand and a concrete causeway to Brandy Rock."

Drivers will head for the large car park at the busy little tourist centre of Outer Hope and its cafés, shops and friendly pub (the Hope and Anchor). The quieter beach, Mouthwell Sands, is opposite the car park, but two minutes south is Hope Cove's larger beach, locally called Harbour Beach. It is particularly attractive, with boats drawn up on to the sand and a concrete causeway to Brandy Rock, popular with fishermen. Overlooking the beach is the enormous Cottage Hotel (anything but a cottage). Tucked in below the hotel is the rather good **Lobster Pod Bistro** (⟨ lobster-pod.co.uk ⟩ Wed–Sun) with tasty food,

particularly fish, and the option of dining in one of their glass pods in the garden.

If you want to stretch your legs, then you might like to walk south around Bolt Tail (about 2 miles): just follow the South West Coast Path signs. This invigorating walk soon reaches the top, giving you great views along the coast. Continue along the coast path for about half a mile past Bolt Tail and look for the footpath left that takes you inland, back to Inner Hope.

15 THURLESTONE & SOUTH MILTON SANDS

It's about a mile by coastal path to the next significant beach, with the iconic **Thurlestone Rock** posing prettily in the bay – the name Thurlestone comes from this rock ('thurled' being another word for 'pierced'). South Milton Sands seldom gets crowded, perhaps because it's less sheltered than Hope so can be quite windy. Consequently it's a good beach for wind-surfing.

If arriving from Thurlestone village with its thatched cottages, you'll come to the car park above **Leas Foot Sand**, a quieter beach than South Milton Sands. The small and unassuming **Beach House Café** at South Milton Sands (TQ7 3JY) has, according to a friend, 'the most amazing seafood you will ever eat'. Consequently, booking is essential ($\mathscr{O}$ 01548 561144 $\mathring{\mathscr{o}}$ beachhousedevon.com).

16 BANTHAM

Bantham is a rarity – the whole village is privately owned. It was bought from its previous owner in 2014 by Nicholas Johnston, who declared that he had no intention of changing the character of the village and its beach. Today, Bantham is a lovely quiet village of whitewashed thatched cottages with a narrow lane funnelling visitors down to the best surfing beach in South Devon. And talking of funnelling, each year the Bantham Swoosh takes place down the River Avon. Promoted by the Outdoor Swimming Society, this is a 6km swim from Aveton Gifford to Bantham, and includes the Swoosh, where the river narrows, propelling swimmers towards the sea on the receding tide. And you don't have to wait for the

◀ **1** Leas Foot Sand is a quieter alternative to some of the busier southern beaches. **2** The striking Thurlestone Rock. **3** The beautiful coastline from Hope Cove. **4** Bantham offers the best surfing beach in Devon.

BANTHAM COMES TO PAKISTAN

In May 2017 a picture appeared on a news channel of children in the coastal village of Mubarak in Pakistan holding their 'surfboards' – trays, ragged bits of chewed-up polystyrene, rough planks of wood – which they used to ride the waves. Now, after an initiative by a local doctor, Aftab Aziz, and surf coach Dave Renaud, they have proper surfboards donated by surfers in Bantham, plus a video showing them how to use them. They take their own videos to show the surfers in Bantham how well they're doing and even have a Facebook page.

official Swoosh date to do this! Start at the little pink boathouse near the ferry, check that the tide is going out and start swimming.

There's a car park by the beach at Bantham (card payments only) where a mobile café, the Gastrobus (again, card payments only), provides tasty snacks. But the Gastrobus is the only sort of bus here – there's no public transport.

Bantham village has an exceptional pub, the Sloop Inn (see opposite), which serves quality food. If the pub is closed, the Village Stores up the road doubles as a café, serving coffee and snacks.

FROM THE AVON TO THE ERME

It's confusing, to say the least, that the small River Avon that rises in Dartmoor has the same name as the much larger one that flows through Bath and Bristol. A few hundred years ago it was called the Aune, Awne or Aume, and most local people still pronounce it Awne. When and why it changed its name is open to conjecture. The river is very scenic, with sandy shores, gnarled oaks overhanging eroded banks, plenty of birdlife and quite a few boats. There's a marked Avon Estuary Walk which, however, mostly follows paths high above the river. It is clearly marked on the Croydecycle map of Bigbury.

If coming from Bantham you will need to cross the river by ferry (✆ 01548561196). This operates in the summer months, on request, so be prepared to stand and wave until the boatman sees you.

BIGBURY-ON-SEA

The names Bigbury and Burgh both derive from the original name of the island, Borough. This seems to have been in use at least until the early

20th century, perhaps later. Almost as old is the general disapproval of Bigbury-on-Sea by visitors looking for 'unspoilt Devon'. Writing in 1907 the author of *The South Devon Coast*, Charles Harper, describes the estuary thus:

> Wide stretch the sands at ebb, but they are not so wide but that the prints of footsteps have disfigured them pretty thoroughly; for where the land slopes down to the shore in grassy fields, the Plymouth people have built bungalows, and are building more. Burr, or Borough, Island is tethered to the mainland at ebb by this nexus of sand. It is in these circumstances a kind of St Michael's Mount, and like it again in that it once owned a chapel dedicated to St Michael. The chapel disappeared in the lang syne, and when the solitary public-house ceased business, civilisation and Borough Island wholly parted company.

Harper was being unfair. This is a typically family-friendly beach with broad sands where children can safely play and their parents relax. More secluded bays lie a short walk away for those of a more solitary nature. There is a nice café, the Venus, which is open all day. If you decide this is the time to learn how to surf, check out the South Devon Discovery Surf School (✆ 07813 639622 ♂ discoverysurf.com).

The comment that 'Borough Island' has 'wholly parted company with civilisation' is particularly ironic given that one of Devon's most exclusive hotels is here, along with a pub, which is partly open to the numerous visitors who stroll across the sand to the island or take the historic sea tractor there.

¶ FOOD & DRINK

The Oyster Shack Milburn Orchard Farm, Bigbury TQ7 4BE ✆ 01548 810876 ♂ oystershack.co.uk. Tucked away at the end of the tidal road off the A379 or access from St Ann's Chapel if the tide is in, the seafood here is terrific, especially – of course – the oysters. Good wine list too.
Sloop Inn Bantham ✆ 01548 560489 ♂ thesloop.co.uk. This characterful pub serves seriously good food at very reasonable prices. They also have five comfortable rooms.

17 BURGH ISLAND

⌂ **Burgh Island Hotel** (page 339)

A hotel that can cost over £1,000 per night seems, at first acquaintance, to be the antithesis of Slow. But once I saw it for myself I realised that it is as true to the spirit of this book as anywhere listed because to stay at

the Burgh Island Hotel you must step back in time, to the 1930s, when life was indeed much slower.

First, some history. **The Pilchard Inn** has been serving ale to visitors, on and off, since 1395. In its smuggling heyday there was supposedly a tunnel running from a cave on the beach where Tom Crocker, the king of smugglers, hauled his booty to the pub where it could be safely stored. Apart from a few fishermen's cottages, the first accommodation on the island was a wooden summer house built by a famous music-hall artist, George Chirgwin, who bought the island in the late 19th century as a retreat from his adoring fans.

The **hotel** was built in 1929 by Archibald Nettlefold, who commissioned the architect Matthew Dawson to design him a 'Great White Palace'. Until the war, the luxurious hotel drew the rich and famous from all *"Complete with a private sun deck and hot tub, it's just the place to write your own murder mystery."* over Britain. Among its visitors were Amy Johnson, Agatha Christie (who wrote *And Then There Were None* here; page 132), Noël Coward, Winston Churchill and royalty: the Mountbattens stayed here, as did the Prince of Wales with Wallis Simpson. Then came a period of non-investment, so when Deborah Clark and Tony Orchard bought it in 2001 it took years to gradually restore it to its full Art Deco-style glory, even restoring the outdoor 'mermaid pool'.

As well as staying in the hotel, you can also stay in Agatha Christie's 1930s two-storey beach house, which sits against the island's rock face on the edge of the water. Complete with a private sun deck and hot tub, it's just the place to write your own murder mystery.

The hotel is unique. It's not just the place itself that is in the 1930s style, but everything about it is in period. For instance, there are no TVs in the bedrooms, nor mobile phone reception, though there is Wi-Fi. The background music is, of course, of the era. Guests dress for dinner, as they would in its heyday. That means black tie. 'You should never worry that you might be overdressed, as this is simply impossible' states the information leaflet. Non-residents can usually dine in the hotel, but reservations are essential.

◄ **1** & **2** Burgh Island is home to a historic hotel, which can be reached by sea tractor. **3** Aymer Cove is lined with silvery-grey cliffs. **4** Ringmore village is filled with thatched cottages.

SHIPWRECKS IN BIGBURY BAY

One night in February 1760, the old 90-gun warship *Ramillies* was sailing from Plymouth to join the English blockade of French ports when a fierce storm arose, carrying her eastward up the Devon coast; waves crashed against her ageing timbers and her captain feared for her survival. Passing a small island in the darkness, he identified it as Rame Head just west of Plymouth, so turned the ship to run for shelter into Plymouth Sound. Too late, he realised the storm had in fact swept him well beyond Rame, and what he had seen was Burgh Island in Bigbury Bay – where there was no shelter from the turmoil, just a line of sheer, forbidding cliffs. The vessel's anchors could not hold her as she pitched and shuddered in the huge seas. She lurched landward and smashed into the cliffs just beyond Bolt Tail.

Her 700-odd men stood little chance in the churning water. Only 26 survived. The *Ramillies* broke up, and one survivor described her as 'drove into such small pieces that it appears like piles of firewood'. As dawn broke, watchers on shore saw Hope Bay littered with bodies, and more drifted in on every tide.

Bounty from the sea was a bonus in a hard existence, and word of the tragedy spread quickly. Looters were soon at work. It's said that several of the old houses in the area still contain timbers and other fittings from the *Ramillies*.

She was by no means the only ship to end her days beneath the waters of Bigbury Bay: the remains of the *Chantiloupe* lie near Thurlestone Rock, where she was wrecked in 1772 with a cargo of rum, Madeira wine, sugar and coffee from the West Indies. There was only one survivor. A sad story tells of a woman washed ashore wearing finery and many jewels, presumably to keep them safe when abandoning ship, who may have reached the beach alive only to be killed there for her riches. Even a century later, it was said that a local woman still had a piece of her fine muslin apron. No murder was ever proved, but villagers had strong suspicions. Earlier, in 1588, during the rout of the Spanish Armada, the *San Pedro el Mayor* had gone down with the loss of 40 lives. Tin ingots from a wreck uncertainly dated back to the Iron Age have been found in the Erme Estuary, and a wreck from 1671 lies nearby. The 19th and 20th centuries saw more. But it's the *Ramillies*, with her dramatic end and tragic loss of life, that features most strongly in the area's history.

AYRMER COVE, WESTCOMBE BEACH & RINGMORE

Flanked by craggy silvery-grey cliffs, **Ayrmer Cove** is nicely secluded, with enticing tide pools. It's owned by the National Trust so is utterly unspoiled and is also only accessible on foot, which keeps the crowds away. To the west, up and over a headland, is the steep descent to

Westcombe Beach. Pronounced Wiscombe, this beach has the same rock pools, grey sand and pebbles as Ayrmer Cove but is even quieter, being further from the car park at Ringmore. Descend to Ayrmer Cove down Smugglers Lane and have a choice of footpaths back to the village (the Croydecycle map *Bigbury, Avon & Erme* shows these).

Apart from the seclusion beloved of Slow travellers, these two beaches give you the opportunity to visit one of the region's prettiest villages, **Ringmore**, and its **Journey's End Inn**. This is a classic Devon village with lots of thatch and tall, crooked chimneys. The church has a funny little spire plonked in the middle of the tower like an afterthought. If the name of the pub sounds familiar to theatre-goers it's not surprising: the playwright R C Sherriff wrote his play in the 1920s while staying there, and the pub was named after it. In its colourful past the inn was thick with smugglers and they say there was a false wall behind which their booty was stashed.

More innocently, the pub hit the headlines by nurturing a piglet called Incredible. Born prematurely just after the war, Incredible's dad was a champion, and the pub's owner was not prepared to let him die like his siblings. During his infancy he consumed three bottles of brandy mixed with glucose and milk, and was kept snug by the Journey's End stove. He flourished, but there was, for a while, a downside: he was addicted to alcohol and refused his unfortified feed.

18 AVETON GIFFORD

The pleasant village of Aveton Gifford (officially pronounced 'Awton Jifford' though most locals give up and pronounce it 'Averton Jifford') with its **Fisherman's Rest** pub (01548 550284 thefishermansrest. co.uk) and well-stocked village shop, is a convenient starting point for riverside walks, including the 7½-mile Avon Estuary walk described (along with lots of other walks in the area) on southdevonaonb.org. uk, which uses paths along both banks and the ferry across the river mouth. If it's low tide you can walk along the tidal road from Aveton Gifford, which brings you eye to eye with swans and is slippery with seaweed. If you are beginning the walk here and continuing down the west side of the estuary to Bigbury-on-Sea, keep a keen eye out for a turning where the path leaves the shore and turns right up some concrete steps. At low tide it's possible to walk along the shore but it can be dispiritingly muddy.

MODBURY & AREA

19 MODBURY

⌂ **Plantation House** (page 339)
⛺ **Brackenhill Glamping** (page 339)
Tourist information: available on their excellent website ⊘ modburytic.org.uk, which also has walking options in the area including the self-guided Heritage Trail – the town was a Royalist stronghold during the English Civil War

Modbury made a name for itself for being Europe's first plastic-bag-free town in 2007, making a small charge for a bag long before the rest of the country caught up. It's a pleasant town, with a good selection of shops, including the excellent St Luke's Hospice charity shop, which specialises in vintage stuff. The town became wealthy through glove making, and the annual May Fair, held during the week beginning with the May Bank Holiday, features a Glove Ceremony among other festivities.

Northeast of Modbury, down a tiny road, is **Calancombe Estate** (PL21 0TU ☎ 01548 830905 ⊘ calancombe-estate.com ⊙ 11.00–17.00 Thu–Sun; booking recommended) which boast a vineyard, a distillery and a rather good restaurant. Caroline and Lance Whitehead came here in 2012 and a year later started planting vines – there are now over 22,000 of them spread over 23 acres. There are also cider apple trees (they have plans to make calvados) and blackcurrants – for cassis! The restaurant is set in the heart of it all, with the winery to its left and the distillery above it on the balcony. On the balcony is also where you can try your hand at blending your own gin – and tasting Calancombe's gins too. Tapas-style dishes are offered at lunchtime, along with English cheeses and charcuterie and, of course, the full range of their award-winning wines. A tour and tasting really gives you a complete understanding of how Calancombe works, or you can just follow one of their walking trails for a stroll around the vineyards after your meal. There is also a range of self-catering accommodation.

South of Modbury is a network of steep, narrow lanes ambling down to the coast, constrained to the west by the unbridged River Erme. This

---

1 Kayaking on the picturesque Erme Estuary. 2 Almost every inch of wood in Holbeton's All Saints Church is carved. 3 The pretty town of Modbury. 4 Mothecombe beach is a peaceful spot. ▶

is the attraction for walkers or cyclists. Walkers on the South West Coast Path can wade across the river at low tide (see opposite). To the east of the river are **Kingston** and **Ringmore** (page 183), with paths and lanes running down to meet the coast path, and on the west side is Holbeton (see below) and the lovely private beaches of Mothecombe and Coastguards (see opposite).

¶¶ FOOD & DRINK

Cool Beans Coffee Poundwell St ☎ 01548 830022 ⌂ coolbeanscoffeebar.co.uk. A popular coffee shop renowned for its breakfasts & a range of paninis & sandwiches.

The Little Kitchen 35 Church St ⌂ tlkgroup.co.uk/modbury. This place is great for breakfast or brunch all the way through to dinner – the tapas is good. As well as tea and coffee, they serve wine, beer, cider and even cocktails!

The School House Mothecombe ☎ 01752 830552 ⌂ schoolhouse-devon.com. Near the car park for Mothecombe Beach (see opposite), this used to be a simple café satisfying the needs of the visitors who arrived on the few days each week that the private beach was open to the public. Now open every day, the restaurant is under the same ownership as the terrific Beach House Café at South Milton Sands (page 177).

20 HOLBETON

This little village is en route to the lovely beaches belonging to the Flete Estate. It has a pub and the Village Stores, but it is the **church of All Saints** that is special. It appears in Simon Jenkins's *England's Thousand Best Churches*, so any Jenkins devotee will want to see it. What makes it remarkable is that it's an example of Victorian restoration that has enhanced a church rather than spoiled it. The restoration was done by J D Sedding in the 1880s and is typical of the Arts and Crafts movement. The elaborate lychgate, porch and doors give you an idea of what is to come, and the impression on entering is that someone has gone mad with a chisel. Every possible surface of stone or wood is carved. The stone pulpit is dense with apostles, vine leaves and ears of wheat. The bench ends are a tangle of flora and fauna, and the screen is so intricate that it needs concentration to take it all in. It's admirably done but, to me, lacks the surprises and primitive appeal found in older churches; realism is everywhere, with creatures and plants correct in every detail so leaving little to speculation.

"The impression is that someone has gone mad with a chisel. Every possible surface of stone or wood is carved."

The knight propped up uncomfortably on his elbow has more appeal because of the large number of children he appears to have fathered. In fact, three generations of the Hele family are here, all called Thomas. Even so, 22 offspring was not bad going, in between fighting wars and the like. The earliest Thomas died in 1613 and his grandson in 1670. All but the armoured Sir Thomas are kneeling devoutly in prayer.

The church is perched on a hillside overlooking the village, its 120ft steeple heralding its presence as you descend the suicidally steep hill. The views from the graveyard down to the Erme Valley towards Mothecombe are splendid.

21 MOTHECOMBE & COASTGUARDS BEACHES

Part of the Flete Estate, the gorgeous and quiet beach of **Mothecombe** used to be open only on Wednesdays and weekends during the summer. Now open daily, with a restaurant (see opposite), it is likely to become far more popular; it has everything: sand, tide pools and a backdrop of craggy cliffs and greenery. No dogs are allowed during the summer months.

Coastguards Beach, further up the estuary, is quieter, more spacious (at low tide), and dogs are allowed so it's popular with walkers.

CROSSING THE ERME

At low tide it's usually possible to wade across the river using the old ford. Unless it has been raining heavily this should be only knee deep and more of a paddle than a wade. Heading east, the ford is from Coastguards Beach to upstream of Wonwell Beach (pronounced Wonell) where you can meet the coast path for the rugged and very scenic three-mile walk to Ayrmer Cove. Continuing west of the Erme, we move into *Chapter 5.*

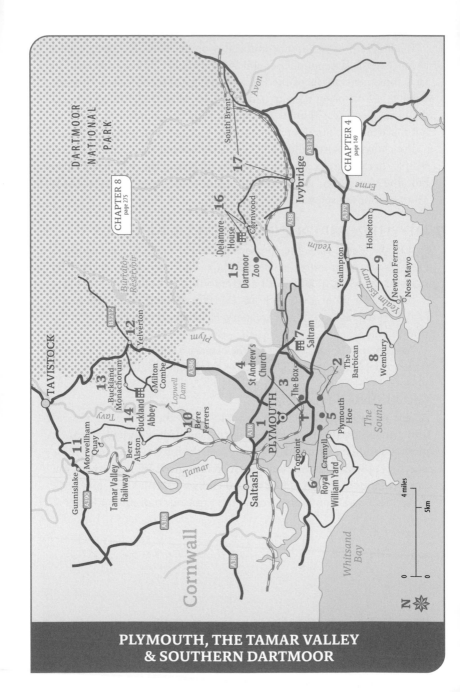

PLYMOUTH, THE TAMAR VALLEY
& SOUTHERN DARTMOOR

5
PLYMOUTH, THE TAMAR VALLEY & SOUTHERN DARTMOOR

Plymouth in the last century was a poor village inhabited by fishermen. It is now so increased in buildings and population, that it may be reckoned among the best cities of England...This great advantage it derives from the capaciousness and convenience of a large bay, which, extending itself inland between two promontories, not only admits ships to a tranquil and secure sheltering place, but conveys them with the tide, which is here very powerful, into two other bays still further inland, being the spacious channels of two rivers.

Cosmo III, Grand Duke of Tuscany 1669, as recorded by Count L Magalotti

More than 400 years before the duke's appreciation of Plymouth, one of the 'spacious channels' he mentions, the River Tamar, was carrying tin, lead and silver ores seaward from Dartmoor's mines. Then copper was discovered and, by the 19th century, the Tamar Valley was Europe's largest source of copper ore and Morwellham Quay was briefly England's busiest port. Today Morwellham has dwindled into historic tranquillity, whereas Plymouth has 'increased in buildings and population' so that the Elizabethan seafarers would have a hard time finding their way around.

Some of the leafiest lanes and prettiest moorland of Dartmoor National Park lie only a few miles from Plymouth. Dartmoor Zoo is here, the artistic delights of Delamore House, and the gateway villages of Yelverton and Ivybridge. The coastline also has some beautiful bays and beaches.

 ## WET-WEATHER ACTIVITIES

Plym Valley Railway (page 192)
Plymouth: Black Friars Distillery Tour (page 193), **Mayflower Museum** (page 193),
National Marine Aquarium (page 194) & **The Box** (page 196)
Tamar Valley Line (page 210)
Buckland Abbey (page 216)

GETTING THERE & AROUND

The **A38** links Plymouth and the surrounding area to both Cornwall and Exeter. Plymouth has **rail** connections from most parts of Britain, and regular daytime services from London Paddington. From Exeter, sit on the left-hand side for a wonderfully scenic stretch along the shores of the Exe and Teign estuaries. Locally, the Tamar Valley Line covers the 15 miles between Plymouth and Gunnislake. Long-distance **buses** and National Express **coaches** serve Plymouth, often with a change at Exeter, and there's a good network of local buses.

SELF-POWERED TRAVEL

For cyclists, the Tamar Valley offers great possibilities, from moorland on Dartmoor's fringes to the deep lanes near the river. The largely traffic-free **Plym Valley Cycle Trail** has been joined with **Drake's Trail** to provide a scenic cycling route between Plymouth and Tavistock (21 miles). Now generally known just as Drake's Trail (⌀ drakestrail.co.uk), it's one of the best cycle routes in the county. It's the first part of the 99-mile **Devon Coast-to-Coast** Route 27 that runs from Plymouth to Ilfracombe, and officially starts at the Plymouth ferry port; but, to save struggling with city traffic, it's better to start from Marsh Mills at the Coypool Park and Ride (where you can also hire bikes; see opposite). The trail then runs for seven miles along an old railway line. It follows the Plym Estuary past Saltram House and through bat-hung tunnels, ferny railway cuttings and shady woodland, then on to Bickleigh Vale and Clearbrook near Yelverton. From there you're ideally placed to explore the Tamar Valley and Bere Peninsula. Continuing to Tavistock, the trail mostly follows a disused railway line again, with some spectacular views from the new viaduct (Gem Bridge) and then down to this ancient town. **Mountain bikers** can enjoy the wooded acres of the **Tamar Trails**, hugging the river on the western edge of the county. Saturday 5k **parkruns** are held here and in the Plym Valley.

Drake's Trail ends at Tavistock but the Coast-to-Coast Cycle Route continues on-road to Lydford, where it becomes the **Granite Way** (page 253) until Okehampton and then heads north to Ilfracombe. Don't confuse this cycle route with the **Two Moors Way**, a 102-mile walking trail from Ivybridge northward to Lynton across Dartmoor and Exmoor (page 283), which also becomes 'coast-to-coast' by adding the Erme–

Plym Trail, a further 15 miles from Wembury to Ivybridge. A map of the cycle route is available from Croydecycle or the Sustrans website ⊘ sustrans.org.uk.

Bikes can be hired from **Plymouth Bike Hire** (⊘ 07577 279928 ⊘ plymouthbikehire.co.uk) based in the Coypool Park and Ride (PL7 4TB) off the A38 at Plympton junction (bus 200 from the city centre). Their website has advice about trails.

Of **walking trails**, the most rewarding named one in the area is the **Tamar Valley Discovery Trail**, a 35-mile route from Tamerton Foliot, just north of Plymouth, to Launceston in Cornwall. Its logo, an apple, represents the fruit grown locally. If you follow it for 12 miles as far as Bere Alston, via Lopwell Dam and Bere Ferrers, a train on the scenic Tamar Valley Line will take you back to Plymouth afterwards. You do need to be aware that Lopwell Dam cannot be crossed for two hours either side of high tide.

The trail beyond Bere Alston relies on a Tamar ferry that was not running when we were writing this book; instead one has to take the train from Bere Alston to Calstock from where the trail can once again be walked. There are also fine walks and some spectacular views along the area's coastline.

1 PLYMOUTH

🏰 **Crownhill Fort** (page 339) & **1 Elliot Terrace – Lady Astor** (page 339)
Tourist information: 3–5 The Barbican (opposite Mayflower Steps) ⊘ 01752 306330 ⊘ visitplymouth.co.uk ⊙ Apr–Oct daily, Nov–Mar closed Sun. Well stocked with information & offers a good range of tourist services. Also contains the Mayflower Museum (page 193).

Cities aren't generally Slow, but big, bustling, maritime Plymouth – 'Britain's Ocean City' – holds so much history. At dusk, looking seaward from the Hoe, it's easy to imagine great high-masted ships turning gently at anchor in the bay, their sails curving to some ancient evening breeze. Sir Francis Drake (page 200) sailed from here, along with Raleigh, Grenville, Hawkins and so many other Elizabethan seafarers; the Pilgrim Fathers finally set off for their 'promised land' from here, and England's battle-fleet of galleons surged from the harbour to defeat the Spanish Armada. Captain James Cook began his voyage around the world here, in 1772, as did Sir Francis Chichester in 1966.

It originated as the 'littel fishe towne' of Sutton, owned by the monks of Plympton Priory until the 15th century, and its deep harbour (still known as Sutton Harbour) offered safe anchorage to the English fleet during the Hundred Years' War. In 1439 Plymouth became the first town in England to receive its charter by Act of Parliament, and it was a prosperous naval and trading centre in Elizabethan times. The Royal Naval Dockyard at next-door Devonport was completed in 1698 and brought further prosperity.

Severe bombing during World War II destroyed around 20,000 buildings. Massive post-war reconstruction introduced some characterless architecture but also reduced congestion; enough old buildings have survived or been restored, and more of the post-war replacements are listed than in any British city except London. The centre feels spacious, while the historic Barbican area still echoes with its Elizabethan past.

In 2020, Plymouth celebrated the 400th anniversary of the voyage of the *Mayflower*, the little storm-tossed ship that in 1620 sailed into the history books and left so indelible a legacy. Some 102 passengers and 30 crew sailed on the *Mayflower* to Massachusetts; families from all over Britain and even some from the Netherlands. Today, more than 30 million people can trace their ancestry to those pilgrims ⊘ mayflower400uk.org.

GETTING AROUND THE CITY

Plymouth has several **car parks** but they get busy. Three **Park and Ride** bus services run from the outskirts to the city centre: Coypool (PL2 3DE) near Marsh Mills roundabout off the A38; the George (PL6 7HB) opposite the George Hotel in Tavistock Road; and Milehouse (PL2 3DE) by Plymouth Argyle Football Club. In Royal Parade they link with the very convenient network of **Citybuses** (⊘ plymouthbus. co.uk). Bus maps are available from the tourist information centre and bus station. There's also a good car park at Ivybridge railway station, just a 15-minute train ride from Plymouth. For a quick chuff on a **heritage steam train**, hop aboard the Plym Valley Railway (Marsh Mills Station, Coypool Rd, PL7 4NW ⊘ plymrail.co.uk), run by volunteers on the rebuilt 1½-mile stretch of line between Marsh Mills (opposite Coypool Park and Ride) and Plym Bridge. Check the website for current times and dates.

Plymouth City Council encourages **cycling** and walking and has produced the leaflet Enjoy Plymouth by bike & on foot. A map of routes across the city can be downloaded from ⊘ plymouth.gov.uk (search for 'cycle routes'). Various designated **walks** cover the main places of interest. The tourist office has helpful leaflets, and the steepest hill you'll need to climb is up from the Barbican.

2 THE BARBICAN

The surviving cobbled streets and quaysides of the Barbican were the heart of ancient Plymouth, stamping ground of sea captains, sailors, merchants and even pirates. Now speciality shops, workshops and restaurants jostle together among the old port buildings and alleyways. Pause at a café, and you could be sipping your coffee on the spot where Elizabethan explorers planned their next voyage over a glass or three of fine French brandy.

You'll find everything from secondhand bookshops, a button emporium, baby clothes, antiques, jewellery, competing varieties of Devon and Cornwall ice cream, galleries displaying local art and crafts and lots more. In New Street, the Tudor House, built in 1599, sells Liberty prints; while the Parade Antiques and Curios Museum has rare military memorabilia, antiques of all kinds and TV relics including a life-size Dalek.

At 60 Southside Street is the **Black Friars Distillery** (⊘ 01752 828967 ⊘ plymouthdistillery.com), the working home of Plymouth Gin since 1793 and before that (among other things) a debtors' prison, a non-conformist meeting place and – as you might expect from the name – a monastery. The gin is still made by one man in one Victorian copper still, using natural ingredients such as juniper berries, citrus peel, orris root, cardamom and coriander seeds to create its smooth rich taste. Tours will take you through the process

"The Barbican was the heart of ancient Plymouth, stamping ground of sea captains, merchants and even pirates."

and you can sample it in the striking refectory bar. The distillery is said to be where the Pilgrim Fathers spent their last night in September 1620 before embarking on the *Mayflower*. The **Mayflower Steps** are reputedly close to the spot where they boarded the ship the next day to start their voyage, and the **Mayflower Museum,** in the same building as the tourist information centre opposite the steps, tells their story. Most fascinating are facsimile pages from William Bradford's original handwritten journal, *Of Plimoth Plantation*, written between 1630 and 1647; the history of the first 30 years of the colony, it's the single most complete authority for the pilgrims' story and the original was a great treasure. The history of the pilgrims starts with the story of the Wampanoag culture, an Indigenous American tribal nation, and tells the story of the emergence of modern America. There is also a trail for children to follow.

And if, on the quay nearby, you should spot a giant prawn clinging to the top of a pillar – it's actually a sea monster, representing the Barbican's rich maritime history.

The **National Marine Aquarium** (PL4 0DX ✆ 08448 937938 ⌨ national-aquarium.co.uk ⏱ year-round, online booking required), across a small footbridge from the Barbican, is the UK's largest aquarium and the first set up solely for purposes of education, conservation and research. It advised on the BBC's *Blue Planet* TV series, among other productions. The scale is impressive: the Eddystone Reef tank has the UK's largest single-tank viewing panel, while the Atlantic Ocean tank is the deepest in the UK, with 2.5 million litres of water; it contains large nurse sharks, sand tiger sharks, lemon sharks, zebra sharks and two species of ray. In the Great Barrier Reef tank

"There are lionfish, unicornfish, pufferfish and many other colourful wonders."

are lionfish, unicornfish, pufferfish and many other colourful wonders. Then there's the sea life of Plymouth Sound itself, including octopus, lobsters and spider crabs. Behind-the-scenes tours are held every day, when you can see the technology and sheer hard work that hold the whole enterprise together, or, if you are feeling brave, you can snorkel in the Atlantic Ocean tank and swim with the stingrays, sharks and a friendly green turtle. The Waves Café provides a wide range of hot and cold food, using ethically sourced local produce, or there are a few places to picnic. Ironically, the **Plymouth Fish Market** is only a stone's throw away!

The number 25 bus from Royal Parade stops nearby. By car, follow the brown 'fish' signs. Main parking is in the Harbour car park.

PLYMOUTH: **1** The Hoe features the Royal Citadel, Smeaton's Tower and a huge Art Deco lido. **2** There's plenty to see at The Box, including restored figureheads from warships. **3** Spot the sea monster on a pillar at the Barbican. **4** St Andrew's Church dates from the 15th century, although its roof was replaced after World War II bombing. ▶

AROUND THE CITY

Of other historic attractions, the **Merchant's House** just up from the Barbican is Plymouth's largest and finest 16th-century home, 'modernised' in the early 17th century by seafaring adventurer William Parker, who later became Mayor of Plymouth. **The Elizabethan House**, with its low ceilings and creaky sloping floors, was the home of an Elizabethan sea captain or merchant; the rooms have been atmospherically restored to recreate the conditions of the time.

Plymouth City Market at Frankfurt Gate (⊘ plymouthmarket.co.uk ⊙ closed Sun) has a mass of indoor, family-run stalls selling everything from Devon lamb and locally made cheese to fish, suitcases, clothing and electronics. Streets around it have many small independent shops.

3 THE BOX
Tavistock Pl, PL4 8AX ⊘ 01752 304774 ⊘ theboxplymouth.com ⊙ 10.00–17.00 Tue–Sun & bank holidays

'The Box' isn't a very inspiring name but it is a truly inspiring museum and art gallery. It has won more than 20 awards in the short time that it has been open and it is easy to see why.

As you enter The Box, your attention is immediately drawn to the 14 huge, restored figureheads from British warships suspended above you. The maritime theme is taken up in the 100 Journeys gallery, with tales of explorers whose travels started in Plymouth. From Sir Francis Drake through Scott of the Antarctic to Sir Francis Chichester, you can see their routes on the huge illuminated globe. Further on you can operate a submarine periscope, and an audio-visual display brings to life the perils of the sea, showing the number of shipwrecks off the coast.

The Box is not all maritime, however. In the next gallery, a full-size woolly mammoth called Mildred greets you; its size contrasts with the display of beetles, butterflies and spiders – the latter looking far too alive.

Upstairs is the Media Lab where you can film yourself presenting the news and weather. The sheer size of the old film and video cameras and editing machines is astonishing. Across the landing is the Living Archive, a place to research all things related to Plymouth. There are also art galleries on this floor and another across the street in an old church. The galleries display ever-changing collections; details on their website.

The Box is free, though there is a small charge for some visiting art shows, and there is a good café and, of course, a shop.

4 ST ANDREW'S CHURCH

This minster church dates in its present form from the 15th century, although a Christian community has been there since the 8th century and the first vicar, Ealphage, was named in 1087. Elizabethan seafarers including Drake, Grenville and Hawkins worshipped there, as did Catherine of Aragon and (it is said) both Charles I and Charles II. War is no respecter of history, however, and two nights of heavy bombing in 1941 left it a burnt-out shell. The next morning, a local schoolmistress placed a wooden board over the north door with the inscription *RESURGAM*, meaning '*I will rise again*'. For some years it remained a roofless 'garden church' with services held in the open air, but then was indeed rebuilt, with stained-glass windows in gloriously rich colours designed by John Piper. On the feast day of St Andrew in 1957 a moving service of reconsecration was held, attended by around 2,000 people. Behind St Andrew's is the **Prysten House**, dating from 1498; it was built by Thomas Yogg or Yogge, a wealthy merchant involved in the French wine trade. It's not regularly open; ask in the church about seeing inside. Next to the church in Royal Parade, the impressive Guildhall with its tall, landmark tower is a relative newcomer: completed in 1874 and then restored after bomb damage. If you like neo-Gothic carvings, it has them aplenty.

5 PLYMOUTH HOE

Plymouth's must-visit attraction is of course the historic **Hoe** (the name comes from a Saxon word meaning 'high place'), where Sir Francis Drake is said to have been playing bowls when told of the approaching Spanish Armada. Nowadays people stroll there, fly kites, putt, picnic, walk their dogs and gaze out across Plymouth Sound from helpfully placed benches. The large island in the bay, **Drake's Island** (∂ drakes-island.com), is now open to the public; the ferry leaves from the Barbican landing stage – booking essential for both the tour of the island and, separately, the ferry. The tour will introduce you to the island's past – it has been a refuge for Protestants, a gun battery for Royalists and a prison for military commanders and clergy. You might even meet some of the island's 15 ghosts.

The **Royal Citadel** at the Hoe's eastern end, with massive 70ft walls, was built in 1665 by Charles II and remained England's most important coastal defence for around a hundred years. Today it's used by the military but bookable tours are available (☎ 07876 402728 ⊙ Apr–Oct 14.00 Sun, Tue & Thu; English Heritage). **Smeaton's Tower**, 72ft high, was built in 1759 as the Eddystone lighthouse, but all but its base was moved from the Eddystone rock to the Hoe in the 1880s because of sea erosion. From 1937 until decimalisation, its image appeared behind Britannia on the English penny coin. The interior has been restored and is open to visitors (⊙ Apr–Oct daily), its Lantern Room giving fantastic panoramic views over the bay.

The Hoe has various **war memorials**: the large naval memorial, in Portland stone, contains dozens of plain, neatly lettered bronze panels recording the names of the 22,443 (yes, that many) men and women of the Commonwealth navies who lost their lives at sea during both world wars. In the autumn of 2017 it was movingly decorated with a massive wave of ceramic poppies, the creation by Paul Cummins and Tom Piper, seen earlier at the Tower of London.

At the seaward side of the Hoe thrusting out into Plymouth Sound is the huge Art Deco lido, the **Tinside Pool** (♂ plymouthactive.co.uk/centres/tinside-lido ⊙ May–Sep). It's a wonderful place to swim, in natural salt water surrounded by harbour views.

6 ROYAL WILLIAM YARD

This fascinating area towards the western end of the waterfront was formerly the old Royal Naval victualling yard, built to supply the Navy with everything from gunpowder to rum and ship's biscuits. It would have been named the Royal George Yard, but George IV died of dropsy and cirrhosis in 1830 five years before its completion and was succeeded by his brother William IV. In olden times it was a strictly secret area, its storehouses and manufacturing areas closed to the public eye. Then, up to 100 bullocks could be killed in a day at the slaughterhouse to provide the naval rations of salt beef; the Mills Bakery with its 12 giant ovens and heavy millstones could produce 20,000 loaves of bread daily and the brewhouse 137,000 litres of beer. Now the majestic old buildings have been opened for development; cafés, galleries, boutiques, offices and other enterprises fill their rooms, and diners spill out colourfully on to the once-silent quaysides. In the old cooperage, where barrels for storing the mass of food and drink on

"In olden times it was a strictly secret area, its storehouses and manufacturing areas closed to the public eye."

board ship were once built, a £3.2 million makeover has created Ocean Studios, with working space for up to 100 artists and craftspeople and where regular exhibitions are held. An open-air food market is held on The Green on the first Sunday of the month in summer, involving many local producers (royalwilliamyard.com).

About a 20-minute walk from Royal Parade, Royal William Yard is served by Citybus 34 and has a central parking area. In season, the Royal William Yard Ferry (page 203) runs there regularly from near the Mayflower Steps.

ANNUAL EVENTS

These include a half-marathon and Lord Mayor's Day in May, Armed Forces Day in June, the spectacular British Firework Championships in August and, in September, the popular Seafood and Harbour festival. In the Sound, every July, the Sail Grand Prix takes place; it is Formula One on water! High-tech, high-speed hydrofoiling F50 catamarans fly across the water at speeds approaching 60mph, manned by the world's most athletic sailors. Also in May there's a lively Pirate Extravaganza weekend in the Barbican; last time I visited I unexpectedly found myself surrounded by swashbucklers large and small.

FOOD & DRINK

Plymouth (and particularly its waterside areas) has no shortage of bars, cafés and restaurants. Many are in the Barbican area, particularly in Southside Street, plus there's a selection of Greek and Turkish restaurants to the west of Armada Way and a few rather good places to eat around the Hoe. Meanwhile, with its cafés and restaurants and convenient parking area, Royal William Yard has become a popular place to eat (page 201).

Barbican & Hoe

Marco Pierre White Steakhouse Bar & Grill (on the top floor of the Holiday Inn Crowne Plaza, Armada Way 01752 639937 mpwrestaurants.co.uk). Offers the quality & standard that you would expect, with a top-class menu & pleasant, professional staff. The view over the bay is superb.

Ocean View Hoe Rd 01752 393777 oceanviewplymouth.co.uk. This waterfront bistro & cocktail bar in the Dome nearby also offers great views if you can get a window table. It's a stylish place on the cliff just below Smeaton's Tower, with competitive prices & inventive menus.

Barbican Kitchen Brasserie (60 Southside St 01752 604448 barbicankitchen. com) in the Black Friars Distillery, is run by celebrity TV chefs James & Chris Tanner. Their

SIR FRANCIS DRAKE

Born around 1540 in a small leasehold farmstead near Tavistock, the young Francis Drake first 'went to sea' some ten years later when his parents travelled by boat from Plymouth to Kent, and found lodging in one of the old hulks moored in the Medway Estuary near Chatham. The youngster was now surrounded by maritime life, from small fishing and cargo vessels to the towering men-o'-war in the naval dockyard. In his teens he was apprenticed to the captain of a small merchant boat, and inherited her some years later when her owner died. His cousin, the wealthy Plymouth ship-owner John Hawkins, had trading links with the New World; Drake thus sold his boat and enlisted in Hawkins's fleet.

Drake's father Edmund, a farmer, was an ardent Protestant lay preacher in turbulent religious times, so the young Francis probably acquired strong anti-Catholic attitudes. He encountered (Catholic) Spaniards on a voyage to the West Indies and the contact wasn't friendly; dislike turned to hatred after a Spanish attack in 1568 destroyed three English ships. Thereafter he sought revenge against Spain.

With the Queen's blessing, he became a thoroughly successful pirate, capturing Spanish vessels and bringing home rich spoils. In 1577 he embarked on his famous circumnavigation of the globe (pausing to raid the Spanish harbours in Cuba and Peru on the way); he then claimed California for England, sealed a treaty with the sultan of the Moluccas (now part of Indonesia) for spice trading, sailed home with a glittering amount of treasure – and was knighted. He also became Mayor of Plymouth, bought Buckland Abbey as well as other manors and businesses, and entered parliament as MP for Bossiney in Cornwall.

In 1585 the Queen sent him off to raid Spanish settlements in the Caribbean. The Spaniards prepared to counter-attack, but in 1587 Drake sailed into Cádiz harbour and did immense damage, 'singeing the King of Spain's beard'. Spain retaliated the following year with its Armada, a massive fighting force

consistently good food is focused on local ingredients, some collected for them by their forager. It's upstairs, but there's a lift for those with mobility issues.

Jacka's Bakery (38 Southside St ✆ 01752 262187 ☉ 08.30–14.30 daily) has wonderful bread (particularly sourdough) & other baking, tasty breakfasts & light lunches, & good coffee. The oldest working commercial bakery in the UK, this family-run spot is small & very popular, so tables get crowded.

Quay 33 (33 Southside St ✆ 01752 393457 ⊘ quay33.co.uk) provides tasty homemade food in a cheery atmosphere.

The Village Restaurant (32 Southside St ✆ 01752 667688 ⊘ thevillagerestaurantplymouth. co.uk), one of Plymouth's oldest seafood restaurants, serves a fine selection of fish dishes, as well as good-value local meat, poultry & game with a Grecian twist.

of 151 warships and almost 30,000 men. The high-born Lord Thomas Howard was appointed admiral of the English fleet, the lowlier but more flamboyant Drake a vice-admiral. For almost a week, fierce battles raged along the English Channel. Finally England outmanoeuvred the Spaniards, 'drummed 'em up the channel' and routed them, to huge popular acclaim.

Drake was lauded in prose and poetry, and souvenir-makers had a field day. However, his star was waning and his final voyage was a failure. He had set off from England to Panama in August 1595, with a fleet of 26 ships, hoping to take Panama City for the Queen; but the Spanish force proved too strong. While retreating, Drake contracted dysentery and died; he was buried at sea, off Panama. It was a sadly inglorious end to a colourful and courageous life.

To the public Drake was a hero; to his peers less so. An arrogant, flamboyant, self-made man of relatively lowly birth, he was looked down on by some of the aristocracy.

A favourite of the Queen, he revelled in his glittering social status, yet one of his main land-based undertakings was the very practical construction of a leat (channel) to bring fresh water to Plymouth from the River Meavy. An old legend tells that he rode off to Dartmoor and located a suitable spring, then turned his horse about, spoke some magic words to the spring, and galloped back to Plymouth with it bubbling along obediently behind him. Such was his popular image.

Queen Elizabeth called him 'my pirate', a Spanish ambassador called him 'the master-thief of the unknown world', and the Elizabethan historian John Stow wrote: 'He was more skilful in all points of navigation than any.' Tristram Risdon, writing 20 years or so after Drake's death, went even further: 'Could my pen as ably describe his worth as my heart prompteth to it, I would make this day-star appear at noon day as doth the full moon at midnight.' And reputedly he also played a mean game of bowls.

Platters (The Barbican ✆ 01752 227262 f), is a deservedly popular, unpretentious waterfront restaurant known for its very fresh seafood, with 'catch of the day' specials straight from the bay. Try our favourite, the 'platters trio', which lets you sample three different grilled fish and their great chips, too. Tables can get crowded at peak times so you might want to book.

Royal William Yard

Le Bistrot Pierre (✆ 01752 262318 bistrotpierre.co.uk) is part of a small chain but a very classy one, serving restaurant & bar meals. It has quality French-influenced food, a warm, relaxed atmosphere & hard-working, friendly staff. Good value. Another branch is in Torquay (page 75).

PLYMOUTH & SURROUNDINGS FROM THE WATER

Thanks to the various boat trips and ferries available, this is a very pleasant way of spending anything from an hour to a day. The Torpoint Ferry is the only ferry that carries cars.

⚓ FERRIES & CRUISES

Plymouth Boat Trips Commercial Wharf, Barbican (near Mayflower Steps) ☏ 01752 253153 ⟨ plymouthboattrips.co.uk. This company offers harbour, wildlife & eco cruises as well as short & longer fishing trips. It also runs Cawsand, Cremyll & Royal William Yard/ Mount Edgcumbe ferries. The scenic Calstock Cruise (see below) takes you past the Dockyard & Brunel's rail bridge, & up through the leafy Tamar Valley to visit Calstock. The Harbour & Breakwater Cruises show you Plymouth Sound (including Drake's Island) as well as Devonport Naval Dockyard. In summer there are trips up the River Yealm. The Boathouse Café, directly by their Barbican slipway & looking over the water, serves fish freshly caught by their own boats.

Cawsand Ferry ⟨ plymouthboattrips.co.uk ☉ Apr–Oct daily. This service, said to have been running for more than 100 years, carries people, prams, bicycles & dogs between

THE TAMAR ESTUARY: A GUIDE FOR BIRDERS

Tony Soper

Taking the four-hour Calstock Cruise offered by Plymouth Boat Trips will reveal the astonishing variety of scenery and birdlife on the Tamar Estuary. These are general-interest cruises, so if you're a birder don't forget your field guide and, whatever your interest, carry binoculars.

As you pass the imposing Citadel and see the grassy expanse of the Hoe, the sheltered anchorage of Plymouth Sound opens on your port hand. Maybe you'll spot a fleet of racing dinghies or yachts; certainly there will be some naval warships or auxiliaries, for you are about to enter the Hamoaze, the deep-water anchorage that serves the Naval Base. Check the upper rigging of any laid-up vessels, for

cormorants delight in colonising ships that sit here for more than a season or two. This part of the trip showcases the marine industrial history of the city, from its 18th-century slips and dry-docks to the nuclear facility.

The twin suspension bridges mark the beginning of the wildlife-rich middle section of the estuary. As you work up on the rising tide there will be exposed mudflats on either side. Shorebirds with short legs probe the soft mud for lugworms and assorted invertebrates, while those with long legs wade in the shallows and pounce or sweep for shrimps. It's along these wet mudscapes that the elegant avocets show up in early winter.

the Barbican & the beach beside the quaint old Cornish fishing (& formerly smuggling) villages of Cawsand & Kingsand on the Rame peninsula, where there are enjoyable walks & magnificent scenery. The sturdy little red vessel, the *Weston Maid*, was originally built as a lifeboat for the elegant ocean liner *Canberra*.

Cremyll Ferry 🖉 01752 822105 (office) 🖱 plymouthboattrips.co.uk ⊘ year-round. An eight-minute trip between Admiral's Hard (near the Royal William Yard, Citybus 34 from Royal Parade) & Mount Edgcumbe in Cornwall, carrying passengers, bicycles & walkers on the South West Coast Path. There's thought to have been a ferry here since 1204. Mount Edgcumbe Country Park is open year-round & has plenty to explore. An alternative is the Mount Edgcumbe Ferry below.

Royal William Yard/Mount Edgcumbe Ferry 🖱 plymouthboattrips.co.uk ⊘ daily Apr–Oct, weekends Nov–Mar. This runs between the Barbican (near the Mayflower Steps), Royal William Yard & Mount Edgcumbe, with impressive views of Plymouth's sea frontage. Much nicer than the bus for getting from the Barbican to Royal William Yard.

Torpoint Ferry 2 Ferry St, Torpoint PL11 2AX 🖉 01752 812233 🖱 tamarcrossings.org.uk. This large car ferry, crossing the Tamar between Plymouth & Torpoint in Cornwall, also takes buses & lorries. It's a regular, 24-hour, daily, all-year service, with ferries only ten minutes apart at peak times. Free for foot passengers & bicycles.

In early summer, parties of young shelducks hoover their way across the mud, finding sustenance in the uncountable numbers of tiny Hydrobia snails. Herons, jealously guarding the riparian rights to their allotted stretch of foreshore, stand knee-deep in water and wait patiently for the fish to come to them. Cormorants jack-knife to chase an eel or a flatfish on the muddy bottom. As the tide rises and covers the mud, the birds find a safe roosting place ashore until the ebb reveals their hunting grounds again. The herons, solitary fishermen, now enjoy some sociable company. Check the waterside trees as you sail higher into the narrower reaches to find a communal cormorant roost. And at each end of the summer comes the time when an osprey, passing by on migration, may stop for a week or two to plunge for a take-away mullet.

The upper reaches of the tidal Tamar offer fine reed beds, alive in summer with the chatter of warblers. There will be otters here as well, but you'll be lucky to see one. Devonians call them 'dim articles', a reference to their invisibility not their intelligence. And around the Cotehele bend at last you reach the waterside village of Calstock. There's time to stretch your legs ashore and go for a cream tea before you return down a high-water scene, totally transformed from that of the upward journey.

Incidentally, if you want to be a proper Devonian, be sure to say Tamar as 'tamer'!

SOUTH & SOUTHEAST OF PLYMOUTH

If you're near Plymouth it goes without saying that you're near the water, and this section stretches from the River Plym to coastal Wembury, with its rock pools, walks and wide-reaching seascapes, and the twin waterside villages of Newton Ferrers and Noss Mayo beside the Yealm Estuary. The nearby River Erme and its pretty villages of Holbeton and Mothecombe are in *Chapter 4* (pages 186 and 187).

7 SALTRAM

Plympton, nr Plymouth, PL7 1UH ✆ 01752 333500 ⊙ Feb 11.00–15.30, Mar–Oct noon–16.30 (house); National Trust

🏠 **Boringdon Hall** (page 339)

The park around Saltram, perched high above the River Plym on the outskirts of Plymouth, is one of the city's valuable 'green spaces'. Bus 21A from Plymouth will drop you half a mile or so away; cycle path NCN 27 and the West Devon Way run along the bank of the Plym (in the park) from Plymouth's Laira Bridge. There's a spacious car park.

The magnificent Georgian **house** – it played the part of the Dashwoods' home, Norland Park, in the film of *Sense and Sensibility* – has exquisite Robert Adam interiors, original furnishings and fascinating collections of art and memorabilia. It has been the home of the Parker family for 300 years and one-time owner Lord Boringdon was a close friend of Sir Joshua Reynolds, so naturally the latter's paintings are featured.

The striking landscaped **gardens** attached to the house are dotted with follies and a fine array of shrubs and trees, but the real delight is the surrounding **park**, open daily from dawn to dusk and offering a range of walks, cycle rides and gentle strolls, whether inland or along the river. Maps are available from reception or you can follow your nose and the signs. Dogs are allowed in the woods and parkland.

The gift shop has local arts and crafts, plants, books (including secondhand) and more; the Chapel Tea Room and the Park Café between them serve snacks, light lunches and traditional afternoon teas.

8 WEMBURY

Wembury's **beach** is the perfect seaside escape. With shale/shingle at high tide and a wide expanse of sand at low tide, it offers safe, clean bathing and paddling as well as surfing. Views are stunning, of sea and cliffs. Rock-pool browsing may reveal sea anemones, starfish, crabs, shrimps, limpets, tiny fish, variously coloured seaweed and more; beach-combing should yield several varieties of shells, including cowries and blue-rayed limpets. By the beach are a café (page 207), a small Marine Conservation Centre and public toilets. From Plymouth, bus 48 goes to Wembury village, 10–15 minutes' walk from the beach, or you can follow the South West Coast Path from Bovisand in the west or (via a summer ferry) Newton Ferrers and Noss Mayo in the east. For drivers, there are car parks outside St Werburgh's Church and near the café. The National Trust owns the whole area; Wembury Beach and its surrounding coast and sea are designated a Special Area of Conservation and a Voluntary Marine Conservation Area. It's a short stroll from the beach out to Wembury Point, with spectacular views across the bay and coastline to the historic Mewstone, a tiny triangular island that is now a bird sanctuary but in times gone by was a haunt of local smugglers and a prison.

"A tiny triangular island is now a bird sanctuary but in times gone by was a haunt of local smugglers and a prison."

The **Marine Conservation Centre** (Church Rd ✆ 01752 862538 ⌖ wemburymarinecentre.org ☉ roughly Easter–Oct) has good, family-friendly explanations of flora and fauna, illustrations of local sea life, hands-on exhibits, quizzes and leaflets about nearby attractions. Regular rock-pool rambles are held in the summer; other events and talks are listed on the user-friendly website.

St Werburgh's Church stands above Wembury bay looking out towards the Eddystone Lighthouse. It's believed there was a Saxon church on the site in the 9th century; the present one is described as 14th century on a Norman foundation. The oldest item is the Norman stoup (12th century) inside the north door; there is also a great deal of carved oak, probably 16th century. Among interesting memorials, one chattily commemorates 'a most vertuous Pious Charitable Religious Sweet & lovinge Lady Mightily afflicted with a cough & Bigge with child'.

Wembury does have some attractive old buildings but also a lot of new homes. The website of the active **Wembury Local History Society** (⌖ wemburyhistory.org.uk) is strong on – naturally! – its history, and has an ancestry section that is helpful for visitors wanting to trace their roots.

Although the original **Two Moors Way** (page 283) starts in Ivybridge, walkers wanting to do it as Devon's Coast-to-Coast route can add an extra 15 miles by starting in Wembury; making a total of 117 miles via Dartmoor and Exmoor to Lynmouth on the north Devon coast.

¶¶ FOOD & DRINK

Old Mill Café Wembury Beach ✆ 01752 863280 ☉ Apr–Oct 10.30–16.00 daily, Nov–Mar 11.00–16.00 Sat–Sun (may close in bad weather). Run by the National Trust in a centuries-old stone mill house by the beach, with large grindstones as outdoor table tops & wide-reaching seaward views, this friendly place offers hot & cold snacks, light meals, good baking & the usual range of drinks. A small shop sells beachy things including shoes suitable for rock-pooling.

9 THE YEALM ESTUARY
Yealmpton

This small town – attractive once you escape from the A379 that runs through – contains Old Mother Hubbard's Cottage, the former home of the woman who inspired the Old Mother Hubbard rhyme written in 1805. Its parish **church** of St Bartholomew, which John Betjeman called 'the most amazing Victorian church in Devon', was largely rebuilt in 1849–51 (with a great deal of marble and ornateness) to plans prepared by renowned Victorian architect William Butterfield. It contains the basin of a Saxon font, and rather improbably the old town stocks. In the churchyard is a chunk of Cornish granite with the rough inscription TOREUS or GOREUS. It's thought to be a memorial to a British chieftain who embraced Christianity some 1,500 years ago. There are similar (but slightly later and better carved) stones in Lustleigh and Tavistock (page 302). The first mention of an earlier church is in a charter of 1225, but there's likely to have been one in situ at the time of the Domesday Book, where Yealmpton is mentioned as Elintona. Just outside town on the A379 from Plymouth is **Ben's Farm Shop** (✆ 01752 880925 ⌀ bensfarmshop.co.uk), with a café and a good array of local produce including organic meat and sausages.

◀ **1** The grandiose Georgian house Saltram on the outskirts of Plymouth. **2** Rock-pooling at Wembury can be rewarded with finds such as this cushion star. **3** St Bartholomew's Church in Yealmpton. **4** White-washed houses and a pretty harbour make Newton Ferrers a lovely spot.

This was the first of Ben's shops which you may now spot in Staverton, Exeter and Totnes.

Newton Ferrers & Noss Mayo

These two pretty waterside villages face each other across Newton Creek, a small and sheltered inlet branching off the Yealm, and are linked by a bridge a little way upstream. It's also possible to cross from one to the other over the bed of the creek, when the tide is low enough. White houses are dotted amid greenery on the steep banks and it's a popular mooring for visiting yachts, buzzing with watery activity in summer. The twice-daily bus from Plymouth (no 94) squeezes its way there along twisting narrow lanes.

Small places can have big histories, and this one is well covered on ⊘ theyealm.co.uk/local-area/history-of-the-villages. **Newton Ferrers** was mentioned as Newton in the Domesday Book, and by 1160 had been acquired by the Ferrers family, who came over with William the Conqueror. **Noss Mayo** crops up in 1198 as part of the manor of Stoke, which in 1287 was given by Edward I to one Mathew Fitzjohn, hence the village was named Noss Mayo or 'Mathew's nose'. So they say. Its church of **St Peter the Poor Fisherman**, now a semi-ruin looked after by the Churches Conservation Trust, was built in 1226 on the cliffs above Stoke Bay, a lovely cove, good for swimming, where you can sometimes spot dolphins and seals. St Peter's remained in use until 1840, when it was badly damaged by a storm. It's a peaceful, atmospheric little place, hidden among trees, with some beautiful stone carving and a hint of monastery about it. Meanwhile Newton's Holy Cross Church was built in the 13th century and, after many alterations, is still in use, across the estuary from the new (19th-century) St Peter's Church in Noss Mayo.

"It's a peaceful, atmospheric place, hidden among trees, with beautiful stone carving and a hint of monastery about it."

Slow visitors will appreciate the lack of brash entertainments: walk in beautiful coastal scenery or ancient woodland, relax over a meal in one of the waterside eateries (see opposite) (they're all open daily) or just watch the comings and goings in the creek. Newton Ferrers Equus (✆ 01752 872807; ⊘ newtonferrersequus.com) offers hacks in woodland or with views of distant Dartmoor. In summer, a local water taxi or ferry carries visitors across the various creeks and to Warren

Point, from where it's possible to walk to Wembury (page 204) via a stone-based track across fields or (better) along the coast path.

FOOD & DRINK

The Dolphin Inn (Newton Ferrers ℘ 01752 872007 ◊ dolphininn.weebly.com), **The Ship Inn** (Noss Mayo ℘ 01752 872387 ◊ nossmayo.com) & **The Swan Inn** (Noss Mayo ℘ 01752 873115 ◊ swaninnnossmayo.com) are friendly, traditional pubs with good menus & tremendous views across the water. The Dolphin & The Ship are on the waterside so you can have a paddle while waiting for your meal.

THE TAMAR VALLEY

> **For the fruit markets, cherries, pears, and walnuts are raised in great abundance; especially in the township of Beer Ferrers; which is said to send out of it a thousand pounds worth of fruit (including strawberries) annually.**
> *The Rural Economy of the West of England* by William Marshall, 1796

Bere means spit of land, and this peninsula, locked between the Tamar and the Tavy, is less accessible today than it was two hundred or so years ago when ships regularly carried cargoes of fruit down the river to Plymouth. The railway provides the only direct connection between Bere Ferrers, the village near the apex of the triangle, and Plymouth; for car drivers it's a cul-de-sac and they must make a wide detour to Denham Bridge, near Buckland Monachorum, to reach the city, a journey of about 20 miles. This enforced peacefulness means that the walker or cyclist can stroll or pedal the lanes with little danger from cars. It's deservedly one of Devon's Areas of Outstanding Natural Beauty (◊ tamarvalley.org.uk).

The Bere Peninsula is still a major fruit producer, and walkers will see apple orchards galore, as well as the ever-present river views with clusters of sailing boats. A few centuries back this land between the rivers became valuable for its silver mines; when the silver ran out, lead was discovered. Then, in 1890, the railway arrived and visitors poured in. It is probably quieter now than at any time in its history.

Bere Ferrers has an exceptionally interesting church, a 'Heritage' railway station with displays of memorabilia, and a friendly pub with a beer garden overlooking the Tavy. **Bere Alston** is larger and less picturesque, though it's made an effort with its multicoloured terraced houses. You can buy provisions here and there's a good pub.

Continuing north, the Tamar remains unbridged, save for the railway, until Gunnislake in Cornwall. Once-bustling **Morwellham Quay** is now an intriguing open-air museum. The Tavy's first bridge, Denham, opens up the western fringe of Dartmoor and the picturesque village with the grand name, **Buckland Monachorum**. To its south is **Buckland Abbey**.

THE TAMAR VALLEY LINE

This delightful railway, from Plymouth to Gunnislake, is a commuter service with its roots firmly in yesteryear. On its flower-bedecked and old-fashioned stations you must hail the oncoming train by raising your hand; yet it rescues the residents of Bere Ferrers and its surroundings from a long detour by road to reach workplaces in the city.

The Tamar Valley Line (✆ 01752 584777) is only 15 miles long, but the changing scenery from viaduct to fruit orchards to rivers is always diverting. The summer service is two-hourly and the line even has a **Rail Ale Trail** (⌂ railaletrail.com) for the terminally thirsty, with information about distinctive pubs all within walking distance of the stations.

10 BERE FERRERS

⌂ **Tamar Belle** (page 339)

The Ferrers were a leading family at the time of the Norman Conquest and Henry de Ferrers was chairman of the Domesday Commission. When he received the Bere estate from Henry II it would have been prime land, situated so close to the river and Plymouth harbour. Now it is cherished by those seeking tranquillity. Standing on the platform here waiting for a train gives you an *Adlestrop* moment: complete silence save for all the birds of Devon and Cornwall.

The Tamar Belle Heritage Centre (⌂ tamarbelle.co.uk) has a boxy-looking blue locomotive, the *Earl of Mount Edgcumbe*; various old artefacts; a display of old photos and documents in a revamped 1950s sleeping carriage; and vintage carriages converted into accommodation. From the station it's about a mile downhill to the **Olde Plough Inn** (✆ 01822 840358 ⌂ theoldeploughinn.co.uk), a nicely sited pub with a

---

1 Costumed staff will show you round the exhibits at Morwellham Quay. **2** The Calstock Viaduct is part of the Tamar Valley Line through this peaceful corner of Devon. **3** Bere Ferrers's St Andrew's Church includes the tombs of Sir William de Ferrers, who died in 1280, and his wife Isolda. ▶

sunny beer garden overlooking the river. It has log fires in winter, local guest ales and occasional live music in the evenings. Next to the pub is the church, so the two provide a pleasant way to spend the hour before the train returns to Plymouth. The **church of St Andrew** was built – or rather rebuilt, since the tower is earlier – by Sir William de Ferrers, who died in 1280. His monument is one of its treasures. He lies, with his wife Isolda de Cardinham, next to the altar, dressed in chainmail, his legs crossed (though he has lost his feet) and a shield at his side. Both hands are on his sword, ready to draw. His wife wears a simple robe and on one shoulder is a small, disembodied hand, said to be that of a child, although it's hard to see where the arm or body could have been. And the fingers are too long for a child; a mystery. The stone canopy is decorated with strange carved heads, perhaps male and female.

The memorial to his father, Sir Reginald, who died in 1194, lies next to the altar and seems to have been carved by the same sculptor. This gentleman lies with his body half-turned, his shield over his hands, which are also poised to draw his sword. His knee raised, he appears ready to leap from his tomb and defend his honour. Sadly both lower legs are missing, as is the lion on which his feet rested, although the paws and curly tail remain.

Another notable feature of the church is the stained glass in the east window, claimed – rightly or wrongly – to be the oldest in the county apart from some in Exeter Cathedral. The window was a gift of William de Ferrers, and one of the lights shows him – or one of his family – holding a model of the church.

THE BERE FERRERS RAIL ACCIDENT

In 1917 ten servicemen from New Zealand were mown down by an express train at Bere Ferrers. The men (aged 20 to 36) had disembarked from their troopship in Plymouth and were on their way to Salisbury Plain for training. They had been told that when the train made its first stop, at Exeter, two men from each carriage should alight and go to the back of the train to distribute rations. When the train made an unscheduled stop at Bere Ferrers they jumped on to the line and were struck by the Waterloo–Plymouth express. They are commemorated by a centenary shelter and rose garden at the station, unveiled by the New Zealand High Commissioner, and also on a brass plaque in the church accompanied by the New Zealand flag. Their names have been added to the village war memorial, and a special memorial ceremony was held in 2017.

Elsewhere St Andrew's has Tudor carved bench ends, the design echoing the shape of the windows, and a Tudor fireplace to keep the gentry warm in the winter. The screen has gone, as have the saints in the panels, scraped off at the time of the Reformation.

In the graveyard is a sad little tombstone which has no name, just the inscription 'Cholera 1849'.

11 MORWELLHAM QUAY

Nr Tavistock, PL19 8JL ✆ 01822 832766 ⌂ morwellham-quay.co.uk

Morwellham Quay is on the River Tamar, four miles west of Tavistock. Its nearest rail stations are Gunnislake (three miles away) and Calstock. By car it's just off the A390 between Tavistock and Gunnislake, and there's masses of free parking space. Or you can cycle.

Looking at the beauty and tranquillity of Morwellham Quay today, it's hard to believe that in Victorian times it was known as 'the richest copper port in the Queen's Empire'. Originally built in the 10th to 11th century by the Cistercian monks of Tavistock Abbey as a means to transport goods and themselves to and from Plymouth, it quickly developed; by the late 12th century ships came to load up with locally mined tin, lead and silver ores. Later, the Industrial Revolution caused a huge demand for metals of all kinds; the hills of west Devon and east Cornwall were

"It became a busier port than even Liverpool. Vessels from Europe and further afield came to collect their precious ore."

rich in tin, lead, copper, arsenic and manganese, and these were shipped via Morwellham to south Wales, with its substantial coal supplies, for smelting. It was said that Morwellham's quayside sometimes held enough arsenic to poison the entire world! A canal was laboriously dug from Tavistock to facilitate transport.

In 1844, Europe's largest known copper lode was discovered just four miles from the quay, and Morwellham became a busier port than even Liverpool. Vessels from Europe and further afield came to collect their precious loads of ore. But then the copper began to run out. Eventually the company running the mine was forced to close, with huge loss of employment. The Great Western Railway's arrival at Tavistock superseded river transport; the great quays gradually fell silent, machinery rusted and the waterways silted up. After 1,000 years of activity, Morwellham Quay slept. In 1933 the canal was bought by the

West Devon Electric Supply Company, and the hydroelectric plant they built there still provides power to the National Grid.

Restoration began in 1970 and UNESCO designated the quay a World Heritage Site in 2006. Nowadays, costumed staff show off the quay's exhibits and help to recreate its 19th-century heyday. A riverside train carries visitors deep into the heart of the old George and Charlotte copper mine; children can dress up in period costume and join in with period activities; various traditional crafts (pottery, blacksmithing, etc) are demonstrated and the old cottages have been reopened, showing the furnishings of earlier times. The old Assayer's Workshop is there, and the Cooper's Workshop, and the Victorian village school. Echoes of the past are everywhere and staff work hard to bring it alive for visitors. Despite all the displays and demonstrations, it's hard to imagine the hectic buzz and clatter of earlier days when the great machines were turning; there's an enveloping sleepiness about the place. But it's still one of Devon's most unusual, atmospheric and historic sites.

EAST OF THE TAVY

Probably best known for Buckland Abbey, this area has plenty of other treasures. Dartmoor's heather and spacious views are only a mile or so away, but it's still an area of woodland and deep valleys, impregnated with the name of Drake.

12 YELVERTON

🏠 **Barnabas House** (page 339)
⛺ **Starbed Hideaways** (page 340)

This busy little village, a useful access hub for the surrounding area, is thoroughly geared towards passing traffic, with its petrol station, supermarket, pub (the Rock Inn), deli, post office and ATMs, but retains a lot of charm. A handy cycle hire/repair place is Rockin Bikes (Harrowbeer Mews ✆ 01822 258022). Frequent buses pass through to either Plymouth or Tavistock. Close by, as you take the main turning towards Buckland Abbey from the A386, you pass the old **RAF Harrowbeer Airfield** (⌖ rafharrowbeer.com, rafharrowbeer-dartmoor.org.uk), now grassed over and scenic with some chunky, Dartmoor-style outcrops of rock. Harrowbeer became operational in 1941 and was an important wartime RAF base; shops in Yelverton's main street had to have their upper storeys removed because of low-flying aircraft. Commemorative events are held annually, and there's an explanatory board at the site. In 1960 there was talk of it becoming Plymouth's airport, but there was strong local opposition and it was eventually demolished.

A few miles northeast of Yelverton on the Princetown road is **Burrator Reservoir** (✆ 01566 771930 ⌖ swlakestrust.org.uk), a multi-terrain area with walks, cycle rides or drives around the lake's perimeter, a dam, an arboretum, a lively interactive discovery centre and a network of footpaths, bridleways and off-road trails in the surrounding area. This is the very edge of Dartmoor, as the ponies ambling around it will remind you; you can enjoy open moorland or climb nearby Sheepstor, one of Dartmoor's most spectacular. I came across a pony suckling her very small and spindly foal. There are birds (robins, nuthatches, great tits...) along the wooded trails, as well as bluebells and primroses in season. You could spend as much of a day as you wanted here, just wandering across the different terrains. It's looked after by the South West Lakes Trust, as is Lopwell Dam (page 218), and there's news of current activities on their website.

WILD SWIMMING IN THE TAVY & WALKHAM RIVERS

Joanna Griffin

About two miles due north of Buckland Monachorum is Double Waters, where the River Walkham meets the Tavy. It's a lovely 1½-mile walk along the Walkham from Grenofen Bridge, through oak and birch woodlands, passing the chimney of the ruined West Down Mine, which was active for only 10 years and never profitable. The river is shallow and fast-flowing and tumbles its way towards the Tavy in a series of rapids, with some calm stretches in between. It is too shallow for swimming but it is possible to wallow in the shallows for a natural jacuzzi on a warm day.

There are better swimming areas around the confluence itself. As the Tavy curves round to meet the Walkham, there is a short calm stretch near the bank, but the current can be strong in parts and sweep you downstream if you're not careful. A wooden bridge takes you almost all of the way across the Walkham just before the rivers meet – it doesn't reach the other side so you'll have to paddle – and downstream there's a calmer stretch for swimming.

From here you can walk up on to West Down for far-reaching views, or to avoid a steep climb simply retrace your steps.

13 BUCKLAND MONACHORUM & AREA

The approach street of this village is so narrow that you proceed at your peril, but it broadens out at the church and the grand Lady Modiford's School, which she endowed in 1702 with an annual allowance for the schoolmaster of £7.10s.

The **church of St Andrew** is, at first glance, plain inside with a simple barrel roof, but then you notice the angels. They hang on the horizontal beams, wings half open, merrily playing a range of musical instruments. There's a Saxon font, looking like a cottage loaf, and the rather alarming Drake Chapel (not Sir Francis, but descendants of his brother Thomas) to the south of the nave. The huge Gibraltar Memorial to General Elliot, who successfully defended The Rock against Spain in 1779–83, is thickly planted with dead bodies and heroic words. There's no question which side God was on. The general married into the Drake family.

Close to Buckland Monachorum is **The Garden House** (PL20 7LQ ✆ 01822 854769 ⏣ thegardenhouse.org.uk ☉ end Mar–Oct 10.30–17.00 Tue–Sun), with a gorgeous mixture of formal and informal gardens. The colours are superb. Its ten acres include an arboretum, a wildflower meadow, a two-acre walled garden with smaller gardens inside, lawns, wonderful wisteria and a glade of acers which blaze red in the autumn. Perfect for strolling. The head gardener, Nick Haworth, was previously head gardener at Greenway, Agatha Christie's old home on the River Dart (page 133). There's a **tea room** serving light lunches, sumptuous cream teas and good home baking, or you can just sip a glass of wine and enjoy the view from the terrace. The house itself is the elegant former home of the vicars of Buckland Monachorum, built in the early 19th century.

14 BUCKLAND ABBEY

Yelverton PL20 6EY ✆ 01822 853607 ☉ house 11.00–16.30 Mar–Oct; National Trust

'The outside looks like a church but the inside feels like a home' says one of the introductory displays, and a home is indeed what Buckland Abbey became in the hands of Sir Richard Grenville of *Revenge* fame (page 218). His grandfather (also Richard) had bought the 270-year-old abbey plus 570 acres of land from Henry VIII in 1541, but did little to it.

The estate passed to three-year-old Richard in 1545 when his father Roger, captain of the *Mary Rose*, drowned when she sank. In the 1570s he began developing it, and decided to make his home in the church itself.

He demolished cloisters and monastic buildings, inserted fireplaces and added a new kitchen wing, as well as dividing the interior into three floors and creating the well-proportioned rooms. The great hall, with its fine plasterwork ceiling and decoration, was completed around 1576. Then in 1581 his money ran out and he sold the whole property – reluctantly, by all accounts – to Sir Francis Drake, who paid for it with spoils from his capture of the Spanish galleon *Nuestra Señora de la Concepción* in 1579. Drake also owned around 40 other properties and, although he lived there on and off for some 14 years, made no particular mark on it; but it remained in the Drake family (although with periods of disuse) until 1940 when it was presented to the National Trust.

On the way to the house you pass the **Great Barn**, a relic of the original Cistercian monastery that was founded here in 1278. 'Great' is inadequate: it's truly massive, with an amazing beamed roof and a huge cider press at one end. The spirit of the old monastery is evoked most strongly in this building; cowled monks could well be padding on soft sandalled feet through the shadows, their robes swishing in the dust.

Inside the house, there are paintings, documents, fine furniture, objets d'art, maps, weapons, ornaments – and of course Drake's drum, which, according to legend, will summon the old swashbuckler back to fight for England if his country ever needs his help. One of the paintings shows the surrender of the *Nuestra Señora del Rosario* (page 77).

The cavernous old kitchen gives some idea of the scale of the feasting, with space enough for cooks to handle whole carcases of meat. The Ox Yard Restaurant in the courtyard uses somewhat more modern equipment! Outside there are also craft workshops and a secondhand bookshop.

There's a full, year-round programme of events, including several for children, from bluebell and woodland walks to charcoal making, weaving, storytelling, concerts, a bug trail and historical re-enactments. Buckland Abbey is a place for all seasons – and for all weathers too, since you'll be well sheltered inside the house on a rainy day.

If you don't want to visit the house itself, for a reduced entrance fee you can just park and stroll around the grounds: meadows, orchards and three woodland walks along the River Tavy. There's a large car park. Trampers (mobility scooters) are available for hire. To reach Buckland Abbey by bus you'll need the 55 from Yelverton (not Sun), which you can reach by bus from Plymouth or Tavistock.

SIR RICHARD GRENVILLE & THE *REVENGE*

As a young man Richard studied at London's Inner Temple, then (aged 24) joined a brief 'crusade' against the Turks who had invaded Hungary. Next he bought land in Ireland and became involved in organising settlements there. He comes across as a somewhat obstinate and domineering character but a loyal and courageous leader, respected by his peers, although lacking Drake's easy charm.

Unlike his cousins Humphrey Gilbert and Walter Raleigh, he was not (apart from his father) from a particularly seafaring family, but he yearned for adventure, and in 1574 sought the Queen's permission to seek new lands and treasure south of the equator. However, she did not grant it. He owned ships and financed voyages but spent little time at sea, until in 1585 he was offered command of a voyage carrying 100 settlers to today's North Carolina, newly acquired for the crown by Raleigh. He embraced this new maritime career, for 'the pleasure of God on the seas', but it proved short-lived, as other commitments then kept him at home for several years. He became a commissioner for the coastal defences of Devon and Cornwall.

Finally, in 1591, came his finest hour. Captaining the *Revenge*, he was second-in-command to Lord Thomas Howard of a small squadron sent to tackle Spanish treasure ships off the Azores. The superior Spanish fleet caught them by surprise when they were at anchor; Howard ordered his ships to flee to safety but Grenville lagged behind to pick up

MILTON COMBE & LOPWELL DAM

About a mile south of the abbey is the almost inaccessible little village of **Milton Combe**, folded into a ravine like a pressed flower. The white cottages find a footing where they can, a stream runs through it and the pub stands in the square ready to reward your efforts to get here. It's called the Who'd Have Thought It.

Lopwell Dam and Nature Reserve (PL6 7BZ ✆ 01566 771930 ⌂ swlakestrust.org.uk) is also signposted from the A386. The superb river views (salt water meets fresh water here) make it worth the detour. It's also good for birdwatching, and is a designated Site of Special Scientific Interest. You may spot grey seals or otters, and it's one of the best areas in Devon for kingfishers. Across the river via a causeway is the 12-acre local nature reserve, an important habitat for a variety of saltmarsh species, with a woodland and marsh-side nature trail. The impressive mineshaft of Wheal Maristow dates back to the 13th century, as does Lopwell's history of lead and silver mining.

The small snag is that the causeway is above water for only two hours each side of low tide, so you'll need to check the tide table beforehand crew who were ashore ('waiting to recover the men that were upon the Island that had otherwise bene lost', wrote Raleigh later in his *Report of the Trueth of the fight about the Isles of the Açores*). He then tried to run the *Revenge* forward through the 15 advancing Spaniards but the great ships blocked his way and his wind. Still he could have escaped by turning tail but 'Sir Richard utterly refused to turne from the enemie, alleaging that hee would rather choose to die, than to dishonour himselfe, his countrey, and her Majesties shippe'. An astonishing 15 hour battle then raged, the little *Revenge* firing fiercely into the Spanish galleons and fighting their men hand-to-hand when they swarmed aboard. By dawn next day her masts and rigging had been shot away and she was badly holed. Sir Richard, grievously wounded, called on his gunner to sink her rather than let her fall into Spanish hands; but his seamen struck a bargain with the Spaniards, deserted their captain and surrendered. Sir Richard was taken to the Spanish flagship *San Pablo*, where he later died.

As the *Revenge* – a considerable prize – was being towed back to Spain, 'the water began to heave and the weather to moan' and a fearful storm arose. The *Revenge* was smashed on to rocks and broke apart, and many Spanish ships and men were also lost. Confrontation had turned to tragedy, Spain had suffered a grievous blow, and Sir Richard Grenville passed into heroic history.

and get the timing right. You can also pick up the Tamar Valley Discovery Trail (page 191) from here, going either northward (via the causeway) towards Bere Alston or else southward towards Tamerton Foliot and Plymouth.

SOUTHERN DARTMOOR

Head south from Yelverton and you'll quickly find yourself in a maze of high-banked narrow lanes that plunge down to river valleys and across gorse-bright moorland. There are some enjoyable walks in the area, perhaps the best being near **Shaugh Prior**, where the River Plym meanders its way eastward. The village itself has a pub, the White Thorn Inn, and St Edward's Church is worth a look for its unusual carved wooden font cover.

The best walk in the area is through the National Trust's **Dewerstone Wood**, a Site of Special Scientific Interest. Nearby, to the east, is Dewerston Rock, the remains of an Iron-Age fort. It's popular with rock climbers though they should bear in mind that the Devil (dewer is one

of his ancient names) is said to have a particularly jolly time around here, galloping about on a black horse with his equally dusky hounds, looking for hapless souls to chase over the rock to their deaths.

Continuing south by car or bike towards **Wotter** you'll pass through a lovely area of moorland, which in May was stunning in its gorse yellowness and scent.

15 DARTMOOR ZOO
PL7 5DG ☎ 01752 837645 ⌕ dartmoorzoo.org.uk

This zoo is only five miles from Plymouth near the village of Sparkwell, via a turning off the A38. It was the subject of the book *We Bought a Zoo* by Benjamin Mee, subsequently turned into a Hollywood film starring Matt Damon and Scarlett Johansson. It's a pleasantly laid-back place, and the helpful staff are happy to talk to visitors about the animals – which seem relaxed and well-cared-for.

Quite a bit of walking is involved as the enclosures are well spaced out; it's also a stiffish uphill walk from the car park, although the compensation is a good view of a family group of happy capybaras when you're halfway up. Notices pointing out how long it would take a cheetah or a frog to make the distance will either encourage or discourage you. There's parking for visitors with disabilities at the top. As well as the smaller animals (including meerkats and several reptiles and amphibians) there are most of the big cats – lion, tiger, jaguar, cheetah – plus otters, lynx, wolves, tapirs, zebras and ostriches. Regular events are held each day (feeding time, talks, close encounters and so on) and are listed on a board at the entrance. There's generally plenty for children to enjoy. The Jaguar Restaurant serves hot and cold meals and snacks.

Bus 59 from Plymouth's Royal Parade runs to the zoo four times a day (not Sun); see the zoo's website for times.

16 CORNWOOD & DELAMORE HOUSE
A few miles east of the zoo is the little village of Cornwood, a delightful place with an interesting church and a pub, and nearby is Delamore House

◄ **1** Garden House near Buckland Monachorum has a wonderful mix of formal and informal gardens. **2** The historic main house of Buckland Abbey. **3** Lopwell Dam is an excellent spot for birdwatching. **4** Enjoy the picturesque countryside around Cornwood. **5** RAF Harrowbeer in Yelverton was an important base in World War II.

and gardens (open only in May), worth travelling across the county to see if you love gardens and art. Here there is the perfect combination.

First, **Cornwood**. The village has a Raleigh connection: Sir Walter's grandfather lived in Fardel Manor and probably worshipped in the 13th-century **church of St Michael and All Angels**, which was looking particularly lovely when I visited, with the flower ladies out in force preparing for their flower festival. There's plenty of interest, from the driftwood cross at the altar to the intricately carved Jacobean pulpit: more flowers, but this time Tudor roses. Worshippers are watched over by a heavenly host of gilded angels on the ceiling and in a side chapel is the very touching effigy of a child, John Savery, who died in 1696. Part of the inscription reads: 'That he has taught us by his hasting hence / That the earth's too vile for soe much innocence / Reader relent since thou noe more shall see / This matchless childe but in his effigie.' Opposite little John is an Elizabethan couple, wearing ruffs.

"There's plenty of interest, from the driftwood cross at the altar to the intricately carved Jacobean pulpit."

Delamore House (PL21 9QT ☏ 01752 837236 ⌨ delamore-art.co.uk ⊙ May 10.30–16.30 daily), built in 1859 from Dartmoor granite, was designed by James Piers St Aubyn, who was best known as a church architect, which explains the somewhat ecclesiastical feel of the house. For one month each year it plays host to local, national and international artists whose work is on display in both the house and gardens, where sculptures vie for attention with the magnificent azaleas and rhododendrons, and lurk beside woodland paths. All the work is for sale at very reasonable prices, and the proceeds go to charity. The former servants' kitchen serves as a **café** with soup, sandwiches and a delicious selection of home baking.

17 IVYBRIDGE & SOUTH BRENT

While they may lack the charm and interest of the region's other small towns, these two do their job as gateways to Dartmoor, with convenient shops and pubs.

Ivybridge

Tourist information: The Watermark, Leonards Rd, PL21 0SZ ☏ 01752 879035 ⊙ closed Wed & Sat afternoons & all day Sun. (It's a desk inside the public library, with leaflets & helpful staff.)

Ivybridge is well served by trains and buses and beautifully located, right on the edge of Dartmoor. It's the starting point of the original Two Moors Way (page 283), and is also on NCN 2. The River Erme runs through the town and the original stone Ivy Bridge, dating back to 1250 and painted by Turner in 1813, is still in situ. The paper mill built in 1787 produced fine paper, even foreign banknotes, for more than 250 years, closing in 2013. The viaduct in Longtimber Woods on the edge of the town was designed and built by Sir James Inglis in 1892 to replace an earlier viaduct from 1848 built by Isambard Kingdom Brunel. Its railway station has ample parking space and is an unofficial 'park and ride' site for Plymouth, just 15 minutes along the line. There are a couple of good places to buy lunch. The **Country Maid** on Fore Street offers a good range of sandwiches and paninis, while **Warrens Bakery** in Glanville Road is the best place for pasties; they have been making them since 1860.

South Brent

Described in *The King's England* as 'a grey little town', South Brent, around five miles north of Ivybridge along the A38, has brightened up considerably since the 1960s with some gaily painted houses and shops. The **church of St Petroc** contains interesting items: St Petroc himself is shown in a carving near the choir, accompanied by his faithful dog (or tame wolf), and there are some good modern carvings. A set of stocks stands in the porch.

Half a mile north of the town, on the edge of Dartmoor, is an exceptionally pretty ancient packhorse bridge, **Lydia Bridge**, which spans the River Avon, with its tangled overhanging greenery and splashy waterfalls.

Two miles southwest along the Dartmoor Way is **Lady Wood**, managed by the Devon Wildlife Trust particularly for the conservation of hazel dormice. At the far end is an impressive Brunel viaduct, a twin to the one in Ivybridge. The bluebells here provide a wonderful display in the spring although, I'm sorry to say, they are hybrid.

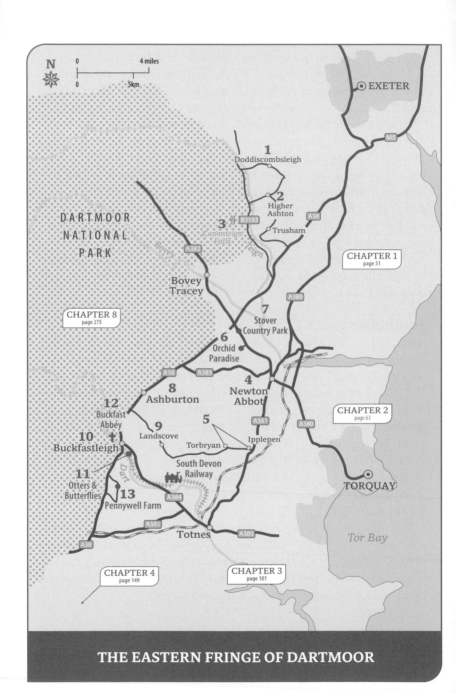

N

0   4 miles

0   5km

⦿ **EXETER**

M5

1 Doddiscombsleigh

2 Higher Ashton

A38

⦿ Trusham

3 *Canonteign Falls*

B3193

Teign

DARTMOOR NATIONAL PARK

Bovey

A382

Bovey Tracey

CHAPTER 1
page 31

A380

7 Stover Country Park

CHAPTER 8
page 275

6 Orchid Paradise

A38   A383

8 Ashburton

4 Newton Abbot

1·2 Buckfast Abbey

5

A381

CHAPTER 2
page 63

A380

9 Landscove

Torbryan

Ipplepen

10 Buckfastleigh

Dart

South Devon Railway

⦿ **TORQUAY**

11 Otters & Butterflies

13 Pennywell Farm

A384

A385

CHAPTER 4
page 149

A38

Totnes

A385

CHAPTER 3
page 101

Tor Bay

THE EASTERN FRINGE OF DARTMOOR

6
THE EASTERN FRINGE OF DARTMOOR

The River Teign turns south at Dunsford and forms the eastern border of Dartmoor National Park before its final journey to Kingsteignton and Teignmouth. Although technically some of the towns and villages in this section lie within the national park, their gentler, leafier character fits better here. Despite their relative proximity to Exeter and Newton Abbot, it's surprising how remote some of them feel.

Along the river are some of the prettiest wooded areas of Dartmoor, splashed by waterfalls and networked by footpaths and narrow lanes. England's highest waterfall, Canonteign Falls, is here, as are Stover Park with its inspirational Ted Hughes Poetry Trail and nearby the unique Orchid Paradise in Burnham Nurseries. Then there's popular Buckfastleigh, whose attractions include the South Devon Railway, Buckfast Abbey, the Valiant Soldier (known as 'The pub where time was never called') and the enchanting miniature pigs at Pennywell Farm. The 14th-century stannary town of Ashburton offers intriguing glimpses of its past, while Ipplepen and Torbryan have exceptional churches. And you may more than once catch a passing echo of Conan Doyle's great detective himself, deerstalker at the ready and John Watson hot on his heels.

 ## WET-WEATHER ACTIVITIES

GETTING THERE & AROUND

Drivers will find this one of the most easily accessible regions, with all the places described lying near the A38 from Exeter. It's once you leave that dual carriageway to track down the little villages that you're in trouble without a satnav.

Buses from Exeter serve Newton Abbot, Ashburton and Buckfastleigh and pass near Stover Country Park; others call at Ipplepen, Landscove and Doddiscombsleigh; but reaching some attractions involves a bit of walking too. You need the Teignbridge bus timetable or the interactive map on ⊘ traveldevon.info.

Newton Abbot is on the direct **railway** line from Exeter to Plymouth, but the cream of the getting-there options in terms of charm is the steam train run by the South Devon Railway between Totnes and Buckfastleigh (page 240).

SELF-POWERED TRAVEL

For walkers and cyclists this region's lanes are typically hilly and narrow, but with strong legs you could see all its major sights in a day. The Stover Trail is a flat, traffic-free, 3½-mile multi-use route which connects Newton Abbot to Bovey Tracey, crossing the busy A38 on a bridge. Created as part of the £4.4 million Granite and Gears project that created new walking and cycling opportunities on Dartmoor, it passes alongside Stover Country Park and connects with the Wray Valley Trail to Lustleigh and Moretonhampstead. Otherwise, there's not as much scope as in some other areas, but more good possibilities can be devised using the Teignbridge bus timetable and Ordnance Survey Explorer map OL110 (for the north of the region) along with Explorer map OL28. None of the excellent Croydecycle maps cover this region. Walkers can access Haytor on Dartmoor along the Templer Way (page 309), which runs through this region from Teignmouth.

THE NORTHERN TEIGN VALLEY

🏠 **Cridford Inn** Trusham (page 340) & **Nobody Inn** Doddiscombsleigh (page 340)

Hidden in the hills of the east side of the Teign, Doddiscombsleigh and Higher Ashton have exceptional churches, while Canonteign Falls provide a dramatic cascade of water in cool, ferny woodland.

1 DODDISCOMBSLEIGH

This little hidden village attracts both church crawlers and pub crawlers. 'Everybody knows the Nobody', they say, and indeed the Nobody Inn (page 231) has been there for centuries, although prior to the mid 18th century it was a cottage. The name evolved from The New Inn to The No Body Inn 'with reference to an unfortunate episode concerning a dead landlord'.

St Michael's Church has been providing spiritual refreshment for even longer: it has the finest medieval stained-glass windows in the county, and the original church probably predates the Norman Conquest. It's built from an aesthetically pleasing mixture of local stone of various colours, including granite from nearby Dartmoor. Inside it's curiously square, with two aisles, and the famous windows can be observed at eye level since they and the wagon roof are exceptionally low. This makes it easy for the visitor to appreciate their craftsmanship and imagination, and brings a feeling of intimacy. To quote the Shell Guide, 'the artist has looked at men without romanticising but with much charity'.

"It has the finest medieval stained-glass windows in the county; the original church probably predates the Norman Conquest."

Indeed. I loved the tired face of St Paul, shielding his right eye with one hand. And also St George's cute little horse, which looks more like a sheep. Then there's St Michael, weighing souls. A little demon is trying to tip the balance but the good are apparently heavy

THE DEVIL'S BITE

Carved at the top of one of the stone capitals in St Michael's Church is a face. It's not a green man, nor a saint or angel. It has funny pointed ears, unusual foliage, and something strange about its mouth. Dr Michael Tisdall is a medical doctor with a passion for the unusual in Devon churches, so he has teased out the (probable) truth here. This carving is at the west end of the church, often called the Devil's End (indeed, some old churches have a little opening through which the Devil can escape during services), and he has a hare lip. As a young doctor studying children's diseases, Dr Tisdall came across the expression 'Devil's bite' to describe a hare lip. And the foliage isn't the usual rose leaves, it's *Succisa pratensis*, or Devil's bit scabious. So there we have it. A medieval carver portrayed the Devil in an instantly recognisable form – to the villagers of his day – but for us it takes the detective work of a knowledgeable enthusiast to get to the truth.

enough to defeat his efforts. The complicated seven sacraments window at the east end of the aisle is more difficult to see, but there's a good description of it in the church booklet, and photos on the wall showing the detail.

The capitals at the top of the columns are finely carved with foliage; the two that are partially set into the walls at each end of the north aisle are worth studying. At the altar end is a frowning green man, and at the west end, near the organ, is the very intriguing harelipped Devil, which would escape anyone's notice if it hadn't been pointed out by Dr Michael Tisdall (page 227).

Surprisingly, given the remoteness of this little village, the 360 bus from Exeter runs here four times a day (Monday to Saturday), so you can view the church and have lunch at the inn without the worry of either finding the place or parking.

2 HIGHER ASHTON

About 1½ miles south of Doddiscombsleigh, Higher Ashton is a pretty village of thatched, whitewashed houses set on a steep hill. The **church of St John the Baptist** is renowned for its medieval rood screen, intricately carved to set off the 32 panels with their painted saints. The church leaflet is helpful in explaining who's who. You'll easily identify well-known saints such as St Sebastian with his arrows (although he is headless), and a baby-faced St George in full armour killing a tiny dragon. This seems a particularly unfair contest since the dragon is depicted with a dog's body and looks as though it's just been woken from a nap. Among the more obscure ones is St Apollonia (page 230) looking speculatively at a huge tooth held in the blacksmith's pincers. There is a wall monument to smug Sir George Chudleigh (1657) who fathered nine sons and nine daughters, and a fascinating commemorative stone embedded in the floor, crudely carved, with September and October written as 7ber and 8ber – the first time I have seen this abbreviation. By the entrance is a list of rectors from 1249 to 1996.

There's nowhere to park near the church; leave your car in the village car park.

---

1 This part of the Teign Valley has a gentle, leafy feel. **2** Doddiscombsleigh's church has the finest medieval stained-glass windows in the county. **3** Canonteign Falls is the highest waterfall in England. ▶

ver of water of life
ar as crystal

The leaves of the tree wh
for the healing of the nati

PETER J HATCHER/A

PETER BROOKS – MOOR & MORE IMAGES

ST APOLLONIA & ST BARBARA

It's not clear to me why a woman who had all her teeth smashed with giant tongs becomes the patron saint of dentists. However, she appears on so many Devon rood screens that it's worth knowing something about her.

Apollonia lived in Alexandria in the 3rd century AD. She led an exemplary life, preaching the gospel during a time when this held considerable risks. Emperor Philip was none too keen on Christians, especially those like Apollonia who gave succour to his political prisoners. In AD249 she was arrested and, inevitably, tortured to persuade her to renounce her faith. All her teeth were smashed and then pulled out with iron pincers. When this had no effect, her torturers piled up firewood, intending to burn her to death, but she leapt into the flames all by herself, thus presenting the church with something of a dilemma: did she commit suicide (a sin) or was she a true martyr, dying for her faith? They chose the latter and sanctification.

Devon has 14 depictions of St Apollonia holding her torturer's pincers (the kind used by blacksmiths, so not really suitable for dentistry). These are usually on painted rood screens or stained glass but one of those, in Stokeinteignhead, is carved into a stone capital.

If explosives are your thing, then St Barbara is your patron saint. Possessed of exceptional beauty and intelligence, she was kept locked in a tower by her father who had a rich suitor in mind. Here she converted to Christianity and managed to escape, only to fall into the hands of a shepherd. Before he could have his wicked way with her, divine punishment turned his sheep into beetles. Her father then contrived that she should be paraded naked throughout the region, but God supplied her with a robe. Frustrated, Dad then got fed up and killed her with his sword, whereupon he was struck dead by a thunderbolt. So St Barbara is now the patron saint of artillerymen and their like, also 'those in danger of sudden death'.

3 CANONTEIGN FALLS

EX6 7RH ✆ 01647 252434 ⊘ canonteignfalls.co.uk ⊙ Mar–Oct 10.00–16.00 daily

⋏ Hennock Hideaways (page 340)

This is one of Devon's superlatives, the highest waterfall in England (220ft), but it's also manmade, which takes the gloss off a bit. Nevertheless it's popular with families who relish the challenge of climbing the 90 steps to the top of the falls. And hats off to the enterprise of the ten generations of Lords of the Manor who have played their part in creating this tourist attraction. The house is on the site of a monastery owned by the canons of St Mary du Val in Normandy, hence the name Canonteign. After the Dissolution of the Monasteries it was converted into a manor house, which was eventually bought by Admiral Edward Pellew, later Lord Exmouth. His descendants enjoyed a period of prosperity in the 19th century through the nearby lead and silver mines, respectively Frank Mills (named after its owner, a banker) and Wheal Exmouth. In the 1880s the mines fell into decline and the miners found themselves out of a job. But then the third Lady Exmouth stepped in with the idea of putting them to work again by diverting the leat that formerly serviced the mine to create a waterfall tumbling over natural rocks for the enjoyment of family and friends. It, and the nearby paths, fell into disrepair after World War II and it was not until 1985 that the tenth Lord Exmouth rediscovered the walk and decided to open it to the public.

In the grounds are a couple of lakes with resident waterfowl, and some gentle paths for those unwilling to tackle the climb up to the falls. Helpful labels tell you what you're looking at, and there's a recreation of a Victorian fern garden complete with tree ferns. There is also a small dog-friendly café and a shop.

On leaving, if you turn left at the road you'll see the tall chimneys of the former Wheal Exmouth lead mine adjacent to the engine house, now a thoughtfully converted three-storey private home. There are two chimneys, one circular with finely worked corbels, and the other octagonal, topless and with trees billowing out of its ragged opening instead of smoke. The whole complex is both scenic and historic, spanning the commercial history of the area from mining to 'grand design' conversion.

¶¶ FOOD & DRINK

Cridford Inn Trusham TQ13 0NR ✆ 01626 853694 ⬨ thecridfordinn.co.uk. The village (just south of Lower & Upper Ashton) has some thatched cottages plus this charming pub (also thatched, & a former longhouse). It claims to be one of the oldest inns in the country & contains what is thought to be Britain's oldest domestic window. Its restaurant (with a mural dating back to 1081) serves seriously good food, & its bar offers own-label beer & over 90 gins. It also has B&B rooms & a holiday cottage (page 340). Worth a detour.

Nobody Inn Doddiscombsleigh EX6 7PS ✆ 01647 252394 ⬨ nobodyinn.co.uk. The food at this curiously named place (page 227) is terrific & has won many awards. A cosy pub with an open fire in winter, a beer garden in the summer, cheery staff & happy locals, it competes with the nearby Cridford for a gastronomic treat. Plus an alcoholic one: the pub can offer you around 240 different whiskies (!) & quite a few gins. Also has rooms (page 340).

NEWTON ABBOT & AREA

Attractions in this area are easily reached from either Newton Abbot or Ashburton, and include butterflies, railway museums, Sherlock Holmes and Roman remains.

4 NEWTON ABBOT

Tourist information: 6 Indoor Market, Market St ✆ 01626 215667 ⊙ 09.00–13.30 & 14.00–16.00 Mon–Sat

Although this busy town is a bit hectic for Slow visitors, it's the starting point for the Haytor Hoppa (page 280), and there's a big outdoor market on Wednesdays and Saturdays. The modern **Newton Abbot Museum** (Wolborough Street ✆ 01626 201121 ⊛ museum-newtonabbot.org. uk ⊙ 09.30–16.30 Tue–Fri, 09.30–13.30 Sat) is a fine example of how engaging modern museums can be. The museum is in a beautifully restored Victorian church and has exhibits relating to (among many other 'notable Newtonians') Isambard Kingdom Brunel and the 18th-century wreck-salvage pioneer and inventor John Lethbridge, complete with his 1715 underwater diving machine. Many of the displays are 'hands on': there is a GWR signal box, with working levers and signals, and an original section of Brunel's atmospheric railway, together with a model of the atmospheric system. Newton Abbot's railway history began in 1846, when Brunel and South Devon Railway board agreed to open Newton Station the following year, and developed so energetically that the town became known as the 'Swindon of the West' because of all its workshops and sheds. Interactive map displays show how dramatically the town was changed over time by the railways. There are also easily accessible audio, film and photo archives that bring the history of Newton Abbot to life.

"A past winner of CAMRA's Cider Pub of the Year award, this is one of the country's few remaining true cider houses."

Cider lovers should head for **Ye Olde Cider Bar** in East Street (✆ 01626 354221 🅵), a basic traditional pub with lots of atmosphere and a huge array of ciders from local independent producers; occasional live music too. A past winner of CAMRA's Cider Pub of the Year award, this is one of the few remaining true cider houses in the country.

5 IPPLEPEN & TORBRYAN

These two villages, only a few miles apart, are remarkable for their churches, which give us so much superb carving in such a small area, yet their medieval congregations probably considered each other to be far away.

Ipplepen

St Andrew's Church is huge; it has a particularly magnificent rood screen, with inset saints and fan vaulting, and a 15th-century carved and painted pulpit resting on an old millstone. Sir Arthur Conan Doyle visited the village before writing his well-known *Hound of the Baskervilles*; living there at the time were his friend Bertram Fletcher Robinson, who lent Doyle his coachman Henry Baskerville to drive him around; and the Reverend Robert Duins Cooke (1859–1939), who regaled him with tales and information about Dartmoor. Robinson's home at Park Hill House and Baskerville's at 2 Wesley Terrace both still exist, and the gravestones of Cooke and Robinson can be seen in the churchyard. See also the box on page 334 by Cooke's great-grandson, Alex Graeme.

Ipplepen is also helping to rewrite Roman history. It was previously thought that Roman influence in Devon had not extended far south of Exeter. However, a series of archaeological excavations, prompted by the discovery (by metal detectors) of many Roman coins in Ipplepen in 2009, unearthed traces of a Roman road (possibly heading towards the Totnes area), and early remnants of bowls and amphorae from France and the Mediterranean that once held wine and olive oil. An early Christian cemetery (mid 7th century) beside the road indicates continued occupation of the site.

Torbryan

🏠 **Old Church House Inn** Torbryan (page 340)

This tiny hamlet was described by Hoskins in 1954 as having 'perhaps the most uniformly attractive village church in Devon'. Unusually, it was built in a single span of 20 years, from 1450 to 1470, making the resulting structure far more unified than one completed over a longer period. Also unusually, workmen would still have been young enough to finish the work that they started. What makes **Holy Trinity Church** exceptional, however, is that there has been no architectural messing around with its interior since it was built in the 15th century. It has the lime-washed exterior characteristic of Devon, and clear glass windows that let in plenty of light to set off the carved, polychromed oak screen, said to have been among the best-preserved medieval rood screens in Britain. But in 2013 two of its painted panels – representing St Victor of Marseilles and St Margaret of Antioch – were hacked out roughly by thieves, leaving a gaping hole. Two years later a sharp-eyed art collector spotted them in an online sale and alerted the police; in 2016, after £7,000-worth of repairs (to woodworm as well as damage from the theft) they were replaced, to great local delight. Together with many other panel paintings of saints in Devon churches they are reproduced in *A Cloud of Witnesses* by Diane Wilks (page 27). Holy Trinity is now cared for by the Churches Conservation Trust.

The old church house, dating from the 14th century or earlier, is now the Old Church House Inn, which is no longer open as an inn but can be rented as self-catering accommodation sleeping 24 (page 340), for those who don't mind ghosts! Retaining a host of old features, it's said to be one of the most haunted pubs in the southwest. It has one of England's oldest bread ovens, and panelling retrieved from a ship of the Spanish Armada.

6 ORCHID PARADISE

Burnham Nurseries, Forches Cross TQ12 6PZ ✆ 01626 352233 ⌂ orchids.uk.com ⊙ 10.00–15.00 Mon–Fri & one weekend a month

Anyone who loves the variety and beauty of orchids should be extremely happy here. Burnham Nurseries has a 'growing area' of interconnecting greenhouses containing orchids that are for sale, with careful instructions as to what conditions they prefer; while Orchid Paradise itself, in a smaller area, is crammed with delights: a private collection of rare (and sometimes amazing) plants accumulated over many years. It includes specimens from around the globe, many of which are nowhere else to be seen in the UK. Apart from the colours, the aroma is astonishing: a mixture of sweet, earthy and indefinable.

---

1 Enjoy a walk around peaceful Stover Country Park. **2** Newton Abbot Museum is in a beautifully restored church. **3** The exceptional 15th-century Holy Trinity Church in Torbryan. **4** Ashburton still holds an annual ale-tasting and bread-weighing ceremony. **5** Orchid Paradise features orchids from around the world. ▶

A family business since 1949 and 20-time gold-medal-winners at the Chelsea Flower Show, they have also contributed to the survival of orchids, propagating many rare species threatened with extinction. Arthur, the nursery manager, told me proudly that he has been working there for 46 years, and his boss is the third generation of her family to run it.

Masterclasses in orchid-keeping are held, plus orchid clinics. If you fall in love with a plant (and they are so seductive!) but can't take it with you on holiday, ask about mail order. The light and airy café, Café Vanilla, has good home baking and snacks, and also sells a selection of locally produced goods together with vanilla items (of course, since vanilla is an orchid…).

7 STOVER COUNTRY PARK
TQ12 6QG ℘ 01626 835236 ⊘ devon.gov.uk/stovercountrypark/visitor-information

Whoever thought up the idea of linking poetry with nature in this country park deserves an award. Stover is one of those agreeable places which has 'nothing to see' yet everything to observe. Within its 114 acres it brings you over heathland thick with gorse and heather, through deciduous trees and coniferous forests, along the banks of a river, adjacent to a tumbling stream and around a lake where herons stand sentinel among the reeds. A 100yd wheelchair-accessible aerial walkway overlooks ponds and woodland. The interpretation boards and the visitor centre are informative, and the place is child-friendly in the right way – for example, they have their own brass-rubbing trail, ten plaques with creatures on them hidden around the lake. No coloured plastic, just an attention-grabbing introduction to the wonders of nature. And then there's the Ted Hughes Poetry Trail and a short Children's Poetry Trail. You may not have thought that you liked his poems (indeed many of them are pretty gloomy) but the 16 chosen here – about birds, fish and animals,

"The trail's poems are accessible and perfect for the surroundings. It's a wonderfully Slow and peaceful occupation."

and the natural world in general – are accessible and perfect for the surroundings. Sadly, for copyright reasons, they haven't been published in a booklet, so you need to read them carefully in situ. It's a wonderfully Slow and peaceful occupation that takes about two hours. The park is 300yds south of the Drumbridges roundabout on the A382 and bus 39

(Exeter to Newton Abbot) passes by. Cycle routes link it to Bovey Tracey and Newton Abbot: the 3½-mile Stover Trail (page 226) runs alongside, and Stover's 4½-mile circular Heritage Trail (waymarked from near the visitor centre) links up with the Templer Way (page 309).

8 ASHBURTON

🏠 **Over Lemon River** (page 340)
Tourist information: Kingsbridge Ln, TQ13 7DX (behind Town Hall) 𝒜 01364 653426
𝒸 ashburton.org ⊙ 10.00–13.00 Tue–Sat

One of Devon's four 14th-century stannary towns (page 279), along with Tavistock, Chagford and Plympton, Ashburton manages to combine its historic past with some energetic modern bustle. It's Slow only if you're trying to ease your car through its busy streets – but there are some attractive old buildings, a good scattering of unusual independent shops and a warm sense of community. The small **Ashburton Museum** (𝒜 08081 203865 ⊙ May–Sep 14.00–16.00 Tue, Thu & Fri–Sat), housed in a former brush factory in the centre of town, has a collection of miscellaneous local memorabilia and – rather surprisingly – North American artefacts. The 13th-century **Chapel of St Lawrence** in St Lawrence Lane, one of Ashburton's oldest buildings, started life as the private chapel of the Bishop of Exeter, then for more than 600 years was the town's grammar school. Some of the detail on its 18th-century decorative plasterwork is among the most impressive in any public building in Devon. It's now a heritage centre, open for a couple of hours four days a week from May to September, and also for talks and concerts (𝒸 stlawrencechapel.org.uk). Henry Baskerville, the coachman who drove Sir Arthur Conan Doyle around Dartmoor (page 334), lived in Ashburton and is buried in the churchyard of St Andrew's.

The mixture of shops includes just about everything, from a guitar maker to Gnash, a shop dedicated to graphic novels, with some good-quality clothing, crafts and house furnishings. It's also becoming consciously quite a foodie town (the Food Festival in September is a big and colourful affair; 🇫), in the sense that excellent local meat, fish, delicatessen and vegetables are available. A great treat (or temptation) is **Moor Chocolate** at 18 East Street, with its array of traditional and newer sweets and chocolate, and if you value really good baking do buy homemade breads and cakes from **Briar Bakery** (9 West St ⊙ Wed–Sat), but get there early – she sells out. All the banks have closed, but the

ALE TASTERS, SCAVENGERS & PIG DROVERS

Ashburton is one of only a handful of towns in Britain to have retained the old Saxon office of Portreeve, dating back to AD820 and meaning the 'reeve' or supervisory official of a 'port' or trading centre. In those days the portreeve was often the only person in the community who could read and write, and his chief duty was to represent the king in legal transactions. Today Ashburton's portreeve may have rather less need to represent His Majesty but is still elected annually, in November, along with their bailiff, bread weighers, ale tasters and other lesser officers such as Viewers of the Market, Viewers of Water Courses, Tree Inspector, Searcher and Sealer of Leather, Scavengers and Pig Drovers. You'll understand how vital these are for the smooth running of any 21st-century town.

Before Magna Carta there was no official check on the quality of ale or bread, and the first Ale Connors were appointed in London in 1276. Soon afterwards, there are records of brewers in Ashburton being fined for selling substandard ale. The tradition is renewed annually with an ale-tasting and bread-weighing ceremony in July, followed by a colourful medieval fair. Special breads baked for the fair are auctioned off for local charities. One woman told me: 'As soon as there's a celebration of any kind, everyone pitches in and we have a right knees-up.'

For more on this, see ⊘ ashburton.org.

post office on St Lawrence Lane provides what banking facilities it can (including an ATM) and also houses the public library.

On the front of the Old Exeter Inn in West Street is a painting of Sir Walter Raleigh who was apparently a regular drinker at the Inn, as allegedly was Sir Francis Drake. Sir Walter was arrested here in 1603 before being taken to the Tower, accused of plotting against King James I.

9 LANDSCOVE

Between Ashburton and Buckfastleigh and four miles or so from each, this small village is home to **Hill House Nursery** (TQ13 7LY ℘ 01803 762273 ⊘ hillhousenursery.com ⊙ Mar–Oct 11.00–17.00 daily), which has been described as being 'awash with treasures and temptations' in the several greenhouses and well-tended nursery. It also has pleasant gardens – you may spot a magnolia that came from Dame Agatha Christie's garden at Greenway (page 133). The nursery is tucked away behind the village church of St Matthew; in fact Hill House (which is not open to the public) used to be the church's vicarage. The network of lanes leading to Landscove are a bit of a tangle and some signs are hard to spot; if you miss the turning from the A38 southwest of Ashburton, then from Buckfastleigh follow the A384 towards Totnes and about quarter of a mile after the Dartbridge Inn take the first turning left, signposted Landscove and Hill House. If you find yourself at the church – its steeple is easily seen from afar – you can leave your car in the car park opposite and walk through the graveyard to the gardens.

Lunch at the Nursery Tea Room (☉ summer only 11.00–17.00) is a treat, with outdoor tables and a terrific selection of salads, sandwiches and scrumptious cakes as well as cream teas. To drink there are organic fruit juices and a good variety of wine and cider.

⍩ FOOD & DRINK

Ashburton Cookery School Old Exeter Rd, TQ13 7LG ✆ 01364 652784 ⟁ ashburtoncookeryschool.co.uk. The school runs a variety of cookery courses, from half a day to a week or weekend. B&B accommodation is available too, & the receptionist told me that some couples split their holidays so that one partner cooks by day while the other – the cookery widow or widower – follows some alternative pursuit. Courses cover a huge range: bread making, chocolate making, macarons, Indian, Mexican, Thai & much more. Several of the chefs whose food you will taste around Devon were trained or refreshed here.

Hill House Nursery Tea Room (see above).

Tea at Taylors 5 North St, Ashburton ✆ 01364 652631 ⬛ ☉ Mon–Sat, hours vary. A welcoming, traditional English tea room renowned for its delicious selection of homemade cakes. The carrot cake is so good that Mary Berry, who tried some when she was passing through Ashburton, asked for the recipe & included it in her next cookery book. Also cream teas & light savoury dishes.

The Old Library Restaurant North St, Ashburton ✆ 01364 652896 ⟁ theoldlibraryrestaurant.co.uk ☉ 09.00–16.00 Tue–Sat. Attractively designed to give a light & airy feel to a smallish space, this is run by a couple who really care about food & add innovative touches to their European-influenced dishes. Vegetarian friendly. First come, first served – no bookings.

BUCKFASTLEIGH & AREA

Tourist information: 80 Fore St, Buckfastleigh ✆ 01364 644522 ⟁ buckfastleigh.gov.uk ☉ Apr–Oct 10.00–15.30 Wed–Sat

Here we have attractions ranging from otters, caves and miniature pigs, through a pub in a time warp and a vintage steam railway to leaf-cutter ants and prehistoric bones. No shortage of variety!

10 BUCKFASTLEIGH

Buckfastleigh is a tourist hub which deserves its popularity. Its name – buck-fast – indicates a stronghold, traditionally where deer were kept. Today it's a pleasant and somewhat sleepy town, but with many attractions within easy reach, and is the terminus/start of the steam train that runs between here and Totnes. This tranquillity contrasts with its earlier life as a buzzing industrial centre, with woollen mills, corn and paper mills and a tannery: in 1838 it had 700 looms in action, more than any other town in Devon.

"It offers the older generation a burst of nostalgia: the pub area is still as it was more than 50 years ago."

The tourist information centre is conveniently next to **The Valiant Soldier** (✆ 01364 644522 ⌖ valiantsoldier.org.uk ⊙ Apr–Oct 10.00–15.00 Wed–Sat), the town's most unusual attraction and well worth a browse. It's known as 'The pub where time was never called'. When the brewery withdrew its licence in 1965 it seems that the landlords, Mr and Mrs Roberts, who'd run the pub for 27 years, simply said 'sod this', locked up, and walked away. They continued to live upstairs, but left the pub area as untouched as if their last customers had only just stepped out into the street. It was only after Alice Roberts, then widowed, sold the property in the mid 1990s that anyone realised what had happened, and Teignbridge council stepped in and bought the premises. Now owned by the Buckfastleigh Trust, it offers the older generation a burst of nostalgia: the pub area is still as it was more than 50 years ago, when Bass was 1/2½ (less than 6p) a bottle. The only nostalgia you can't indulge in is an actual pint. Upstairs, the rooms have been turned into surprisingly touching representations of village rooms of that period, with personal and household items – clothing, toiletries, a vintage radio playing old tunes, an old Singer sewing machine, framed family photos – that those of us of a certain age remember so well. There is one room where the display changes each year; currently the exhibition is about the history of the local pubs.

The South Devon Railway

✆ 01364 644370 ⌖ southdevonrailway.co.uk

Continuing the nostalgia theme, the South Devon Railway has it in dollops. Just a peep through the carriage windows at the compartments brings back a flood of memories to oldies, as do the acrid smell of

SQUIRE RICHARD CABELL
& THE HOLY TRINITY CHURCH

Buckfastleigh's Holy Trinity Church is now an evocative ruin, though its spire can be seen for miles around as a reminder of the devilish forces at work on Dartmoor. The church was burned down beyond repair in 1992 when an intruder lit a fire beneath the altar. Was this the work of Satanists? Read on...

In the graveyard is what looks like a summerhouse with a grille over the window. This is the burial chamber of the Cabell family. Richard Cabell was lord of the manor in the 17th century. He married a local heiress whom he is said subsequently to have hunted to her death with a pack of ferocious black hounds.

Another version is that he had his throat torn out by his wife's loyal hound as he stabbed her to death. They say that he is buried in the family tomb, weighed down with a large stone to prevent him from getting out – not that this worked, since his headless ghost still haunts the moor. Sir Arthur Conan Doyle heard the stories when he was staying with a friend in Ipplepen (page 233), and was driven around the area by coachman Henry Baskerville!

That's the stuff of legends, but the reality is that this clearly unpleasant man, who took his wife's money and probably drove her to her death even if he didn't actually kill her, interred her in the tomb with the inscription: 'Here lies Susannah, wife of Richard Cabell, who was buried in linen.' Linen was the fabric of the nobility. The lower orders were required to wrap their corpses in wool to keep the local industry going, so Richard was openly flouting this rule. The tomb's iron grille was left in place, at the pleading of the villagers, during World War II when the government was requisitioning all iron railings; the parishioners of the Holy Trinity Church were taking no chances with their local villain. And when the church burnt down some local people said that it was the curse of Richard Cabell, and the floor of the tomb was strewn with home-made 'Palm Sunday' crosses.

These days youngsters dare each other to come up to the tomb after dark, walk round it 13 times (or maybe seven, accounts vary) in an anticlockwise direction, and then put their hand through the bars to see whether Squire Cabell (or the Devil) bites their fingers off.

the steam and the breathy toot of the whistle. The scenic branch line of the Great Western Railway running alongside the River Dart, built in 1872, was axed by Dr Beeching in 1958, but only 11 years later it was reopened – ironically by Dr Beeching himself – and this service between Buckfastleigh and Totnes is now run by a charitable trust and operated by volunteers.

Buckfastleigh's vintage railway station is a delight, with its evocative advertisements and memorabilia. A venerable old engine named *Lady*

Angela, built in 1926, was parked there when I visited, with a notice saying that she was 'in the queue for a full boiler overhaul'. I felt a surge of sympathy. There's also a spacious refreshment room, a shop and the refurbished Railway Museum (𝒟 08433 571420 ⊙ year-round). Well-presented displays here include *Ashley*, a steam engine built in 1942, which shows children – and adults – how a steam train works. The only surviving broad-gauge locomotive, *Tiny*, is also here; the line was later converted to standard gauge. There are descriptions of the stations on the line and their history, and of Brunel's literally 'atmospheric' railway, which used air pressure to drive the train (page 44).

Steam locomotives make the return trip (via Staverton Station, which appeared in a BBC adaptation of *The Hound of the Baskervilles*) four to nine times a day: a comprehensive timetable is on the website and you can book tickets online.

A perfect day out is to enjoy the 30-minute train ride between visits to Buckfastleigh and Totnes. Otters & Butterflies (page 245) is just two minutes' walk from Buckfastleigh Station, as is the Valiant Soldier (page 240), and Totnes Rare Breeds Farm (page 110) is just a minute's walk from Totnes Station. Both these unusual animal attractions are small and owner-run.

Buckfastleigh Caves

William Pengelly Cave Studies Trust, Russets Ln, Buckfastleigh TQ11 0DY 𝒟 01752 775195 𝒹 pengellytrust.org

A visit to the little-known Pengelly Centre is a serious but highly rewarding undertaking. There is no attempt here to provide entertainment – the museum with its informative displays and the 1½- to two-hour tours are aimed at adults and bright children who want to know about local history, geology and palaeontology.

Most of the work here is scientific, and volunteers from the William Pengelly Cave Studies Trust are only available to give tours a few times a week, normally Wednesday and Thursday in the summer, so check their website or phone before making plans.

The caves were discovered by local men exploring the disused quarries in the 1930s. On the floor of one cave they found some bones and took them to the museum in Torquay. 'Nothing of importance – just pigs and cows', they were told. Not satisfied by this explanation, they sent them to the Natural History Museum in London. This time the reaction was quite different, and the area was cordoned off until the experts, who had correctly identified the fossilised bones of elephant, hippopotamus and hyena, could take a look. These huge animals, all larger than present-day species, thrived in Devon during the warm period that preceded the last ice age, around 120,000 years ago.

The tour starts with a video explaining the geology of the area and a description of the greater horseshoe bats (page 246) which roost in one of the caves. The nub of the tour is a visit to Joint Mitnor Cave, now easily accessible via a system of boardwalks, where the most exciting finds were made – over 3,000 bones, dug out of the cave floor and walls. A long-ago earthquake opened a hole in the roof of the cavern, and animals fell in.

Herbivores such as bison were followed by their predators: hyenas. These two species provided the majority of bones found, but there were also wild boar, hippopotamus, bear and rhinoceros, as well as four straight-tusked elephants – two adults and two calves. The adults, in fact, were too large to fall through the hole but probably became wedged and unable to escape. These elephants were far larger than present-day African elephants, the adults standing at around 15–20ft high. Together with them were found the bones of brown bears and animals familiar in the British countryside today: foxes, voles, badgers, red deer and fallow

SOMETHING OLD, SOMETHING NEW...

In September 2015, thieves broke through the huge steel door to the Joint Mitnor Cave and stole some of its precious bones, including an elephant's tooth. They seem to have been professionals, possibly working for a private collector, as it was a slick job and they knew what to take. Despite enquiries throughout the caving and museum communities, no item from their haul has yet been found.

Technology to the rescue! When the cave reopened to the public in August 2017, all seemed to be as it was before the theft; but any palaeontologist unknowingly inspecting the bones would have been very startled by

their composition. In fact, bones excavated from the same cave in the 1960s had been copied on a 3D photocopier at the University of Birmingham, and the resulting polymer plastic replicas were then cast in gypsum in Cornwall. The elephant's tooth, a far more complex item than the average university 3D photocopier generally encounters, actually broke two machines in the process. London's Natural History Museum, which already had a Joint Mitnor collection, also contributed its expertise and high-tech scanning facilities.

And thus a little scrap of prehistory was re-created by the present day.

deer. Quite a few bones have been left to add interest to what is already a fascinating visit. Eventually the cave filled up with animal remains and debris and was no longer a death trap. The last ice age, which ended around 20,000 years ago, probably covered it completely until the 20th-century quarry men opened it.

11 DARTMOOR OTTERS & BUCKFAST BUTTERFLIES (OTTERS & BUTTERFLIES)

TQ11 0DZ ℰ 01364 642916 ℰ ottersandbutterflies.co.uk ⊙ Apr–Oct 10.00–17.00 daily
It's signposted from the station & is just off the A38, about one mile from Buckfastleigh.
Satnavs may take you past the turning so watch for signs.

The butterfly centre was founded in 1984 by David and Sue Field, who added the otter part in 1988 because of the proximity of the River Dart. 'It seemed an obvious thing to use this in some way. Originally we wanted to divert a stream to run through the grounds to create otter pools but this wasn't permitted, so the water is pumped out and in each day so they are swimming in river water.'

Completely protected from the elements by their thick, waterproof fur, the otters

> "As you watch the chrysalises, one or another may start to twitch, and it's a huge temptation to stay until they hatch."

are particularly lively before feeding times: 11.30, 14.00 and 16.00. The three species here are North American, Asian short-clawed and British, all displaying different characteristics.

If you wear glasses, they'll steam up in cool weather when you move from the otters to the butterfly house. Even on a gloomy autumn day there were plenty of eye-catching butterflies in evidence, but Sue said that they are far more active on bright, warm days. More easily studied are the rows of chrysalises attached to bamboos, showing the range of colours and sizes of these pre-butterflies. As you watch them, one or another may start to twitch, and it's a huge temptation to stay until they hatch.

Equally enthralling is the colony of Costa Rican leaf-cutter ants in the reception area, holding their leaves aloft like tiny sails as they file

◄ 1 Buckfast Abbey's garden includes around 150 species of lavender. 2 The romantic ruin of Buckfastleigh's Holy Trinity Church. 3 Explore the fascinating Buckfastleigh Caves. 4 Asian short-clawed otters at Otters & Butterflies.

GREATER HORSESHOE BATS

My thanks to Geoff Billington of Greena Ecological Consultancy for information.

In Britain, this bat is found only in the southwest of England and in Wales. The colony at the Buckfastleigh Caves (page 242) is the largest in the UK, and particularly important since this species is in decline. It's a strange-looking animal with its large mobile ears and fleshy 'noseleaf' (looking like a horseshoe, hence its name) which amplifies the bat's calls; it makes these through its nose with its mouth closed, so that it can judge the distance of its prey. These bats have small eyes, but the expression 'blind as a bat' has little truth as bats can see fairly well, although only in black and white. However, in complete darkness they have to rely mainly on their echolocation 'sonar'.

Greater horseshoe bats are among the largest European species of bats, and can live for 30 years. They mate during the autumn but delay fertilisation until they have emerged from hibernation in the spring. Their impressive wingspan is about 16 inches and, as with all bats, their wings are versatile.

Apart from enabling them to fly – bats are the only mammals that have evolved this way – the wings act as a cooling system in flight, since they contain innumerable blood vessels, and are a means of finding underground sites by detecting temperature changes from draughts emerging from entrances. Dozing bats wrap their wings right round their bodies. And when it comes to birth, the wings are more like an open umbrella, allowing the newborn baby to drop from its upside-down mother into safety. At times the baby hangs from a false nipple, positioned at the lower end of the abdomen, while the real nipples are near the armpit (or wingpit). The mother can fly with her infant thus attached, though she also parks it in the roost, hanging upside down, while she goes hunting. The young can fly and catch insects from about three weeks.

Bats emerge from their roosts about half an hour after sunset. Sit quietly and watch them, but do not disturb this protected species.

unswervingly along the walkway to their fungus garden. Apart from leaves, they apparently like fruit cake, Rice Crispies, used teabags and cooked ham or chicken, which must make for pretty exotic fungus.

Finally, there are over 200 terrapins, mainly the red-eared variety who breed at the centre, and a green iguana called Izzard.

12 BUCKFAST ABBEY

TQ11 0EE ☎ 01364 645500 ⊘ buckfast.org.uk

The brochure says that Buckfast Abbey, founded in the 11th century and demolished in the 16th following the Dissolution of the Monasteries, is now 'home to a community of Benedictine monks who lead a life of prayer, work and study'. I don't doubt it, but they've also created a thriving commercial enterprise teeming with visitors who happily pay high prices at the well-stocked gift shop, and flock to the modern abbey in numbers exceeding those to our great cathedrals. It's utterly commendable in the sense that the profits from tourism undoubtedly sustain the life of prayer. Nevertheless, something about it leaves me feeling a little uncomfortable.

That said, entrance to the site is free, as is parking; it's a peaceful setting and there's a wonderfully relaxed feeling about the place, with people strolling contentedly, quietly enjoying all it has to offer without any laid-on entertainment. There's also the extraordinary achievement of the abbey church, rebuilt by just a handful of the monks themselves, starting around a hundred years ago. By hand they cut the great stones to shape, lashed wooden scaffolding together, hauled the stones up on rudimentary pulleys... It took them 32 years, and the imposing St Mary's Church that you see today is the result.

Beekeeping here is also an interesting story, and Brother Adam, who worked with the abbey's bees for over 70 years, is world famous for breeding a new strain that was a high honey producer, relatively gentle and resistant to disease. Over four decades he travelled some 100,000 miles to isolated areas of Europe, Asia and North Africa, persuading local beekeepers to give him queens from their indigenous strains; these he posted back to Buckfast. The result is known as the Buckfast bee, and its products are sold in the Monastic Shop – along with the famous Buckfast Tonic Wine, which made headlines a few years ago because of its rather incongruous popularity among young and anti-social drinkers. Beekeeping courses are held for both beginners and improvers.

"Brother Adam, who worked with the abbey's bees for over 70 years, is world famous for breeding a new strain."

Bees are contented visitors to the lavender garden, which has around 150 species of lavender (when it's in flower, the perfume is wonderful). There are also sensory and physic gardens and spacious lawns, as well as some fine mature trees. There is a separate shop, 'The Green Hub', selling an interesting and varied selection of indoor and outdoor plants. Meanwhile retreats of various lengths are available in the monks' guest accommodation.

The Grange Restaurant, which incorporates the 12th-century arch of the old north gate and whose outdoor patio has a wonderful view of the abbey, provides a good range of food (lunches, teas, snacks) in pleasant surroundings.

Buses serve Buckfast from Newton Abbot, Ashburton and Buckfastleigh and, if you would like to stay, the Abbey has a 33-bedroom hotel and some self-catering cottages.

13 PENNYWELL FARM

TQ11 0LT ✐ 01364 642023 ⌘ pennywellfarm.co.uk ⏱ Feb–Oct 09.00–16.00 daily; booking essential

Forget conservation and endangered species, this hands-on animal place is just that – its aim is to bring humans and animals as close together as possible and as such it offers one of Devon's most rewarding experiences for children. Just look at the expression of a little girl gently stroking a tiny dozing piglet, and you'll see how well it works. Or sometimes doesn't, as disgruntled squeals then make very clear; but whenever a baby cries there are nursemaids – or nursemen – on hand to retrieve it for a soothing word or two.

Pennywell has been selectively breeding miniature pigs since 1992, with the result that a piglet weighs just eight ounces at birth and grows

PENNYWELL'S MINIATURE PIGS

I talked to the ebullient Chris Murray about his miniature pigs. 'I've always loved pigs. I studied Agriculture at Seale-Hayne [agricultural college] and got interested in breeding pigs then. They're ideal animals for selective breeding because they have two litters a year and up to 18 piglets per litter. Of course in those days we were breeding for improved meat, and we wanted our pigs to grow fast. Now it's the opposite – we want small, slow-growing pigs. All sorts of traditional breeds have been used in our breeding programme: Iron Age wild boar, Gloucester old spot and Tamworth for colour, Berkshire, middle white because they're small with smiley faces, kune-kune which have a nice temperament, and English lop, which are docile. We aimed for other small details too – for instance we wanted prick ears rather than lop. But not too small because tiny ears look mean. And we wanted a short snout, because it's more appealing, and the right mouth. It took us 16 years to breed the smile!

'Yes, we sell them. As pets, of course. We have some lovely customers here. One lady has a pig that sits on the sofa and watches television with her and there's a man who takes his pig on bike rides.'

to about the size of a springer spaniel. It's not just the miniature piglets you can hug. The rabbits and older piglets are remarkably tolerant of human attention too, and selected ones are held in pens where visitors can join them for a stroke. As a pig enthusiast I was just as thrilled as the little kids around me when a piglet collapsed on its side in ecstasy as I scratched it under the chin.

Every half hour there is something different happening, such as ferret racing, pig racing (the contestants nonchalantly pause in their canter from time to time for a nibble of grass), bottle feeding or pony pampering, and there are plenty of non-animal activities for children too, as well as a café and gift shop. A plus on wet days is that many of the pens and activities are under cover.

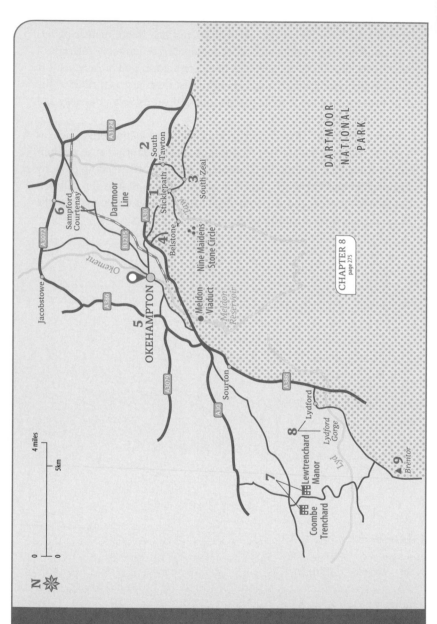

THE NORTHWESTERN FRINGE OF DARTMOOR

7

THE NORTHWESTERN FRINGE OF DARTMOOR

This is an area where the ancient underlies the merely old. Medieval thatched cottages, centuries-old inns and much-loved little village churches occupy land where prehistoric monoliths, hut circles and burial cairns once stood, and the footprints of early people stretch back a long, long way. Sheep and red Devon cattle graze in the fields, and crops ripen through deepening shades of green to dusty gold. Between gaps in the trees, the hills and tors of Dartmoor appear as a distant backdrop.

Parts lie away from the tourist routes, allowing the occasional hamlet to be unselfconsciously unadorned. In one tourist information centre the assistant told me: 'The cottages down there are lovely because they haven't been titillated,' leaving me to wonder what a titillated cottage might get up to. Others are in their full thatched and whitewashed finery, with competitive gardens and cats dozing on windowsills.

WET-WEATHER ACTIVITIES
Finch Foundry Sticklepath (page 253)
Museum of Dartmoor Life Okehampton (page 261)

GETTING THERE & AROUND

Drivers will find this an easily accessible region, with most of the places described lying near the dual-carriageway A30 from Exeter. West of Okehampton, the A386 heads south to Lydford Gorge on its way to Tavistock. Once off these main roads, the lanes are often narrow and you'll need to be reading your map or using a satnav.

Okehampton has a national **rail** network station with an hourly service to Exeter, taking just 35 minutes and calling at Crediton on the way. Alternate trains arriving from Exeter connect at Okehampton

Station with the 118 Rail Link bus to Tavistock via Sourton and Lydford (⊘ dartmoorline.com).

The appropriate **bus** timetable for the area is *West Devon*. Okehampton is covered by buses 5A, 6 and 6A from Exeter, 118 from Tavistock and 178 (only twice daily) from Newton Abbot. The 178 also goes to the 'beacon villages', apart from Belstone, which has the 670 from Okehampton (once each way, only on Thursdays). Sampford Courtenay is served by the 5A from Exeter and (two or three times a week) by the 631 and 648 from Okehampton.

SELF-POWERED TRAVEL

Roads are good throughout the area and it's not excessively hilly. The **Granite Way** (⊘ drakestrail.co.uk or look for the leaflet in TICs) is an 11-mile walk/cycle route from Okehampton to Lydford, mostly following the course of the old Southern Region railway line so gradients are gentle. This route gives an unbeatable view of ruined Okehampton Castle (page 261) down below in the West Okement River valley. If you would like a refreshment stop, the Highwayman Inn (page 259) is on the route and the Bearslake Inn (page 340) is just 500yds west of Lake Viaduct. There is **cycle hire** at the station (page 263). The Granite Way is part of the Devon **Coast-to-Coast** cycle route (National Cycle Network route 27) from Ilfracombe via Barnstaple and Okehampton to Plymouth (page 190), and much of it lies within Dartmoor National Park. It's relatively easy going, entirely off-road for six miles between Okehampton and Lake Viaduct, and ideal for families and those whose cycling is rusty. There are numerous smaller walks, some on lanes and some on footpaths. The relevant OS maps are Landranger 191 and Explorer OL 28 (Dartmoor). It's also shown in adequate detail (and with all pubs marked!) on the handy Croydecycle *South Devon* map (page 19).

For walkers, the 24-mile **Two Castles Trail** links the Norman castles of Okehampton and Launceston, which was the ancient capital of Cornwall. It never strays far from bus or train routes so you can easily break it into sections. Devon County Council's very comprehensive guide is available in TICs or you can download the PDF from ⊘ visitdartmoor. co.uk/get-active/the-best-dartmoor-walks/two-castles-trail. Sampford Courtenay is another pleasant walking area, and historically interesting (page 264), while from nearby Jacobstowe with its 12th-century church the southernmost tip of the **Tarka Trail** leads south along the bank of the Okement River to Okehampton.

CYCLE HIRE

Devon Cycle Hire Sourton Down EX20 4HR ✆ 01837 861141 ⌂ devoncyclehire.co.uk
Granite Way Cycle Hire Youth Hostel, Klondyke Rd, Okehampton EX20 1EW ✆ 01837 650907 ⌂ granitewaycycles.co.uk. Also has an on-site café.

COMBINATION TRAVEL

The new railway service to Okehampton has opened up some great options for combination travel. The railway's dedicated website offers three ideas for walks from two to seven miles ⌂ dartmoorline.com. Walkers on the 11-mile Granite Way from Okehampton to Lydford can use the 118 Rail Link bus to bring them back to Okehampton from either Sourton or Lydford.

From the Granite Way it is just 41 miles south to Plymouth or 43 miles north to Barnstaple on the Coast-to-Coast (NCN 27) route. The train will get you, and your bicycle, back to Okehampton from either end in under two hours.

THE BEACON VILLAGES

The four 'beacon villages' – Sticklepath, South Tawton, South Zeal and Belstone – are so named because they're all located at the base of **Cosdon Beacon**, a broad 1,804ft hill where signal fires were lit in medieval times; it was thought to be the highest point on Dartmoor. Extensive prehistoric remains, including hut circles and cairns, have been found on its slopes; during the 19th century, many were robbed of their stones by villagers seeking free building materials. Roads leading from one beacon village to the other are a bit labyrinthine, but the signposting is reasonably clear. Driving or walking between them you'll be playing hide-and-seek with the outline of Dartmoor in its various moods, one minute looming as a backdrop and the next nowhere in sight.

1 STICKLEPATH

⚑ **Fallows Leap** Ash Park Farm (page 340)
Sticklepath has some fine thatched cottages, but its main point of interest is the **Finch Foundry** (✆ 01837 840046; National Trust; booking desired

Bus-assisted walk: Okehampton to Finch Foundry, Sticklepath

✾ OS Explorer 113; start: Okehampton Mill Road car park, EX20 1PR ♀ SX590950; just under six miles; mostly level, with just one climb

The walk follows the deep wooded valleys of the two main rivers of the area – the East Okement and the Taw – and a short stretch of open moorland affords fine views across Dartmoor. The pretty villages of Belstone and Sticklepath have good cafés and pubs.

Return to Mill Road from the car park, turn right and then take the first fork left on to **Courtney Road**, which leads to Okehampton College's back entrance. Here turn left, signed as a footpath and as the Dartmoor Way.

Now keep ahead, initially below fields and then through Ball Hill conservation area. After about ¾ mile you emerge at a T-junction. Turn right to cross Charlotte's Bridge and then curve left to pass under the five-arch **Fatherford railway viaduct** and the A30 viaduct. Keep ahead through the **Halstock Wood** alongside **East Okement River** for about half a mile, when you cross the footbridge over Moor Brook.

Keep ahead again – look for the gap in the fine stone wall – and keep your eyes open for the sometimes spectacular waterfalls; it rather depends on how wet it has been. After half a mile

but walk-ins are accommodated), which isn't actually a foundry at all but the last working water-powered forge in the country. In its heyday it made around 400 tools a day (sickles, scythes, shovels and more) for local farmers and miners. You can watch the machinery in action, and the precision of the great handmade wheels, cogs and other parts is amazing. Tucked away behind the forge is a peaceful little Quaker graveyard, probably dating from soon after 1700. The small thatched arbour there was built by a certain Thomas Pearse (yes, that's the one, and presumably he had a grey mare) who was himself buried in the graveyard, in 1875, aged 81. Opposite the foundry is the Sticklepath Stores and Café, recommended for a cup of tea and a slice of home-made cake. Sticklepath also has an energetic team of female Morris dancers, **Cogs and Wheels Ladies Morris**, who may be found performing in local venues between May and September.

"Watch the machinery in action: the precision of the great wheels, cogs and other parts is amazing."

you come to a second footbridge, this time over the East Okement. Cross, then turn sharp left to ascend gently; when a track is reached near the top turn sharp right to keep the stone wall on your left.

After a further half mile the wall turns sharp left and this is your signal to do the same, climbing over the ridge of **Belstone Common**. Soon a track is reached: turn left to descend into Belstone. In the village turn right down the side of **The Tors Inn** (page 260) and fork left as soon as you reach the open common to descend; keep the walls on your left and the moor on your right.

At the bottom yet another footbridge is reached and, after crossing the **River Taw**, turn left and follow it downstream. The path crosses the river twice more before the village of **Sticklepath** may be spotted on the far bank. You may see the **old mill**, once owned by Tom Pearce of Widecombe Fair fame.

When a gate is reached, turn left and look for the final footbridge to cross the Taw, leading you into the rear of **Finch Foundry** (page 253).

Buses number 6 or 6A will return you to Okehampton in about 15 minutes from the bus stop in front of the Devonshire Inn.

2 SOUTH TAWTON

South Tawton was a royal manor at the time of the Domesday survey and its fertile land made for successful farming; wealth from the wool trade expanded a smaller, probably 11th-century chapel into the mainly 15th-century granite **church of St Andrew**, a listed building that towers above the village today and has some exceptional medieval carved bosses above the nave and aisles. Unfortunately they're hard to distinguish from below because they're covered with some kind of brown stain (binoculars and a strong torch are helpful), but they've been painstakingly photographed for the Church House website (see below).

Beside the church the picturesque thatched **Church House** (☏ 01837 840418 ◈ thechurchhouse.uk ◷ Jun–Sep 14.00–17.00 Sun) was built soon after 1490 as a parish centre where all parishioners could gather to enjoy 'Church ales'. These were parties organised to fundraise for the church's upkeep and to help the poor, in much the same way that churches hold fundraising coffee mornings today. It was 'ale money' that paid for the roof carvings, in the late 1400s. On the ground floor was the kitchen where ale was brewed and food was cooked in the great fireplace; the feasting hall upstairs with massive roof trusses and a large window could have housed a great deal of medieval jollity. In the 17th century the hall was used as a school, and from 1804 through Victorian times as a poorhouse. During World War II, soldiers were billeted there after Dunkirk.

3 SOUTH ZEAL

🏠 **The Oxenham Arms** (page 340)

In the mid 13th century, the de Tony family who held the manor of South Tawton were granted royal permission to form a borough – a 'new town' – straddling the main route between Exeter and Cornwall: that town became South Zeal. In 1298 it was granted a charter for two annual fairs and a weekly market. The 'strip' layout at right angles to the single broad main street, still visible today, allowed householders street access in front, with a narrow strip of land continuing behind the house where gardens and workshops could be sited. South Zeal also has a number of medieval through-passages and Tudor houses, and the history of the town has

"There's a 14th-century market cross and the appealing St Mary's Chapel with its unusual 15th-century bell turret."

been carefully researched; the South Tawton and District Local History Group has produced a booklet *South Zeal: A glimpse at the Village's Past*, on sale in the **Country Store and Tea Room** (itself in a through-passage house, with a splendidly large fireplace). There's a **14th-century market cross** and the appealing little **St Mary's Chapel** with its unusual 15th-century bell turret, as well as two pubs. In August the annual Dartmoor Folk Festival (⊘ dartmoorfolkfestival.org.uk) erupts into the village, as it has done since 1981, filling it with music and activity. Tinners Morris (⊘ tinnersmorris.com) are a group of men's Morris dancers based in South Zeal. They dance with handkerchiefs, sticks and sometimes even iron bars. You might catch them practising on a Sunday morning in the Victory Hall or later taking refreshment in the King's Arms.

---

1 South Tawton's fertile land has made it successful for farming since the Domesday survey. **2** A blacksmith at work at Finch Foundry in Sticklepath. **3** South Zeal hosts the annual Dartmoor Folk Festival. **4** Belstone's Grade II-listed stocks. **5** The lavish interior of the Highwayman Inn, Sourton. ▶

🍴 FOOD & DRINK

King's Arms South Zeal ✆ 01837 840300 🅵 ⊘ closed Tue. This cheery place with friendly staff dates back to the 16th century but is very involved in today's village activities: you may find local folk groups playing here, or seasonal themed evenings. Their cider is made at a farm less than 20 miles away. Hearty pub food is available noon–14.00 & 17.30–20.30. There's also a simple campsite (toilets are available but no showers) with a good view of the moor.

Oxenham Arms South Zeal ✆ 01837 840244 🖋 theoxenhamarms.com ⊘ closed Mon. The oldest heritage inn in Devon & Cornwall & probably originally a monastery, it is thought to have been built by 12th-century lay monks – & they incorporated a 5,000-year-old standing stone into one of its inner walls. Another room has a similar menhir supporting the ceiling. It's a rambling place, visibly full of history. Lunches are available noon–14.30, evening meals 18.00–21.00, & cream teas all afternoon (booking advised). There's also luxury B&B in beautifully furnished period rooms, some with four-posters (page 340).

4 BELSTONE

🏠 **The Tors Inn** (page 340)

This peaceful, charming, leafy village right on the edge of Dartmoor is mentioned as Bellestan or Bellestam in the Domesday Book. It's full of history and moorland atmosphere, with some traditional old stone and thatched cottages, grazing ponies, dramatic Dartmoor views, a Norman church and an incised granite ring-cross dating from the 7th to 9th centuries, suggesting a much earlier place of worship. Similar crosses have been found and dated in south Wales and early Christian sites in the southwest of Ireland. Unusually for a village church, in the 19th century men and women were separated during services here, with men on the south side of the nave and women on the north.

The old stocks (now a Grade II-listed monument) still sit on the village green – slats of wood between two granite pillars – as if awaiting some lingering medieval miscreant, and one house still has its old iron pump outside. Belstone is popular with walkers, out on a moorland ramble and heading through to visit a nearby prehistoric stone circle, the somewhat unimaginatively named **Nine Maidens** stone circle (I counted 21), which is actually a prehistoric cairn: a burial place within a circle of stones. Or, it's a circle of maidens who were turned to stone for dancing on the Sabbath. Your choice. According to one story you'll always count a different number, as one or other skips outside the circle when your back is turned. It's marked on OS Explorer map 28. Once you're through the gate at the end of the road, follow the track to the end of the stone wall, then head uphill and you'll see it.

'The cakes are just arriving,' a man called out cheerily, as he bustled past me with a large box. I was standing by the village green outside the **Old School Tearoom** (℘ 01837 840498 ⌨ belstonetearoom.co.uk), waiting for it to open. His box's contents were on the counter by the

THE HIGHWAYMAN INN & COBWEB HALL

Philip Knowling

Highwayman Inn Sourton EX20 4HN ℘ 01837 861243 ⌨ thehighwaymaninn.net
☉ noon–15.00 & 18.00–21.00. Ales, meals & snacks in its Aladdin's cave of artefacts & curios. Also B&B & a self-catering cottage (page 340).

Putting the lie to the idea that follies are useless is the Highwayman Inn at Sourton, on the bleak west side of Dartmoor. Sourton is the sort of place you could pass through without noticing if it weren't for the hard work, imagination and enthusiasm of the late John 'Buster' Jones, who over a 40-year period transformed two of its key buildings into fabulous, fascinating and accessible architectural wonders.

What makes this pub a folly? Well, it's the most lavishly and imaginatively decorated inn you could ever visit. Inside and out there's wit and whimsy, imagination and inspiration – plus a little macabre kitsch. The Highwayman is a fantasy blend of pirate ship, church, museum, junk shop and fairytale.

In 1959 Buster Jones moved his family to Devon and took over Sourton's New Inn – a small, run-down pub in a 13th-century building. He and his wife Rita changed the name to the Highwayman Inn and, to promote it, Buster acquired the old Okehampton–Launceston stage coach and set it up as a lobby at the front door of the pub.

He hauled pieces of bog oak off the moor and used them as bar tops; the dartboard is fixed to a tree stump set into the wall. There are bits of ship (a carved door from an old whaling ship called *Diana*) and pieces of church (from Plymouth).

One room has a nautical theme – it's below decks on an 18th-century sailing ship cum bric-a-brac shop with bar facilities. Elsewhere, there's an indoor grotto full of stuffed animals (an inventive use of roadkill). Cartwheels and lanterns and sewing machines also feature.

Buster also turned the former Sourton village hall, just across the road, into a fairytale Gothic cottage orné – despite a certain amount of conflict with the planning authorities. Today Cobweb Hall is a unique holiday let, standing on the edge of rising moorland.

The two buildings are now in the good care of Buster's daughter, Sally. The Highwayman is world-renowned – and rightly so. If you visit it, you'll never see your own local in quite the same way again.

time I went in: some lovely fresh, sticky home baking. On shelves and dressers along the walls were rows of differently sized teapots wearing colourful knitted tea cosies (I couldn't resist one shaped like a sheep), with various other bits of vintage china. Vases of bluebells brightened the tables, and wooden benches were softened by cushions. Jars of homemade jam and chutney were for sale. I loved it! My pot of tea was hot and strong, and my slice of fruit cake was delicious. Opening hours, posted outside on a blackboard, may vary seasonally (when I visited they were 14.00–17.30 Fri–Mon); check their website.

"On shelves and dressers along the walls were rows of differently sized teapots wearing colourful knitted tea cosies."

For something a bit stronger than tea, The **Tors Inn** (𝒫 01837 840689 𝄞 thetorsinn.co.uk ☉ 17.00–23.00 Tue–Sat) is a friendly, unpretentious, traditional Dartmoor pub, popular with locals and walkers. Meals are freshly cooked and generous, and it also does B&B (page 340). At the rear is The Shed (☉ noon–17.00 Tue–Sun) an outdoor beer and burger bar with great views, and they move into the pub if it is wet.

OKEHAMPTON & AROUND

The past plays a big role in this section, what with the Dartmoor Line's beautifully restored railway station, the Museum of Dartmoor Life in Okehampton, echoes of the Prayer Book Rebellion at Sampford Courteney and the dramatic ruin of 11th-century Okehampton Castle. So prepare for some gentle nostalgia!

5 OKEHAMPTON

🏠 **Bearslake Inn** Sourton (page 340)
🏰 **Cobweb Hall** Sourton (page 340)
⛺ **Honeyside Down** (page 340)
Tourist information: The Okehampton TIC has closed, but the Museum of Dartmoor Life (3 West St 𝒫 01837 52295 𝄞 dartmoorlife.org.uk ☉ Apr–Oct 10.00–16.00 Mon–Fri & 10.00–13.00 Sat) has information & a good website

This is one of only two market towns mentioned in the 1086 Domesday survey of Devon, and in medieval times was an important centre. Its surprisingly wide main street was once the old London Road to Cornwall and held a third row of buildings, which included an ancient guildhall and a 17th-century covered market. These were demolished in 1850. The 15th-century St James's Chapel is the oldest building, and one of only five in England that is strictly non-denominational. Pigs were once used to hoover up the garbage in the streets and were housed near the chapel; the pig-shaped cycle-stands nearby are a reminder of this.

Economically the town is struggling and some high-street shops have closed; but several small independent shops and boutiques down side alleys are flourishing, particularly those offering fresh local produce: baked goods, meat, vegetables, fruit, etc. There's also the **Red Lion Yard Retail Village,** which has a pleasantly boutiquey feel; there's very good coffee at Grants and a wide selection of local food is available at the Harvest Workers' Cooperative Farm Shop (⊘ harvestworkerscoop.org. uk). This is a not-for-profit social enterprise that grows much of the food it sells. Everything that can be sourced locally is, including the rather good organic ice cream. Across Fore Street is the small Victorian shopping arcade, a miniature version of London's Burlington Arcade and an extra treat.

The **Museum of Dartmoor Life** (see *Tourist Information*, opposite) is well worth a visit. It's housed in an old mill (dated 1811) with a restored waterwheel, tucked away down an alley with cobbles down the middle and mosaics on the sides, roughly opposite Lloyds Bank. Its three floors of exhibits cover around 5,000 years, from prehistoric times to the present day. You'll find Bronze Age, Roman and Saxon collections, as well as historic Dartmoor trades and industries, transport and the military – with quirky personal links bringing history to life.

Perched on a hillside about a mile from the centre of town is 11th-century **Okehampton Castle** (⊘ 01837 52844 ⊙ Apr–Oct; English Heritage), an atmospheric and allegedly haunted ruin that is said to have been Devon's largest castle. Built soon after the Norman Conquest and originally a motte-and-bailey construction with a stone keep, in the 14th century it was converted into a private residence by the Earl of Devon. In the 16th century, after his descendant fell into dispute with Henry VIII and was beheaded, it was left to decay. The walls are feeling their age now, but the view of its ancient stonework silhouetted against the sky is dramatic, and there are attractive woodland and riverside walks nearby. When I approached in February the grass below its walls looked frosty, until I realised that the 'frost' was a mass of snowdrops.

Okehampton Station & Meldon Viaduct

A ten-minute stroll from town is the beautiful **Okehampton Station** (⌂ dartmoorline.com). The station reopened in 2021 and has been restored to how it might have looked in the 1950s, the heyday of rail travel. It is now more than just the terminus of the hourly train service to Exeter. On Platform 3 there is a Dartmoor National Park visitor centre staffed by friendly and knowledgeable volunteers, and at the other end of the platform is the Bulleid Buffet tea room (☉ 07.00–1700 Mon–Sat, 09.00–16.00 Sun), run by the Amazing Brownie Bakers. The café serves drinks, snacks and light meals, and has many photographs of the station from 1950s on its walls. On Platform 2 is the Dartmoor Railway Association's museum and shop (☉ 11.00–16.00 Sat–Sun). Dedicated to railwayman Arthur Westlake, who helped to keep the station in Okehampton open, the museum is focused on the history of the area and its railway. The adjoining shop has a huge range of secondhand railway books and memorabilia. On the south side of the station is a cycle hire and repair shop (page 253) and Okehampton's youth hostel.

"Meldon Viaduct, a scheduled ancient monument with spectacular views, is a dramatic example of Victorian engineering."

Nearby **Meldon Viaduct**, a scheduled ancient monument with spectacular views, is a dramatic example of Victorian engineering: one of only two examples in Britain of a wrought-iron truss-girder viaduct. Spanning the deep, steep river gorge required a strong but flexible structure; the wrought-iron and cast-iron frame consisted of six 90ft warren trusses on five wrought-iron lattice trestles, riveted together. It was built in 1874 for the main line between Waterloo and Plymouth, then doubled in width (to allow a second track) in 1878 and finally closed to trains in the late 1960s. Now it's a part of the Granite Way (page 252). **Meldon Reservoir**, accessible by road and via a diversion from the Granite Way, is 900ft above sea level; it was created in 1972 by a dam across the West Okement River, and offers fine views over the moors and to the viaduct. It's managed by the South West Lakes Trust

◀**1** The 11th-century Okehampton Castle is allegedly haunted. **2** Constructed of wrought iron, Meldon Viaduct is a spectacular example of Victorian engineering. **3** St Andrew's Church in Sampford Courtenay was involved in the Prayer Book Rebellion of 1549. **4** The Museum of Dartmoor Life includes displays on historic Dartmoor trades and industries.

($\oslash$ swlakestrust.org.uk). **Black-a-Tor Copse National Nature Reserve**, on the bank of the West Okement as it flows into the reservoir, is one of Britain's best examples of high-altitude oak woodland, nationally important for the great variety of lichens on its trees and rocks. The only comparable one in Devon is Wistman's Wood (page 331).

6 SAMPFORD COURTENAY

This village five miles or so north of Okehampton is known mainly for its involvement in the Prayer Book Rebellion of 1549 (see below). It's accustomed to visitors and presents itself well, having 70 or so listed buildings and monuments. As Arthur Mee wrote 70-odd years ago: 'It is charming, with white cottages and thatched roofs and a lofty pinnacled tower. Old crosses keep watch by the road, and another guards the 15th-century church.' That church, **St Andrew's**, rebuilt from an earlier building in 1450 and mentioned in Simon Jenkins's *England's Thousand Best Churches*, has some fine bosses in its wagon

THE PRAYER BOOK REBELLION

As part of the Protestant reforms instigated under the boy king Edward VI, the familiar prayer book in Latin was declared illegal and, from Whit Sunday 1549, churches in England were required to adopt the new *Book of Common Prayer* in English and to adapt their traditional rituals. Resistance to this was particularly strong among the villagers of Devon and Cornwall, as people saw their traditional methods of worship under threat. At Sampford Courtenay they likened the English prayer book to a 'Christmas game', something like a Nativity play without true substance; initially their priest obeyed orders, removed his robes and conducted the 'new' Sunday service, but vocal parishioners quickly forced him to revert to the Latin form. Others dissented, a fracas developed, and in the melee a local man was stabbed with a pitchfork on the steps of the Church House and then hacked to death.

Villagers in their thousands, armed with no more than farm implements and staves, then rose in support and marched to Exeter, laying siege to the city and demanding the withdrawal of the English version. The siege lasted six weeks, but in the end the rebels were no match for the well-armed military force sent to quell them: more than 3,500 died in skirmishes in Devon, including 1,300 in a final stand at Sampford Courtenay. The militia continued into Cornwall and, by the time the rebels were crushed, some 4,000 from both counties had died – and to little eventual purpose, as, when Edward's half-sister Mary, who was a devout Catholic, succeeded him in 1553 she re-legalised the Latin version anyway.

roof, including a sow suckling seven rather elongated piglets, and a permanent descriptive display about the Prayer Book Rebellion. There's also a venerable old oak chest, made from a single block of wood, and a rare walnut pulpit.

The Church House nearby, which will have been used, like South Tawton's, for communal feasting and 'Church ales', probably dates to around 1500.

LYDFORD & AROUND

From photogenic country houses to a folly, a gorge and a 12th-century tor-top church, this is an area of contrasts, and of gentle meandering lanes once you leave the main roads.

7 LEWTRENCHARD & COOMBE TRENCHARD

🏠 **Lewtrenchard Manor** (page 340)

It's unusual to find two such perfect, traditional country houses, set in extensive and typically English gardens with lawns and terraces, only a ten-minute walk from each other; both have intriguing histories and contain some impressive period art and furnishings. With sun on their classic stone frontages and flowers splashing their borders with colour, they're an artist's or photographer's delight. The main difference is that while Coombe Trenchard was built in 1906, Lewtrenchard is around three centuries older. Although wonderfully secluded they're actually only a few miles from the A30, and also lie fairly close to the Two Castles Trail (page 252).

Lewtrenchard Manor

Lewdown, nr Okehampton, EX20 4PN ✆ 01566 464070 ⬡ lewtrenchard.co.uk

The Domesday Book mentions a royal manor here, but the core of the present house seems to have been started around five centuries later. It was a simple oblong building, only the width of a single room, until Sabine Baring-Gould (page 266) in the 19th century began transforming it into this colourful, imposing and graceful building, now a family-run hotel. Inside it's opulent; Baring-Gould was a great collector and brought treasures from far and wide: oak and leather, gilt and carvings, knick-knacks and heavy period furniture. It's a delight just to walk from one well-proportioned room to another.

In the gardens, beyond the palm trees and colourful flowerbeds, is little **St Peter's Church**, originally St Petroc's but dedicated to St Peter when it was rebuilt in 1261. Barely a trace of that old church remains; the present one dates from 1520 and again Baring-Gould brought additions from far and wide to embellish it: a medieval triptych and 15th-century brass chandelier from Belgium, the lectern from France, the altar painting from Switzerland, the east window from Germany and so on. On his memorial stone is carved *Paravi Lucernam Christo Meo,* or 'I have prepared a lantern for my Christ' – and indeed it burned brightly.

Lewtrenchard Manor has an excellent restaurant, open to non-residents for lunch, afternoon tea (including cream teas) and dinner. It's top-class cuisine; the chef works closely with local producers, and vegetables mostly come from the hotel's own walled garden. Menus change frequently to make use of whatever is freshly available. For an

THE REVEREND SABINE BARING-GOULD (1834–1924)

Squire, parson, scholar, antiquarian, novelist, hymn-writer, collector of folk songs…and Sabine Baring-Gould's father had hoped he would be just a mathematician. When he was 34 he married Grace, the 18-year-old daughter of a Yorkshire mill-hand; in the next 21 years they had 15 children and their marriage lasted 48 years. He had carved on her tombstone *Dimidium Animae Meae,* meaning 'half my soul'. In 1872 when he was rector of East Mersea in Essex his father died, and he inherited the Lewtrenchard family estates. The manor house at the time was only one room wide; Sabine extended it, filled it with artistic treasures and created today's stately Lewtrenchard Manor (page 265). As squire, he could appoint himself parson of the parish – and did so; he called himself a squarson. He wrote numerous articles and papers on subjects as diverse as Icelandic folklore and candle-snuffers. He was also a prolific novelist (some tales were quite racy for a clergyman, with a fair bit of bosom-heaving and moustache-twirling), wrote the words of the hymns 'Onward Christian Soldiers' and 'Now the Day is Over', and painstakingly tracked down and transcribed old English folksongs that he feared might otherwise be forgotten. His huge collection, one of the most significant West Country collections of the Victorian era, has now been digitised; for details see ⊘ sbgsongs.org.

He lovingly restored St Peter's Church on the estate, adding art and beauty to it in his own unrestrained style, and is buried in its churchyard; the parishioners installed electricity in his memory. He would no doubt be satisfied that it's now listed in Todd Gray's *Devon's Fifty Best Churches.*

extra treat, you can arrange a private dinner with the kitchen's activities relayed to you on a large flatscreen TV, giving you the opportunity to interact with the head chef and his team. The place is popular locally, and booking is strongly recommended.

Coombe Trenchard

Lewdown, nr Okehampton, EX20 4FA ✆ 01566 783179 🌐 coombetrenchard.co.uk

Friends of Sabine Baring-Gould had been renting the old rectory on the Lewtrenchard estate, while he lived next door in Lewtrenchard Manor. Sabine then offered them that portion of the land and they bought it, demolished the rectory and in 1906 began building this elegant Arts and Crafts house, using architect Walter Sarel and Devon church builders Dart and Francis.

The interior (only accessible by arrangement) has fine oak panelling, ornate ceilings, gracious rooms and period furnishings – and somewhat surprisingly an ingenious disappearing wall, thought to be unique, which can be slid down to the basement, rather in the manner of a sash window, to make space for large gatherings. When the current owners bought the property in 2007 the large gardens, originally designed and laid out by Walter Sarel, were badly neglected; now, after a huge amount of work, the forgotten paths, glades, woodland garden, terraces, steps and other structures are back in view.

"It has period furnishings – and somewhat surprisingly an ingenious disappearing wall, thought to be unique."

The **gardens** can be visited through the annual National Gardens Scheme (page 24). Otherwise they are not regularly open to the public, but private group visits to the gardens and some rooms in the house can be arranged by request. They're also accessible through Historic Houses (🌐 historichouses.org), an association that organises visits to stately homes.

8 LYDFORD GORGE & LYDFORD

🏠 **The Dartmoor Inn** (page 340)
🏡 **Foxtor & Haretor Barns** (page 340)

Hidden away on a feeder road off the A386, this is one of those happy places with plenty to see and an hourly bus service, the number 118 between Okehampton and Tavistock. People have always loved waterfalls, and **Lydford Gorge** (EX20 4BH ✆ 01822 820320 ⊙ ticket office 10.00–16.30, closed Mon, trails close Nov–Feb & in bad weather; National Trust) has been enticing visitors to its White Lady Waterfall for around 300 years, although it was the arrival of the railway in 1865 that put it within reach of holidaymakers. Now owned by the National Trust, the 1½-mile stretch of river deserves its popularity – it really does live up to expectations.

The gorge walk is designed as a circular route and follows a one-way system – necessary because the paths are narrow – so from the main entrance you walk in a clockwise direction, above the river and through the woods to the waterfall, returning close to the river. The three-mile walk has some steep sections so you need to be fit enough, and have the time (allow two hours) to do the whole thing. There are alternatives, however. On my last visit I parked at the waterfall entrance and walked the lovely river section to the main entrance. Bus number 118 runs hourly so if you get your timing right you can enjoy the facilities of the tea room and take the bus back. It stops outside each entrance. There are also short circular walks at each end, the most dramatic being the Devil's Cauldron accessed from the main entrance. Here the river is forced through a narrow space between rocks, with the path pinned against the steep fern-clad rock face so you look down on the churning white water. Even after a dry period it's impressive, and breathtaking (and slippery) after rain.

"The river is forced through a narrow space between rocks, with the path pinned against the steep fern-clad rock face."

The other end, with the **White Lady Waterfall**, is drier and less ferny than the eastern section, and the descent to the falls is down a long flight of steps, although there is a longer, 'easy' path as an alternative. The waterfall is just that – a waterfall – not spectacular but very pretty in its wooded environment. However, the Reverend Stebbing Shaw, who visited Lydford in 1788, was moved to paroxysms of delight. 'You are presented with the finest milky streams imaginable, neither too perpendicular to be one confused heap, nor too much divided to be

1 The church atop Brentor is thought to have been completed in 1130. **2** Lydford Gorge's beautiful White Lady Waterfall. **3** Why not explore the area with a walking companion from Lydford Gorge Alpacas? ▶

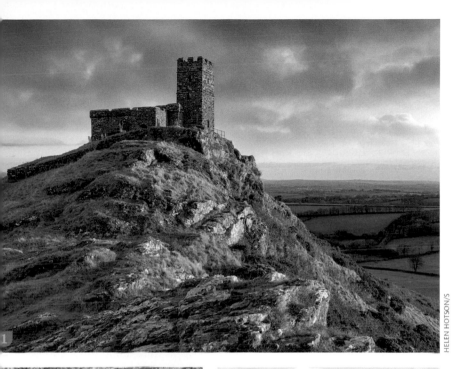

ungraceful; but one continued silvery chain of 200ft [actually it's 90ft]; towards the bottom the rock projects so favourably as to fill the air with aqueous particles, and to imitate the effect of a real fountain, softly falling in a silver shower...'

The paths between the two entrances have a variety of trees and flowers, including swathes of bluebells and pungent wild garlic in May, and allow you to see the different moods of the river, from quiet pools to mini-waterfalls. Dippers and grey wagtails are frequent visitors and, if you're lucky, you may see a flash of blue as a kingfisher whizzes by. It's a lovely, varied walk and well worth doing the whole stretch, whether assisted by the bus or walking in both directions.

Lydford Gorge attracts large crowds so, if you can, avoid the busy summer months. Early spring is a perfect time to visit, when the water is high and the woods are touched with green. Autumn, with its yellows and russets, is equally appealing.

Lydford is more than just the gorge. The village has the remains of a Norman fort (now visible only as a grassy mound) and a little square Norman 'castle' that looks as if it were built by a young child out of Lego bricks. This was used as a stannary court and jail, infamous for the harsh judgements meted out in the 17th century, possibly by Judge Jeffreys. Lydford's position between two ravines gave it a natural defence so the village has prospered since before the Norman Conquest when it had its own mint, producing silver 'Lydford pennies' from 973. The tin boom at the end of the 12th century turned it into a stannary town (page 279). It was also Dartmoor's biggest

"Grey wagtails are frequent visitors and, if you're lucky, you may see a flash of blue as a kingfisher whizzes by."

parish, so decaying corpses had to be transported across Dartmoor, from as far afield as Bellever, to be buried at its St Petroc's Church. **The Lych Way**, running from Powder Mills (between Postbridge and Two Bridges) to Lydford, is the ancient route that they used to take. St Petroc's is early Norman, but it's thought that an earlier, possibly 7th-century building preceded it.

Directly opposite the Lydford Gorge Waterfall car park – that's the southern car park – there is a farm with a difference. Helen keeps a herd of super-friendly alpacas (✆ 07579 218502 ⌂ lydfordgorgealpacas. com). Her farm borders Dartmoor so you, and your favourite alpaca, can trek into unspoilt wilderness. It is a calming, enriching experience – just you, your alpaca and nature all around.

If trekking is not your thing then you might prefer a one-on-one encounter with alpacas where you are guaranteed to be the only people there.

And if love is what you are seeking then Helen runs small-group speed dating treks which include dinner at a local inn.

¶¶ FOOD & DRINK

Castle Inn ✆ 01822 820242 ♂ castleinnlydford.co.uk. Lydford's gastro-pub in the centre of the village has plenty of unforced charm as well as two exceptionally fine stained-glass panels. I wasn't able to find out their history, but possibly they came from a church, since one shows a green man & another the 'tinners' rabbits' or 'three hares' that feature in most stannary town churches (page 280). There is a good beer garden too.

The Dartmoor Inn ✆ 01822 820221 ♂ dartmoorinn.com ⊙ lunch Wed–Sun & dinner Wed–Sat. A classy inn that is more a restaurant than a pub, with B&B accommodation (page 340) as well as seriously special meals. The menu features local produce including Devon venison & moorland steak. There is also a separate menu for vegans. Dining areas are exceptionally cosy with a warming log fire on cold days.

Lydford Farm Shop ✆ 01822 820737 ♂ lydford-farm-shop.edan.io. We were told that people visit Lydford Farm Shop just because their pasties, pies & sausage rolls are so good; we tried them & understood. Marcia & her team were making the pastry when we visited & she explained that the meat comes from her farm just up the road. The shop also stocks a good range of local food including fruit & veg.

9 BRENTOR (BRENT TOR)

The conical hill topped with its proud little church is a landmark throughout western Dartmoor, and the view from the top is, as you'd expect from the highest church in England, magnificent. On a clear day you can see Bodmin Moor and Plymouth Sound. The church is old – some say it was finished in 1130 – and stands at an altitude of 1,130ft, but that sounds a little too neat. There are many legends about why it was built at such a height. One explains that the original intention was to build the church at

"It is a landmark, and the view from the top is, as you'd expect from the highest church in England, magnificent."

the base of the tor nearer to the village. However, the Devil feared this might encourage the villagers to go regularly to worship, so he sent his imps to move the foundation stones to the top of the hill each night after work had finished. At first the builders rolled the stones back to the bottom again, but soon got fed up with this and decided to let the Devil have his way. They named the church after St Michael, who is patron saint of grocers, mariners, the police and other emergency services, paratroopers (that must surprise him) and the sick. The saint came to visit his newest church and took great exception to the fact that the Devil had engineered its position outside the village. St Michael then engaged in a fearsome battle with the Devil, finally hurling a great boulder at him and knocking him head over heels to the base of the tor. The boulder still lies there today, as a reminder of this saintly victory.

It's only a ten-minute climb to the church for a fit person, up a rough path lined with foxgloves, through cow-grazed pasture, dodging cowpats. The church itself is tiny and utterly simple inside. It's the location that makes it so special; and the fact that it celebrates evensong every Sunday in the summer and holds a Christmas carol service.

The award-winning Slow Travel series from Bradt Guides

Over 20 regional guides across Britain.
See the full list at bradtguides.com/slowtravel.

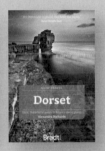

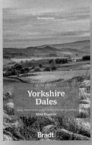

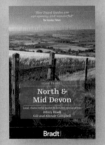

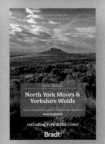

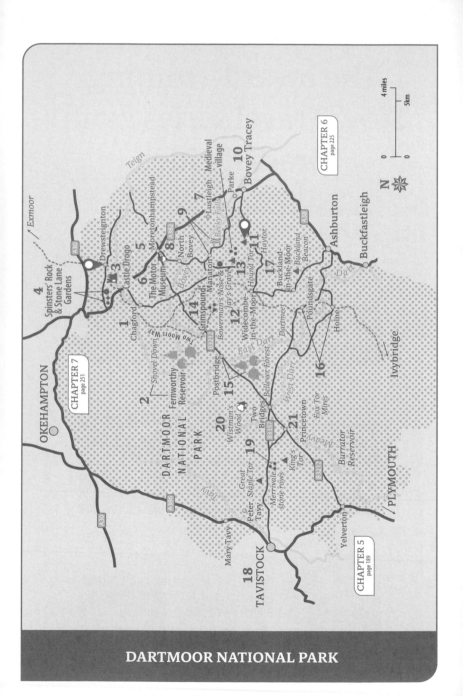

DARTMOOR NATIONAL PARK

8
DARTMOOR NATIONAL PARK

Look at any map of Devon and you'll see the largely roadless blob that is Dartmoor. Literature and imagination give it an air of menace: *The Hound of the Baskervilles*, a bleak prison where the surrounding moor is the best security, and craggy tors emerging from heavy, disorientating mists. This national park is high – the highest land in England south of the Pennines – leaving the visitor exposed to raw winds sweeping in from the Atlantic. There's a softer side to Dartmoor: sheltered, wooded valleys that feel a world away from the typical moor. But if you want Dartmoor bleakness you can find it. Once you cross a cattle grid the hedges disappear, sheep and ponies raise their heads to watch you pass, and the wind catches your hair as you reach for a sweater. You can walk for hours without seeing a road – or a tree. And everywhere you see granite: rocks as large as cars scattered randomly or piled on top of hills to form the tors that define Dartmoor, quarried and dressed in the walls of the ancient village churches, or rough-hewn and arranged in circles or rows by the first humans to make the moor their home.

The low-lying perimeter is another world, however, networked by deep narrow lanes. Footpaths meander through gentle, flower-filled meadows or dark woodland, or along the banks of rivers. The Tavy, Teign and Dart dominate, but all have tributaries and you are never far from a brook. Hidden in the valleys are small villages, their church towers poking through the trees, and welcoming pubs. But no-one visiting here would stay only in the valleys; Dartmoor is the high moor. You may regret venturing up there in mist and rain, but on a sunny day its wildness is alluring. It's aptly called England's last wilderness, and the feeling of space and silence, broken only by the trilling of skylarks and the scrunching of boots on stones, is intoxicating.

Dartmoor also has, uniquely, its visible prehistory in the monuments such as hut circles and stone rows that litter the moor. A newcomer might assume the tors are also the work of prehistoric people. The word comes from the Celtic *twr*, or 'tower', but these are the work of nature – erosion – not of man. And in an area that has blessedly few 'tourist attractions', nature has provided children with some rewarding scrambles and adults with hills to test their stamina, as well as giving Dartmoor its unmistakable horizon.

 ## WET-WEATHER ACTIVITIES

Dartmoor Artisan Trail (page 284)
Chagford Swimming Pool (page 290)
Castle Drogo (page 295)
Vessel Moretonhampstead (page 298)
Motor Museum Moretonhampstead (page 299)
MAKE Southwest Bovey Tracey (page 306)
House of Marbles Bovey Tracey (page 307)
Pannier Market & **Tavistock Museum** (page 327)
Dartmoor Prison Museum Princetown (page 332)
High Moorland Visitor Centre Princetown (page 331)

DARTMOOR: THE HAND OF MAN

There are more prehistoric sites here than anywhere in Europe, and Dartmoor is one of the easiest places in Britain to view the march of history, from Neolithic circles to the neo-medieval Castle Drogo. Most archaeologists believe that the earliest remains on Dartmoor are **Neolithic**, from around 4000BC, and that as true settlers these people had the most profound effect on the landscape by domesticating animals and cultivating crops. Then the Beaker people in the early Bronze Age, around 2200BC, built the Grimspound enclosed village (page 318) and some 2,000 other 'hut circles' on the moor. Bronze is an alloy of tin and copper so tin-rich Dartmoor was an obvious place to settle, the metal being easily extracted from rivers and surface deposits. Later, still a few centuries BC, came the **Iron Age**, whose most tangible heritage is the plethora of hill forts that are found in other parts of Devon, but not Dartmoor; and finally the two millennia of Christianity and its enduring symbol, the English country church, its fortunes tied to those of the tinners who continued to extract the valuable metal from Dartmoor until the mid 20th century. Wealthy tin merchants who endowed a church in a stannary ('tin-workers') town were ensured a short cut to heaven.

Visiting Dartmoor today, you may find it puzzling that Neolithic and Bronze-Age people chose to settle in such an inhospitable region. Probably, in an age where finding enough to eat was the main preoccupation, the attraction was the abundance of game in the woodlands that at that time covered low-lying parts of the moor, and the good grazing for both wild and domestic animals in the higher areas. The climate was milder then, and the soil less acidic; thousands of years of slash-and-burn agriculture impoverished the land and helped create the moor that we see today. The availability of granite for constructing durable, weatherproof homes and the mysterious stone circles and monoliths will have helped the inhabitants, but it frustrates archaeologists, since granite cannot be carbon-dated. But that is part of the attraction: we just don't know what a lot of these structures were used for, nor even when they were built. We can simply enjoy them for what they are.

It's thrilling to come across the signs of early human habitation on the moor, particularly when we really don't know why these people, living up to 4,000 years ago in a warm, forested place that provided for all their basic needs, went to the trouble of moving huge hunks of granite into geometric patterns. It is also a sobering reminder of the effect of deforestation and climate change on a once green and fertile land. Some of the most striking sites are the chambered tomb known as Spinsters' Rock (page 297), the easily reached Nine Maidens stone circle at Belstone (page 258), the stone rows at Merrivale (page 329), the Bronze-Age pound of Grimspound (page 318), and the cluster of prehistoric features on Shovel Down (page 293).

Moving forward to our known history, the **Norman Conquest** in 1066 resulted in tracts of land being set aside for the new king to indulge his enthusiasm for hunting. These areas, rich in game, were called '**forests**', although this did not mean woodland; the moorland of Dartmoor was a royal forest. In those times deer, wolves and wild boar were all plentiful. All have gone now, including most of the red deer. Penalties for harming animals in the royal forests were severe, and in the 12th century King John yielded to pressure and 'deforested' all of Devon apart from Dartmoor and Exmoor. In 1337 Edward III gave the Forest of Dartmoor to his son, the Prince of Wales and Duke of Cornwall.

It remains the property of the Duchy of Cornwall – and the current Prince of Wales – to this day.

DARTMOOR TIN & THE STANNARY TOWNS

Dartmoor, with Cornwall, was the first known source of tin. Some 4,000 years ago, metal workers discovered that by mixing tin (10%) with copper (90%) they created a stronger but easily worked material: bronze. Because tin doesn't rust it is also used to coat other metals. Minerals containing tin are almost always associated with granite, hence tin's abundance on Dartmoor. The ore was originally collected from the streams and rivers, through the simple process of panning or 'streaming'. Once these deposits were exhausted – and streaming continued into the 17th century – the ore was extracted from the ground using pick and shovel, sometimes with the help of leats, or diverted streams, to wash away the debris. Millstones were used to crush the ore and extract the metal, which was then smelted. Dartmoor is littered with evidence of these primitive mines, from the remains of mining cottages to deep pits, protected by guard rails, amid the gorse and bracken. Two smeltings generally took place, one at the site and the second, to produce pure tin, in one of the **stannary towns**. The Latin for tin is *stannum*, hence the term stannary.

Stannary towns in Dartmoor were mining centres where refined tin was collected, weighed and stamped. When sold, the proceeds were passed to the Duchy of Cornwall. In 1305 Edward I established Tavistock, Ashburton and Chagford as Devon's first stannary towns, with the right to organise their own political affairs through the Stannary Parliament and Stannary Courts. Other stannary towns were established later as mining became more organised. Stannary laws were the first legal code of England, affording the miners considerable power – providing they were honest. Legend has it that any tinner convicted of mixing impurities with his metal was to have three spoonfuls of it poured down his throat in a molten state.

◀ **1** A Dartmoor pony foal grazing in the national park. **2** The Long Stone at Shovel Down is one of many signs of prehistoric man on Dartmoor. **3** There are some excellent routes for mountain biking. **4** Three tinners' rabbits on the roof of Chagford's church of St Michael the Archangel.

THE TINNERS' RABBITS

In several places on Dartmoor you can see depictions of three rabbits or hares, so designed that they appear to have two ears each while actually sharing the second ear with their neighbour. No-one really knows their significance. Some say they are a symbol of the Holy Trinity, others that they are a secular symbol of the three elements of the tin trade: tin, market, wealth. One thing is certain: they are not unique to Dartmoor, a similar design being found in Iran, Mongolia and along the Silk Route. So this curious emblem has been favoured by Muslims and Buddhists as well as Christians.

GETTING THERE & AROUND

If there were a better bus service in Dartmoor we'd recommend leaving your car at home rather than tackling the single-track lanes – in the summer months you can spend as much time in reverse as going forward. **Drivers** should be aware that although the national park authorities have been generous with the provision of parking areas, and only charge a fee for the most popular car parks, they are tough on those who park at the roadside; if there's a risk of blocking access for emergency services your vehicle will be towed away. And note: there are no petrol stations within the national park, so fill up in one of the large gateway towns.

CAR-FREE ACCESS TO DARTMOOR

If you're willing to use taxis from time to time you can just about enjoy a car-free holiday on Dartmoor, especially if you're a walker. The nearest mainline **railway station** is Ivybridge (page 222), at the southern end of the national park and handy for the Two Moors Way, and there are two more stations on the park's borders – Okehampton (page 260) in the north and Buckfastleigh (page 240) to the east. Newton Abbot is a little further from the moor, but convenient for the eastern section. From Exeter you can catch the X38 express **bus** to Ashburton, every two hours, or, if you're basing yourself in the north of Dartmoor, take bus 173 to Moretonhampstead or Chagford, running four times a day.

There are a couple of ways to achieve perfect car-free days in Dartmoor. One is the delightful bus 271, the **Haytor Hoppa** (details on ⊘ dartmoor.gov.uk). This follows a circular route through some of Dartmoor's most popular eastern places, including Haytor,

Widecombe, Hound Tor and Becky Falls. With six departures a day from Newton Abbot Station (or Bovey Tracey) you can relax and enjoy the moor. The Haytor Hoppa runs on Saturdays from the end of May to the end of October plus weekdays in August – and dogs are allowed on board.

Another option, and a personal favourite, is the **Dartmoor Explorer** (⏣ firstbus.co.uk/adventures-bus), which runs twice a day in each direction across the moor between Exeter and Tavistock, stopping at all the towns and villages in between.

Other once-a-week offerings are equally rewarding but need more organisation. Spend some time on the handy interactive map on ⏣ traveldevon.info or get creative with the two relevant bus timetables: *Teignbridge* and *West Devon*.

SELF-POWERED TRAVEL
Cycling
Cyclists may find the lanes around the moor too steep and narrow for enjoyable riding (but take heart: electric bicycles are increasingly available), but those with mountain bikes are well served: there are few restrictions to cycling off-road as long as you stick to bridleways and designated cycle tracks. Many of these follow dismantled railway lines

TAVISTOCK COUNTRY BUSES

In the first edition I wrote about 'Britain's rarest bus', which went across Dartmoor on the fifth Saturday of the month, summer only. Which meant that it ran about three times a year. Sadly, it is now extinct, but there are several other equally scenic and enjoyable routes to choose from. The Tavistock Community Transport Association was founded in 1981 to provide transport to areas not serviced by commercial bus companies. It is run entirely by volunteers, and the buses are a joy to ride on for the routes they take and the friendliness of the passengers and drivers.

These buses mostly only run once a week and all start in Tavistock, taking between 30 and 90 minutes for their journey. Most are round-trip (just one, the 113, crosses Dartmoor to go to the shopping centre of Trago Mills, where it waits for passengers to have a wander around the shops and relax over lunch before returning). The routes are varied; some take you round the edge of Dartmoor or venture over the county border into Cornwall. Timetables are available at TICs or online at ⏣ tavistockcountrybus.co.uk; alternatively phone 𝒥 07580 260683. Booking is recommended.

with easy gradients. The national park authority has comprehensive cycling information and maps on ⊘ dartmoor.gov.uk.

Among the several dedicated cycle paths is the **Dartmoor Way**, a 95-mile circuit around the perimeter of the national park, some of it along abandoned sections of railway. Clearly signposted, it is strenuous in parts, but always on hard ground so perfectly manageable for an ordinary cyclist. There are plenty of pubs and B&Bs throughout the route so you can do it in two or three days, using Luggage Transfers (page 18) or taxis to transport your bags. The old Princetown railway track is also a popular route for mountain bikers. Easiest of all is the four-mile circuit round **Burrator Reservoir** in western Dartmoor (page 215).

There are several good bike-hire places. **Granite Way Cycle Hire** (next to the railway station in Okehampton ✆ 01837 650907 ⊘ granitewaycycles.co.uk) and **Devon Cycle Hire** (Sourton Down, Okehampton ✆ 01837 861141 ⊘ devoncyclehire.co.uk) are both popular since they are on the Granite Way and hire out electric as well as pedal bikes. To the east of the moor, in Moretonhampstead, **Dartmoor Bike Hire** (✆ 01647 440628 ⊘ dartmoorbikehire.com) offer pedal bikes, electric bikes, child trailers and even a tandem.

If you like cycling but look at Dartmoor's hills in dismay, consider a guided tour with **Dartmoor Ebikes** (✆ 07772 011519 ⊘ dartmoor-ebiking.com), who do the hard work for you with trips from Okehampton or Princetown. They provide you with an electric bike or you can bring your own.

Walking & backpacking

Until I came to live in Devon I avoided walking on Dartmoor, imagining waist-deep bogs negotiated in driving rain, and being lost for days in landmark-obscuring mists. So I've been excessively pleased by the reality – strolls along tumbling brooks, walks through bluebell woods, striding out along a disused railway with the knowledge that it won't suddenly take me up an energy-draining hill, and grassy paths up to tors with a 360-degree view.

That said, walkers should take the challenges of Dartmoor seriously. On the moor itself there is no shelter from lashing rain, mist can descend suddenly, leaving you with no idea where you are, and to cap it all there's a Dartmoor speciality, 'featherbeds', which are bogs covered by a firm-looking layer of moss. Step on them and you'll feel as though you're balancing on jelly – until you sink in. So stick to well-defined paths and check the weather forecast.

Die-hard hikers can get their teeth into the real thing by tackling the 102-mile **Two Moors Way** (⊘ twomoorsway.org), which runs from Ivybridge on the southern edge of Dartmoor (accessible by train) and across the roadless area of the southern moor, before revisiting civilisation at Scorriton and continuing north to Exmoor. Walkers wanting to do it as a coast-to-coast route, which is how it's sometimes described, can add a further 15 miles from Wembury (page 204) to Ivybridge. (Don't confuse this with another route also described as Devon Coast-to-Coast – the 99-mile cycle trail between Plymouth and Ilfracombe; page 190.) The first stretch from Ivybridge is around 12 miles of moorland with no escape, so a serious undertaking, but the feeling of being utterly alone makes it worth the effort. You will also be walking

"You will be walking through Dartmoor's history, crossing an ancient clapper bridge on the old Abbots Way."

through Dartmoor's history, crossing an ancient clapper bridge on the old **Abbots Way** between Buckfast and Tavistock abbeys, and passing **Huntingdon Cross**, a 16th-century boundary marker and one of the stone crosses that are such a feature of the moor. After Holne the path frequently crosses roads so can be walked as part of a circular route if you are not planning to continue across Mid Devon and on to Exmoor. The easy option for transporting your luggage is to use **Luggage Transfers** (⊘ luggagetransfers.co.uk) who can also arrange accommodation, or choose the cheaper option of arranging for taxis to carry your luggage between B&Bs.

The **West Devon Way** runs for 37 miles between Okehampton and Plymouth, skirting the western edge of the moor, while the **Templer Way** (page 309), from Teignmouth to Haytor, is only 18 miles long and accessible in many places by public transport.

Some **bus-assisted walks** that allow you to go from A to B without returning to your starting point are described in this chapter, and there are others on Visit Dartmoor's Haytor Hoppa website (⊘ visitdartmoor.co.uk/key-information/haytor-hoppa).

Dartmoor is one of the few places in England where true **backpacking** – carrying all your needs for a few days in the wilderness – is both possible and sensible. **Wild camping** was banned in early 2023 but

after vigorous protests that ruling was overturned in July the same
year. Camping is permitted almost everywhere, providing you avoid
farmland, prehistoric sites and enclosed areas, and do not litter or cause
fires. If you'd prefer not to carry your own tent there are a dozen youth
hostels and bunkhouses scattered around the moor. However, to my
mind, once you've experienced the freedom of wild camping, and if
you're strong and fit enough to carry a pack, there's no contest between
it and dormitory accommodation.

Accessible Dartmoor

Miles Without Stiles is a countrywide programme to establish and
promote stile-free routes that enable those with limited mobility to get

DARTMOOR ARTISAN TRAIL

Dartmoor has always attracted creative
people; perhaps it's to do with all that space
and wildness. The Dartmoor Artisan Trail was
established in 2017 to bring together a group
of 20 or so of the most interesting artisans,
artists and food producers to create an in-
depth experience for visitors. Blacksmiths
and beekeepers, potters and painters,
woodturners and weavers, farmers and
brewers – they're all there, and more. The trail
gives you the chance to meet these people,
see them at work, and perhaps try your hand
at creating something yourself. You'll also be
able to buy products directly from the makers.

The Artisan Trail is the brainchild of writer
and photographer Suzy Bennett, who has
sought out the most talented and innovative
people on Dartmoor. She is continually
adding to the list, and this endeavour won
the award for the Best UK Tourism Project by
the British Guild of Travel Writers.

The trail is self-guided: you choose the
artisans that most interest you and, if you

want to participate in a workshop, book
ahead through the website ⊘ dartmoor-
artisan-trail.co.uk. There is no set route for
car drivers but cycling is encouraged, with a
suggested route and bike-hire information.

Suzy explained what inspired her to set up
the trail: 'There is a resurgence of interest in
traditional skills and crafts across the UK, and
Dartmoor is one of the creative hubs of this
new energy. In a world of mass production,
it's wonderful to see that things are still
being made by hand, with passion, honesty
and integrity.' I spent an inspiring day
visiting workshops in Moretonhampstead,
one of the hubs with a variety of artisans
(page 298), and Chagford (page 288) before
heading southwest to meet Jane Deane and
learn about natural dyes and spinning at
Huckworthy Bridge (page 330).

Even if you're not a creative type, the
chance to see so many of these traditional
crafts within reach of each other and amid a
lovely landscape is surely unique.

out into the countryside. The routes are graded using a scheme set up by Disabled Ramblers (⊘ disabledramblers.co.uk) and most are suitable for all-terrain powered mobility scooters or 'trampers'.

There are a few routes on the Dartmoor National Park website (⊘ dartmoor.gov.uk) ranging from one to six miles in length, as well as on the Disabled Ramblers website. Some routes do have gates, but no stiles.

Guided walks

The national park runs these throughout the year, varying in length from two to eight miles and covering every area and aspect of the moor. Led by knowledgeable and enthusiastic guides, they are a great way of getting under the skin of Dartmoor. If you prefer a smaller group (maximum 10), **Keith Lambeth**, of **Out There on Dartmoor**, is your man (✉ outthereondartmoor@gmail.com). He is a team leader for Dartmoor's Search and Rescue team, and his knowledge of the moor is encyclopaedic. Keith has devised a variety of walks, choosing the most suitable when he has gauged participants' interests and abilities, and also with the weather in mind. Specialities are full-moon night walks and circular walks around Dartmoor's historic sites. Afterwards he emails you the route with GPS points, mileage and summaries of what you've seen.

Llama Walks, based near Widecombe-in-the-Moor (✆ 01364 631489 ⊘ dartmoorllamawalks.co.uk), offers guided walks where your luggage and picnic are carried by llamas or alpacas, and custom-made guided tours are offered by **Dartmoor Walks This Way** (✆ 01364 654471 ⊘ dartmoorwalksthisway.co.uk), which organises walks specifically to suit your interests and ability. Finally there's the **Dartmoor Walking Festival** (⊘ moorlandguides.co.uk/dwf) in late August to early September with a choice of guided walks, short and long, to choose from.

Walking & cycling maps & guides

The arrival of six large-scale Croydecycle maps for Dartmoor is excellent news, with Fingle, Chagford, Bellever, Holne, Haytor and Lustleigh covered in the minute detail for which these maps are renowned. In addition the *South Devon* one (page 19) at a scale of 1:100,000 is perfect for cyclists (and drivers), giving an overview of the moor and its roads and lanes, plus the main sights and pubs. The double-sided OS Explorer map OL28 is also useful. However, we call it 'the tablecloth' because of its size, and find it too unwieldy; there are more user-friendly alternatives available in the visitor centres at Haytor and Princetown. These include the OL28 (1:25,000) in a booklet, *Dartmoor A–Z*, and the *Yellow River Maps* (scale 1:16,000) for various popular areas in Dartmoor using OS cartography. Other good maps for walkers are Harvey's *Dartmoor* (separate maps for north and south) at 1:25,000, and Harvey's *British Mountain Map: Dartmoor*. The scale is 1:40,000 but there's enough detail for a variety of walks. By the same publisher and at the same scale is *Dartmoor for Cyclists*. It's double-sided, with one side showing routes for cycle touring and the other for mountain biking. Several walking guides with clear maps are available. Recommended ones include the six Bossiney walking guides for Dartmoor and Pathfinder's *Dartmoor: Outstanding Circular Walks*, but there are several others for specific areas.

"A couple of hours on horseback, in such a varied landscape, is far superior to a normal hack along rural bridleways."

RIDING

Several specialist companies offer riding holidays on Dartmoor, varying from a weekend to a full week. **Liberty Trails** (*𝒷* 07967 823674 *𝒷* liberty-trails.com) do luxury weekends on quality horses, but if you fancy trying something really different you can release your inner cowboy at **Dartmoor Riding Holidays** (*𝒷* 07966 522363 *𝒷* dartmoorridingholidays.co.uk), whose Western-style holidays on American quarter horses include a seven-day ride around the moor and cattle drives.

Climbing Dartmoor's hills on someone else's legs has an obvious attraction, and a couple of hours on horseback, riding through such a varied landscape, is far superior to a normal hack along rural bridleways. The riding stables listed opposite offer a variety of rides ranging from one hour to all day. When booking, riders need to be honest about their abilities. I was told that riders who could count themselves experienced at home were sometimes unprepared for a hack in such rugged terrain so it's better to underestimate your proficiency. Complete beginners are welcome at most places – the ride will be tailored accordingly. If you are fit an all-day ride is superb, allowing you to experience varied countryside and have a good pub lunch.

DARTMOOR PONIES

In contrast to Exmoor, where all ponies on the moor are similar in appearance (as you would expect of a distinct breed), Dartmoor's ponies are much more varied. There are few true Dartmoor ponies left now, the result of generations of cross-breeding, there being no rules on which ponies may graze Dartmoor common land as long as the stallions do not exceed 12.2 hands (4ft 2in) and are believed by a vet to be fit for surviving the often harsh conditions found on Dartmoor.

Since no pony is truly wild, and many will be sold on at some point, there are commercial considerations. 'Coloured' (piebald or skewbald) ponies attract higher prices than bay or brown, the original Dartmoor pony colour, so they are replacing the less strikingly coloured animals.

Pony drifts, when the animals are rounded up and marked for ownership before being sold on, take place once a year in the autumn.

A pony market is held in Chagford on the second Thursday in October.

The Dartmoor Pony Heritage Trust (DPHT) was set up to preserve the unregistered Dartmoor pony gene pool, and to maintain traditional native herds on Dartmoor. It aims to increase the value of the annual foal crop by handling, castrating colts not suitable for breeding and promoting the good temperament and versatility of these moor-bred ponies. Every year the DPHT, supported by the Dartmoor Pony Society, assesses the quality and conformation of the foals and awards the cream of the crop Heritage status.

The trust's visitor and education centre is in the Parke Estate near Bovey Tracey (TQ13 9JQ ✆ 01626 833234 ⌂ dpht.co.uk) where they run 'meet the ponies' afternoons. The trust also runs guided walks twice a month, April to October. All events are run by volunteers, so check the website for dates.

 RIDING STABLES

Babeny Farm Riding Stables Poundsgate ✆ 01364 631296 ⌂ babenystables.co.uk
Cheston Farm Wrangaton ✆ 01364 388188 ⌂ chestonfarm.co.uk
Cholwell Riding Stables Mary Tavy ✆ 01822 810526 ⌂ cholwellridingstables.co.uk
Shilstone Rocks Riding Centre Widecombe-in-the-Moor ✆ 01364 621281
⌂ dartmoorstables.com

CHAGFORD, CASTLE DROGO & THE NORTH

This is one of the prettiest areas of Dartmoor, with more than its share of river gorges, tors and prehistoric ruins, as well as the delightful Stone Lane Gardens, which are close to **Spinsters' Rock**. Chagford makes a perfect base for exploring the region, as it has reasonable bus services: the number 173 from Exeter and the 178 from Okehampton or Newton Abbot.

1 CHAGFORD

🏠 **Gidleigh Park** (page 341) & **Mill End Hotel** (page 341)
Tourist information: No office but see 🖱 visitchagford.com

Chagford can strike one as almost too perfect. It sits in an ideal location, sandwiched between the River Teign and Chagford Common, which is cluttered with prehistoric remains, and the village has a satisfactory shape with a defined centre dominated by the 16th-century 'Pepper Pot' market house in The Square. The shops are varied and concentrate on local produce, such as **Black's**, the very good deli which sells everything a food lover could ever want, whether it be ingredients, ready meals or just something special for a picnic. There is also an enormous hardware shop, **James Bowden**, where DIY enthusiasts can disappear for hours. Notable among the many arty shops is **The Artisan** (🖉 01647 432414 🖱 artisanmakers.store), part of the Dartmoor Artisan Trail (page 284); indeed it is a mini artisan trail itself, showing the work of dozens of local artists and craftspeople. There are ceramics and glass,

TO BOLDLY GO...

If this guide tempts you to explore Dartmoor, beware! It holds many and fearsome hazards. Take the pixies, for a start. They're friendly little beings on the whole, but if you mock or disbelieve in them they turn distinctly nasty. Visitors who are 'pixie-led' can lose all sense of direction and wander alone for days through the mist or be drawn to their death in marshes. Be particularly careful not to trample foxgloves or stitchwort, as these are their special flowers, and avoid their cave on Sheepstor. If you do feel threatened, quickly turn your jacket inside out (or your pockets, if you're not wearing a jacket) as this will appease them.

Then there's the Devil. Despite its many churches, Dartmoor is one of his favourite haunts. He and his Wisht hounds, huge and fearsome black creatures with eyes like glowing coals, hunt in the dead of night by Dewerstone and Hound Tor, and you may hear their ghostly baying in the darkness. His frying pan is near Mis Tor, so if you catch an appetising whiff of crispy bacon don't be tempted to investigate; he'll be cooking up his breakfast.

Witches are another risk. To mix her potions, the Witch of Sheepstor uses the water from Crazywell Pool, and Bowerman the Hunter was turned to stone (Bowerman's Nose) because he and his hounds disturbed metalwork and wood, paper and jewellery, stone and textiles. Two more Chagford participants in the Artisan Trail are Linda Lemieux and Ed Hamer. Linda gathers her own rushes and willow for basket weaving and rush chair seating; she runs courses and day workshops on her craft (℘ 01647 231330 ♂ woodandrush.net). Ed is a community farmer supplying local villages with his organic produce: members pay an annual fee and receive a regular supply of vegetables. Sort of like having an allotment

"It's in an ideal location, between the River Teign and Chagford Common, which is cluttered with prehistoric remains."

but without the work. You can have a tour of the farm or volunteer for the day in return for a free lunch and veg box (℘ 07858 381539 ♂ chagfood.org.uk).

When I asked a passerby for directions to **Bellacouche**, another participant in the Artisan Trail, I was taken aback when she said, 'Oh yes, the coffin lady.' But indeed, while I was to learn felting, Yuli Somme's main job is making felt coffins. So while I worked at creating a picture using the technique called needle felting, I chatted to Yuli about death. Scattered around her studio in a beautiful converted chapel are gorgeously decorated sections of white felt. 'It's an updated version of

a witches' coven. In fact, being turned to stone isn't unusual, so watch your step, particularly on Sundays: it happened to the Nine Maidens at Belstone Tor and The Dancers near Cornwood because they danced on the sabbath.

If you're driving or cycling along the moor's roads, beware the Hairy Hands: they'll grab the steering wheel or handlebars and try to force you off the road. Mostly they frequent the B3212 near Postbridge, although they've also appeared near Exeter. Making the sign of the cross is said to discourage them. UFO encounters have been reported on Dartmoor too, so watch out for aliens.

Ghosts can appear anywhere. A headless coachman drives Lady Mary Howard across the moor from Okehampton at midnight, in a coach made of the bones of her four husbands, and the infamous Judge Jeffreys haunts Lydford Castle in the form of a black pig. On Merripit Hill, little ghostly piglets trot sadly to and fro in search of food. Finally, be careful in Ashburton: the malevolent red-eyed watersprite Cutty Dyer, who lives by King's Bridge, accosts drunks and other undesirables and throws them in the river. Normally he tolerates tourists, but one never knows...

And you'll find many other Dartmoor legends at ♂ legendarydartmoor.co.uk.

an old tradition,' she said. 'It used to be the law to bury the dead in a woollen shroud to protect the wool trade.' The felt coffins are supported by a wooden frame with carrying handles, but no conventional coffin is so beautiful. Yuli decorates the top cover with pictures appropriate to the person being buried. After interment the family can keep the cover or leave it in place over the grave and let it gradually rot down and become part of the earth. 'Thinking outside the box', she calls it, and what a beautiful way to leave this world. Yuli's studio ($\mathscr{D}$ 07763935897 $\mathring{\partial}$ bellacouche.com) is in the Stableyard, just southeast of the village centre. She sells a range of felt items, such as tea cosies and slippers, so not just coffins.

Chagford was a stannary town and shows its former tin wealth in its **church**, which has some 'tinners' rabbits' (page 280) on one of the bosses adorning the splendid wagon roof. Although much restored, with some very modern additions, the church has great appeal; its features include a 400-year-old stone carving of an archangelic St Michael with luxuriant locks, slaying a 'nasty little demon'. This has been placed just inside the door. The list of benefactors is interesting: it ends with one pound seven shillings' worth of bread to be delivered to the poor every Good Friday 'to be continued for ever'. Look out, too, for the painstakingly done needlework hanging in the south aisle: showing the history of the region, this was made by the Chagford Women's Institute.

Chagford has the largest **outdoor swimming pool** in Devon ($\mathscr{D}$ 01647 432929 $\mathring{\partial}$ chagfordswimmingpool.co.uk $\odot$ May–Sep afternoons only). Fed by the River Teign, heated by solar power to 27 degrees, this is something special. The Tea Shed serves hot and cold drinks and snacks.

On the approach road to Chagford from the north you'll pass **Proper Job** (TQ13 8DR $\mathscr{D}$ 01647 432985 $\mathring{\partial}$ proper-job.org) on your left. This wonderful not-for-profit recycling place is absolutely crammed with goodies. There's a room stacked full of books, another with good antiques, and three rooms of quality clothing plus furniture, curtains, tools, toys and much more. If you're a natural scavenger you'll love it.

---

1 Fernworthy Reservoir is a beautiful place for a walk. **2** Castle Drogo may look austere but you'll find yourself warming to its human story. **3** Some springtime visitors to Spinsters' Rock Neolithic burial chamber. **4** Wander among the birch, alder and sculptures of Stone Lane Gardens. **5** Chagford's 16th-century 'Pepper Pot' market house. ▶

Fingle Bridge & the Teign Gorge

✽ OS Explorer map OL28; start: Fingle Bridge ♥ SX743899; 3½ miles; easy

This 'circular' (oblong, really) walk, one of the most popular on Dartmoor, is a walk of two halves, initially following the riverside before returning through woods and moorland.

1 Start at the picturesque **Fingle Bridge**, south of Drewsteignton, heading along the **Fisherman's Path**, which hugs the north side of the **River Teign**, passing through deciduous woodland and mossy rocks.

Joanna Griffin, wild swimming enthusiast, recommends places where you can swim in the deep pools of the river. Just upstream from Fingle Bridge, there is a small deep pool above Fingle Weir which is great for a quick dip. A mile and a half upstream is a long, calm, shady (and rather bracing) stretch of water above Drogo Weir, just downstream from an iron bridge.

2 From the bridge the **Hunter's Path** will take you on the long wind up to the **Castle Drogo Estate**. Just below the weir is a series of pools – Salmon Leaps – built by Castle Drogo's original owner, Julius Drewe, to assist the upward migration of salmon, which doubles as a natural whirlpool for wild swimmers.

3 The return along the Hunter's Path takes you through open moorland with gorse, heather and stands of silver birch, eventually forking right down to Fingle Bridge. There are opportunities to access the Castle Drogo Estate at the western end of the circuit, and the walk can begin from

---

🍴 FOOD & DRINK

The Birdcage The Square, Chagford ✆ 01647 433883 ⬛ ◷ 09.00–15.00 Mon–Tue & Thu–Sat. A lovely little café/restaurant which is a popular choice for coffee as well as meals.

Gidleigh Park nr Chagford TQ13 8HH ✆ 01647 432367 ⬦ gidleigh.co.uk. Set in its own 45 acres, yet near Chagford, this is a seriously posh hotel with a two-Michelin-star restaurant. Come here for that very special treat when you don't care how much you spend. Or maybe come for their afternoon tea, which gives you that glimpse of luxury without going the whole hog.

The Globe Inn ✆ 01647 433485 ⬦ theglobeinnchagford.co.uk. A relaxed & good-value inn by the church in Chagford, popular with the locals, offering accommodation as well as meals.

The Old Forge Caffe The Square, Chagford ✆ 01647 433226. Renowned for its great breakfasts & brunches – our favourite was the avocado, mushroom & poached egg but there is plenty of choice.

the Castle's car park instead of Fingle Bridge; here you can find a good selection of walking guides and maps and the café serves drinks and light meals all day. Variations of the walk can be done by taking bus 173 to Drewsteignton and catching it again at Castle Drogo.

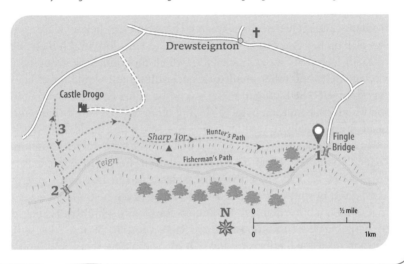

Three Crowns High St, Chagford ✆ 01647 433444 ◇ threecrowns-chagford.co.uk. A fine thatched inn in the centre of town with excellent food. Pricey, but it's a lovely place for a bit of a treat.

2 SHOVEL DOWN & FERNWORTHY RESERVOIR

For a total immersion in prehistoric sites, have a walk on to **Shovel Down** near Scorhill, at the end of tiny lanes west of Chagford. It has bits of everything, but you need to follow the OS map carefully to locate them – a clapper bridge (Teign-e-ver Bridge), Scorhill stone circle, several stone rows, a standing stone aptly known as the Long Stone, and Round Pound (an Iron-Age animal enclosure). Park near Scorhill Farm (♥ SX661877), walk southwest past the stone circle, then southeast over the clapper bridge to Batworthy Corner and the Long Stone, then head northeast up Kestor for a splendid view over the whole area – it is about two miles each way.

About four miles southwest of Chagford, on a good road, is **Fernworthy Reservoir**, looked after by the South West Lakes Trust (⌂ swlakestrust.org.uk). Although an artificial lake and surrounded by introduced conifers, it is a beautiful, peaceful place for a walk and some birdwatching (there are bird hides), with much to see including an impressive double stone row. When the water level is very low, submerged clapper bridges are visible. The reservoir can also be accessed from the car park just north of Warren House Inn (see below) where you can pick up the Two Moors Trail which takes you close by. I joined one of Keith Lambeth's walks (page 285), which took our little group here via hut circles and other prehistoric curiosities that I would never have found myself. The highlight was **Assycombe stone row** in a clearing in the woods, but walking back to the inn along a faint path bright with heather was equally rewarding.

Warren House Inn (PL20 6TA ☎ 01822 880208 ⌂ warrenhouseinn. co.uk ☉ summer 11.00–22.00 daily, shorter hours in winter) is a curiosity in its own right: the most isolated inn in Dartmoor, one of the highest in southern England, and with so much history and legend that there is a book about it. It's famous for having a fire that is alleged to have burned continuously since 1845 (despite, it must be said, patrons' occasional efforts to dowse it by readjusting their fluid intake and output). And there's the legend about the corpse. The story goes that, sometime in the 18th century, a traveller was caught in a snowstorm and asked for a room in the inn. There was only one available, sparsely furnished, but with a large wooden box at one end. Curious, the traveller lifted the lid

"It is one of the highest inns in southern England, and with so much history and legend that there is a book about it."

and saw, to his horror, a well-preserved corpse. Next day he got his answer from the landlady's son: 'Tis only fayther! The snaw being so thick, and making the roads so cledgey-like, when old fayther died, two weeks agon, we couldn't carry un to Tavistock to bury un; so mother put un in the old box, and salted un in: mother's a fine hand at salting un in.' Another version has it that 'we'd just killed the pig and we was saltin' 'un down, so mother, 'er put father in too.'

Warren House Inn is a welcome sight for walkers looking for warmth and food. It serves a great rabbit pie, appropriately, given that its name comes from the commercial rabbit warren nearby.

3 CASTLE DROGO

EX6 6PB ✆ 01647 433306 ◷ Mar–Oct 10.30–16.30 daily, Nov–Dec 10.30–15.30 Sat–Sun;
National Trust

I overheard a visitor liken the castle to a Stalinist gulag, and indeed, some find it hard to warm to this monument to 20th-century extravagance and megalomania. But warm I did, and I think it's worth the effort, and, indeed, the eight years of effort by the National Trust to stop the roof from leaking. It's always leaked. It leaks because Mr Drewe specified that there should be a flat roof and no windowsills or guttering. Asphalt was used, and it cracks.

Drogo was conceived by Julius Drewe, who made his money as founder of the Home and Colonial Stores which he and his partner sold in 1889 for £3.5 million – around £193 million today. Retired at the age of 33 and needing a way to use up his money he decided, without any evidence, that he was descended from the Norman Baron Drogo de Teign who had given his name to Drewsteignton. Now he needed an ancestral home, so he bought the Drogo estate in 1910 and employed Edwin Lutyens to make his dreams reality. Not a bad commission, even for the most renowned architect of the 20th century. Drewe wanted a castle of 'heroic size', which must have made Lutyens very, very happy.

I never thought that granite could look identical to concrete, but that's the impression given by the precisely cut blocks of stone. Inside, the plasterless walls are the same austere grey and even the garden is all right angles, although many of the castle's ceilings are curved to carry the huge weight of the higher storeys. The feeling of incarceration is not helped by the muted light. But as you make your way through the house you'll start to appreciate what you're seeing. The library is impressively laden with books and one can imagine settling down by the large fireplace with a volume or two and a glass of port. The view from the drawing room, with windows on three sides, allows you to appreciate the castle's magnificent location: ahead lies craggy Dartmoor and to the side is the Teign Valley. Make use of the enthusiasm and knowledge of the National Trust volunteers: they really know their stuff. The human side of this story is what makes a visit to the castle ultimately rewarding: the children's toys, eye-popping in their extravagance; look out for the horse-drawn carriage which could be pushed like a pram. There's a beautiful dolls' house too, though it was explained to me that what we call dolls' houses were not for children to play with, but rather

SIR EDWIN LUTYENS 1869–1944

The home-schooled architect of Castle Drogo was uncomfortable with his wealthy public-school-educated patrons, preferring to sketch ideas for mansions on napkins when seated next to their wives at dinner parties. The commissions that followed were traditional in style but always demonstrated some unique features; Lutyens was as involved in the interiors as with the buildings themselves, including designing furniture. Budgets held little interest for him, and he made it almost a point of honour to exceed them. In 1897 he married Lady Emily Bulwer-Lytton, the daughter of a former Viceroy of India, which must surely have helped him secure his greatest commission: to design the new administrative centre in New Delhi, a task which took him nearly 20 years.

Among Lutyens's best-known designs are the Cenotaph in London and Liverpool Cathedral, but perhaps his most appealing was Queen Mary's Dolls' House, which is on permanent display in Windsor Castle and was created as a showcase for the craftsmen of the time.

He was knighted in 1918.

used as decorative objects and to teach household management. The most poignant memorabilia are for Adrian Drewe, the first-born son who died in 1917 at Ypres, at the age of 26, having been married for just one year. As the oldest boy he had been involved in the planning of Castle Drogo from the beginning. It's clear from the lovingly displayed items how deeply missed he was, and one imagines that his father's enthusiasm for the great castle died along with his son; the reduction of the original plan by two-thirds could not have been purely for financial reasons. Tired visitors might be relieved to see the model of the house as planned compared with the one actually built.

Castle Drogo is served by **bus** 173 between Exeter and Moretonhampstead (but not on Sundays).

FOOD & DRINK

Fingle Bridge Inn Drewsteignton EX6 6PW ✆ 01647 281287 ⊘ finglebridgeinn.co.uk. The verdant location by the river is the main draw here.

The Old Inn ✆ 01647 281276 ⊘ old-inn.co.uk. Right in the centre of Drewsteignton, this 17th-century inn is a real find. Fine dining with locally caught fish & Dartmoor lamb on the menu when we visited. Also three en-suite rooms.

4 SPINSTERS' ROCK & STONE LANE GARDENS

The carved stones in these two sites may span 5,000 years, but in their own way they are equally mysterious and appealing. How convenient that they are within walking distance of each other (less than two miles), and accessible by the 173 bus, although of course most people will drive.

Spinsters' Rock (TQ13 8JT SX701907) is a Neolithic burial chamber which stands nonchalantly in a meadow full of buttercups and, occasionally, cows. This chambered tomb or cromlech would once have been visible only as a mound of earth, which has either eroded away or been removed to reveal the 'chamber' (now more like a shelter) comprising three upright stones forming a tripod, capped by a huge domed piece of granite. The sign tells us that it was allegedly built by three spinsters one morning before breakfast. Take the A382 off the A30, pass the sign to Venton on the left, and at the next crossroads you'll see it signposted. The gate leading to the site is opposite the yard of Shilstone Farm (a shilstone is the 'lid' of a cromlech). If coming by bus you will need to ask the driver to let you off at the turnoff, half a mile beyond Venton, from where it's a very pleasant walk up the hill to Shilstone Farm.

Stone Lane Gardens (TQ13 8JU 01647 231311 stonelanegardens. com year-round; sculpture exhibition Jul–Oct; free on Fridays for RHS members) is home to the National Collection of Birch and Alder, collected by the late Kenneth Ashburner from around the world. There are over a thousand trees, with 47 species of birch including *Betula ashburneri*, named in memory of Ken, and 33 of alder. Their white trunks give the five acres of woodland and water an ethereal appearance.

The gardens are a joy to stroll in at any time of year but the surprise and pleasure of the summer **Sculpture Exhibition** makes this the best season for a visit.

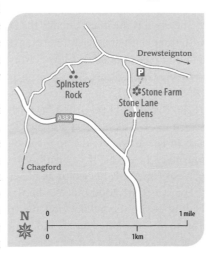

To reach the garden on foot or car from Spinsters' Rock, carry on up the lane to the T-junction and turn right, then either continue to the car park from where there's a short cut to Stone Farm or, if on foot, turn right again down the lane to the gardens. There are some parking places in the Stone Farm yard for visitors with disabilities. There are maps to guide you round the woodland paths and a printed list of the sculptures, and you're on your own to enjoy this perfect blend of the work of man and nature.

THE EAST

At each end of the oblong formed by the northern apex of the A382 and the B3212 are two of the gateway towns to the high moor, Moretonhampstead and Bovey Tracey, contrasting with some of the most remote-feeling yet accessible valleys in Dartmoor and two of its prettiest villages.

5 MORETONHAMPSTEAD

Tourist information: New St ✆ 01647 440043 (☉ summer 09.30–17.00 daily, winter 10.00–16.00 Thu–Sun). Staffed by enthusiastic volunteers who love their town, it has a comprehensive stock of local information.

This small town sits right in the centre of Devon, surrounded by some wonderful countryside and with the moor on its doorstep. It has a few attractive old buildings (among them arcaded 17th-century almshouses and a fine 15th-century granite church) but it is as a centre for the arts that it excels. The artist-led arts and heritage centre, **Green Hill Arts** on Fore Street (✆ 01647 440775 🖰 greenhillarts.co.uk ☉ 10.00–16.00 Wed–Sat), has a changing exhibition of local artists, an art shop and art and craft courses.

The town is the main hub for the **Dartmoor Artisan Trail** (page 284), with three of their artisans working here: a blacksmith, a shoemaker and a tanner (see opposite). All well worth a visit.

At 44a Court Street you can find **Vessel**, Jilly Russell's ceramics studio (✆ 07989 887717 🖰 vesselceramics.co.uk ☉ 14.00–16.30 Tue, 10.00–16.30 Thu–Fri, 11.00–14.30 Sat), where there is a small shop selling a selection of work by local potters. Upstairs, Jilly runs pottery workshops that last from two hours to a full day, and longer courses that last for four to eight weeks. If you get hooked, then you can become a member of Vessel and have access to all of her facilities.

For street art, look out for the wrought ironwork outside the Parish Hall opposite the gallery and the sparrowhawk in the central square. The main street has small independent shops with some good local produce – baking, meat, cheeses etc – and cafés.

THE ARTISANS OF MORETONHAMPSTEAD

Moretonhampstead hosts some of the most interesting and diverse participants in the Dartmoor Artisan Trail (page 284). I visited **Green Shoes** where one of the team of shoemakers was busy doing a final fitting for a woman with green hair and a happy smile. I hadn't planned to buy shoes, but when I saw how meticulously they were made, how mismatched feet of different sizes could be catered for, and the joy of seeing a normally mass-produced item made by hand, I was hooked. My feet were measured, style and colours chosen, and they are now one of my favourite pairs for both looks and comfort. I was shown what remained of an old pair of shoes, shaped to every bump of the wearer's feet. 'I've finally persuaded her that it's time for a new pair,' the shoemaker said. 'She's had these for 20 years and they've been resoled twice. But she loves them.' The workshop is in a lovely converted chapel (26A Cross St ✆ 01647 440735 ⊘ greenshoes.co.uk ☺ 09.30–16.00 Mon, Wed & Fri–Sat for browsing). If you want a fitting it's best to make an appointment.

Most popular of all on the Artisan Trail for 'having a go' is **Greg Abel** the blacksmith, also on Cross Street (no 27 ✆ 01647 440331 ⊘ moretonforge.co.uk). Working in his old forge full of the implements used by his predecessors, Greg makes a variety of traditional forged items such as gates, railings and fire sets. You can book a workshop with Greg to learn blacksmithing techniques or, best of all, learn how to make a small item yourself. I know how rewarding this is since I regularly go on blacksmithing courses to make scrap-metal sculpture, so do try it.

Jessie Watson-Brown's traditional tannery (✆ 07780 977058 ⊘ oakandsmoketannery. co.uk) can be found on Moretonhampstead's western edge. Jessie collects hides that would otherwise have been thrown away and uses smoke to tan them. She then crafts these skins into wonderfully soft bags and pouches and even hats and drums. Jessie's courses cover all aspects of tanning, including deer hides, sheepskins, rabbit fur and fish skin.

What struck us most about Moretonhampstead was its friendliness. Certainly some places are prettier, or richer in visible history, or more spectacularly located; but everyone we spoke to was so pleasant and so ready to spend time answering our questions that we continued on our way afterwards with a great feeling of warmth.

6 THE MOTOR MUSEUM

This is a great little museum (Court St, TQ13 8LG ✆ 01647 440636 ⊘ moretonmotormuseum.co.uk ☺ Mar–Oct 11.30–15.30 Tue–Thu & Sat–Sun; check website for other times) just five minutes' walk west out of Moretonhampstead. It will have any classic car enthusiasts purring with happiness and the rest of us saying 'I remember those' or even 'that's my first car!' Created and run by Frank Loft and housed in the old bus depot is a collection of 150 vehicles, including such rarities as a D-type Jaguar with a racing speed of 178mph, and a stately 1918 charabanc with a basket for umbrellas on the the dashboard. Necessary, I should think, when the rain blew horizontally through the glassless windows. Some bonnets are raised so you can gaze knowledgeably at the engine, and the signage is informative and comprehensive. There are also historic motorcycles and even some children's toy vehicles. It's hard to believe that so many vehicles are housed in such an apparently small building.

> *"It will have any classic car enthusiasts purring with happiness and the rest of us saying 'I remember those' or even 'that's my first car!'"*

LUSTLEIGH & NORTH BOVEY

Here are two classically picturesque villages of thatched cottages, only a few miles from the A382 but cut off from mainstream traffic by the nerve-rackingly narrow approach lanes.

7 Lustleigh

Lustleigh would probably feature in most shortlists of Devon's prettiest villages, sitting at the base of the Lustleigh Cleave escarpment with narrow car-free paths winding around thatched cottages. There is a well-stocked village shop, The Dairy, which also houses the post office. The village has a long May Day tradition, celebrated with aplomb on the first Saturday of the month, with maypole dancing and a brass band in The Orchard, which is reached by keeping St John the Baptist's Church on your right and going straight ahead at the (road) T-junction past the old post office. The names of all the May Queens since the 1960s are recorded on a rock in the centre of the Orchard. Carry on to the gate at the far end for the footpath to Lustleigh Cleave.

---

1 Bovey Tracey is home to MAKE Southwest, which showcases Devon's artists. **2** Parke's 205 acres are great for walking around – or for joining the Saturday parkrun! **3** Stop for a picnic by Becky Falls. **4** Moretonhampstead's diverse Dartmoor Artisan Trail participants include Green Shoes shoemakers. **5** Lustleigh is one of Devon's prettiest villages. ▶

DOM MOORE

CHRIS PARKER

HONOURABLE/AND3OLD/D

HILARY BRADT

LUSTLEIGH COMMUNITY ARC-HIVE/ROD LATHAM

LIGHT ON THE DARK AGES

Current thinking defines the span of Britain's 'dark ages' as roughly the two centuries following the final departure of the Romans, so around AD400–600, and relatively few artefacts from that period have been found.

In Yealmpton churchyard (page 206), a granite slab like a small standing stone, roughly engraved with the word TOREUS or more probably GOREUS, has been dated by past local historians to between the 3rd and 6th centuries, and described as a memorial to either a Christianised Roman or a converted British chieftain. Holes in its back suggest it was also used as a doorpost or fence post.

A similar but better-engraved stone in Lustleigh Church, with the inscription DATUIDOCI CONHINOCI FILIUS (of Datuidoc son of Conhinoc), is put at around AD550–600. The names are British but the language is Latin.

In Tavistock (on private land) are three more, roughly 6ft high, described as 5th–6th century, whose Latin inscriptions translate as 'Sabinus son of Maccodechet', 'Nepranus son of Conbevus', and 'Dubunnus the smith son of Enabarrus'. They were retrieved at different times in the 19th century, from Buckland Monachorum, Roborough Down and Tavistock. One had been used as a farm gatepost, one served as a footbridge over a leat and one was lying beside a road, so it's fortunate that they were spotted and taken to safety.

The men they commemorate remain a mystery (what type of smith would merit so important a memorial?), and more undiscovered ones may well exist, so, if you unexpectedly come across a similar slab of granite, do check whether or not it has been inscribed!

The **church** is well worth a visit for its beautiful wood carvings. The pulpit is by Herbert Read, a fine wood carver who contributed to the beauty of several Devon churches at the end of the 19th century, and the bench-ends are more recent, with figurative carvings of various animals including a rather jolly lion and an elephant. The screen is equally finely carved (though the painted panels have been defaced) and it has a modern (1929) rood (crucifix) above it, as would have been the case with all churches before they were removed by Cromwell's henchmen.

Two 13th-century stone effigies of a knight and his lady have been repositioned on their sides, and quite a few centuries later the stonemason (probably) carved a portrait of his gloomy-looking wife above the west window. A piece of granite against the west wall is described by Arthur Mee in 1965 as 'a mysterious stone inscribed with strange characters which have not been deciphered'. More recent research has solved some of the mystery – but created more (see above).

¶¶ FOOD & DRINK

The Cleave Lustleigh 🕿 01647 277223 🖉 thecleavelustleigh.co.uk. This lovely 15th-century thatched pub – dogs welcome – has a well-deserved reputation for good food & a varied menu. In the rear is a beer garden for summer lunches.

Primrose Tea Rooms Lustleigh 🕿 01647 277365 **f**. Serves excellent lunches & classic cream teas in its primrose-yellow, thatched cottage.

8 North Bovey

🏠 **Bovey Castle** (page 341)

🏨 **Bovey Castle** (page 341) & **The Chapel & Sanders** Lettaford (page 341)

With its spacious green surrounded by whitewashed thatched houses and backed by a church, this is a classic English village and exceptionally tranquil. The green is shaded by oak trees of different sizes, each planted to commemorate an event: variously Queen Victoria's Jubilee, George V and Queen Mary's Silver Jubilee, several coronations, and the smallest tree of all – the Millennium. At the edge of the green is a Dartmoor stone cross which was retrieved from Bovey Brook in 1829 by the Rev Pike Jones, known as Bovey Jones, and hauled into position. The famous thatched pub, The **Ring of Bells** (🕿 01837 871400 🖉 eversfieldorganic.co.uk/pages/ring-of-bells ⊙ closed Mon, Tue & Sun evenings), burned down in 2016 and several medieval features were discovered and retained during its two-year, £1.5 million restoration. It is an organic pub; the Eversfield family also own an organic farm and organic shops/cafés in Totnes and Tavistock.

"With its green surrounded by whitewashed thatched houses and backed by a church, it is a classic English village."

The **church** (St John the Baptist) is delightful, with worm-eaten pews and mainly clear glass to let Dartmoor in. There's an elaborate carved pulpit, donated by parishioners in 1910 to commemorate the vicar's 80th birthday and 45 years of service. The intricately carved screen is a few hundred years older, but the painted saints have been removed. The old pews in the centre have carved bench ends, mostly with architectural designs, but there are two in the south aisle of particular interest. One is carved with the initials WP, which could have been William Pipard, who was Lord of the Manor in the 14th century. The other is described in the church information sheet as 'a bearded Renaissance man with a jaunty feather in his hat.' He appears to have a string of beads emerging from his mouth: one of those enigmatic bench-end carvings the meaning of which we can only guess at.

The floor of the nave is almost covered with crudely lettered memorial stones to parishioners who died in the 1700s, and overhead is a splendid wagon roof with some brightly painted roof bosses; look for the 'tinners' rabbits' (page 280) above the altar rail.

9 MANATON & BECKY FALLS

Manaton was once two villages, Manaton Magna and Manaton Parva, which explains its fragmented nature. Upper Manaton, around the church, is perfection: a spacious green sets off the fine church of St Winifred, dressed in traditional Devon white, with a row of thatched houses behind it. One splendid house, Wingstone Manor, was, for a time, the home of John Galsworthy, who wrote *The Forsyte Saga*. The village green was bought in 1928 from its previous owner, Lord Hambledon (who owned a huge swathe of the region in the early 19th century), for £75 collected from parishioners. Last time I visited a game of village cricket was in progress.

The interior of the **church** has some rather splendid pillars of Devon granite, carved bench ends (mostly foliage and coats of arms) and a fine wooden screen defaced during the Reformation: every carved saint and angel has had its face chiselled away. The coffin wagon on display doubles as a handy surface from which to serve tea. The view from the churchyard across the moor to Haytor must be one of the best on Dartmoor.

"The view from the churchyard across the moor to Haytor must be one of the best on Dartmoor."

The local pub, **the Kestor Inn** (TQ13 9UF ℘ 01647 221204 ℘ thekestor.com) is actually in a little hamlet called Water, a half mile outside Manaton. It has views from the conservatory area, and a mix of locals and hikers enjoying the homemade bar food. There is a nice beer garden and five rooms if you'd like to stay longer.

A little over a mile to the southeast is **Becky Falls** (TQ13 9UG ℘ 01647 221259 ℘ beckyfalls.com ☉ Feb–Oct 10.00–17.00 daily), a good place to bring the family to see the meerkats, owls and, new arrivals, Sully and George (giant tortoises) and two Mangalitsa pigs. You can pet the rabbits, pygmy goats and miniature ponies, before visiting the reptile house to squeal over the huge boas and other snakes, and one of my favourite animals, a Madagascar hissing cockroach. Throughout the day, animal keepers host short sessions to explain more about the animals. The waterfall itself is pleasant rather than dramatic in the summer, but makes a good focal point. There are three walking circuits of varying difficulty, so you can suit your visit to your abilities. It's worth spending half a day here; there is a woodland café serving light lunches. Do make time to enjoy the birdwatching (we saw a dipper bobbing about on the rocks) and the mossy quietness (which you might not get during the school

LETTERBOXING & GEOCACHING ON DARTMOOR

In 1854, a Dartmoor guide named James Perrott placed an empty glass pickle jar by Cranmere Pool. He told hikers and other guides about it and encouraged them – if they reached it – to put some record of their visit inside. People began to leave postcards and letters, addressed either to themselves or to others, which the next visitor would take and post: the Dartmoor equivalent of throwing a bottle into the sea containing an address. By the early 1900s the Cranmere pickle jar had been replaced by a tin box containing a more formal visitors' book, and in 1937 a granite box was erected there.

Gradually letterboxes were placed in other parts of the moor, each with a notebook and appropriate rubber stamp. **Letterboxers** now 'collect' these when they find them by marking the stamp into their own notebooks; when their total reaches 100 they can join the '100 Club'. Letterboxes today range from solid structures to jars and tins to plastic sandwich boxes, generally well concealed. There are strict guidelines about their maintenance, choosing sites considerately and not damaging the landscape; make sure to read them on ⊘ letterboxingondartmoor.co.uk before placing a box of your own.

Remember, too, that a box placed in winter may be hidden by vegetation when you return to check it in the summer. A friend described how the growing bracken swallowed up not only the box but her smallest grandchild who was hunting for it: they found him when a little voice piped up from deep in the fronds: 'Grandad, where are you?' Children love the challenge of letterboxing, and another friend told me that her three would be seriously grumpy in the car on the way home if they hadn't managed to find a box.

From Dartmoor, letterboxing has spread to several other parts of Britain. It also caught on in the United States in 1998, then reached New Zealand and various European countries. A new and more technological version called **geocaching**, using GPS co-ordinates, started in the US in 2000 (⊘ geocaching. com) and now has well over 3 million geocaches worldwide. The Geocaching Association of Great Britain was established in 2003; its website ⊘ gagb.org.uk is full of useful information.

So, if you spot an unexpected container on the moor, you may have taken the first step towards becoming a fully fledged Dartmoor letterboxer or geocacher!

holidays). The Haytor Hoppa bus runs four times a day to Manaton and Becky Falls (Jun–Sep Sat), and the 671 makes a single journey on Wednesdays all year. The timing allows you to explore Becky Falls and Manaton and have a meal at the Kestor Inn before catching the return bus.

10 BOVEY TRACEY

🏠 **Ilsington Country House Hotel & Spa** (page 341)
Tourist information: Station Rd lower car park ✆ 01626 832047 ⏁ boveytracey.gov.uk
🕐 10.00–16.00 Tue & Thu, 10.00–13.00 Fri–Sat. Run by (very helpful) volunteers, so may sometimes be unexpectedly closed.

Bovey (pronounced Buvvy) Tracey is a lovely town to spend time in. If you approach from the A38, you'll be able to park next to the TIC and near the town's outstanding attraction: **MAKE Southwest** (Riverside Mill, TQ13 9AF ✆ 07507 671914 ⏁ makesouthwest.org.uk 🕐 10.00–17.00 Tue–Sat). The displays here are top quality, with a shifting exhibition showcasing the best of Devon's artists and craftspeople, from jewellery and stained glass to sculpture, pottery and ceramics, not to mention fabulous clothing. There is a shop full of beautiful handmade items and a small café. MAKE also holds events and workshops including some aimed at children.

Some of Bovey's shops, too, are aimed at creative visitors. One of the most popular is **Spin a Yarn** (26 Fore St ✆ 01626 836203 ⏁ spinayarndevon.co.uk), which stocks a huge range of wools. This shop is a painter's palette of colours, all softly blending with each other. The yarns come from around the world and the shop attracts visitors from far and wide. Further up the road is the new shop of **Serendipity** (56 Fore St ✆ 01626 836246 ⏁ serendipityquilts.co.uk), which focuses on patchwork and quilting. Myriam Van de Pas and her daughter Sunny sell a huge range of fabrics, patterns, buttons and other sewing supplies as well as finished goods, and run courses. While I was in the shop an old fellow came in for two more yards of material. He told us that a heart attack had put an end to his long walks on the moor so he'd taken up sewing instead. 'I've been making some amazing stuff,' he said.

Keeping on up Fore Street, you'll come to the Old Town Hall, which is now being put to much better use than politics – it is a whisky and gin distillery. **Dartmoor Whisky** (✆ 01626 832874 ⏁ dartmoorwhiskydistillery.co.uk) produces three whiskies; downstairs there is a small shop and upstairs a single large room houses their bar and, in pride of place, their hand-beaten copper still. The still is a work

DARTMOOR DIALECT

The late Tony Beard, 'the Wag of Widecombe', who was born and bred on Dartmoor, told me some of the local words still used in rural areas. 'There are lots of different words in the Devon dialect, and these can even vary from region to region within the county. For instance, that little creature the woodlouse has several different names: round here it's called *granfer grigg*. A blue tit is an *ackermail* and a wren is a *tit-e-tope*. We call a thistle a *daishel*, and sometimes we swap letters around so a wasp is a *wapse*.'

of art: originally a cognac still, its unique shape adds a particular softness and sweetness to Devon's only whiskies. You can book a whisky or gin tasting experience, which explains the whole process and gives you the chance to sample all three whisky 'expressions'.

All the delights of Bovey seem to be clustered together near the river at the eastern end of town, but the **House of Marbles** is some way away, near the roundabout on the Newton Abbot road (Pottery Rd, TQ13 9DS ℘ 01626 835285 ⊘ houseofmarbles.com). This is a working glass factory with a large shop selling just about everything, some fine exhibitions of glass and a small museum devoted to marbles. It opens at 09.00 (10.00 on Sunday), which puts it a step ahead of most attractions, and it's free so is popular with coach parties. There's plenty to enjoy here apart from shopping. You can watch the glass-blowers at work and, best of all, gaze mesmerised at the giant marble run at the top of the stairs. It's the biggest in the world, created to mark the Millennium, and I could happily have spent an hour watching the giant marbles progress along an intricate maze propelled by nothing more than gravity. There are smaller marble runs in the museum, equally enjoyable, and an interesting display of marbles from earliest times, when they really were marble, to the present day. There is also a small indoor and outdoor restaurant.

PARKE

TQ13 9JQ ℘ 01626 834748 ⊙ year-round, dawn–dusk; National Trust

This peaceful 205-acre estate, about a mile out of town on the B3387, is one of the National Trust's unsung properties. The walled garden is of particular interest, being run jointly by the National Trust and Bovey Climate Action (⊘ boveyclimateaction.org.uk), raising warm-climate produce such as peaches, apricots and almonds, as well as salads; there's a solar-powered pump for irrigation.

People come to Parke to stroll in the gardens or walk in the woods – or for the energetic, to do the Saturday parkrun – and to eat in the excellent café. The Dartmoor Pony Heritage Trust is here (page 287) and the Dartmoor National Park Authority has its offices in the old manor house.

¶¶ FOOD & DRINK

The Brookside Station Rd ✐ 01626 832254 ⌀ brooksiderestaurant.co.uk. Robin & Mark's café is also a restaurant. At times it is full of locals, in for a cup of tea & a chat & maybe a scone or two; for lunch you can get a fine chicken curry or chef Phil's pie of the day.
Creeping Thyme 5 Fore St ✐ 01626 923020 ⌀ creepingthyme.co.uk. Local lad Louis opens a restaurant with friends using local suppliers & wins two awards in his first year. Interesting dishes & great service, but only 20 seats so booking is a good idea.
Home Farm Café Parke Estate ✐ 01626 830016 ⌀ homefarmcafe.co.uk. This is a bustling & popular place, with freshly cooked meals & snacks using locally sourced & mostly organic fairtrade ingredients. Good coffee, too. Open in the daytime plus some weekend evenings.

THE HIGH MOOR

My favourite approach to the high moor is from Bovey Tracey. Cyclists toil up the three-mile hill, overtaken by drivers in third gear, but their goal is the same: the sudden view of Haytor and the feeling that you've arrived in the 'real Dartmoor'. With Widecombe-in-the-Moor as its focus, this region has bleak, open moorland, craggy tors and farms. Some of Dartmoor's oldest prehistoric sites are here, including **Grimspound** and well-known landmarks such as **Jay's Grave** and **Bowerman's Nose**.

11 HAYTOR

🏠 **The Rock Inn** (page 341)
Tourist information: Dartmoor National Park Visitor Centre, TQ13 9XT ✐ 01364 661520 ☉ Apr–Jun 10.00–16.00 daily, Jul–Sep 10.00–17.00 daily, winter opening times vary. Helpful & informative, with an extensive selection of leaflets, maps & books.

Four miles west of Bovey Tracey, Haytor is the best known of all of Dartmoor's tors. Easily accessible from the road, the 1,499ft summit is almost always topped by the silhouettes of scramblers who have reached the peak of this huge granite outcrop. Nearly two centuries ago some steps were cut and a handrail provided (now removed) to make the ascent easier, to the disgust of a local doctor who commented that the steps were 'to enable the enervated and pinguitudinous scions of humanity

THE TEMPLER WAY: THE GRANITE TRAMWAY

This 18-mile trail is more than just a long-distance footpath from Teignmouth to Haytor; it is an extraordinary example of using a local material – granite – in hitherto unimaginable ways.

James Templer was born in 1722. An orphan, he ran away to sea and made his fortune in India. On returning to England he bought the Stover estate (page 236) and built Stover House.

In the 1820s his grandson, George Templer, bought a granite quarry on Haytor, Dartmoor, and needed to find a way of moving the blocks of stone to a seaport so they could be transported to London (at that time Dartmoor granite was used for a great many of the capital's buildings and even London paving stones). So he built a granite tramway, using grooved granite instead of metal rails. Even the points and sidings were made out of granite. Teams of up to 19 horses pulled the huge, flat wooden trucks. The braking mechanism for going downhill was primitive, to say the least, but history does not tell us about the accidents that must surely have happened.

The granite tracks are still visible along parts of the Templer Way; on Dartmoor you can see them on a popular walk near Haytor and near Bovey Tracey.

of this wonderful 19th century to gain its summit'. It is no coincidence that the granite tramway (see above) ran from here; the granite is of exceptionally high quality, although erosion has now reduced Haytor's once single stone to two, with an avenue running between them.

There are some good walks from here, including the popular one to Hound Tor and the Templer Way, and a choice of circuits. The walk described on page 309 is one of our favourites.

¶ FOOD & DRINK

The Rock Inn Haytor Vale TQ13 9XP ℘ 01364 661305 ⌂ rock-inn.co.uk. A 300-year-old inn standing high on Dartmoor. Run by the same family since 1983, it offers convivial surroundings & local produce. Beer garden for fine summer days. See also page 341.
Ullacombe Farm Shop & Café Haytor Rd (between Bovey & Haytor), TQ13 9LL ℘ 01364 661341 ⌂ ullacombefarm.co.uk. A terrific farm shop & butchery selling everything, including their own organic produce. Excellent café; dogs welcome.

12 WIDECOMBE-IN-THE-MOOR

⌂ **Brimble Cottage** (page 341)

To most visitors this village is the capital of Dartmoor, with a cathedral to boot. Its popularity as a tourist honeypot stemmed from the traditional

A short walk around Haytor Down

❄ OS Explorer map OL28; start: Haytor car park, TQ13 9XY 📍 SX759767; three miles; generally easy, with a couple of steepish climbs.

The two or three (or is it four) main rocks of Haytor are perhaps the most prominent landmark on Dartmoor. They are very popular with tourists, few of whom stray far from the road. This short walk allows you to see more of the moor, enjoy great views from two tors and explore the remains of the 19th-century granite quarries and tramways.

There are two main car parks at Haytor and this walk starts from the smaller one closest to the rocks. If you park in the larger car park in front of the visitor centre, which does have the advantage of toilets, then directions still work fine.

1 Head for the most prominent, right-hand **Haytor** rock and keep to its left to pass in front of the rock wall. This area between the two rocks is grandly named 'the Avenue'.

2 Pass right around the front of the rock and then look for a main track left downhill, leading to **Haytor Quarry**. While the remains of the quarry are still very clear, it is hard to imagine that this tranquil place was once a hive of activity. In the 1800s, the granite from Dartmoor was used for buildings all over London. The foundations of London Bridge came from this very quarry.

3 Pass the two trees and keep left around the quarry. You soon find you are walking on the remains of the old tramway track built in 1820 – two long lines of granite. Horse-drawn trams transported the quarried rock to the **Stover Canal** from where they were taken by boat to Teignmouth. The track curves right to reach a junction.

4 At the junction of granite tracks, turn left to cross a shallow cutting. This cutting is known as the **Streamworks** and is the remains of tin workings. Tin was exposed by using water to wash away the soil – spoil heaps were used to channel the water to each area in turn. Tin working on Dartmoor dates back to the 12th century.

5 When the stone tracks fork again, take the right fork heading towards the tor ahead, Holwell Tor, and then curving around to the right into **Holwell Quarry**. The evidence of quarrying is all around, with five ruined buildings and a sheer rock face. Many of the granite boulders are covered in lichen: over 60 species thrive here despite the often harsh conditions.

song about Widecombe Fair: it's the one place in Dartmoor everyone's heard of. And once the tourists came they needed to be provided for; Widecombe must, for its size, have more tea rooms and car-parking space than any other village in Dartmoor. Despite the coaches and crowds its charm is undiminished, making it a good base for exploring

6 Retrace your steps and then fork right to climb **Holwell Tor** from where the view is spectacular across the combes and tors of Dartmoor. Hound Tor is very clear to the north and Honeybag and Chinkwell tors to the northwest. To the south is Saddle Tor and, about 550 yards away, you will spot the rocks of Haytor.

7 Pass across Holwell Tor, turning left behind its rocks. You are now heading for the ridge ahead, **Emsworthy Rocks**, beyond which Rippon Tor is clearly visible on the horizon. The good track wanders about a bit but as you reach the top of the ridge you are rewarded with a great view ahead.

8 Turn left along the ridge, soon seeing perhaps the best view of Haytor. Keep ahead towards the right hand end of the Haytor rocks and the car parks.

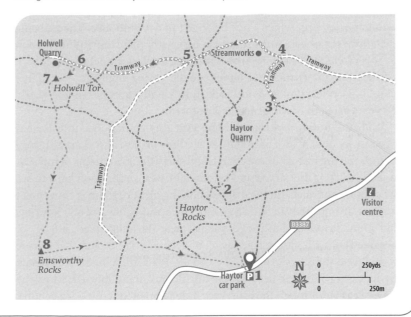

the moor and the valleys even without a car. With transport – car or bicycle – all of Dartmoor is within easy reach.

The village sits in a hollow, with the extraordinarily high tower (350ft) of the **church** visible from the surrounding hills and giving it the popular name of the Cathedral of the Moor. Much of the church dates from the 14th century, but the tower was added later and reputedly paid for by well-to-do tinners. The church is dedicated to St Pancras, who most people associate with a London railway station rather than a child martyr. This orphan was beheaded in AD304 as a 14-year-old for proclaiming his faith, and is patron saint of children; he can also do his bit for headaches and cramp. And for perjury, although I'm not sure how that works... Quite a few of his relics ended up in England, which explains why there are several churches dedicated to him. Widecombe Church has two depictions of Abraham and Isaac (relevant to child martyrdom): a painting near the south door and a carved panel displayed at the west end of the church. The sign identifies this as a tester, or bedhead from a four-poster bed, which once belonged in a farmhouse. There's some delightful detail here, with Abraham being stopped from killing his son by a very chubby angel. Nearby is an unattributed model of the church made from matchsticks. Another model, at the opposite end of the church, is Widecombe's 'Old Uncle Tom Cobley and All', made nearly 60 years ago and now rescued and restored.

"There's some delightful detail here, with Abraham being stopped from killing his son by a very chubby angel."

With the number of tourists who visit this church, the interior has become as much of a museum as a place of worship. Large display boards tell the history of the church and show the main items of interest, one of which is the carved and coloured bosses on the roof: hard to see by craning your neck so the display showing most of them is convenient and rewarding. They include a green man, a scapegoat and a pelican-in-her-piety, as well as the 'tinners' rabbits' near the altar (page 280).

Mixed up with all the legends of Widecombe is the fact that during a dramatic thunderstorm on 21 October 1638, the church was struck by lightning and four people were killed, and many injured, when the tower crashed through the roof. Very little happened in the 17th century that wasn't the work of God or the Devil. In this case, an innocuous-looking gentleman had popped into a Poundsgate inn for a glass of ale and asked the way to Widecombe. The landlady remembered afterwards

1 Widecombe's church is known as the Cathedral of the Moor thanks to its 350ft tower.
2 Widecombe Fair, originally a livestock show, now offers all sorts of entertainment.
3 Haytor is the best known of Dartmoor's tors. ▶

WIDECOMBE FAIR

Widecombe Fair (⊘ widecombefair.com), the popular market that enticed Bill Brewer, Jan Stewer, Peter Gurney, Peter Davy, Daniel Whiddon, Harry Hawk, Old Uncle Tom Cobley and all to borrow Tom Pierce's grey mare to transport them from their homes in north Dartmoor to the fun and revelry, is always held on the second Tuesday in September when the village operates a one-way system for traffic. Originally a livestock show, it has now evolved into more of a tourist attraction, with exhibitions and a funfair. The restored Uncle Tom Cobley model with its working parts, which was last exhibited 50 years ago, made its reappearance in 2009 and is now housed in the church.

that she heard his drink hiss as it went down his throat. In Widecombe the Devil, for it was he, tethered his horse to a pinnacle of the tower while he went about his mischief with some local lads. Some say he was involved in a tussle to gain a soul, others that he simply forgot that his black steed was still tethered, and galloped away, toppling the tower. The pious congregation disregarded the fact that God had, perhaps, selected a time when a service was being held to do a bit of smiting, and the church records their gratitude and praise.

Next to the church is the original **Church House**, which was once an ale house to refresh travellers, and then a poorhouse. It is now the village hall and headquarters of the local National Trust, with a shop and information centre. On the last Saturday of every month a **food market** is held here with lots of local produce for sale.

On the spacious green is a **Millennium Stone** under which are buried photos of every house and every family in the parish. However, they are on CD/DVD so whether the people who unearth it centuries hence will be illuminated or puzzled remains to be seen.

¶¶ FOOD & DRINK

The Rugglestone Inn ⊘ 01364 621327 ⊘ rugglestoneinn.co.uk. Named after a local logan stone (a wobbling stone that has become detached from its base), this small & very popular inn on the outskirts of Widecombe has been a favourite with locals & visitors for many years, & is one of the best on Dartmoor. The listed building is charming, the food excellent & the location sublime. Reservations essential.

Café on the Green ⊘ 01364 621720 ⊘ thecafeonthegreen.co.uk ⊙ 10.00–16.00 Tue–Sun. Indoor & outdoor seating, a very good & varied menu & fast service make this an excellent choice for lunch or tea.

The Old Inn ☎ 01364 621207 ⊘ theoldinnwidecombe.com. Situated in the centre of the village, it is indeed old (14th century) & has a spacious car park. The food is simple but good, & reasonably priced.

13 HOUND TOR, JAY'S GRAVE & BOWERMAN'S NOSE

Northeast of Widecombe are some of the high moor's most iconic attractions. Park at Swallerton Gate (TQ13 9XF ♥ SX739791), near Hound Tor, reached from either Widecombe or Bovey Tracey. If you visit on a Saturday, the Haytor Hoppa provides the perfect transport, or if you're a keen walker there's a popular three-mile walk from Haytor to Hound Tor which takes in part of the granite tramway (page 309) and the medieval village (see below). Pick up a walks leaflet from the Haytor Information Centre for a description of the route.

Hound Tor

Hound Tor is a wonderful jumble of rocks, often less busy than Haytor and providing plenty of scrambling for children. It is the starting (or finishing) point of several walks including from Manaton (page 304).

It's also the site of a ruined **medieval village**, although this can be so hidden among the vegetation in summer that it's easy to miss. From the car park, walk up the track that runs to the right of the tor and continue to the top of the rise; then as you pass the tor bear slightly left so that you're descending into a valley rather than heading for level moorland. You'll come to the low, broken foundations of around 12 buildings, some showing recognisable features.

"Hound Tor is a wonderful jumble of rocks, often less busy than Haytor and providing plenty of scrambling for children."

Without a plan or some archaeological knowledge they're hard to identify but there's a good description of the village and its history on the English Heritage website (⊘ www.english-heritage.org.uk).

Activity on the land pre-dates the ruins: it was farmed for a while at least as early as the Bronze Age, then abandoned after a series of cold wet years when the climate deteriorated. Several centuries later, in about AD500, Saxon farmers on the lookout for good agricultural land began to work it, as it had conveniently been cleared of boulders by its previous inhabitants; they built rough homes of wood and peat, which

haven't survived but can be identified archaeologically by post holes. Sometime in the 13th century, these were replaced by more solid stone buildings with wooden doors and thatched roofs. Some were traditional 'longhouses', on a slight slope so that the family could live at the higher end and the animals at the lower; drainage channels from the animals' quarters are still visible. They had barns, gardens, ovens – and the people probably enjoyed a healthy diet from their crops, livestock and nearby game.

The scope of the buildings suggests that it was a comfortable little farming community for a while, but in the 14th century the climate deteriorated again: persistently cold wet weather destroyed crops, leaving both animals and people hungry. Then came the Black Death, sweeping its murderous way across the country. Some families may have struggled on for a time, but almost certainly by the early 15th century the homes were abandoned. Today it's a peaceful place, protecting the memory of moorland farmers from long ago.

Jay's Grave & Bowerman's Nose

From the car park take the left, northwest, fork to walk to **Jay's Grave**. I first heard about this from my neighbour on the Haytor Hoppa. 'I haven't been for a while but there always used to be fresh flowers laid there every day.' The grave belongs to Kitty Jay, a girl who took her own life after being seduced by a local lad. As a suicide victim she was buried outside the parish boundary, but exhumed in 1860 and reburied in a proper grave in its current position at a crossroads. And there are indeed always fresh flowers there, and often other items such as coins. Treat the grave with respect or you may regret it (see some of the comments on legendarydartmoor.co.uk).

From here it's a pleasant and easy walk along a footpath to the lane that runs north of Swallowton Gate, and then over a grassy hill to Hayne Down from where you can take a look at **Bowerman's Nose** before returning to your car. Despite the misfortune of having been turned to stone when inadvertently disturbing a coven of witches while out with his hounds, the hunter does not look unhappy. Indeed, he has the

◄**1** The jumble of rocks that make up Hound Tor are great for scrambling. **2** Bowerman's Nose rock stack. **3** Grimspound is the best-preserved Bronze Age walled enclosure on the moor. **4** Bellever Forest is a great spot for families.

expression of a twitcher who has just spotted a rare bird. After all, he has an idyllic view of patchwork fields to look out on for eternity, and his faithful hounds are nearby, also turned to stone, on Hound Tor.

If you time it right, you can continue walking to Manaton and pick up the Haytor Hoppa bus (page 280).

14 GRIMSPOUND

About four miles north of Widecombe, and roughly the same distance from Moretonhampstead, is Grimspound, the best-preserved Bronze-Age pound, or walled enclosure, on the moor and only a short, though steep, walk from the road. The rather fanciful speculations that this massive circle of stones was a Druid temple or Phoenician settlement were quashed when excavations in the late 19th century concluded that the large external wall was nothing more exotic than a corral for cattle, and the smaller stone circles within it the remains of huts, some of them dwellings and others food stores. Considering their age, the huts were quite sophisticated: you can still see the stone beds, which were probably covered with bracken or animal skins. Grimspound, in its moorland setting, is incredibly atmospheric. Alex Graeme (page 4) says: 'It's my favourite place on Dartmoor and every guest I bring there loves it. As you look back across the valley you can see lynchets [medieval irrigation systems] on one of the hillsides and the remains of the tin-mining industrial landscape on another hill. So it's a perfect place to see the sweep of Dartmoor's history in one spot.'

A sign on the B3212 points towards the site (TQ13 7UB ♥ SX697808) but a better alternative is to walk there from Widecombe, taking the Two Moors Way (about three miles one-way); it runs above the site, thus giving you the best view of the circle and huts in this wild and desolate place. Imagine the time it would have taken to haul all those stones into position. Then visualise the hillsides

covered in trees, providing cover for wildlife and edible plants, and the cattle safe inside the compound. Maybe it wasn't so harsh a life after all.

15 POSTBRIDGE & BELLEVER FOREST

🏠 **Lydgate House Hotel** (page 341)

Heading south along the trans-moor road, the B3212, you come to **Postbridge**, where there's an accessible **clapper bridge**, and one of the few post offices on Dartmoor. There's also a national park visitor centre here providing information, maps etc (PL20 6TH ✆ 01822 880272 ☉ Apr–Sep 10.00–16.00 daily, winter opening times vary).

THE SNAILY HOUSE

Once upon a time, as one version of the story goes, two spinster sisters living near Widecombe existed for many years on a diet of snails. Their small two-storey cottage, named Whiteslade, became known locally as 'the snaily house', and the crumbled lower part of its ruin is still visible today. The surrounding vegetation is tangled now, with gorse and nettles growing up among the stones, but 200 or so years ago it was part of a working farm. The snail legend (which started some time before 1840) possibly referred to the thick black slugs that thrive in damp areas; locally they are sometimes known as snails. They may have been pickled or salted, as was done long ago in the Hebrides to provide food during the bleak Scottish winters. Probably some snails were involved too, perhaps spiced up with the wild garlic that grows nearby.

It is said that the two sisters were negligent farmers and produced poor crops, yet they appeared healthy and well fed even when times were hard; some villagers suspected them of stealing sheep or other livestock, while others whispered furtively of witchcraft. Few visited the isolated cottage. Then one day someone braver (or nosier) than the others sneaked along the muddy track to peer through the window as the sisters were sitting at their meal, and saw with horror what was on their plates. For the story to have survived for almost two centuries and given the cottage its nickname, the discovery must have caused lively local gossip and consternation, and yet there are old records of slugs being eaten in other parts of Dartmoor too when food was short. It's a mystery how legends develop. But there we have the two old women in their isolated cottage, hunched together over their wooden table by the light of a smoky lamp, tucking in to something highly unlikely to feature as an example of fine medieval dining. What happened next? We don't know. One version of the tale says they were so shamed by the discovery that they 'just faded away'; or perhaps good-hearted villagers took their diet in hand. Choose your own ending!

Southeast of Postbridge is **Bellever Forest**, owned by the Forestry Commission and consisting mainly of conifers. Nevertheless, this is a deservedly popular place for families and picnickers, with a good car park and walks along the Dart riverbank, with swimming possibilities.

If you return to the road from the car park and turn right you come to Bellever Bridge with, next to it, an old clapper bridge. Turn right again down the path next to the river and, after about half-a-mile, you'll reach some stone walls and, marked on the OS map, the ruins of the **Snaily House** (page 319).

SOUTHEAST DARTMOOR

This region of woods and deep river valleys reveals the gentler side of Dartmoor, ideal for a drizzly day when the mists are hanging low over the tors. There are riverside walks with swimming possibilities, as well as the lovely walk to Buckland Beacon for one of the best views on Dartmoor. **Dartmeet**, as you would expect, is where the two branches of the River Dart meet. It lies deep in the woods, with sunlit meadows and wild swimming possibilities nearby. It's a popular picnic place and can get crowded in the holiday season.

The main towns here are **Holne** and **Buckland-in-the-Moor**, both easily accessible from Ashburton or Buckfastleigh.

BRIMPTS FARM
Between Two Bridges & Dartmeet, PL20 6SG ℰ 01364 631450 ⟁ brimptsfarm.co.uk
⋀ **Brimpts Farm** (page 341)

Look at any old map or book about Dartmoor and Brimpts is there. William Crossing (1909) describes it as 'one of the ancient tenements, and in 1307 is referred to as Bremstonte' before charting its progression through several names to the present day. Andy Bradford and his wife Gabrielle now run the farm, which is an example of successful diversification from way back. Andy's mother got the tenancy of the farm in 1947, but it has provided accommodation since World War I. In 1969 the Bradfords became leaseholders for £1 an acre, to the disapproval of some locals who thought this too high a price. Andy loves green technology

"This region reveals the gentler side of Dartmoor, ideal for a drizzly day when the mists are hanging low over the tors."

ST RAPHAEL'S CHAPEL & VICTORIAN SCHOOL

St Raphael's Chapel, Huccaby, nr Hexworthy, PL20 6SB

What a wonderful piece of serendipity to come upon this charming place as I made my way towards Holne from Dartmeet. First I noticed the tall chimney and then the sign on St Raphael's Chapel noticeboard caught my eye: 'It's summer. Son Screen prevents Sin burn!' It was worth a look. I learned that the simple chapel was built in 1868, initially to provide local farmers with a place of worship on Sundays, saving them the journey to St Michael's in Princetown, and to be a school for their children during the week, thus ensuring that the new building was put to full use.

What makes a visit so worthwhile is that the chapel has many reminders of its previous use as a school. The pews adapted to desks are there, with a quill pen stuck in each inkwell, and slates. The headmistress's desk sits high in a commanding position, and to ensure discipline there is a dunce's cap and a swishy cane. It's altogether delightful.

The chapel is the only Anglican one in the whole of England that is dedicated to Archangel St Raphael, who is a patron saint of travellers. The chapel is still used for monthly services.

('He's the one with vision,' says Gabrielle; 'I look after the practical side.') One of the fruits of this vision is the biomass boiler and the Dartmoor Wood Co-operative to harvest the woodchips for it; diseased or dead trees such as larch and ash are often used.

In the 1990s some barns were converted to accommodation and group spaces for conferences including popular literary weekends (ask Gabrielle about these). Traditionally, however, Brimpts is for beef cattle (South Devon crossed with Limousin). 'Dartmoor wouldn't be Dartmoor without the farms,' said Andy, before the conversation turned to Brexit and his worry about imports from the USA. 'There are uncertain times ahead.'

16 HOLNE TO POUNDSGATE

Holne's attraction is its notable feeling of community, a lively place with plenty happening – and a lovely walk there with an option to cool off in the river. Park at **New Bridge** (TQ13 7NT ♥ SX711708) – not very new: it dates from the 15th century – and take the footpath south through National Trust property for about a mile. The track initially follows the River Dart through flower-filled woodland and then meanders uphill, crossing a field or two before emerging near the village. As the main track leaves the river you can take a small path to the swimming area where flat slabs of rock channel the stream into deep, cool pools (page 123).

Charles Kingsley, who wrote *The Water-Babies* and *Westward Ho!*, was born here. His father was the vicar, and Charles is commemorated in a stained-glass window in **St Mary's Church**, which is worth visiting in its own right. A splendid lightning-blasted yew stands in the graveyard, so hollow it resembles scaffolding rather than a solid tree. The church entrance is a little wonky – it seems to lean to the left – but inside all is as it should be. There's a fine wagon roof and a striking rood screen, beautifully restored, which depicts 40 saints of varying obscurity. A helpful loose-leaf binder explains who's who and what they were patron of, including St John the Apostle, who is patron saint of authors, booksellers and typesetters. I'm sure he'd add publishers if asked nicely. The pulpit, richly carved in 1480 from a single block of oak, has had its polychrome restored.

The village has an excellent community-run **village shop and tea room** (✆ 01364 631188), providing coffee and a good selection of cakes and light lunches as well as tourist information.

Just north of New Bridge is **Poundsgate**, just a scatter of houses and an inn with a history. **The Tavistock Inn** (✆ 01364 631251 🕸 tavistockinndartmoor.co.uk) is one of the oldest in the county, and it was here that the Devil had his glass of ale before heading for Widecombe (page 312). Nearby is **Higher Uppacott**, a historic Devon longhouse (page 324), which is owned by the national park and has kept its original features.

17 BUCKLAND-IN-THE-MOOR & BUCKLAND BEACON

From the high moor the village is approached via single-track lanes so it's quite a relief to see the tower of the famous church and know you've reached your destination (it's easier to access it from Ashburton, three miles away). It's the church clock that is famous – the numerals

---

1 The 15th-century New Bridge near Holne. **2** St Raphael's Chapel in Huccaby doubled as the village school. **3** St Peter's Church in Buckland-in-the-Moor has 'my dear mother' on the clock face rather than numerals. **4** The Ten Commandments are carved into the granite of Buckland Beacon. ▶

HELEN HOTSON/S

CASSIE LONG

PEEWAM/D

SIMON DELL

HIGHER UPPACOTT: A DARTMOOR LONGHOUSE

There are plenty of longhouses on Dartmoor, but none that has preserved its original features as well as Higher Uppacott in Poundsgate. The function of a longhouse was to house animals and people in the same building, using the warmth of the animals to provide primitive central heating – a perfect concept in a harsh environment like Dartmoor. These houses were usually built on a slight slope so animal waste could drain out.

Higher Uppacott was probably built in the 14th century and retains the shippon, or animal quarters, as used by the medieval farmers, with the cattle tied up in parallel rows, their backsides over a drain running down the middle of the floor and out on to the dung heap in the adjacent pasture. Hay was stored on racks made from branches and, since the building was probably running with rodents, an owl window was built to allow these predators in.

Originally the human living quarters were extremely simple, with a fire in the middle of the room, the smoke rising to the thatch above (this open-hearth arrangement can still be seen in Africa, and is effective in killing insects that would otherwise infest the thatch). Later, in the 17th century, an upper storey was created and the fireplace moved to the wall where a chimney stack was built.

There are details of guided walks on ⬙ dartmoor.gov.uk or you may choose to buy a copy of the booklet *Higher Uppacott: The evolution of a Dartmoor longhouse* from one of the park's visitor centres.

have been replaced by the words 'MY DEAR MOTHER' in Gothic lettering by 19th-century landowner William Whitely (more of him later) who also arranged for the bells to chime a rough version of 'All things bright and beautiful'. But the **church of St Peter** is much more than the clock and worth visiting in its own right. As one description puts it, 'The church on its sloping site looks as if it were carved from a natural granite outcrop or perhaps risen over time fully formed from the rock of Dartmoor'. Before entering, look for the tomb of a soldier who died 'succouring a foeman'. It's touching how proud the community obviously was of this demonstration of humanity.

Once inside, you can appreciate the contrast between the rough-hewn granite pillars and the intricately carved wooden rood screen showing traces of gilding. Its narrow uprights end in fan vaulting – a characteristic of Devon churches. Some of the painted saints remain in the panels, but half have been scraped off, no doubt in the Puritan era. More recently there's been a strong Royalist tendency. Above the south door is the coat of arms of George II, dated 1745, and along the wall are framed telegrams from the congregation congratulating a series of monarchs on their coronations and jubilees. They are mostly undated but the earliest is probably George V, with later ones to George VI and Queen Elizabeth.

Up on nearby **Buckland Beacon** are two granite slabs on which are carved the **Ten Commandments**. These were provided by the same benefactor as the unique church clock: William Whitely of Buckland Manor. Mr Whitely was one of many Devonians who felt strongly about the attempted introduction of a new prayer book (thought by many to have 'popish trends') in 1928. The proposal was rejected, and the Ten Commandments remind parishioners of God's unchanging laws – and landowner Whitely's influence.

The Beacon is not easily accessed from the village. With a car it is easiest to drive towards Cold East Cross and park just over the cattle grid (TQ13 7HQ ♥ SX740741). A good track runs close to a wall on your left and leads to the rocks that mark the Buckland Beacon (one of many such 'beacon hills', where fires were lit to commemorate the Silver Jubilee of 1935). The walk is level and easy, taking only 15 minutes, and from the top you have one of the choicest views on Dartmoor, a mixture of woods, river and moorland. On a clear day you can see the English Channel. The two slabs of rock inscribed with the Ten Commandments are just below the Beacon and, although nearly 100 years old, after restoration the text is easily read. The combination of easy walking, splendid views and a focal point makes this one of the best short walks on Dartmoor.

"The combination of easy walking, splendid views and a focal point makes this one of the best short walks on Dartmoor."

THE WESTERN MOOR

Much of the area north of the B3357 is used by the Ministry of Defence as a firing range (no doubt under the watchful eye of St Barbara – page 230). If a red flag is flying, you can't go there. This uncertainty restricts the number of visitors, which perhaps gives it extra appeal for those who like to be alone. One of Dartmoor's most interesting and popular ancient sites is here, but outside the 'danger area': the **Merrivale stone rows**. The B3357 leads to **Tavistock**, the gateway town to the region (so described first in this section), and just south of Two Bridges is Princetown, famous for its prison and the headquarters of the national park.

18 TAVISTOCK

🏠 **The Bedford Hotel** (page 341)
⛺ **Langstone Manor Holiday Park** (page 341)
Tourist information: in the Guildhall, just up from the river bridge 📞 01822 813946
🖥 tavistockguildhall.org 🕐 10.00–16.00 Tue–Sat

One's heart lifts on entering this ancient town. There is no urban sprawl, just an arrival over a humped stone bridge with the view of the stately Victorian Gothic of Bedford Square. The first building of significance here was the Benedictine abbey, built about a hundred years before the Norman Conquest on the banks of the River Tavy. *Stoc* is old English for a farm or settlement. The abbey became wealthy, and the town's success was cemented when it was made one of the first stannary towns.

> *"One's heart lifts on entering this ancient town. There is no urban sprawl, just an arrival over a humped stone bridge."*

Fragments of the abbey wall still remain; some are clustered by the river and one piece is even incorporated into the wall of The Bedford Hotel.

On the Dissolution of the Monasteries the abbey's land and the nearby town were bought by the Russell family, who later became the dukes of Bedford. The tin ran out, but a burgeoning cloth industry filled the gap before that too failed. However, just when the town seemed destined for oblivion, large deposits of copper were found at Mary Tavy at the end of the 18th century, and the new wealth of Tavistock was assured.

William Marshall, travelling in 1796, thought Tavistock had the potential to 'rank high among the market towns of the kingdom,' adding: 'At present, though meanly built, it is a tolerable market town.' His prediction came true. It is now one of the most architecturally homogenous towns in the West Country, thanks to the money lavished on it by the 7th Duke of Bedford.

The Victorian Gothic architecture is most evident in Bedford Square, the centre of the town, where you will find the magnificent **Guildhall**. This houses the tourist information centre and the Gateway Heritage Centre (🕐 10.00–16.00 Tue–Sat). Tavistock was the centre of copper and arsenic mining in the 19th century and it seems that not everyone was well behaved during Tavistock's boom times. The Guildhall housed a combined police station, courthouse, jail and fire station – all now open to the public.

For a deeper appreciation of the town, join a guided walk led by experienced guides, usually on Saturdays. Ask in the Guildhall or check on their website ⊘ tavistockguildhall.org.

Leading from the square is the covered **Pannier Market** (⊙ Tue–Sat), which has been held here since 1105. Though you should forget picturesque visions of shoppers clustered round horses with loaded panniers: this is more than a standard market. There are permanent small shops and temporary stalls selling everything from plastic dinosaurs to organic bread. A busy **farmers' market** is held on the second and fourth Saturdays of the month, but on any day of the week you'll find some fresh produce or plants for sale in Bedford Square. Each year in October the annual **Goose Fair** spreads along Plymouth Road where you can buy just about anything – except, possibly, geese. Historically these markets will have been just as their names suggest. The Reverend Stebbing Shaw, writing in 1788, describes the approach road to Tavistock: 'This being market day we met numbers of the people flocking hither with grain, a few sheep, and an abundance of Michaelmas geese. The common vehicles in this country are panniers and horses; nor did we meet a single carriage the whole day.'

> "Permanent small shops and temporary stalls sell everything from plastic dinosaurs to organic bread."

Tavistock has a fine 15th century church, dedicated to the converted Roman, **St Eustachius**. It is full of carved beams and angels, and monuments to the town's historic dignitaries. Most notable is Sir John Glanville, a judge, leaning uncomfortably on his elbow. John Fitz is laid to rest under a carved canopy, having survived being lost on the nearby moor, where a carved stone with his initials covers the spring that he drank from to protect him from mischievous pixies who might have misled him further (page 288).

Sir Francis Drake is said to have been born in Tavistock in 1542, in the Crowndale area about a mile from the centre; his statue is on Plymouth Road. The little **Tavistock Museum** (Bedford Sq ✆ 01822 611264 ⊘ tavistockmuseum.co.uk) is open from April to October and has changing exhibits on the town's history. The town is mercifully free of large chain stores, and has plenty of small independent shops including a good bookshop, Book Stop, on Market Street.

If you have time to spare in the town, take a stroll along the **canal**. Built to transport copper ore to Morwellham Quay (page 213), it runs

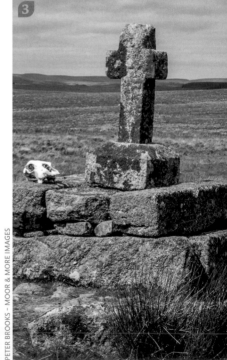

for 1½ miles before going underground. You can also walk across the viaduct, which is such a prominent landmark in the town.

As you would expect for a town of this size, Tavistock is easily reached by **bus** from Plymouth, and also by the 118 from Okehampton. Tavistock is also the western terminus of the Dartmoor Explorer (⌂ firstbus. co.uk/adventures-bus) which runs twice a day in each direction across the moor to Exeter, stopping at all the towns and villages in between. You can also enjoy the 21-mile scenic cycle ride on the Drake's Trail from Plymouth (page 190).

¶¶ FOOD & DRINK

Taylors Bistro 22 Market St, PL19 0DD ✆ 01822 613045 ⌂ taylorstavistock.co.uk. Exceptional food in a cosy setting in the centre of Tavistock.

The Bedford Hotel Bedford Sq ✆ 01822 613221 ⌂ bedford-hotel.co.uk. Bang in the middle of town with a quiet restaurant serving great locally sourced food whose suppliers are listed on the menu. Evening meals are creative & interesting with a slightly unusual take on traditional dishes. See also page 341.

OFF THE B3357

🏠 **Two Bridges Hotel** (page 341)

Between Tavistock and the crossroads at **Two Bridges** there are several places of special interest: a textile artisan, a fairytale wood, Merrivale's enigmatic row of stones and Princetown.

19 Merrivale stone rows

These are thought to date from between 2500 and 700BC and comprise two double rows of stones, with a third single row at an angle to the others. A standing stone, or *menhir*, marks each end of the rows and there's also a small burial chamber. The second row is just beyond it, running parallel, and the small burial chamber is about halfway along. As with all stone rows, it is assumed that these had a ritual purpose.

To reach the stones you need to park at Merrivale car park (PL20 6ST ⚲ SX553750). Get your bearings from the television mast that supplies Princetown and walk towards it; you should find them.

◄ **1** The Merrivale stone rows, thought to date from between 2500 and 700BC. **2** Tavistock's magnificent Gothic Guildhall. **3** One of Dartmoor's iconic stone crosses at Childe's Tomb on Fox Tor Mires. **4** Wistman's Wood looks straight out of Tolkien.

WOAD & WENSLEYDALES

South of the B3357 near Sampford Spiney, and next to the painfully narrow Huckworthy Bridge over the River Walkham, is Jane Deane's **dyeing, spinning and weaving** workshop (✆ 01822 612338 ⌗ janedeane. co.uk). Jane is part of the Dartmoor Artisan Trail (page 284); she runs weekend natural dyeing, spinning and weaving courses. I found it fascinating seeing the plants in her garden which produce the vibrant or subtle colours of the unspun Wensleydale fleece piled up in baskets. I now know what woad looks like (a bit like spinach) and learned that the blue from this plant is a mild antiseptic so that those blue-painted ancient Britons that we learned about at school were just treating their sores and flea-bites. Maybe. Blue is a hard colour to achieve. Most plants, whatever the colour of their flowers, give shades of yellow or brown.

After viewing the stones you can, of course, just retrace your steps, but this can be part of an interesting four-mile **bus-assisted walk** if you park in Princetown and take the number 98 bus to Merrivale car park. Then you can do a linear walk back to your car, through a satisfyingly chronological slice of Dartmoor's history, from prehistoric times to the 19th century, with the option of a dip in a quarry lake en route. Bus 98 currently runs up to four times a day (but not on Sundays); check the timetable.

If heading for Princetown from Merrivale you need to find a standing stone adjacent to a wall, then set your sights on **King's Tor** (and the television tower) to the north. This involves a certain amount of cross-country walking, but the disused railway track circles round it, so you can't really go wrong. After that it's easy – just follow the old railway track to Princetown. You are walking on a nice piece of history here. The **Plymouth and Dartmoor Railway** was built in the 1820s to transport granite from the quarries. When this became uneconomical in the 1880s the route was sold to the Great Western Railway. The last passenger service ran in March 1956. The track passes the disused Swell Tor Quarry, and if you have the time and energy it's worth investigation; look for the stone corbels that were cut in 1903 for the widening of London Bridge but never used. You can also take a short detour to Fogintor Quarry, and the possibility of a swim, by taking a left turn towards the somewhat forbidding ruins of the old mining buildings. From here, the quarry is down a short track to the right. Wild swimmers can walk around the left side of the quarry wall and enter the water from there. It's deep in parts but very shallow in others, with large rocks just below the surface. It isn't ideal for anything too enthusiastic but it's great for sheer atmosphere, and offers a different perspective on the imposing faces of the quarry.

20 Wistman's Wood

'It's straight out of Tolkien,' a friend remarked. 'You wouldn't be surprised to meet a hobbit there.' Concealed on the western side of the B3212, this small grove of stunted oaks is one of the few remaining examples of the forest that once covered much of Dartmoor, and one of the most wonderful sights on the moor. Perhaps I'm biased, having visited it on an intermittently sunny day in April, when the banks of the approach track were covered with primroses and the gorse was in bloom. From the **Two Bridges car park** it's a two-mile walk north to the grove, first up a farm track and then across the moor where you scan the barren hillside ahead for anything resembling a tree. Suddenly there it is, a green-coated fairyland of gnarled and twisted boughs, festooned in epiphytes, ferns, liverwort and moss, the oaks finding footholds between moss-covered boulders. It's as though some fanatical knitter has been at work with miles of green wool. In early spring the low sun gave the leafless green branches an almost golden outline.

21 Princetown

⚠ **Dartmoor Hill Farm Glamping** (page 341)

Tourist information: High Moorland Visitor Centre, PL20 6QF 𝒥 01822 890414
⌛ dartmoor.gov.uk ⊙ Apr–Sep 10.00–16.00 daily, winter opening times vary. The main TIC for the national park, housed in the old Duchy Hotel where Conan Doyle stayed, has a fund of local information (accommodation, routes, weather conditions, etc) as well as interpretive displays & exhibits, & all the books & maps that you need.

At around 1,340ft Princetown is the highest settlement on the moor; this and its well-known prison suggest a wild, bleak place with echoes of *Wuthering Heights*, but in fact it's a neat, functional little town geared to the needs of moor walkers and visitors. Rather than chain-gangs and fleeing convicts it has pubs, shops, eating places, B&Bs, its own Dartmoor Brewery (the highest in England) and an excellent, and unusual, museum.

The town is not particularly old. In 1785 Sir Thomas Tyrwhitt, secretary to the Prince of Wales, leased a large area of moorland from the Duchy of Cornwall, intending to convert it into profitable farmland. The road from Tavistock was built and a settlement gradually grew, named Princetown after the Prince of Wales. When French prisoners from the Napoleonic Wars were too numerous for Plymouth jail, Tyrwhitt suggested that a prison be built in his 'new town' to house them; the French were soon followed by American sailors from the War of 1812. The warders and other prison staff needed accommodation, so that was constructed, and in 1812–15 prisoners built the simple granite **church of St Michael and all Angels**, which is now looked after by the Churches Conservation Trust ($\mathcal{O}$ visitchurches.org.uk). It wasn't until 1850 that the old POW camp was converted into a prison for the most dangerous convicts; before that they were dispatched to Australia. So the small town and its prison have always coexisted, their histories closely linked.

The **Dartmoor Prison Museum** (PL20 6RR $\mathcal{O}$ 01822 322130 $\mathcal{O}$ dartmoor-prison.co.uk $\odot$ Feb–Dec 09.30–16.00 daily) is housed in the old prison dairy just past the main prison entrance on the road to Tavistock. Extensively enlarged and refurbished in 2017, exhibits in this exceptionally interesting museum range from items made by French

SHEEP ON DARTMOOR

Most visitors to Dartmoor are only vaguely aware of the sheep that graze the moor and wander over the road in front of their cars. A conversation with Jane Deane (page 330), who uses their wool for a variety of crafts – dyeing, spinning and weaving – told me how much they vary in both the quality of their wool and their suitability to moor life. 'Rare breeds are rare for a good reason!' says Jane. For instance, the rare local Devon and Cornwall longwool sheep are reputed to be terrible mothers, giving birth and then relinquishing all responsibility for their offspring.

The best wool comes from blue-faced Leicester sheep, which Jane describes as looking 'a bit like Victorian clergymen, with a bare head and Roman nose'. But they are too delicate for the moor. The Greyface Dartmoor has been developed to thrive on the moor but their wool is coarse and mainly used for carpets. Even scratchier are the Hardwick sheep from the Lake District, which Jane says have wool like Brillo pads.

Most of the sheep that you see on the moor are the hardy Scottish blackface. All sheep must be clearly marked to identify their owner, and the marks registered with the Commoners' Council. Sheep are marked with a splash of paint on their fleece, the position and colour being unique to the owner, and a distinguishing notch in their ear.

prisoners of war, including a model of Notre Dame Cathedral, to the brutal punishment implements from years gone by. These include a flogging frame, last used in 1952, and a 'man-hauling belt', with the aid of which prisoners could pull carts around the prison and village. Old Pathé News clips reporting on 'the toughest prison in the country', riots and escapes contrast with interviews with present-day prisoners describing the modern regime with a positive spin. A description of Moor Trees, where prisoners help in reforestation projects, reinforces the message of how much the prison has changed.

"With its enthusiastic staff this is an absorbing and different museum – and one that children will love."

With its knowledgeable and enthusiastic staff this is an absorbing and different museum – and one that children will love.

Another option for those with children is to try a bit of rock climbing, abseiling and weaselling. **Crag2Mountain** (⊘ crag2mountain.co.uk) offer all sorts of outdoor activities and courses, some aimed at families but others for adults who would like to have a go at something a little more challenging with the guidance of local experts. Sessions last from a couple of hours to a few days.

There's a cash machine (not free) outside the village store in the main street, and the post office counter inside offers free withdrawal services during normal hours. The Dartmoor Brewery Shop (⊙ 09.00–16.00 Mon–Fri) sells its own Jail Ale, Legend, Dartmoor IPA and Dartmoor Best as well as seasonal 'specials' including Santa's Secret, Dragon's Breath and the very warming Christmas Ale.

Princetown is served year-round (Mon–Sat) by bus number 98, four times a day from Tavistock and three times from Yelverton. The 113 between Tavistock and Newton Abbot only runs once each way on the first and third Wednesdays of the month; booking advised (⊘ 07580 260683).

Yelverton and the Burrator Reservoir are described in *Chapter 5*.

¶¶ FOOD & DRINK

Fox Tor Café 2 Two Bridges Rd ⊘ 01822 890238 ⊘ foxtorcafe.com. Snacks, full meals & cream teas; comfy sofas. Indoor & outdoor seating & free Wi-Fi. Also has a bunkhouse.
The Old Police Station Café Tavistock Rd ⊘ 01822 890415 ⊘ theoldpolicestation. uk. A friendly café with traditional all-day food (good breakfasts, including vegetarian) & take-aways.

THE HOUND OF THE BASKERVILLES

Alex Graeme, of Unique Devon Tours & uniquedevontours.com

What a story! One of detective fiction's finest, the most popular of the Sherlock Holmes novels, and famous all around the world. And yet the story behind the story is just as intriguing as the tale itself, and stems from this part of Devon. Spending the day visiting all the places that inspired Sir Arthur Conan Doyle when writing his book, with their combination of historic churches, dramatic country views, tranquil old towns and iconic Dartmoor locations, makes for the perfect Slow visit.

First, **Ipplepen** introduces us to some of the real-life characters who contributed to the story. Bertram Fletcher Robinson, a friend of Conan Doyle, lived here, and it was he who told Doyle the legend that inspired the story: that of Squire Richard Cabell III, a 17th-century brute of a man who lived near Buckfastleigh, supposedly murdered his wife, and terrified the locals while out hunting with his devilish pack of hounds. His coachman, Henry Baskerville, drove Conan Doyle around the area during his visits. Finally, Robert Duins Cooke, the local vicar at Ipplepen from 1897 to 1939, also happened to be an expert on Dartmoor, and suggested which Dartmoor locations Doyle should visit when he came to Devon to do his research. These three were all in Ipplepen while the story was being constructed, and their homes can still be seen. The headstones of Bertram Fletcher Robinson and Robert Duins Cooke are both in the graveyard at St Andrew's Church, as are those of Henry Baskerville's parents and brother.

The Prince of Wales Tavistock Rd ℘ 01822 890219 ⓦ princeofwalesbunkhouse.co.uk. Hearty pub meals, generous helpings, friendly company, log fires in winter, bunkhouse & campsite.

Fox Tor Mires

If you take the minor road south from Princetown you will come, at the very end, to Fox Tor Mires, an area so desolate that you can believe all the legends associated with it. Most famous is that it was the inspiration for Grimpen Mire in *The Hound of the Baskervilles* (see above) and, being probably the most treacherous 'featherbed' bog on Dartmoor, it is the stuff of other legends. One story (from ⓦ legendarydartmoor.co.uk) goes that a fellow was heading home across the moor when he saw a rather splendid top hat sitting on a green patch of featherbed. The lad gingerly approached the mire to retrieve the

"You will come to Fox Tor Mires, an area so desolate you can believe all the legends associated with it."

Baskerville eventually moved to **Ashburton**, where we can still see the red brick house where he lived. His headstone is there in the graveyard of St Andrew's Church, not far from the headstone of a certain James Mortimer, whose name also appears in Doyle's story.

We continue to **Buckfastleigh** to visit the unique Holy Trinity Church, both tragic and fascinating in its history and very different from any other church in Devon. This is where the Hound of the Baskervilles story really began (page 241).

Next the mystique of Dartmoor beckons, and it's off to the high ground, passing Brook Manor where the notorious Squire Cabell lived. We come to the extraordinary Bronze-Age settlement of **Grimspound** (page 318), which inspired Conan Doyle's reference to 'prehistoric man' in the story, as well as the prehistoric huts that an incognito Sherlock stayed in when he came to the moors. In **Princetown**, the most central town on Dartmoor and without a doubt the bleakest, with its prison and higher-than-average rainfall, what is now the national park visitor centre was once the Duchy Hotel, where Doyle stayed while exploring the moors. **Fox Tor Mires**, one of Dartmoor's most desolate and atmospheric places, inspired him to create Grimpen Mire, described by Watson as a melancholy place and the most evocative of the locations in his story.

I have followed this circuit many times, since a Hound of the Baskervilles Tour is among those that my company offers. After all, the Reverend Robert Duins Cooke was my great-grandfather!

hat. As he picked it up he was astonished to find that under the hat was a head, which smiled courteously, introduced itself and asked if the lad might, perhaps, try to pull him out of the bog. Regaining his composure the fellow gave it his best effort but to no avail. The gent then offered a suggestion: 'If you wouldn't mind waiting a moment I'll try to take my feet out of the stirrups; I'm still on my horse.'

I was taken here by Alex Graeme, who described it as 'a huge bowl of granite through which the water never really drains away'. One of Dartmoor's stone crosses, marking **Childe's Tomb**, is near here, and the remains of tin-miners' houses and the mining pits all contribute to the feeling of desolation and abandonment.

ACCOMMODATION

The places to stay that are listed in this section have been chosen either because of their location, because they are in some way unusual, or because they encapsulate the Slow approach. Since the first edition, glamping has really come into its own, so that is included too. The suggestions below are just a small selection of the many places that we happened to find or hear about as we researched; an internet search will reveal hundreds more.

In Devon by far the most popular accommodation is self-catering, offered by a large number of agencies. We have listed some alphabetically in the box opposite.

The hotels, pubs and B&Bs featured in this section are indicated by ♠ under the heading for the town or village in which they are located. Self-catering is indicated by 🏠, campsites by ⋀ and glamping by ⋀. For complete listings and fuller descriptions, go to ⊘ bradtguides.com/southdevonsleeps.

1 THE EXE & TEIGN ESTUARIES

Hotels
The Ness Shaldon TQ14 0HP ✆ 01626 873480 ⊘ theness.co.uk. Beautifully set on the edge of Shaldon with commanding views over the Teign Estuary. Nine en-suite bedrooms, popular restaurant.

B&Bs
Lammas Park House Dawlish EX7 9JF ✆ 01626 888064 ⊘ lammasparkhouse.co.uk. Super-comfortable Georgian B&B with sea views from all three large rooms & from the two-bedroom suite.

Self-catering
Brunel Holiday Park Dawlish Warren EX7 0NF ✆ 01626 888527 ⊘ brunelholidaypark.co.uk. Five converted railway carriages sleeping up to six. Near beach & good public transport.
Yannon Towers Teignmouth TQ14 9UE ✆ 07805119442 ⊘ airbnb.co.uk. Gothic folly sleeping ten with spectacular views over Teignmouth & the sea.

Glamping
Rocombe Valley Retreat Stokeinteignhead TQ12 4QL ✆ 07563 996496 ⊘ rocombevalleyretreat.co.uk. Quiet retreat, surrounded by woodland & fields, with a safari tent, three yurts & a shepherd's hut – each with a fire pit & a private hot tub.

SELF-CATERING

Airbnb ⚲ airbnb.co.uk. Ubiquitous but useful with a huge number of properties available.

Canopy & Stars ⚲ canopyandstars. co.uk. Sawday's glamping selection.

Classic Cottages ⚲ classic.co.uk. West Country specialists.

Coast & Country Cottages coastandcountry.co.uk. South-Hams-based self-catering holidays.

Cottages.com ⚲ cottages.com. One of the UK's leading providers of holiday cottages.

Dart Valley Cottages ⚲ dartvalleycottages.co.uk. Focuses on the most attractive parts of the River Dart.

Devon Holiday Cottages ⚲ devonholidaycottages.com. Specifically Devon for all budgets.

Helpful Holidays ⚲ helpfulholidays. com. Based in Chagford, with a huge range of places.

Holiday Cottages ⚲ holidaycottages. co.uk. Bideford-based company with cottages across the UK.

The Landmark Trust ⚲ 01628 825920 ⚲ landmarktrust.org.uk. This charitable organisation is quite different from the other accommodation providers listed here. Their role is to rescue historic buildings in danger of dereliction, restore them, & rent them out to holidaymakers. Furnishing is done with an eye for the history & character of the place, & there are no TVs, Wi-Fi or telephones.

Quirky Accommodation ⚲ quirkyaccom.com. Self-explanatory; includes boats & treehouses.

Salcombe Finest ⚲ salcombefinest.com. As the name suggests, they specialise in luxury holiday lets in & around Salcombe.

Toad Hall Cottages ⚲ toadhallcottages. co.uk. An independent, local business offering a wide selection of self-catering holiday properties in sought-after destinations across the South West.

Unique Hideaways ⚲ uniquehideaways. com. Wide selection of unusual glamping.

Unique Homestays ⚲ uniquehomestays. com. Genuinely unique places at the upper end of the market.

2 THE ENGLISH RIVIERA: TORBAY

Hotels

The Cary Arms & Spa Babbacombe Beach, TQ1 3LX ⚲ 01803 327110 ⚲ caryarms.co.uk. Luxury seaside hotel with a prime spot in the bay; a choice of a cottage, sea-facing bedroom or a chic beach hut.

Orestone Manor Maidencombe TQ1 4SX ⚲ 01803 897511 ⚲ orestonemanor.com. Boutique hotel & restaurant set in a quiet location north of Torquay with stunning sea views.

Redcliffe Hotel Paignton TQ3 2NL ⚲ 01803 526397 ⚲ redcliffehotel.co.uk. A hotel folly by the sea with good facilities; there's even a ballroom. Good value.

B&Bs

Albaston Boutique B&B 27 St Marychurch Rd, Torquay TQ1 3JF ⚲ 01803 212100 ⚲ albastonhotel.co.uk. An elegant Victorian house with nine stylish bedrooms; electric vehicle charging points in the driveway.

Breakfasts can be taken on to the terrace on fine days.

The Haytor Hotel Meadfoot Rd, Torquay TQ1 2JP ✆ 01803 294708 ⌂ haytorhotel.com. This elegant villa has twelve comfortable bedrooms; the attractive garden has chairs for lazing on sunny days.

Heathcliff House 16 Newton Rd, Torquay TQ2 5BZ ✆ 01803 211580 ⌂ heathcliffhouse. co.uk. This adults-only B&B was where Agatha Christie took afternoon tea with the vicar who advised her when writing *The Murder at the Vicarage*. Ample off-road parking, well placed for buses & within walking distance of the beach. Eight bedrooms.

The 25 Boutique B&B Torquay TQ2 5LB ✆ 01803 297517 ⌂ the25.uk. Five extraordinary rooms only ten minutes' walk from the seafront & the town. The top in award-winning quality.

Self-catering

Faithful Brixham TQ5 9BW ⌂ canopyandstars. co.uk & others. Converted fishing boat in the marina; sleeps two on a king-size bed beneath a roof window – perfect for star-gazing.

Long Barrow North Whilborough TQ3 1SB ✆ 01803 472930 ⌂ devonwindmills.co.uk. A beautifully renovated windmill tower just four miles from Torbay beaches. Sleeping two or a family of four, a peaceful place to enjoy the wildlife of Dartmoor.

Glamping

Brownscombe Marldon TQ3 1TA ✆ 01803 872532 ⌂ brownscombe.co.uk. A range of glamping options – a tin tabernacle, a roundhouse & safari tents. Small shop & restaurant on site.

3 TOTNES & THE RIVER DART

Hotels

Anzac Street Bistro Dartmouth TQ6 9DL ✆ 01803 835515 ⌂ anzacbistro.co.uk. Three rooms in the centre of town.

Cott Inn Dartington TQ9 6HE ✆ 01803 863777 ⌂ cottinn.co.uk. Old, thatched & beautiful. Five rooms.

Dart Marina Sandquay Rd, Dartmouth TQ6 9PH ✆ 01803 832580 ⌂ dartmarina. com. A luxury hotel & spa with a riverside location. Dog-friendly.

The Sea Trout Inn Staverton ✆ 01803 895395 ⌂ seatroutinn.co.uk. Lively riverside pub with good restaurant.

B&Bs

Dartington Hall Totnes TQ9 6EL ✆ 01803 847147 ⌂ dartington.org. There are 50 rooms around the medieval courtyard.

Kilbury Manor Between Buckfastleigh & Totnes, TQ11 0LN ✆ 01364 644079 ⌂ kilburymanor.co.uk. Four comfortable B&B rooms plus self-catering apartment.

Self-catering

Ashley's Shack Harbertonford, between Totnes & Dartmouth ⌂ classic.co.uk. Rural setting; sleeps two.

Duck Cottage Tuckenhay ⌂ dartvalleycottages. co.uk. Waterside cottage, tranquil river views. Sleeps four.

Kingswear Castle ⌂ landmarktrust.org.uk. Yes, a castle! Sleeps four.

Sandridge Boathouse Stoke Gabriel ⌂ helpfulholidays.com. Right on the River Dart. Getting there involves a half-mile field-&-woodland walk. Sleeps four.

Tuckenhay Mill Tuckenhay ✆ 01803 732624 ⌂ tuckenhaymill.co.uk. Historic paper mill converted to classic cottages in 20 acres of natural landscape. Indoor pools & spa.

Camping & glamping

Dartington Hall Totnes ⌂ dartington.org. Campsite set among the rolling hills & ancient woodland on the Dartington estate. Also wooden camping pods & a fisherman's cabin.

Dittisham Hideaway Dittisham TQ6 0JB ✆ 01803 925034 ⌂ dittishamhideaway.co.uk. Four treehouses, five shepherd's lodges & a 1956 restored American Airstream caravan. All beautifully fitted out.

Hemsford Yurt Camp Littlehempston TQ9 6NE ✆ 01803 762774 ⌂ devon-yurts.co.uk. Four Mongolian yurts & a shepherd's hut in peaceful surroundings.

4 SOUTH HAMS & DEVON'S FAR SOUTH

Hotels

Burgh Island Hotel Bigbury-on-Sea TQ7 4BG ✆ 01548 810514 ⌂ burghisland.com. Unique accommodation in a unique hotel (page 179).

Gara Rock Hotel East Portlemouth TQ8 8FA ✆ 03333 700555 ⌂ gararock.com. This clifftop hotel has a selection of accommodation options, an excellent restaurant & two swimming pools.

Plantation House Ermington PL21 9NS ✆ 01548 831100 ⌂ plantationhousehotel. co.uk. A restored Georgian rectory set in extensive grounds overlooking the River Erme. A comfortable place to relax after a day on Dartmoor.

B&Bs

The Cricket Inn Beesands TQ7 2EN ✆ 01548 580215 ⌂ thecricketinn.com. Waterside pub with good food.

Victoria Inn Salcombe TQ8 8BU ✆ 01548 842604 ⌂ victoriainnsalcombe.co.uk. A traditional pub that is good value considering its location in the centre of Salcombe.

Self-catering

Bowcombe Boathouse Kingsbridge TQ7 1LA ✆ 0154 8559221 ⌂ twocabins.com. This restored boathouse overlooks the Kingsbridge Estuary. Sleeps two; kayak available.

Maberly House Chillington TQ7 2LH ⌂ coolstays.com. An elegant Georgian house that sleeps 12 in seven bedrooms.

The Signal Box Woodleigh TQ7 4DE ✆ 01548 550664 ⌂ loddiswellstation.co.uk. Quirky restored railway building. Sleeps four.

Glamping

Brackenhill Glamping Ugborough PL21 0HQ ✆ 07739 473977 ⌂ brackenhillglamping.com. Two very comfortable safari tents in a 1½-acre field, only five minutes' drive from Dartmoor National Park. One sleeps five, the other six.

5 PLYMOUTH & THE TAMAR VALLEY

Hotels

Boringdon Hall Plympton PL7 4DP ✆ 01752 344455 ⌂ boringdonhall.co.uk. An award-winning Elizabethan manor house with luxurious studios & rooms. Two restaurants & a spa.

B&Bs

Barnabas House Yelverton PL20 6DY ✆ 01822 853268 ⌂ barnabas-house.co.uk. Very comfortable B&B, helpful owners, walks & cycle trails nearby.

Tamar Belle Bere Ferrers PL20 7LT ✆ 07813 360066 ⌂ tamarbelle.co.uk. Have your own *Brief Encounter* in a converted railway carriage.

Self-catering

1 Elliot Terrace – Lady Astor Plymouth PL1 2QL ⌂ cottages.com. On the seafront, this elegant first-floor apartment is ideal for a couple seeking privacy & comfort in the centre of Plymouth close to restaurants, museums & ferries.

Crownhill Fort Plymouth PL6 5BX ⌂ landmarktrust.org.uk. Built in the 1860s. Accommodates eight in the old Officers' Quarters.

Glamping

Starbed Hideaways Buckland Abbey, Yelverton PL20 6EZ ✆ 01822 259062 ⌂ starbedhideaways.co.uk. Two luxury shepherd's huts set in the National Trust estate at Buckland Abbey.

6 THE EASTERN FRINGE OF DARTMOOR

B&Bs

Cridford Inn Trusham TQ13 0NR ✆ 01626 853694 ⌂ thecridfordinn.co.uk. Historic thatched longhouse with four en suite bedrooms. Also a self-catering cottage.
Nobody Inn Doddiscombsleigh EX6 7PS ✆ 01647 252394 ⌂ nobodyinn.co.uk. Five B&B rooms in a historic 'olde worlde' pub.

Self-catering

Old Church House Inn Torbryan TQ12 5UR ⌂ oldchurchhouseinn.uk. A haunted 13th-century pub that you can now rent. Sleeps 24.
Over Lemon River Little Sigford Farm, Ashburton ⌂ uniquehomestays.com. Converted mill house for two with hot tub & wood burner. Well-behaved dogs welcome.

Camping

Hennock Hideaways Hennock TQ13 9QD ✆ 01626 832362 ⌂ hennockhideaways.co.uk. Campsite just for tents with spectacular views across the Teign Valley. Two large bell tents can be rented complete with bedding & towels.

7 THE NORTHWESTERN FRINGE OF DARTMOOR

Hotels

Bearslake Inn Sourton EX20 4HQ ✆ 01837 861334 ⌂ bearslakeinn.com. A traditional thatched country inn with six spacious en-suite rooms, four of which are dog-friendly. The inn is a good base for walking & cycling the Granite Way.

Lewtrenchard Manor Lewdown, nr Okehampton, EX20 4PN ✆ 01566 464079 ⌂ lewtrenchard.co.uk. A gracious Jacobean manor in extensive grounds. It has 13 luxury bedrooms & an excellent restaurant (page 266).
The Oxenham Arms South Zeal EX20 2JT ✆ 01837 840244 ⌂ theoxenhamarms.com. Seven exclusive en-suite rooms with hand-stitched fabrics & antique furniture.

B&Bs

The Dartmoor Inn Lydford EX20 4AY ✆ 01822 820221 ⌂ dartmoorinn.com. Three rooms, good restaurant, convenient for the Lydford Gorge.
The Tors Inn Belstone EX20 1QZ ✆ 01837 840689 ⌂ thetorsinn.co.uk. Good-value B&B in traditional family-run pub on edge of Dartmoor. Good location for walkers (page 260).

Self-catering

Cobweb Hall Sourton EX20 4HN ⌂ booking. com. Located on the edge of Dartmoor, this unique, quirky two-bedroom cottage is well placed for exploring the area. The Highwayman Inn is opposite (page 259).
Foxtor & Haretor Barns Lydford EX20 4BW ⌂ classic.co.uk. These semi-detached barns are in a quiet location surrounded by open moorland. Each barn sleeps four in two bedrooms; there is an interconnecting door so that both properties can be used by larger parties.

Glamping

Fallows Leap Ash Park Farm, Sticklepath EX20 2NG ⌂ uniquehideaways.com. A sophisticated shepherd's hut with a double bedroom & small kitchen, an adjacent bathroom & second outdoor kitchen. There are 20 acres of rewilded fields to explore in your own Ranger all-terrain vehicle.
Honeyside Down Okehampton EX20 1EH ⌂ canopyandstars.co.uk. Honeyside is a few minutes' walk from Okehampton's cafés, shops

& railway station but immersed in woodland. Birdbox, Humble Bee & Nutshell all sleep two & each is a unique rustic hideaway.

8 DARTMOOR NATIONAL PARK

Hotels & B&Bs

The Bedford Hotel Tavistock PL19 8BB ℘ 01822 613221 ⌂ bedford-hotel.co.uk. In the centre of Tavistock. Plenty of parking.

Bovey Castle North Bovey TQ13 8RE ⌂ boveycastle.com. Large luxury hotel ideal for families. Lots of activities.

Gidleigh Park nr Chagford, TQ13 8HH ℘ 01647 432367 ⌂ gidleigh.co.uk. A luxury country house.

Ilsington Country House Hotel & Spa Ilsington (nr Bovey Tracey), TQ13 9RR ℘ 01364 661452 ⌂ ilsington.co.uk. Upmarket, comfortable & gracious.

Lydgate House Hotel Postbridge PL20 6TJ ℘ 01822 880209 ⌂ lydgatehouse.co.uk. Inexpensive & super location on Two Moors Way.

Mill End Hotel Chagford TQ13 8JW ℘ 01647 432282 ⌂ millendhotel.com. Dog-friendly country-house hotel on the B3206.

The Rock Inn Haytor TQ13 9XP ℘ 01364 661305 ⌂ rock-inn.co.uk. Long-established inn; lovely location.

Two Bridges Hotel Two Bridges PL20 6SW ℘ 01822 892300 ⌂ twobridges.co.uk. Large hotel on the River Dart.

Self-catering

Bovey Castle 22 self-catering lodges; see *Hotels*, left.

Brimble Cottage Widecombe-in-the-Moor ⌂ holidaylettings.co.uk. A converted stone barn, part of a 400-year-old longhouse. Sleeps seven.

The Chapel & Sanders Lettaford, North Bovey ⌂ landmarktrust.org.uk. Two quite unique properties. The Chapel is a tiny converted chapel sleeping two; Sanders, is a traditional longhouse sleeping five.

Camping & glamping

Brimpts Farm Dartmeet PL20 6SG ⌂ brimptsfarm.co.uk. Rustic camping pods, sleeping four, with shared facilities & camping fields.

Dartmoor Hill Farm Glamping Princetown PL20 0SL ℘ 01822 890189 ⌂ dartmoorglamping.com. Shepherd's huts with underfloor heating & large bell tents with a double bed.

Langstone Manor Holiday Park Moortown, Tavistock PL19 9JZ; ℘ 01822 613371 ⌂ langstonemanor.co.uk. Camping areas (wooded or meadow) plus wooden pods. 'Green' facilities.

Your local
holiday cottage specialist...

Whether it's a romantic retreat for two or a flexible property fit
for families, Toad Hall Cottages offer over 1,300 holiday homes
throughout South Devon, Dartmoor and the rest of the stunning
South West. Choose from traditional country cottages, beachside
apartments, dog friendly homes and large properties with luxury
extras like hot tubs and swimming pools.

www.toadhallcottages.co.uk | 01548 202020

NOTES

INDEX

Entries in **bold** refer to major entries; *italics* refer to maps.

INDEX OF ADVERTISERS

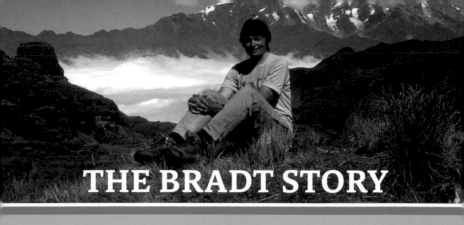

THE BRADT STORY

In the beginning

It all began in 1974 on an Amazon river barge. During an 18-month trip through South America, two adventurous young backpackers – Hilary Bradt and her then husband, George – decided to write about the hiking trails they had discovered through the Andes. *Backpacking Along Ancient Ways in Peru and Bolivia* included the very first descriptions of the Inca Trail. It was the start of a colourful journey to becoming one of the best-loved travel publishers in the world; you can read the full story on our website (**bradtguides. com/ourstory**).

Getting there first

Hilary quickly gained a reputation for being a true travel pioneer, and in the 1980s she started to focus on guides to places overlooked by other publishers. The Bradt Guides list became a roll call of guidebook 'firsts'. We published the first guide to Madagascar, followed by Mauritius, Czechoslovakia and Vietnam. The 1990s saw the beginning of our extensive coverage of Africa: Tanzania, Uganda, South Africa, and Eritrea. Later, post-conflict guides became a feature: Rwanda, Mozambique, Angola, and Sierra Leone, as well as the first standalone guides to the Baltic States following the fall of the Iron Curtain, and the first post-war guides to Bosnia, Kosovo and Albania.

Comprehensive – and with a conscience

Today, we are the world's largest independently owned travel publisher, with more than 200 titles. However, our ethos remains unchanged. Hilary is still keenly involved, and **we still get there first**: two-thirds of Bradt guides have no direct competition.

But we don't just get there first. Our guides are also known for being **more comprehensive** than any other series. We avoid templates and tick-lists. Each guide is a one-of-a-kind expression of an expert author's interests, knowledge and enthusiasm for telling it how it really is.

And a commitment to wildlife, conservation and respect for local communities has always been at the heart of our books. Bradt Guides was **championing sustainable travel** before any other guidebook publisher. We even have a series dedicated to Slow Travel in the UK, award-winning books that explore the country with a passion and depth you'll find nowhere else.

Thank you!

We can only do what we do because of the support of readers like you – people who value less-obvious experiences, less-visited places and a more thoughtful approach to travel. Those who, like us, take travel seriously.

Bradt GUIDES
TRAVEL TAKEN SERIOUSLY